D1081966

Psalms and Practice

A "Connections" Book

Psalms and Practice
Worship, Virtue, and Authority

Stephen Breck Reid
Editor

A Michael Glazier Book
THE LITURGICAL PRESS
Collegeville, Minnesota
www.litpress.org

BS
1435
P73
2001

A Michael Glazier Book published by The Liturgical Press

Cover design by Ann Blattner. Watercolor by Ethel Boyle.

As cited in this volume, the Scripture quotations are from a number of translations of the Bible, including the New Revised Standard Version Bible, Catholic edition, © 1989 by the Division of Christian Education of the National Council of Churches of Christ in the U.S.A. Used by permission. All rights reserved.

The Scripture selections that are taken from the New American Bible copyright © 1991, 1986, 1970 by the Confraternity of Christian Doctrine, 3211 Fourth Street, N.E., Washington, D.C. 20017-1194 are used by license of the copyright owner. All rights reserved. No part of the New American Bible may be reproduced in any form or by any means without permission in writing from the copyright owner.

© 2001 by The Order of St. Benedict, Inc., Collegeville, Minnesota. All rights reserved. No part of this book may be reproduced in any form or by any means, electronic or mechanical, including photocopying, recording, taping, or any retrieval system, without the written permission of The Liturgical Press, Collegeville, Minnesota 56321. Printed in the United States of America.

1   2   3   4   5   6   7   8

Library of Congress Cataloging-in-Publication Data

Psalms and practice : worship, virtue, and authority / Stephen Breck Reid, editor.
    p. cm.
   "A Michael Glazier book."
   Includes bibliographical references and index.
   ISBN 0-8146-5080-5
   1. Bible. O.T. Psalms—Liturgical use. 2. Bible. O.T. Psalms—Devotional use. 3. Bible. O.T. Psalms—Cristicism, interpretation, etc. 4. Christian life—Biblical teaching. I. Reid, Stephen Breck.
BS1435.P73 2001
264'.34—dc21   00-049559

JKM Library
1100 East 55th Street
Chicago, IL 60615

To
James Luther Mays
and Bernhard Word Anderson

pioneers in the Psalms and Practice in the life of the Church

Contents

Contributors   xi

Preface   xiii
  Stephen Breck Reid

Foreword   xv
  Dorothy Bass

Part I: Psalms and Practice

Introduction   3

1   Psalm, *Bhajan*, and *Kirtan:*
    Songs of the Soul in Comparative Perspective   7
    Terry Muck

2   The Psalms as a Place to Begin for
    Old Testament Theology   28
    W. H. Bellinger, Jr.

3   Power and Practice: Performative Speech
    and Piety in Psalm 132   40
    Stephen Breck Reid

Discussion—Psalms and Practice   52

Part II: Psalms and Practice: Contemplation and Worship

Introduction   59

4   Praying with Psalms:
    A School of Prayer   62
    John C. Endres, S.J.

 5   The Sacramental Function of the Psalms in Contemporary
     Scholarship and Liturgical Practice   78
       Harry P. Nasuti

 6   Burning Our Lamps with Borrowed Oil: The Liturgical Use
     of the Psalms and the Life of Faith   90
       Rolf Jacobson

 7   My Tongue Will Sing Aloud of Your Deliverance:
     Praise and Sacrifice in the Psalms   99
       Kathryn L. Roberts

 8   Thus Says the LORD: "Thou Shalt Preach
     on the Psalms!"   111
       J. Clinton McCann, Jr.

 9   The Psalms in Worship and Preaching:
     A Report   123
       James C. Howell

10   How Long, O Lord! Will Your People Suffer
     in Silence Forever?   143
       Beth LaNeel Tanner

Discussion—Psalms and Practice: Contemplation and Worship   153

     Part III: Psalms and Practice: Virtue and Authority

Introduction   161

11   The Virtues of the Righteous in Psalm 37:
     An Exercise in Translation   164
       Michael Jinkins

12   All God, and Us: Double Agency and Reconciliation
     in Psalms 22 and 51   202
       Cynthia L. Rigby

13   The Cursing Psalms as a Source of Blessing   220
       Larry Silva

14   Songs for the City: Interpreting Biblical Psalms
     in an Urban Context   231
       Gerald H. Wilson

15 Taking Inspiration: Authorship, Revelation,
and the Book of Psalms   244
Mark S. Smith

Discussion—Psalms and Practice: Virtue and Authority   274

Author Index   279

Scriptural Index   282

Contributors

Bernhard W. Anderson is emeritus professor of Old Testament/Hebrew Bible from Princeton Seminary. He is the author of numerous books, including the newest edition *Out of the Depths,* which he wrote with Steven Bishop.

Dorothy C. Bass is director of the Valparaiso Project on the Education and Formation of People in Faith, a Lilly Endowment Project based at Valparaiso University. She edited and contributed to a book that interprets the Christian life through the conceptual lens of practices: *Practicing Our Faith: A Way of Life for a Searching People.*

W. H. Bellinger, Jr. is professor of Old Testament and director of graduate studies at Baylor University. He has written extensively on the Psalms including the book *A Hermeneutic of Curiosity and Readings of Psalm 61.*

Larry Bethune is the pastor of University Baptist Church in Austin, Texas. He is active in the Austin seminary community in the area of racial reconciliation and social justice.

Steven Bishop is co-author of the recent edition of *Out of the Depths.*

John Endres, S.J., is professor of Hebrew Bible/Old Testament at the Jesuit School of Theology in Berkeley. He is the author of several books including a coming volume on spiritual formation and retreats.

James Howell is the pastor of Davidson United Methodist Church.

Rolf Jacobson is an ordained Lutheran minister and assistant professor at Augsburg College.

Michel Jinkins is associate professor of pastoral theology at Austin Presbyterian Theological Seminary and the author of numerous books including *In the House of the Lord: Inhabiting the Psalms of Lament.*

Elizabeth Liebert, S.N.J.M., is professor of spiritual life at San Francisco Theological Seminary. She is the co-author of a volume on the use of the Psalms in spiritual renewal with John Endres.

James Luther Mays is emeritus professor of Old Testament at Union Theological Seminary in Richmond. He is the author of several books on the Psalms, including *The Lord Reigns.*

J. Clinton McCann is professor of Old Testament at Eden Theological Seminary. He is the author of several books on the Psalms, including *A Theological Introduction to the Psalms.*

Esther Menn is assistant professor at University of Virginia. Her work on the interpretation of the Psalms is appearing in a coming volume of *Harvard Theological Review.*

Terry Muck is professor of mission and world religions at Asbury Theological Seminary. He was for a decade executive editor of *Christianity Today Magazine.*

Harry Nasuti is professor of Hebrew Bible/Old Testament in the department of theology of Fordham University. He is the author of several books on the Psalms, including *Defining the Sacred Songs. Genre, Tradition and the Post-critical Interpretation of the Psalms.*

Irene Nowell, O.S.B., is the book review editor for the *Catholic Biblical Quarterly* and author of *Sing a New Song. The Psalms in the Sunday Lectionary.*

Cynthia L. Rigby is associate professor of theology. She is also the editor of *Power, Powerlessness, and the Divine,* a collection of essays on the Bible and theology.

Kathryn L. Roberts is assistant professor of Old Testament at Austin Presbyterian Theological Seminary. She is ordained in the Reformed Church in America and has extensive pastoral experience.

Fr. Larry Silva serves a multiracial parish in Oakland, California.

Mark S. Smith is professor at New York University. He has written extensively on the Bible and the ancient Near East, including *Psalms the Divine Journey.*

Beth LaNeel Tanner is assistant professor of Old Testament at New Brunswick Theological Seminary. She is also the author of the coming volume *The Psalms Through the Lens of Intertextuality.*

Preface

This project comes from many years of conversations with colleagues at work in the field of Psalms research. The scholars in that conversation are also committed church people. So when the opportunity presented itself to have a conversation with pastors and academics on reading and practice with the Psalms.

We brought together for three days pastors and biblical scholars in academic settings in a collegial and comfortable context. We shared conversation on topics generated by papers written by a number of participants, pastors, and academics alike. The group reflected a broad range of confessional traditions, including Roman Catholic and Baptist. We brought together persons in different stages of their career. We were honored with the presence of James Luther Mays and Bernhard Anderson, senior scholars who contributed significantly to the discussion, while at the same time encouraging the younger readers. I use this term for despite our place of ministry we shared a common commitment to the practice of reading the Psalms in the Church. The reviews by the participants indicate that they all thought that we accomplished this goal. It is our hope that some of these friendships will lead to ongoing collaborations. However, it is too early to know whether that will in fact be the case.

The structure of our time included conversation over papers, but also time of prayer in both Protestant and Roman Catholic traditions. While we were aware that these traditions are much broader and deeper than we could experience, a number of the participants commented that the combination of conversation on the psalms and the practice of reading and praying the psalms in worship enriched the conversation of reading the psalms in the conversation of the papers.

I want to thank Dr. Dorothy Bass program director of the Valparaiso Project on the Education and Formation of People of Faith, who not only funded the project but also participated in it. We would also like to thank Dr. Craig Dykstra of the Lilly Endowment who brought this project to the attention of Dr. Bass. We thank the two of them and the Lilly Endowment for making this conference possible. As we hope the following report demonstrates, the goals of the conference were accomplished.

I would like to thank Jeanne French, the administrative assistant on the project, as well as Valerie Sansing, Sharon Bryant, and Dixie Anders for their work in preparing the manuscript for publication. When Jeanne French became ill, Alison Riemersma pitched in to bring the project to completion. I also need to thank Linda Maloney and Mark Twomey at The Liturgical Press for seeing the manuscript from the conference to completion.

Stephen Breck Reid
Austin Presbyterian
Theological Seminary
Austin, Texas

Foreword

The Psalms pervade the language and the lives of Christians and Jews. In Christianity, the tradition from which this book's authors come and to which they chiefly write, the words of what Dietrich Bonhoeffer called "the prayerbook of the Bible" have enabled generations of believers to give voice to praise and lament, thanksgiving and repentance. The Psalms are shouted by Pentecostals: "This is the day the Lord has made! Let us rejoice and be glad in it!" They are quietly intoned—all one hundred fifty of them—by monks. They are whispered at hospital bedsides. They are married to tunes played on organs or they are lined out to the beat of drums, that they might be sung by congregations at worship.

During the past century, and longer in some academic settings, the Psalms have also attracted attention of a somewhat different kind. These texts, after all, present historians, philologists, and social scientists with intriguing resources for the study of ancient religion, society, and culture. Modern scholarly attention to the Psalms has often helped theological students and religious leaders to understand the Psalms and the communities within which they originated more fully, to be sure. But scholarship on these and other biblical texts has also occurred, not infrequently, in relative isolation from communities of faith.

This volume emerged from Stephen Breck Reid's conviction that such isolation denies both the academy and the church access to important dimensions of the Psalms. He noted, however, that a concept currently attracting considerable interest in the academy—the concept of *practice*—might provide an approach to the study of the Psalms that could incorporate the best insights of both scholars and religious leaders. To test this insight, he invited the authors of the essays here gathered, as well as some twenty other colleagues, to consider the Psalms through this conceptual lens. Among these were several who have devoted their lives to the academic study of the Old Testament. Also included were professors from other fields—philosophy, spirituality, education, theology—and individuals who serve full-time in positions of pastoral or social ministry. In some cases, the vocations of those involved gave the lie to easy categorizations: there were pastors with doctorates in Old Testament and scholars who are active in ministry. Some of the participants had been involved in conversation across the divide between church and academy for many years.

An approach to the study of the Psalms that draws on the concept of *practices* provides several features that encourage integrative conversations of this sort. First, to locate the study of the Psalms within the conceptual terrain of *practice* is to insist upon the social and historical character of the Psalms and their use. Biblical scholars have been interested in the original social and historical contexts of these and other biblical texts for generations, of course, and a practices approach affirms this long-standing emphasis on the relation between texts and the ambiguous, embodied communities that read them. Beyond this, however, a practices approach also provides a way of thinking about the relationships among communities of the past, the present, and the future. A practice is not just any activity, but one that exists over a long period of time, adapting as need be but still recognizably and meaningfully embodied in the lives of human beings. In this sense, a continuous (though surely changing and sometimes disjunctive) practice of reading the Psalms might be said to exist in ancient courts and temples, in rabbinic and apostolic teaching, and in monasteries, congregations, and seminaries, including the communities to which people belong today and to which they will belong tomorrow.

Second, the concept of *practice* provides a way of reflecting on the normative dimensions of reading the Psalms. Every practice has normative dimensions, at least on its own terms. A practice is complex; it requires specific skills and dispositions, and seasoned practitioners can tell excellence from sham. When people of faith treasure and perform a practice over the years, a practice also becomes normative in a larger sense: the practice points beyond itself to the God who is worshiped in and through the practice. Whoever would read the Psalms with excellence today, therefore, will also want to know about the social, historical practice of reading the Psalms, in ancient Israel, contemporary Latin America, and many other places. We will want to know about the forms this practice has taken across centuries and cultures and about how it has become distorted and been renewed. We will want to know this so that we may engage in this practice in as excellent a way as possible today, in our own historical situation.

Finally, to think about reading the Psalms as a practice is to refuse to separate idea from form, thinking from doing, words from social behavior. Every practice requires and engenders knowledge—not abstract knowledge (if there is such a thing) but knowledge that is intrinsic to the social, embodied acts in which practitioners are engaged. For example, the reading of Psalm 51 by penitents is not a matter of abstract declaration about the character of God or oneself. Rather, to read this Psalm is to grasp and be grasped by a knowledge of God and oneself in the midst of a real social world—a social world within which the penitent learned the Psalm, in liturgy or at home or school; a social world in which repentance and reconciliation have specific meanings; a social world in which meaningful gestures accompany the Psalm's plaintive words. To interpret the reading of this or another psalm as a practice, whether in academic or religious settings, is to acknowledge that such a reading entails a profound awareness, a deep knowing in the mind and the heart and the body, that is linked to a community of readers.

The practice of reading the Psalms is as old as the Psalms themselves. Through this stimulating and innovative book, Dr. Reid and his colleagues now invite a much wider circle of readers to join them in this practice. As their essays—including the footnotes—attest, their own reading draws on the work of earlier practitioners in academy, church, and synagogue, including a pastor who spoke Psalm 145 as a table blessing, a composer who gave glorious harmony to Psalm 19, and a scholar who discerned how certain psalms are related to others. In each essay, readers can learn as these authors extend the practice of reading the Psalms into our own time. Finally, these essays become resources for those who will continue this practice in their own religious and scholarly communities.

Dorothy C. Bass

Part I:
Psalms and Practice

Introduction

What do we mean by a psalm and practice?

*A*lasdair McIntyre brought the Aristotelian notion of "practice" back to the conversation about philosophical ethics. The scholars in these articles explore how the notion of practice might help contemporary readers understand psalms in a new way.

"'By practice' I (MacIntyre) am going to mean any coherent and complex form of socially established cooperative human activity through which goods internal to that form of activity are realized in the course of trying to achieve those standards of excellence which are appropriate to, and partially definitive of, that form of activity, with the result that human powers to achieve excellence and human conceptions of the ends and goods involved, are systematically extended."[1] A practice has certain characteristics. (1) It involves an attention to rules. (2) It operates under a standard of excellence. (3) It moves out of a history that governs both the standards of excellence and the rules of engagement. (4) It "requires a certain type of relationship between those who participate in it."[2]

Terry Muck introduces us to the issue by a history-of-religions approach. He stands in the tradition of phenomenological analysis. He examines the psalms of Christianity, Hinduism, and Sikhism. He uncovers traits that recur in these three and notes the places where these diverge in their use in psalm-like poetry. He reminds us of the need to read a psalm not as a mere artifact of theology or literature but a byproduct of practice, a practice with rhetorical rules. He coins a term that points to an important way to understanding the practice reading of psalms as "devotional singing." He excavates interstices of practice and devotional singing in three primary ways cosmological, liturgical, and conversational.

An unexpected consequence of the insights of MacIntyre was the catalyst for a new appreciation of "practice" as a vehicle to understand

Christian life and formation. Herman Gunkel shaped the understanding of Hebrew poetry in general and the psalms in particular. This volume brings together the issues of practice and the reading of the psalms. Each of the articles assumes the interface of theology as a Christian practice. Craig Dykstra and Dorothy Bass pioneered the practice and spiritual formation interface.[3] Muck's article helps us think about texts in practice.

The practice of the Church requires a thoughtful consideration. Sometimes we think of this as biblical theology. W. H. Bellinger, Jr. describes the Psalter as a locus for Old Testament theology. The notion of practices may help us move from the present impasse in biblical theology. History which was the foundation of biblical theology in the twentieth century no longer held sway. This shift from history means a commensurate shift of biblical focus from the mighty acts of God to the language of God in the Psalter. Bellinger refers to the work of Knierim and Brueggemann as demanding that any move toward a theology of the Old Testament must attend to the plurality of witnesses of the Old Testament. This includes strategies of emphasis on creation theology or metaphorical theology. Bellinger notes, following the lead of Levenson, that this is complicated by the fact that Christians share Hebrew Scriptures with the Jewish community. Bellinger puts this present search for foundations for a theology of the Hebrew Scriptures in context of the inheritance of Eichrodt and von Rad. Bellinger finds the future of Old Testament theology suggested by the work of George W. Anderson, who suggests that the diversity of the Psalter commends that we start there with the practice of faith called theology.

When we do this Bellinger uncovers three affirmations: (1) God is involved in the world by coming to deliver, (2) God blesses in life, and (3) God speaks to the people in liturgical instructions. Bellinger notes the rules of Hebrew poetry at work in the Psalter that embodies a standard of excellence for what constitutes the devotional songs of Old Testament theology. Bellinger in his outline of the problem likewise makes the case for the history that governs both the standards of excellence and the rules of engagement. Further the liturgical connection points to the relational aspect of practice.

Stephen Breck Reid like Muck wants to ask a phenomenological question, "what is a psalm?" He uses the philosophical study of speech outlined by J. L. Austin and John Searle and Nicholas Wolterstorff which Reid calls "performative speech." The next part of his argument presents the rudiments of practice suggested by MacIntyre. Reid notes that the category "practice" and the philosophical/theological category "agency" interpenetrate. This royal psalm embedded in the Psalms of Ascent has been a focal point for a debate on the method of dating a psalm. Reid rehearses the two positions early and late dating of the material. Then he moves to ask "so what?"

NOTES: INTRODUCTION

[1] A. MacIntyre, *After Virtue*, 2nd ed. (South Bend, Ind.: University of Notre Dame, 1984) 187.

[2] Ibid., 191.

[3] D. Bass, *Practicing Our. A Faith. A Way of Life for a Searching People* (San Francisco: Josey-Bass, 1998).

1

Psalm, Bhajan, *and* Kirtan
Songs of the Soul in Comparative Perspective

Terry Muck

*F*rom a history of religions point of view, psalm, *bhajan,* and
kirtan are religious devotional songs used in liturgical and individual worship by adherents of Christianity, Hindu, and
Sikh, respectively, as aids to think, feel, and act in ways appropriate to
their traditions' understanding of transcendent reality.

From a history of religions point of view, psalm, *bhajan,* and *kirtan*
are distinct from each other to the extent that their religious traditions'
understanding of transcendent reality are distinct, and they are evaluated as true/false, good/bad, and right/wrong by the extent to which
they generate effective ideas and practices to connect adherents with
the transcendent.

For each of the religious traditions these religious devotional songs
represent (Christianity, Hinduism, Sikhism), the songs and their
singing are central acts of worship. They encompass central features of
their history, beliefs, and practices.

Psalms

Psalms are ancient Hebrew songs of praise and lament addressed to
God. Specifically, Psalms refers to a book of 150 songs included in the
Hebrew Bible or Old Testament. The word itself is a Greek rendering of
a Hebrew word that means "a song accompanied by string plucking."[1]

Background

The 150 songs that make up the book of Psalms were collected over a long period of time in the Middle East, coming into their final form in the first century C.E.[2] Most psalms have headings that either name an author, give musical instructions, or indicate what type of song it is.

Five authors (or collections) are mentioned: David, Korah, Asaph, Moses, and Solomon. Nearly half are attributed to David, although it is unlikely he wrote them all himself. At various times in both Jewish and Christian history, David has been considered the author of all the psalms.[3]

The psalms offer both communal and individual praise and lament to God. They are personal in form even when they are in communal or hymnodic voice. Because of this voice, they lend themselves readily to both devotional singing and liturgical use.

Within the parameters of ethical monotheism, the psalms offer a balanced theology. God is at times pictured as awesome and transcendent, at other times as pastoral and immanent. Whether awesome or pastoral, God is forever just. The timing of God's justice may be uncertain, but its inevitability is sure. To be sure psalms does not present a systematic theology but an interweaving of familiar biblical themes.[4]

The psalms have been used variously in Jewish liturgy and Christian worship. The early Essenes at the Dead Sea used them as their hymnal.[5] They were chanted in the early Temple as a rehearsal of the mighty deeds of God, especially God's creative acts.[6] They were used, depending on their subject, as regular features of various early liturgies.[7] And they were used pastorally, recited on behalf of the seriously ill and dying.

The early Church continued most of these indigenous uses, especially when it was remembered that Jesus recited psalms. In the Middle Ages many clerics and most monastics were required to memorize all 150 Psalms.[8] In many orders, over the course of a week, the entire Psalter would be recited. (Psalter is a name taken from psaltery, a stringed instrument often used to accompany the singing of the psalms.)[9]

Modern Jews and Christians continue to use the psalms in public worship, meditation, and even revelation, attempting to discern God's will and ways from the teachings of these poetic texts. The overall role that the psalms play in Jewish and Christian life is probably best summed up in Augustine's definition of a hymn: "A song with praise addressed to God."[10] The psalms fit in the overall monotheistic structure as an attempt by religious adherents to articulate their praise and laments to God and thereby enhance reconciliation.

Practice

There is enough evidence from early sources to indicate these songs were sung both liturgically and devotionally; there is far too little evidence to tell us exactly how this was done or even what the music sounded like.[11] As far as showing how this music was used then, we are left with inference from what evidence we do have and a history of how they have been used throughout church history.

As for inference, some musical directions are attached to some of the psalms. These directions vary as to songs. Further, the content of the songs—different types of praise (general and specific) and different types of lament—indicate the psalms each had different uses. Finally, content and context indicate that some psalms were used communally, some by individuals, some by both.

Historically, the Psalms have been read and sung liturgically and devotionally. For the community at Qumran they were the heart of worship. Benedictines read them daily in community.[12]

Today the Psalms may be used in as many ways as scripture and song are used. Psalms may be read in a number of translations as *lectio divina,* praise, prayer, or lament. They may be read together in groups or alone in individual devotion.

The key to using psalms is to remember that they are first person speech to God. Narrative parts of Scripture tell about God's mighty deeds, prophesy tells of the promises of the life lived in devotion to God, wisdom literature and theology explain God's deeds and God's promises. Psalms are the believer's speech to God.

The most frequent misuse of the Psalms is to treat their secondary uses—as history, theology, wisdom—as primary. The psalms are primarily prayer, speech to God. This means their primary uses are as liturgical prayer (praise) and as devotional mediums. A great deal of valuable history and theology may be mined from the Psalms, but lessons learned must be first appropriately filtered through their genre—devotional song.

Bhajan

Bhajans are popular Hindu devotional songs, especially popular in northern India from Rajasthan to Behar.

Background

The place of *bhajan* in the popular religious devotion of Hindu India must be understood in the context of two larger Hindu issues: one philosophical, the other historical. The philosophical issue is the cosmological role of sound in Indian thought overall.[13] The historical issue is the rise of a devotional movement called *bhakti* at the beginning of the second millennium C.E.[14]

For Indians, sound embodies the power of the universe.[15] The scriptures of the earliest Hindus, the Vedas, make frequent references to *nāda brahma,* literally the sound god. Sound emanates from Brahman, the essence of all the universe. The primordial sound constitutes the power of the universe. Thus, all sounds that replicate this holy sound— music, chant—put its producer—singer, chanter—in direct contact with the reality of all that is. This theological importance of sound can be seen in the meditative and iconographic importance of the sacred syllable OM and the genetic reference to the sacred scriptures as *śruti,* "that which was heard" (analogous to divine revelation).[16]

In this context of holy sound, a second historical development produced the Hindu devotional songs known as *bhajans. Bhakti,* or fervent devotion to a god, first arose in the classic Indian text, the *Bhagavad-Gita.*[17] As a popular religious movement it was resisted by the Vedic-oriented, elite brahmans because it encouraged a religiosity somewhat independent of ceremonial ritual. *Bhakti* focuses on a single god who is but a manifestation of the all encompassing Lord Isvara. This manifest god represents qualities of the divine Isvara. Devotion to this single god constitutes a path that leads to union with Isvara. *Bhakti* is the divine-human relationship as experienced from the human side.

The relationship is a passionate one. *Bhakti* is a striking contrast to other forms of Indian spirituality, such as yoga, which stress detachment from both positive and negative emotions.[18] Sometimes translated as devotion, the *bhakti* relationship seeks both love and union. It is both communion with and full identity with the chosen god.

The earliest devotional poetry of this sort is probably that written in praise of the Tamil god Murukan about 200 C.E.[19] From there it spread throughout India.

The singing of *bhajans* is a primary *bhakti* ritual but not the only one. Contact with the god is also made through the ritual meal, *puja,* the performance of dance, drama, and rituals of the heroic deeds of Visnu or Siva.

The goal of these songs is to create conditions where the personal religious experience of closer and closer communion with the divine are realized.

Practice

Bhajan singing may be done individually but is more commonly a communal affair. Songs often tell stories and in general celebrate the presence or close communion of the god or lament the god's absence.

It is the singing of the words that increase their power. By singing of love to one's god, a purification takes place. The purification then leads to a mystical union: "Lover and believer become one in ecstatic song."[20]

Often the song is sung over and over again. In the late 1960s and 1970s, *bhakti* singers sung on street corners in the United States:

> Hare Krisna, Hare Krisna
> Krisna, Krisna, Hare, Hare
> Hare Rama, Hare Rama
> Rama, Rama, Hare, Hare[21]

These lovers of Krishna and Rama could not contain their love and joy in their beloved gods.

Each singer and listener of a bhajan are paradoxically separate from and identical with Brahman, the all encompassing reality. *Bhajan* singing and listening helps resolve this paradox.

Over time, the singing of *bhajan* takes a person through four stages of devotion:

1. Ordering religious devotion;
2. Instrumental devotion attainable by special external efforts;
3. Emotional devotion resulting from spontaneous inward feeling;
4. Loving devotion, maintained reciprocal devotion.[22]

Kirtan

Kirtan is the Sikh devotional practice of singing God's name with religious feelings. Literally, it means "singing the praises of God."[23]

Background

In the late fifteenth and early sixteenth century, Nanak, a wandering mystic in northwest India began teaching primarily through devotional songs called *kirtan,* a religious practice/tradition that emphasized worship of a single God he often called True Name.[24] At that time, northwest India (modern Punjab) was the place where Muslims migrating from the west met the traditional religions of India, a grouping usually called Hinduism. In Nanak's unique conception of a single true God we can see the influences of Islamic monotheism; in his insistence in the ineffable nature of that God (and in his overall world view) we can see the influences of various forms of indigenous Hinduism. Nanak himself came from the Hindu *sant (sadhu,* saint) tradition.[25]

The devotional songs called *kirtan* also reflected this dynamic syncretism.[26] The words of the songs invariably praise God or True Name. The music, however took traditional indigenous tunes, called *rajas,* and replaced the words *(bani)* with Nanak's poetry.[27] The importance of these songs to the Sikh religious tradition can be seen in the make up of their holy scriptures called the *Adi Granth.*[28] The scriptures are made up almost entirely of these songs. Many (947) of the songs are composed by Nanak, the remainder by subsequent leaders of the tradition (called gurus): 907 by Aman Das, 679 by Ram Das, 2218 by Arjan, 62 by Angad, and 116 by Teyh Bahadur.[29]

Guru Nanak was in effect a traveling religious minstrel, spreading his message through song in every village and town along the way. His lifestyle was not at all odd, differing little from other wandering holy men called *sants* or *sadhus.* Nanak traveled with another musician named Mardano. Both were known as composers of *niguna bhajans* or songs about a deity without form (as opposed to *saguna bhajan,* composers who write songs about deities with form).[30] Nanak's distinctive element uses his admonitions (probably derived from Islam) that the proper response to True Name was an attitude of surrender to the deity, whereas the traditional *bhakti* singers of *bhajans* longed for unity with their deity.

In essence Nanak taught a theology of song.[31] The first element of this theology was the words of the song the *bani.* Nanak understood these words as aids to overcoming basic human sinfulness *(kaumai)* understood as ego-centeredness. The second element was the music itself, the *ragas.* These tunes created a receptive spirit *(wismad)* that opened the heart to truth. Especially effective in this function was the recitation of the various names of God *(nam).* Third, the actual singing of these songs was the core experience of worship. Many texts describe *kirtan* as the only hope a Sikh believer has of overcoming self-centered ignorance of God. Fourth, the ultimate goal was a mythic sense of unity with God, a continuous sense of

God's presence and direction. Sikhs who are able to consistently achieve this state are called *gurmuch* or religious saints/statesmen. They experienced a true communion of the inner spirit with the outer world.

Practice

Kirtan may be done devotionally, either communally or in private worship.[32] A typical ensemble today is made up of two harmonium players and a drummer. In a communal setting *(kirtan maryada),* a group of musicians usually begin by playing a tune on their instruments *(rebeck saranda).* This sets the proper mood. Next, someone says an introductory prayer to prepare humble hearts and minds in the singers. Then follows a series of *kirtans* sung to traditional ragas. Only songs from the *Adi Granth* may be sung in *kirtan.* The service ends with a reading from the *Adi Granth* and a final prayer. The service is often followed by a meal.[33] Guru Nanak taught that in the company of other earnest seekers/singers the soul more easily made progress toward God.

In private, *kirtan* is usually done at bedtime and most often is made up of a collection of five hymns found on pages 12 and 13 of the *Adi Granth.*[34] The first hymn speaks metaphorically of death to self and "marriage" to God; the second of the unity and diversity of God; the third of adoration of God; the fourth of reconciliation with people; and the fifth is a call to spiritual effort.

It is a short cycle of hymns taking perhaps fifteen minutes in all. Traditionally there are four times for services of *kirtan:* early morning, forenoon, sunset, bedtime.

The hymns are arranged in the *Adi Granth* according to the raga or tune to which they are to be sung. There are only thirty-one *ragas,* so hundreds of *kirtans* are sung to the same tune. As far as possible hymns are to be sung to the correct *raga,* at the appropriate tempo and rhythm. The tempo is slow; words are reverently pronounced. It is important that every single word be accurately pronounced.[35]

Hand gestures, clapping, and dancing are prohibited. In communal *kirtan* no applause for the musicians is permitted. Since the very purpose of *kirtans* is to assist the religious in refocusing his or her attention from self to God, Nanak was adamant the singing be done reverently and slowly with musical excellence but sans adornment. Guru Arjan put it this way in the *Adi Granth:* "The praising of the Beautiful One and the singing of his excellence is not obtained by any skill nor by any religious practice . . . he obtains it to whom it is decreed by destiny itself."[36]

Religious Songs, Devotional Songs

One might profitably ask whether or not there is such a thing as "religious" song.[37] The world's religions use "songs" of extraordinary diversity in their respective cultures. In some the line between sacred and secular music appears to be sharply drawn; in others the line appears to be almost nonexistent. In such cultures can one even speak meaningfully of religious songs, much less attempt to identify its essence across cultures? Is there such a thing as religious song?

To answer such a question we must begin with the recognition that sound, music, and song play central roles in all known religions.[38] In some religions sound itself is a cosmological starting point. As such, it represents the essence of the universe and to be in harmony with the universe means to hear accurately its sound. Music, that is, ordered sound, can be used in such systems to unify the believer with the universe or to get the god's attention. Further, sound may be the medium of revelation by which the gods have chosen to make themselves known. Further still, sound may be the believer's means of communication to the gods and/or preparing oneself for such communication. The content of this preparation and communication is combined with the music to become songs, that is music with an articulated goal. Music has been used cosmologically, liturgically, and devotionally in all the world's religions.

But has it been used in a distinctively religious sense so that a genre, religious music, and religious song may be identified? Some answer this question negatively. There is no such genre as religious song, they say, only songs that are used for religious purposes. Others argue that religious song is distinct but distinct because the words of the song are religious.[39] Thus classical, popular, rock, country—all may be used in the service of one's religion because the words are religious. Others identify the righteousness in the music itself, at least in the effects it produces in its listeners. If those effects produce both joyous glorifying in and awe of the transcendent, say, then the music is religious.[40]

This is a complex subject and I'm not sure that either of these answers do justice to the question's complexity. The negative answer does not seem to acknowledge the phenomenon of religious song and its clear identification in the world's religions; the positive answer seems to run the danger of the exception—surely some religious songs produce neither joy nor awe, yet are centrally religious. One thinks, for example, of Native American music or the Christian's psalms of lament.

The difficulty in identifying defining characteristics of religious song is that these characteristics are precisely those that go beyond definition. Religious song refers one to the sublime dimensions of life, the ineffable, the beyond, the undefinable. Perhaps the best definition is one that acknowledges it is really no definition at all because it admits that its subject is undefinable. In other words, an essential definition is impossible and one is left with two other ways of delineating the boundaries and scope of the musical genre called religious song.

The first way is to attempt to discuss the undefinable by talking about how it relates to other areas of human knowing, feeling, and acting. Let's call the area in question the sublime and suggest that religious songs are religious to the extent that they refer to the sublime. What is the sublime? Jean-Francois Lyotard describes it this way:

> (The sublime) takes place . . . when the imagination fails to present an object which might, if only in principle, come to match a concept. We have the idea of the world . . . but we do not have the capacity to show an idea of it.[41]

Religious songs, then, are those that have the capacity to present the unpresentable, the sublime.

Not that these songs are content-less. They do stimulate content and images, often cultural icons, but they are presented in full recognition of their ultimately symbolic nature, with no hope of exhaustive knowledge even in a theoretical sense. Religious songs create feelings and emotions that Kant described as an admixture of both pleasure and pain, but feelings that not only cannot be traced to definite emotion-producers, but clearly communicate the bittersweet recognition that they cannot be affixed to any presentable cause or idea.[42] Religious songs may tell stories and describe events and stimulate actions of worship, but do so in such a way that the actions seem other motivated and beyond rationale. The realm of the sublime is not irrational, a-emotional, or passive; on the contrary, the sublime is that perception that combines all three of these human faculties in such a way that ensures that the subject cannot be clearly reduced to any one of the three without violating the reality to which they refer.

Clearly psalms, *bhajan,* and *kirtan* have as their subject matter, their evocative basis, and their performance this area called the sublime. When the psalmist clearly intones a lack of fear or evil even though walking through the valley of the shadow of death, he speaks truth, but a truth that other psalms make clear is beyond human comprehension—the why, how, when, and where of the psalmist's confidence resides in God.[43] When Kabir, perhaps the most famous singer of *bhajans,* sings that the soul leaves the body at death he speaks religious truth.[44] When Guru Nanak speaks of True Name as true in the beginning, in history, now and forever he is not stating a hypothesis to test, but it is as true a proposition as any he knows.[45]

Psalm, *bhajan,* and *kirtan* speak truth and open one to God. Their singing represents one aspect of the quintessence of the religious act. But these religious, devotional songs are more than theology, worship, and liturgy. They are all of these together—and more.

What does it mean to say these religious songs are devotional? To be devotional means to earnestly perform religious duties. Devotion is very common in the world's religious traditions even though the methods and objects of devotion vary greatly. One can be devoted to God, gods, ancestors, gurus, saints, imams, bodhisattvas, and buddhas. One may also be devoted to relics, holy places, creeds, and rituals. The methods of devotion are equally varied: devotion can be meditative and subdued, or passionate and frenzied. The setting can be formal—churches, synagogues, temples, or mosques; or it can be informal—private devotions. Clearly, then, to say that these religious songs are devotional is to say little about their substance. It says a lot about form and function, and form and function can best be described in terms of direction—or better, in terms of prepositions.

Religious, devotional songs are directed *from* human beings *toward* the object of devotion. As John Carmen described the Hindu *bhakti* movement, *bhajans* are "the human side of the divine-human encounter."[46] Humans direct their religious songs to the transcendent object with awe and reverence in the face of sacred power; they are sung with confidence and trust that the transcendent is real; and they are sung with a single-minded concentration that befits the sincerity required of such an endeavor.

In terms of grammar, the preposition "to" is the primary one in describing devotional religious acts: psalms are human cries of praise and lament *to* God; *bhajans* are human musical compositions that open their singers up *to* the all-encompassing reality of Brahman; *kirtans* are the guru's words *(bani)* of praise *to* True Name set to music and sung by Sikhs to God. This is not to say that this means these religions are totally characterized by "to," only that devotion is. In their totality, Christianity, Hinduism, and Sikhism give ample place to "from," "about," and "with."

All three religious traditions, in fact, acknowledge that "from" is the primary preposition. Christians, for example, insist that truth (Scripture) and the initiative for the religious life comes "from" God. In this sense, even the psalms themselves come "from" God. In traditions like Hinduism and Buddhism where the individual human actor is always, to some extent at least, merely a happenstance coming together of *karmic,* historical, and cultural forces, the "from" is implicit in the religious structure. Nanak insisted that it is only through True Name's grace and power that we may respond at all.

Further, a great deal of the substance of all three religions traditions may be summed up in the preposition "about." Narratives and myths tell us about the gods and their mighty deeds. Much of the Bible is writing "about" God and God's work. The Vedas are about the gods and their sacrifices. Although the Guru Granth Sahib is almost all songs of praise to True Name, a clear theology "about" God emerges in the process.

All three religions also include a great deal of content that has to do "with" human action and interactions. Prophets spoke messages aimed at human leaders. Wisdom literature tells us how to live with each other. Apostolic letters direct early religious communities and institutional organization. "With" is crucial to all religions.

What distinguishes the devotional in each of these religions traditions, however is "to." The genre of devotion can be identified by its voice: the psalmist speaks to God, the *bhajan* singer venerates his or her deity, the kirtan singer intones the names of God with reverence designed to change one's whole perspective from ego-centered to God-centered.

Practice

Our definition of psalm, *bhajan,* and *kirtan* as religious devotional songs implies that they too could be used in either an individual or communal setting. Phenomenologically, that is the case. All three types of songs have been used and are used by individuals and in group settings. Because of this variety of use and the way psalms, *bhajans,* and *kirtans* have been used historically in each of the three traditions, it is almost impossible to determine current practice from historical genre studies. Questions of genre are not profitably divorced from questions of content and, eventually, function.

Consider as one example the history of psalms studies. The modern period of psalms studies beginning with Gunkel has focused on classifying the psalms according to genre.[47] Once it became clear that careful historical-critical study of the psalms yielded little in the way of history or systematic dogmatics, attention shifted to classifying just what kind of compositions these writings are. Gunkel did the pioneering and enduring work here. Mowinckel used Gunkel's initial insights to elaborate and outline a provocative hypothesis of his own regarding the cultus origin of the psalms.[48] Westerman amended these schemas, as did Seybold, and Gerstenberger added important sociological analysis and comparative religion insights.[49] Gradually, the original goal of this fruitful approach—to understand the literary history and nature of the psalms in order to understand their meaning for today—has given way to another important insight.

The insight is this: original setting and cultural influence mean much less for interpreting and using the psalms today than the above mentioned psalms scholars seemed to imply.[50] History yields ideas for current meaning and use but does not determine it. Perhaps the best evidence of this is the extraordinarily diverse use to which the psalms have been used historically. Psalms were used originally in cultus settings (Mowinckel) and as private cries of lament of individual sick persons (Seybold). Early Jews used the psalms in Mishnaic argumentation and in Temple ceremonies. Monks at Qumran used them as a hymn book. The *siddur*, the modern Jewish prayer book, relies heavily on the psalms. Early Christian monastics memorized them for personal spiritual practice and communal recitation. The psalms dominate modern Christian liturgies. Clearly, the original use of the psalms, whatever that was, has not been totally determinative of the way they have been used since then. Identifying the original literary genre surely has helped understand the psalms. But modern insights have shown us that it is probably more accurate to turn that statement on its head and say today that what the psalms mean to the Church and the use to which we put the psalms determine the genre of the psalms; that is, how we classify them today. Genre changes.

Consider a second example, a popular cultural use of *bhajans*. In the 1960s the Beatles, the British rock singing group, took a tour of India, searching for what the sixties generation called Enlightenment. They sat at the feet of religious gurus and, being musicians, they sampled the local music, including bhakti devotional songs, *bhajans*. Paul McCartney, one of the song writers in the group of four, discovered a *bhajan* that sang praises to the devotees' god, "my sweet lord." McCartney liked the lyric, at least as it was translated into English for him, and he turned it into a popular rock and roll song that the Beatles sang: "My

Sweet Lord." Talk about genre change. From village *bhajan* to western rock song. Yet McCartney would say it was still a religious song, at least for him an important part of his "enlightenment."

Neither of these examples is given to say that original intent (and thus accompanying genre) is unimportant. Obviously it is, and students of psalms, *bhajan,* and *kirtan* need the insights this kind of study produces. It *is* to say that original intent is not normative for either meaning and/or use today. History, phenomenology, and the "theology" of the respective traditions share and teach something quite different.

Yet the normative question must be asked. What makes a psalm a psalm, *bhajan* a *bhajan,* a *kirtan* a *kirtan?* Clearly the consensus in all three traditions is that religious, devotional songs may be used individually or in groups for purposes of worship, and/or petition with a wide variety of music styles, as long as they are faithful to the religious traditions' understanding of the transcendent and effective in generating ways of connecting singers to that transcendent.

The Importance of Devotional Singing

So why are these songs seen as so central to these three religious traditions?

In his *Confessions* Augustine says, "Oh in what accents spoke I unto thee, my God, when I read the Psalms of David, those faithful songs, and sounds of devotion . . . Oh . . . how was I inflamed toward thee by them."[51] Or Calvin: "The varied and resplendent riches which are contained in this treasury it is no easy matter to express in words. . . . I have been accustomed to call this book, I think not inappropriately, *An Anatomy of All the Parts of the Soul;* for there is not an emotion of which any one can be conscious that is not here represented as in a mirror."[52]

Bhajan for the *bhakti* is the most complete way to relate oneself to the eternal. "The art of 'intoning' sacred sound has been seen (in Hinduism) to both inaugurate and sustain the soteriological quest toward whichever Hindu god, goddess, or heaven is targeted."[53]

Sarabjot Kaur says, "Kirtan is music which is the very embodiment of harmony and the most sublime of all acts. . . . It aids meditation, settles the restless mind into serenity, exalts the feelings and produces the most wonderful and marvelous results. The music soothes the soul and brings the wavering mind into a focus."[54] As Guru Nanak said "When a man is disappointed with all religious practices, philosophies, and other intellectual searches he can find comfort only by kirtan."[55]

Other modes of expression, of course, propel one toward salvation/liberation/release in all three of these traditions. Theology does it. Meditation and/or prayer does it. Good deeds do it. But each of these is limited—intentionally in many cases—in their scope: theology to rationality, meditation/prayer to the affective dimension, good deeds to action. And that means that each in turn is limited in their evaluative or excellence scales: theology to true/false, meditation/prayer to effective/ineffective, good deeds to right/wrong or good/bad.

Religious devotional songs rise above all that. They combine rationality (words) with affect (music), with action (performance) and in so doing propel the religious adherent beyond the narrow limitations of any one of them.

Phenomenologically, music has been related to a religious tradition's beliefs and practices in three primary ways. The first is *cosmological*—music as the underlying theoretical, theological, numerical, or even essential reality of the universe. The second is *liturgical*—music as the most complete tool used to help connect believers with the religion's transcendent reality in public and private worship. The third is *conversational*—music as the medium of "conversation" between a religion's transcendent reality and human beings.

All three of the religious traditions represented by psalm, *bhajan*, and *kirtan* incorporate all three of these dimensions. But in each of the traditions a different one of the three elements predominates: in Christianity the liturgical dominates, in Hinduism the cosmological dominates, in Sikhism the conversational dominates. This emphasis in each religious tradition results from many factors not the least of which is focused in the traditions' understandings of the transcendent which in turn determines how the fundamental problem of existence to be solved by religious action is solved.

In some ways this distinctive emphasis can be shown most effectively when related to each religion's founding days. All three types of religious songs originated in religious-based cultures where the relationships between sacred and profane were not nearly as pronounced as they are today. In that sense the function of music as a religions phenomenon was much more integral in those older cultures. Today the picture is more complicated. The separation of religion and society into distinct spheres of human action has complicated the issues. One result is that within each tradition a much wider range of use of traditional religious music is possible.

Christianity

The Judeo-Christian understanding of God as personal and right-eous—ethical monotheism—is the key factor in the liturgical use of the psalms being the primary one. As has been frequently noted, modern critical studies of the psalms have focused on their use in the early worship of the Israelites. Since Mowinckel's single-minded statement of the idea in *The Psalms in Israel's Worship,* subsequent commentary has been made up of elaborations of the theme.[56] Even when repudiated, the preferred alterations have never strayed very far from the liturgical root.

This primary liturgical use, however, is not simply a sociological phenomenon. It results primarily from the conditions set up by a religious tradition with a personal God. In such dualistic traditions the fundamental problem becomes how to relate the personal divinity to human beings who by definition are not divine. Most of the religious functions in such a tradition are set up to bridge this divide, to solve what amounts to a relational divide. The key words in such a system are relational: we obey God, we love and honor God, we serve God, we long for communion with God. Obedience, commitment, love, fellowship are all relational terms. In such a religious system, it is entirely under-standable that religious music, psalms, are used primarily to worship and otherwise relate ourselves and our problems to God. This finds fullest expression in public services of worship, although it is also a prominent gesture of private devotional acts.

To say that the use of psalms in the Judeo-Christian tradition has been primarily liturgical because of these theological considerations is not to deny that it also has cosmological and conversational usages. In fact it has had both.

The cosmological understanding can probably best be traced back to Greek philosopher Pythagoras' sixth-century B.C.E. mathematical discovery. He discovered an invariable numerical order in the world of sound. Augustine was probably drawing on Pythagoras' theories when he wrote his *Six Books on Music.*[57] The ordered nature of music reflects the most intimate understanding of the mind of God in creation. "In music," said Isider of Seville, "we touch the mystery of creation." In such an understanding, of course, music and the musician, in imitat-ing the divine laws of creation, are inherently theological in nature. Gottfried Wilhelm Leibnitz defined music according to this cosmolog-ical use: "Music is the sacred exercise of arithmetic of a soul which does not know it is counting."[58]

In the end, however, this cosmological understanding of the psalms remains secondary to the liturgical. Music's identification with and imitation of creation is not enough. It must go beyond that toward intentional worship of God.

What of the psalms as conversation? Or better perhaps as divine language? Martin Luther for one thought that our hearing produced far more important revelations of God than our seeing: "The miracles which our eyes offer us are far smaller than the miracles we perceive with the ears."[59] For Luther this means that both the gospel and music have a heavenly origin and are best heard, not seen or read. Poets and musicians are those who best have ears to hear the voice of God. The psalms become divine-human conversations.

Hinduism

The Hindu understanding of Brahman as impersonal and unified—as inclusive of all that is and can be—means that the cosmological understanding of music is the primary one. "The common premise of the religious music of India is that sound either invokes or symbolically represents the power of the universe."[60] As Donna Marie Wulff notes, music in India at once has the status of the metaphysical, is accorded divine origin, and has the power for attaining both mundane and transcendent goals. But there is little doubt that the cosmological is primary.[61]

"The highest aim of our music is to reveal the essence of the universe it reflects and the ragas are among the means by which this essence can be apprehended," says the great Indian musician Ravi Shankar.[62] This understanding of music as cosmological has been articulated well in a recent book by Hindu scholar Guy Beck, *Sonic Theology*. He begins his treatise with this: "Hinduism has sacred sound as its heart and soul."[63] Of course, there is a liturgical use tied up with the use of religious music in Hinduism. As Beck notes in his conclusion, "The act of intoning sacred sound—the oral 'sonic act'—has been seen to both inaugurate and sustain the soteriological quest."[64]

But the soteriological quest in Hinduism is in the end indistinguishable from the cosmological. The soteriological quest in Hinduism, despite the many and various forms it might take, all aim at the same union of Atman-Brahman, the joining of soul and Soul, the recognition that all is one. Even those forms of Hindu philosophy that place great value on the individual, in the end advocate a joining together of all. In such a system "liturgy" and ritual becomes indistinguishable from philosophy. The cosmological understanding one begins with becomes more than just the starting point. It becomes goal and means to achieve the goal as well.

Similarly, music as conversation has a very special meaning in Hinduism. It is true that bhajan songs are often, indeed almost always, sung to named deities such as Vishnu, Krishna, Rama, or Siva. Yet these gods are known to be penultimate representatives only of the single ultimate reality Brahman. Even the most unsophisticated village practitioner of bhakti understands that the plaster cast statue of Sarasvati in the elementary school (Sarasvati is the goddess of learning) is merely a representation of an all-encompassing cosmic force. So *bhajans* may very well have the form of conversation and the song itself may appear to be a medium of conversation between human and divine. But the conversation aspect quickly fades away when one realizes one is talking to oneself. Cosmology again asserts itself.

The irony of *bhajan* is that personal songs of the soul end up being sung for purposes of doing away with distinctions between soul and Soul. In other words, personal songs of the soul become soul-less if they achieve their true ends. This irony can only be properly understood if the Hindu cosmological understanding of the world is central.

"Bhajan functions to help people cope with a difficult environment by obliterating the value of the phenomenal world, depriving it of (ultimate) meaning and by advocating bhakti practices that have the same effect."[65]

Sikhism

There can be no question that the primary use of music in Sikhism is conversational. This is not to say that the liturgical and cosmological also play major roles. As we have noted, *kirtan* is best practiced in communal settings where other earnest seekers are present. There is a holiness about those settings that set them apart from other religious gatherings. And it is equally true that Sikhism basically accepts the Hindu cosmology—indeed it is sometimes difficult to distinguish between *kirtan* and *bhajan*—the *Adi Granth* contains many *bhajan* singers' compositions. Still, the conversations dominates. Nanak's great discovery was the joy of heart-to-heart conversations with True Name. It can be said with accuracy that his theology was all music. He sang his "sermons" with Mardana at his side. His followers elevated his music to canonical status when they named the written *Adi Granth* as the guru of all time. Religious, devotional music reaches it apogee in Sikhism.

A Final Note

The psalms are Judeo-Christian devotional songs whose purpose is to stimulate soul growth *vis a vis* the sublime. They are not primarily (1) propositional truths about God, nor (2) practical advice about how to live in the world, nor (3) simple expressions of cathartic release of emotion directed toward God.[66] Each of these three may have been true at one time or another. It is perhaps true that in the religious-based culture of the original hearers all were more or less true. Today, however, certain features of our culture, such as the technology decried by Weber, Habermas, Ellul, and Tracy, or the social complexity described by Durkheim and Bellah, have in some ways narrowed the use of psalms to liturgical and devotional use.

Others would say that the use of the psalms has been broadened. The primary effect of the Psalms is something quite distinct. Singing the psalms waters the seeds of the soul. The music breaks through the hardened crusts and the words nurture our spirits by directing our attention away from self and toward God. It is true we can do theology, both theoretical and practical, from them. But we can only really tell when a psalm has done its work when something spiritually new or fruitful follows.

NOTES: CHAPTER 1

[1] *Theological Dictionary of the New Testament,* Gerhard Kittel and Gerhard Friedrich, eds., Geoffrey W. Bromiley, trans. Abridged in 1 vol. (Grand Rapids, Mich.: William B. Eerdmans, 1985) 1225.

[2] Edward Greenstein, "Psalms," *Encyclopedia of Religion* vol. 12, Mircea Eliade, ed. (New York: Macmillan, 1987) 39.

[3] McCullough, "Psalms: Introduction," in *The Interpreter's Bible* vol. 4 (Nashville: Abingdon, 1952) 8.

[4] James Limburg, "The Book of Psalms," *The Anchor Bible Dictionary* vol. 5 (New York: Doubleday, 1995) 534.

[5] Brevard S. Childs, *Biblical Theology of the Old and New Testaments* (Minneapolis: Fortress, 1992) 191.

[6] Toni Craven, *The Book of Psalms* (Collegeville: The Liturgical Press, 1992) 10.

[7] McCullough, *The Interpreter' Bible,* 16.

[8] St. Patrick, of Ireland, recited the Psalms daily in the fifth century. J. M. Neale and R. F. Littledale, *A Commentary on the Psalms from Primitive and Medieval Writers* (London: Joseph Masters and Company, 1874) 5.

[9] McCullough, *The Interpreter's Bible,* 5.

[10] For Augustine on the Psalms, see *Confessions* IX.4

[11] Klaus Seybold, *Introducing the Psalms* (Edinburgh: T & T Clark, 1990) 81.

[12] Neale and Littledale, 6.

[13] See Donna Marie Wulff, "On Practicing Religiously: Music as Sacred in India," in *Sacred Sound: Music in Religious Thought and Practice,* Joyce Irwin, ed. (Chico, Calif.: Scholars, 1983) 149–172.

[14] John B. Carmen, "Bhakti," *Encyclopedia of Religion* vol. 2, Mircea Eliade, ed. (New York: Macmillan) 130–134.

[15] Guy Beck, *Sonic Theology: Hinduism and Sacred Sound* (Delhi: Motilal Banarsidass, 1995).

[16] Ainslie T. Embree, ed. *The Hindu Tradition* (New York: Vintage, 1966) 6.

[17] A. L. Basham, *The Origins and Development of Classical Hinduism* (Boston: Beacon, 1989) 91.

[18] K. M. Sen, *Hinduism* (New York: Penguin, 1961) 91–96.

[19] *Textual Sources for the Study of Hinduism,* Wendy Doniger O'Flaherty, ed. (Chicago: University of Chicago, 1988) 182.

[20] Harold Coward and David Goa, *Mantra: Hearing the Divine in India* (New York: Columbia University Press, 1996) 61.

[21] See T. R. Sharma, "Psychological Analysis of Bhakti," in *Love Divine: Studies in Bhakti and Devotional Mysticism,* Karel Werner, ed. (Surrey: Curzon, 1993) 85–95.

[22] Sharma, 89.

[23] "Kirtan," *Encyclopedia of Sikh Religion and Culture,* Ramesh Chander Dogra and Gobind Singh Mansukhani, eds. (Delhi: Vikas, 1995) q.v.

[24] Jagjit Singh, "The Philosophy of Divine Name," *Studies in Sikhism and Comparative Religion* (April 1990) 85–96.

[25] Hindus also call some singing *kirtan,* but Sikh scholars and theologians are very careful to distinguish between the two traditions' use of the singing. See Sarabjot Kaur, "Kirtan in Sikhism," *Studies in Sikhism and Comparative Religion* (April 1990) 105–12.

[26] It should be noted that both Sikhs and Sikh scholars use the word "syncretism" very carefully, pointing out the distinctiveness of Sikhism as a religion in itself. See Mark Juergensmeyer and N. G. Barrier, eds. *Sikh Studies: Comparative Perspectives on a Changing Tradition* (Berkeley: University of California Press, 1979).

[27] "Rag," *A Popular Dictionary of Sikhism,* W. Owen Cole and Piara Singh Sambhi, eds. (London: Curzon, 1990) 130.

[28] Robert E. Van Voorst, *Anthology of World Scriptures* (Belmont, Calif.: Wadsworth, 1994) 122–23.

[29] W. Owen Cole, *Sikhism* (London: Hodder, 1994) 103–7.

[30] Teja Singh, "Love of the Name," *Studies in Sikhism and Comparative Religion* (April 1990) 29–30.

[31] "Kirtan," *The Encyclopedia of Sikhism* vol. II, Harbens Singh, ed. (Patiala: Punjabi, 1996) 516–17. For a concise summary of the theology underlying the singing of *kirtan,* see Taran Singh, "Guru Nanak's Conception of Haumai (Ego)," *Studies in Sikhism and Comparative Religion* (April 1990) 97–104.

[32] Raghbir Singh Bir, "Simran," *Studies in Sikhism and Comparative Religion* (April 1990) 59–77.

[33] See "Kirtan," in Dogra and Mansukhani, q.v.

[34] *The Adi Granth,* Ernest Trumpp, trans. (Delhi: Munshiram Manonarlal, 1877) 12–13.

[35] "Kirtan," in Dogra and Mansukhani, q.v.

[36] *The Adi Granth*, Ernest Trumpp, trans. (Delhi: Numshiram Manonarlal, 1877) cvli, n. 7.

[37] See Lois Ibsen al Faruqi, "What Makes Religious Music Religious?" in *Sacred Sound: Music in Religious Thought and Practice*, Joyce Irwin, ed. (Chico, Calif.: Scholars, 1983) 21–34.

[38] See *Enchanting Powers: Music in the World's Religions*, Lawrence E. Sullivan, ed. (Cambridge: Harvard University Press, 1997).

[39] Gerardus van der Leeuw discusses this possibility and others in *Sacred and Profane Beauty: The Holy in Art* (Nashville: Abingdon, 1963) 252ff.

[40] Oskar Sohngen, "Music and Theology: A Systematic Approach," in *Sacred Sound: Music in Religious Thought and Practice*, Joyce Irwin, ed. (Chico, Calif.: Scholars, 1983) 1–19.

[41] Jean-Francois Lyotard, *The Postmodern Condition: A Report on Knowledge* (Minneapolis: University of Minnesota Press, 1984) 78.

[42] Immanuel Kant, *The Critique of Judgement*, trans., J. C. Meredith, (London: Oxford University Press, 1997).

[43] See Psalm 23. See also, *Psalm Twenty Three: An Anthology*, K. H. Strange and R. G. E. Sandbach, eds. (Edinburgh: Saint Andrew Press, 1976).

[44] See a *bhajan* by Kabir recorded in 1989 in Eastern Uttar Pradesh by Edward O. Henry, "The Vitality of the Nirgun Bhajan," *Bhakti Religion in North India*, David Lorenzen, ed. (Albany: SUNY Press, 1995) 236.

[45] See the Mool Mantra—better yet, listen to the Mool Mantra as recorded by Singh Kaur and Kim Robertson, Invincible Music, 1987, Phoenix, Arizona.

[46] Carmen, 130.

[47] For an excellent concise history of psalms interpretation see Patrick Miller, *Interpreting the Psalms* (Philadelphia: Fortress, 1986) 3–17. For Gunkel's position Miller suggests Hermann Gunkel, *The Psalms* (Philadelphia: Fortress, 1967).

[48] Sigmund Mowinckel, *The Psalms in Israel's Worship*, D. R. Ap-Thomas, trans. (Nashville: Abingdon, 1967). "The historical viewpoint from which I regard the psalms is that of form history, a method of approach introduced by Hermann Gunkel—it is necessary to use in addition the cult functional approach. They must be viewed and comprehended in their relationship to the congregation's devotional life" (1).

[49] Claus Westerman, *Praise and Lament in the Psalms* (Atlanta: John Knox, 1981).

[50] See Walter Brueggemann, *Praying the Psalms* (Winona, Minn.: St. Mary's Press, 1982) and *The Psalms and the Life of Faith*, Patrick Miller, ed. (Minneapolis: Fortress, 1989). Or as W. H. Bellinger notes, "Disinterested theologies do not exist." *Psalms: Reading and Studying the Book of Psalms* (Peabody, Mass.:Hendrickson, 1992) 149.

[51] Augustine, *The Confessions of St. Augustine*, trans., J. G. Pilkington, *Nicene and Post-Nicene Fathers of the Christian Church*, vol. 1 (Grand Rapids, Mich.: Eerdmans, 1979) 131.

[52] John Calvin, *Commentary on the Book of Psalms* vol. 1 (Grand Rapids, Mich.: Eerdmans, 1949) xxxvi–vii. Calvin also said something that resonates powerfully with some of Guru Nanak's statements: "There is no other book (than the Psalms) in which we are more perfectly taught the right manner of praising God, or in which we are more powerfully stirred up to the performance of this religious exercise" (xxxix).

[53] Guy Beck, *Sonic Theology*, 212.

[54] Sarabjot Kaur, "Kirtan in Sikhism," *Studies in Sikhism and Comparative Religion* (April 1990) 109.

[55] Sher Singh, "Mam Marga," *Studies in Sikhism and Comparative Religion* (April 1990) 51. See also, John C. Webster, "The Christian Mission to the Sikhs in Punjab," *Dharma Deepika* (June 1998) 5–12.

[56] Sigmund Mowinckel, *The Psalms in Israel's Worship.*

[57] Augustine, "On Music," *Writings of Augustine* vol. II (New York 1947).

[58] Gottfried Wilhelm Leibniz, *Epistolae ad diversos* (Leipzig, 1742) 240.

[59] Martin Luther, *Weimarer Ausgabe,* J. C. F. Knaake (Weimar, 1883) as quoted by Oskar Sohngen, "Music and Theology: A Systematic Approach," *Sacred Sound,* Joyce Irwin, ed. (Chico, Calif.: Scholars, 1983) 11.

[60] David Roche, "Music and Religion in India," *Encyclopedia of Religion,* Mircea Eliade, ed. (New York: Macmillan, 1988) 185.

[61] Wulff, 153.

[62] Ravi Shankar, *My Music, My Life,* 17.

[63] Beck, 6.

[64] Ibid., 212.

[65] Lorenzen, 243.

[66] Although James Luther Mays has noted the important shift in function from "performance in ritual proceedings toward instruction," in the early cultus. *Psalms* (Louisville: John Knox, 19xx) 11.

2

The Psalms as a Place to Begin for Old Testament Theology*

W. H. Bellinger, Jr.

Our Present

*T*he theology of the Hebrew Scriptures has been near the bottom of the list of agenda items in biblical studies in recent decades. What has been called a golden age for this area of study began in the 1930s and continued until about the time I was in seminary in the 1970s,[1] but the last twenty-five years have produced little new on the understanding of Yнwн in the Hebrew Scriptures. Indeed, I had begun to wonder if this area, traditionally known as Old Testament theology, had a future.[2]

Two reasons for the waning of interest in the area are associated with recent hermeneutical developments in biblical studies. The first has been chronicled by Leo Perdue in his volume *The Collapse of History.*[3] He has shown that history had been the basis for theological study of the Hebrew Scriptures, but scholars in the area have moved away from that basis. With the demise of that foundation, searches for new ways forward have not come to consensus. Second, the movements Perdue has chronicled are part of post-modern impulses in contemporary theology and biblical interpretation. Such impulses tend to celebrate diversity and pluralism rather than coherence and unity. Those who study the theology of the Older Testament have usually sought a coherent way to organize that testament's kerygma, an emphasis that runs counter to contemporary trends.

To put the matter another way, a number of scholars who study the Hebrew Scriptures are dealing with texts from theological perspectives, but few have moved in the direction of articulating a theological structure for the whole of the Hebrew canon. For example, Perdue's *Wisdom and Creation* is explicitly theological but limited to Wisdom literature.[4] Among the new visions of Isaiah, holistic readings of the book, are works with profound theological implications.[5] Robert Alter's expositions of texts often carry theological freight,[6] but none of these works exhibits an interest in a full theological structure for the Hebrew Scriptures.

Two recent publications have, however, sparked some renewed interest. The hefty volumes by Rolf Knierim and Walter Brueggemann are salutary developments. They pursue approaches already at hand but do so in a more comprehensive way. I fear, however, that the volumes do not move us forward in pursuit of a viable theology of the Hebrew Scriptures. Knierim's volume *The Task of Old Testament Theology: Substance, Method, and Cases* brings together essays written earlier.[7] He articulates well the problem of bringing some order to the plurality of witnesses in the Old Testament; that is the task of the theologian of the Hebrew Scriptures. In a variety of ways in this volume, he pursues further the recent emphasis on creation theology. That emphasis is a welcome one, for the Old Testament's creation theology has long been neglected by scholars. At the same time, I am left with the impression that Knierim sees the whole of the Old Testament from the perspective of creation theology. I believe the Hebrew Scriptures witness a much more diverse richness.

Brueggemann continues in the vein of what Perdue has called metaphorical theology. He uses a legal metaphor to examine Israel's testimony to Yhwh's ways in the world.[8] I do not object to the use Brueggemann makes of the legal metaphor; he sees its limitations. Still, I worry about its proximity to legalism and other ways the image could be used. Such metaphors seem to work better for those at home in reformed theology than those who stand in the free church tradition. Brueggemann has brought together an enormous amount of theological material within the framework of the history of scholarship and perceptive readings of our contemporary circumstance. The first chapter of *Theology of the Old Testament: Testimony, Dispute, Advocacy* is a compelling argument from the history of scholarship for the centrality of the theological task in the study of the Hebrew Scriptures. He also narrates in clear and certain tones scholarship's loss of innocence and scattering among various proposals. Our setting holds conflicting interpretations that we must negotiate.

Such is the task Brueggemann sets for himself and for us. His volume can fairly be called a first post-modern Old Testament theology. In addition, he has helped us see that creative tension is not only among scholarly constructs but also among portrayals of the divine. He has pointedly narrated the creative tension in the Hebrew Scriptures between divine sovereignty and vulnerability. Still, I find it lamentable that whenever Brueggemann speaks of creation theology perspectives, they are always on the margin and never at the center. They are certainly present but not central. At base, Brueggemann is still a covenant theologian and so I wonder how much his volume really moves us forward in articulating an Old Testament theology.

With all this nay saying and so little progress, you might suggest that I simply give up the pursuit. I would respond that we need to continue theological work on individual texts but as a theologian of the Church, I also believe that both contemporary culture and individuals are much helped by having frameworks within which to consider texts. We read from contexts. Our reading is more informed when we become aware of our contexts and the reading strategies they lead us to employ and when we critically evaluate our assumptions. So I still believe that the search for a satisfying theology of the Hebrew Scriptures is important. The search for coherent Old Testament theological structures is a significant part of biblical theology. I am told that Rolf Rendtorff's theology is soon to appear, and publication of the volumes by Knierim and Brueggemann give us the occasion to consider again directions for formulating such a theology. This paper is prolegomena for such a task.

Here I pause to consider the work of Jon Levenson. In a most interesting essay, "Why Jews Are Not Interested in Biblical Theology,"[9] he notes that the theology of the Hebrew Scriptures has almost universally been populated by Christians. Christian attempts at articulating Old Testament theology inevitably, according to Levenson, include at least some form of supersessionism, the view that the New Testament supersedes the Old. In addition, Jews balk at the notion of universalizing, typically a move in the theological enterprise. Jewish history, philology, and law are more at home in the synagogue with its attention to rabbinic tradition. The church provides a home for systematic theological affirmations, often stated as abstractions. I believe we need to heed Levenson's warning because Christian assumptions can corrupt our attempts to see the theological confessions of the Hebrew Scriptures. Our context can lead us to miss important texts. At the same time, I must confess that my presuppositions come from my place as a theologian of the Church. Moreover, I probably would not be searching the Hebrew Scriptures were it not for those presuppositions. We need to heed Levenson's warning and still, I believe, persevere in the theological task.

The Past

Let me now put the search into context. The two great classical Old Testament theologies of the twentieth century are those of Eichrodt and von Rad. It was Eichrodt's magisterial work suggesting that the center of the First Testament is covenant that set us on the search for a way to present a coherent view of the proclamation of the Old Testament.[10] He suggested making a cross cut through the Old Testament and in so doing found covenant as the unifying notion. Eichrodt understood that the theologian selects and organizes; the Old Testament does not present a theological synthesis. One can, nonetheless, discover the center point as the organizing focus. In Eichrodt's view, the center was Mosaic covenant.

Eichrodt's proposal of covenant for the center of the Older Testament (*die Mitte* in German) gave impetus for a veritable plethora of other proposals for a center around which to organize a presentation of Old Testament theology. Indeed, Gerhard Hasel made a career of tracing these proposals and other issues in Old Testament theology.[11] I mention but a handful. Koehler in the 1930s, for example, proposed the lordship of God as the center while keeping the traditional categories of God, anthropology, and judgment and salvation.[12] Vriezen spoke of communion as the organizing principle in his confessional theology published in the 1940s.[13] In the 1950s Wildberger suggested the theme of Israel's election as the people of God.[14] In the 1960s Horst Seebass returned to the rulership of God.[15] Rudolf Smend spoke of YHWH the God of Israel, Israel the people of YHWH,[16] and Zimmerli suggested that the sentence "I am YHWH your God" provides the starting point for exploring the revelation and response recorded in the Hebrew Scriptures in times of crisis and hope.[17] Herrmann has suggested the book of Deuteronomy as a starting point.[18]

On the other hand, von Rad claimed that there was no center of the Older Testament and so no one organizing principle for an Old Testament theology.[19] Others have pointed out that his Deuteronomic view of history became a kind of secret organizing principle for structuring his two-volume theology.[20] Von Rad has, however, demonstrated the diversity of theological perspectives in the Hebrew Scriptures. Many would still support his view.

Still others have suggested that one center is not sufficient and so take a bi-polar approach.[21] Westermann speaks of the saving God and history and the blessing God and creation.[22] Terrien speaks of the aesthetics of worship and the demand of law.[23] Hanson pursues cosmic and teleological perspectives.[24] I will not recount the rest of the history of scholarship on the debate about whether there is a center of the First Testament and if so, what it is. Suffice it to say that the search for a center has not found a consensus and may have ground to an ignominious halt. I do not wish to beat a dead horse but I do still want to consider resuscitating—probably a more appropriate goal than resurrecting—the study of Old Testament theology. I want to suggest that today we go back to the future and consider an older approach to the issue, an approach that takes some different starting points. We return to the 1960s.

A Future

In 1963 George W. Anderson published in the *Scottish Journal of Theology* the presidential address he had given in that year to the British Society for Old Testament Study.[25] The address was entitled "Israel's Creed: Sung, Not Signed." With a nod to H. Wheeler Robinson's comment that the book of Psalms "supplies the data for an epitome of Old Testament theology,"[26] Anderson seeks to articulate that data. The context in which the article was written is colored by the debate between those who sought to reconstruct the history of ancient Israel's religion and those who searched for an Old Testament theology. Old Testament theology was popular in Anderson's day and he attributes that to the fact that the Old Testament is by nature a confessional document. The Old Testament relates to but is not at bottom an articulation of the history of Israelite religion; that is a task of reconstruction for scholars. The First Testament is rather a collection of documents coming from and molding the life of a religious community. It is thus fair to describe the Hebrew Scriptures as a confessional document from a worshiping community. Were it not for the religious life of the community ancient Israel, we would have no Old Testament. Von Rad and his view that the traditions of ancient Israel are shaped by cultic confessions of faith or creeds also influence Anderson. Israel's creed was sung, and so it is logical to look for the fullest source in which Israel sings its creed to be a representative source for Old Testament theology.

Anderson suggests that a theological synthesis of an important and characteristic kind is found in the Psalter, Israel's sung creed. The range of its content is supremely representative of the Hebrew Scriptures. Here one finds the range of Old Testament literature. The content of the narrative books recounting history and kingship, the voice of prophecy as judgment and instruction, celebration of the torah, and wisdom are all represented here. Wisdom psalms are clearly present. The psalms also give voice to the problems an Old Testament theologian must face. The book includes the various voices of the Hebrew Scriptures and so does not allow one to ignore the multiplicity of the Old Testament's theological witness. How one relates such liturgical documents to the history of Israelite religion and settings therein is also brought to the table. Anderson says,

> The Psalter represents a remarkable concentration of these and other problems of theological interpretation and thus exemplifies uniquely the recalcitrance of the Old Testament material to our attempt to reduce it to a propositional confessional system which adherents might be required to sign.[27]

In addition, the theological themes of ancient Israel are in the psalms: "election and covenant, rejection and restoration, *Heilsgeschichte*, creation, and providence, the way of life and the way of death."[28] This diverse piece is held together as the faith confession of a worshiping community, as the prayer and praises of this community confessing faith in YHWH and so encountering YHWH. The Psalter is not a systematic theology, but it is a concentration and selection of the theological material in the Older Testament made in the context of ancient Israel's worship. The Old Testament theologian is still left with work to do, but the Psalter offers "guidance for that task such as is offered by no other part of the Old Testament."[29] The Psalter is the first of all Old Testament theologies. "This is how, over the centuries, Israel did confess God."[30] Were we to lose the rest of the Old Testament and somehow retain the Psalter, we would still have the basics for an Old Testament theology. The Psalter is Israel's sung creed, a confession representative of the theology of this faith community.

I believe Anderson is basically correct. The Psalter is at the center of the Old Testament and its theological perspective; it is representative of the Old Testament's theology and is sung by a worshiping community. So I am suggesting that we have not so much a center of the Old Testament as one unifying concept or proposition, the German *die Mitte*, but still we have a place to begin, a central place to begin, a textual place to begin, the Psalter. I suggest that we test out this place to begin for Old Testament theology. When I was growing up in the First Baptist Church of McColl, South Carolina, we participated in "sword drills." With "the sword of truth" we practiced to familiarize ourselves with the Bible. The instructions were "attention, draw swords—a text was called such as

Psalm 1:1—charge." Whoever found the text first stepped forward from the line-up, read, and gained the advantage in this cutthroat competition. I look back on that with a smile. I am told these contests persist as Bible drills now. One of the keys to success was to remember that the book of Psalms was in the middle of the Bible. I have, in a sense, made a parable of that clue. The Psalter is central for the theology of the Hebrew Scriptures.

If we begin with the Psalter, what do we find for the task of the theologian of the Hebrew Scriptures? I must first say what I am seeking.[31] We should begin with a broad view. I take theology to be the search for, here, what the Psalter affirms about God in relation to humanity and implications thereof.[32] One might consider such a statement to be self-evident; "theology" has to do with utterances about God. The Hebrew Scriptures certainly make claims about God. But that statement is not sufficient. It is also important to see how the Psalter selects and organizes its confessions about God and God's involvement in the world. The Psalter, and the Old Testament more broadly, primarily speak of the initiative on the divine side of the equation. So I begin to look in terms of divine initiative and human response. What do I find in the Psalter?

First, I find that God is involved in the world by coming to deliver. Several of the psalms recount the history of God's delivering the people. Psalm 105 begins with the ancestral promise and goes on through the entry into the land under the call to remember the wonderful works God has done (v. 5). Psalms 68, 114, and 135 recall the deliverance from Egypt:

> Our God is a God of salvation,
> and to God, the Lord, belongs escape from death (Ps 68:20).[33]

The psalms of individual and community thanksgiving also give praise and thanksgiving to God for delivering from a particular crisis. Psalms 30 and 107 are representative examples:

> Then they cried to the Lord in their trouble,
> and he delivered them from their distress (Ps 107:6).

In addition, the lament psalms, the most numerous type of psalm, presuppose such a theological perspective. These texts operate more from a human cry out of need, but they cry to the God who comes to deliver. But we must now adjust the test thesis of divine initiative and human response; there is human initiative in these psalms. Psalms 6, 13, and 44 illustrate these cries:

> Turn, O Lord, save my life;
> deliver me for the sake of your steadfast love (Ps 6:4).

The dialogical nature of the lament and thanksgiving psalms shows that Israel's worship was connected to the rest of life. The affirmation that God comes to deliver was often severely tested in life. The dialogue is part of Israel's sung creed. God's coming to deliver is the basis of covenant theology which undergirds much of the Hebrew Scriptures, and three strategically placed Psalms—1, 19, and 119—also speak of the covenant avenue of response to the God who delivers, torah.

Second, the Psalms portray God as the one who blesses in life. God is praised as creator and King, the trustworthy God who is present to bless. Psalms 29, 97, and 104 illustrate:

> The Lord sits enthroned over the flood;
> the Lord sits enthroned as king forever (Ps 29:10).

> O Lord, how manifold are your works!
> In wisdom you have made them all;
> the earth is full of your creatures (Ps 104:24).

And wisdom comes from this God as guidance for human response. Here God is not so much the one who comes to deliver as the one who is constantly present to enable the community to grow and prosper in the world, to experience the health of vital living:

> Happy are the people to whom such blessings fall;
> happy are the people whose God is the Lord (Ps 144:15).

The choice of the Davidic line of kings, celebrated in the Royal Psalms, is one such blessing. Such a theological perspective characterizes creation theology in various parts of the Hebrew Scriptures.

Third, the psalms portray God as one who speaks to the people in liturgical instruction as in Psalms 15 and 24 which utter qualifications for worship. God also in the Psalter speaks in prophetic warning such as in Psalm 50:

> Hear, O my people, and I will speak,
> O Israel, I will testify against you.
> I am God, your God (Ps 50:7).

People are to order life rightly under God. This final emphasis is a kind of prophetic theology.

I think of these three as theological perspectives in the psalms.[34] They are not contradictory but do reflect different theological approaches to God's involvement in the life of the worshiping community. I would suggest then that the procedure would be to trace covenant, creation, and prophetic theological emphases through the canon of the Hebrew Scriptures with an eye to ways these theological perspectives interact in the text. But I have suggested that the textual place to start, the Psalter, Israel's sung creed,[35] gives some guidance for our theological search through the canon.[36] We begin with a framework, which we test as we move through the Hebrew Scriptures.

Conclusions

Finally, I need to note that I agree with my mentor Ron Clements who says that theology is not theology unless it has to do with contemporary life.[37] Any serious attempt to articulate an Old Testament theology also has to do with life today. Here I suggest that we attend to two other areas of research. One is narrative theology. One way to define narrative theology is "discourse about God in the setting of story."[38] This area is significant because we all live narratives and can relate to narratives. Much of the Old Testament takes that form, and a number of psalms operate from a narrative impulse. Narrative is not only descriptive but also constitutive of a shape to life.[39] The narrative remembered in Psalm 105 could well provide a framework, an identity, for living. Scott Momaday of the University of Southern California has told how his father took him as a child to spend a day with an older Kiowa woman to hear and participate in the story, ritual, and song of his people. He says he left that woman's house a Kiowa.[40] Narrative can both explode and change lives; narratives that commend the God who embraces pain to deliver, for example, communicate powerful theology for people today.

Second, I call upon the discipline of psychology, about which I know little but which, I am told, has a strain of personality theory called the psychology of personal constructs.[41] Persons view reality through constructs or schemata. The constructs guide the perception and interpretation of experience. For example, the affirmation of God as creator such as we have in the psalms can become part of one's perspective and influence how one relates to nature. The call to a life of justice could become a central construct in shaping relationships with others. These constructs become a part of our memory that shapes how we view life and how we live. And we test these constructs as we move through the experiences of life.

What I have done in this paper is but prolegomena, but I do suggest that we take a renewed look at how to articulate a theology of the Hebrew Scriptures and that we do so from a different vantage point, a textual vantage point, the psalms. I am sure that vantage point is also limited. Still, it gives us a place to begin and then pursue the task of structuring a theology of the Hebrew Scriptures. I suggest that we begin with Israel's pilgrimage songs of faith as guidance for our theological journeys.

Remember also that the Psalter confesses the faith of a worshiping community. Vibrant theologies are most naturally those which derive from worshiping communities. The Hebrew Scriptures tell about the living God encountered in worship. Such a context for theological reflection and confession of faith assures a tie to real life and a tie to the dynamism of a community.

NOTES: CHAPTER 2

* A version of this paper was read as the presidential address at the Southwest regional Society of Biblical Literature meeting in Dallas in March 1999.

[1] Gerhard F. Hasel, *Old Testament Theology: Basic Issues in the Current Debate*, 4th ed. (Grand Rapids, Mich.: Eerdmans, 1991) 26.

[2] This paper will use the terms Hebrew Scriptures, Older Testament, First Testament, and Old Testament as synonymous. The multiplicity of terms is to suggest *awareness* of difficulties with what to call this collection of documents, though not as a solution to the dilemma.

[3] Leo G. Perdue, *The Collapse of History: Reconstructing Old Testament Theology*, Overtures to Biblical Theology (Minneapolis: Fortress, 1994).

[4] Leo G. Perdue, *Wisdom and Creation: The Theology of Wisdom Literature* (Nashville: Abingdon, 1994).

[5] For example, Edgar W. Conrad, *Reading Isaiah*, Overtures to Biblical Theology (Minneapolis: Fortress, 1991); Katheryn Pfisterer Darr, *Isaiah's Vision and the Family of God*, Literary Currents in Biblical Interpretation (Louisville: Westminster/John Knox, 1994); Roy F. Melugin and Marvin A. Sweeney, eds., *New Visions of Isaiah* (JSOTSup; Sheffield: Sheffield Academic, 1996).

[6] Robert Alter, *The Art of Biblical Narrative* (New York: Basic Books, 1981); Robert Alter, *The Art of Biblical Poetry* (New York: Basic Books, 1985).

[7] Rolf P. Knierim, *The Task of Old Testament Theology: Substance, Method, and Cases* (Grand Rapids, Mich.: Eerdmans, 1995).

[8] Walter Brueggemann, *Theology of the Old Testament: Testimony, Dispute, Advocacy* (Minneapolis: Fortress, 1997).

⁹ Jon D. Levenson, *The Hebrew Bible, the Old Testament, and Historical Criticism: Jews and Christians in Biblical Studies* (Louisville: Westminster/John Knox, 1993) 33–61.

¹⁰ Walter Eichrodt, *Theology of the Old Testament*, 2 vols.; OTL (Philadelphia: Westminster, 1961–1967).

¹¹ Hasel, *Old Testament Theology* and "The Problem of the Center in the Old Testament Theology Debate," *ZAW* 86 (1974) 65–82.

¹² Ludwig Koehler, *Old Testament Theology* (Philadelphia: Westminster, 1957); German original (Tübingen: Mohr, 1936).

¹³ Th. C. Vriezen, *An Outline of Old Testament Theology* (Newton: Branford, 1958); Dutch original (Wageningen: Veenman & Zonen, 1949).

¹⁴ Hans Wildberger, "Auf dem Wege zu einer biblischen Theologie," *EvT* 19 (1959) 70–90.

¹⁵ Horst Seebass, "Der Beitrag des Alten Testaments zum Entwurf einer biblischen Theologie," *Wort und Dienst* 8 (1965) 20–49.

¹⁶ Rudolf Smend, *Die Mitte des Alten Testaments*, Theologische Studien 101 (Zurich: EVZ, 1970).

¹⁷ Walter Zimmerli, *Old Testament Theology in Outline* (Atlanta: John Knox, 1978).

¹⁸ S. Herrmann, "Die Konstruktive Restauration. Das Deuteronomium als Mitte biblischer Theologie," *Probleme biblischer Theologie: Gerhard von Rad zum 70. Geburtstag*, H. W. Wolff, ed. (Munich: C. Kaiser, 1971) 155–70.

¹⁹ Gerhard von Rad, *Old Testament Theology*, 2 vols. (New York: Harper & Row, 1962–1965).

²⁰ Hasel, *Old Testament Theology*, 146–51.

²¹ Walter Brueggemann, "A Convergence in Recent Old Testament Theologies," *JSOT* 18 (1980) 2–18 and "A Shape for Old Testament Theology," *CBQ* 47 (1985) 28–46, 395–415.

²² Claus Westermann, *What Does the Old Testament Say About God?* (Atlanta: John Knox, 1979) and *Elements of Old Testament Theology* (Atlanta: John Knox, 1982).

²³ Samuel Terrien, *The Elusive Presence*, Religious Perspectives 26 (New York: Harper & Row, 1978).

²⁴ Paul D. Hanson, *Dynamic Transcendence* (Philadelphia: Fortress, 1978).

²⁵ G. W. Anderson, "Israel's Creed: Sung Not Signed," *SJT* 16 (1963) 277–85.

²⁶ Ibid., 277.

²⁷ Ibid., 283.

²⁸ Ibid., 284.

²⁹ Ibid., 284.

³⁰ Ibid., 284.

³¹ Ben C. Ollenburger, "Old Testament Theology: A Discourse on Method," *Biblical Theology: Problems and Perspectives. In Honor of J. Christiaan Beker*, ed. Steven J. Kraftchick, Charles D. Myers, Jr., and Ben C. Ollenburger (Nashville: Abingdon, 1995) 81–103.

³² Knierim, *The Task of Old Testament Theology*, 78–79.

³³ Biblical quotations are from the NRSV.

³⁴ Note that my description of theological perspectives in the Psalter is rather different from Hans-Joachim Kraus, *Theology of the Psalms* (Minneapolis: Augsburg, 1986) and James L. Mays, *The Lord Reigns: A Theological Handbook to the Psalms* (Louisville: Westminster/John Knox, 1994). Kraus summarizes his view of historical-

critical issues in Psalms study. See my review of Mays' volume in *JBL* 115 (1996) 523–24.

[35] In the distant future, the hymnbook of a church will say more about its theology than will its annual reports.

[36] This approach reflects the influence of Brevard Childs and his important emphasis on canon. See Brevard S. Childs, *Introduction to the Old Testament as Scripture* (Philadelphia: Fortress, 1979) and *Old Testament Theology in a Canonical Context* (Philadelphia: Fortress, 1986) and *Biblical Theology of the Old and New Testaments* (Minneapolis: Fortress, 1992).

[37] Ronald E. Clements, *Old Testament Theology: A Fresh Approach,* New Foundations Theological Library (Atlanta: John Knox, 1979).

[38] Gabriel Fackre, "Narrative Theology: An Overview," *Int*, 343. See 341 for a definition of "narrative."

[39] Perdue, *The Collapse of History*, 231–62.

[40] I first heard this story in a sermon by Roger Paynter at Lake Shore Baptist Church, Waco, Texas.

[41] George A. Kelly, *A Theory of Personality: The Psychology of Personal Constructs,* The Norton Library (New York: Norton & Company, 1963); Robert A. Neimeyer and Greg J. Neimeyer, eds., *Personal Construct Therapy Casebook* (New York: Springer Publishing, 1987) 3–19. This theory can lead to a perspective on the social construction of reality and thus to important questions of power and social location in the interpretation of Old Testament texts. The study of narrative and personal constructs also holds important implications for questions about the authority of texts in faith communities.

3

Power and Practice

Performative Speech and Piety in Psalm 132

Stephen Breck Reid

What I have to say here is neither difficult nor contentious; the only merit I should like to claim for it is that of being true.[1]   Austin

God is in the details. It's the details of texts that resist imposed interpretations. Only by attending to the details does it become likely that one is oneself interpreted by the text—or by that One who is the author of the text.[2]   Wolterstorff

*T*he psalm is a particular type of rhetoric. The historical reconstructions differ in terms of the dating of Psalm 132. Nonetheless, each historical construction makes the same observations regarding the rhetorical language of the passage. The historical-critical discussion begins with the matter of the date of the material as the base line for the discussion. First, I will rehearse the reading of Psalm 132 using well-crafted historical-critical discussions of the psalm. Some argue for an early date of the psalm, by that they mean in the period of the united monarchy. Others suggest a later date for this psalm, by that they mean divided monarchy to a post-exilic construction. Second, I will explore a performance interpretation of the psalm.

I

Early Position

The difficulty of the early dating position is embedded in the language necessary to make the case. "Our earliest witness to the Davidic covenant is found in the lore of Davidic date embedded in Psalm 132."[3] Verse 10 and vv. 13-18 even Cross admits are from a later hand. Verses 2-5 Cross attributes to David.[4] The vocabulary of *yosheb* occurs in early texts (1 Sam 4:4; Exod 15:17 (Song of the Sea), 1 Kgs 8:12) As does the *lamed* as a preposition "from" (v. 8) which was replaced by *min* in early Hebrew.[5] Seow states the theoretical position clearly ". . . the psalm presupposes the monarchy, and there is nothing that compels a late date."[6] One faces a chicken or egg circumstance. Those who posit an early date insist that Psalm 132 is copied in 2 Chron 6:41.[7] However, the converse could be arguable.

One argument for the early dating is its legitimation of Davidic rulers which indicates that they were still ruling at the time of the poem.[8] Further, the advocacy for Zion likewise indicates a time when the Temple was in full function.[9] While Seow designates this as early, he does not follow Cross with a Davidic dating but rather opts for a post-Solomonic date. This passage consoles those who mourn the end of the United Monarchy.

The content of David's oath (vv. 3-5) is similar to that of Egyptian royal inscriptions from the reigns of Amenhotep III and Sethos I. The Mesopotamian cylinders of Gudea reflect the same sort of commitment that is seen in Psalm 132.[10]

The epithet, the bull of Jacob occurs three other places in the Hebrew Bible (Gen 49:24; Isa 49:26; 60:16). Seow suggests an interesting scenario. "If my (Seow's) dating of this psalm is correct, the use of the bull-epithet is hardly coincidental: it is a subtle polemic against any attempt to establish a competing shrine with bull iconography in the north."[11] Now to do this he focuses on Genesis 49. The Genesis text represents an earlier witness than the exilic or post-exilic Second Isaiah reference, thereby providing superior support for a pre-exilic date of the psalm.

Late Position

Even those who hold out for an early date have to concede that the poem is not consistently archaic.[12] Nonetheless, late proposals range from the divided monarchy to the time of Zerrubbabel.

Already in 1968 D. Hillers raises some methodological questions about the early date for Psalm 132. Once again the ANE texts are used as helpful analogies,[13] but as Seow will do some years later, the ANE texts do not speak to the date of the psalm but merely to the genre and provenance.[14] The phrase קוּמָה יְהוָה לִמְנוּחָתֶךָ אַתָּה וַאֲרוֹן עֻזֶּךָ "rise LORD to your resting place, you and the ark of your strength" has been the main element of data for those arguing for a ritual process behind this text. However, such a suggestion is not without problems. Much of the issue revolves around the rendering of the lamed. Should it be "to" or "from." Hillers argues for the latter.[15] While Hillers argues for a time later than Seow, he nonetheless does not go so far as to suggest a post-exilic context such as Zerrubbabel. The language of verse 8 mentions the ark. Conventional wisdom makes the point that the ark was carried away during the Exile and never seen again. Hence, the presence of the ark argues for a pre-exilic era.[16]

A key element to the argument goes to the issue of the shape and shaping of the Psalter. The songs of ascent provide the present canonical context for Psalm 132. However, Psalm 132 does not share distinctive elements of the others psalms in the collection.[17] (1) Psalms 120–131 show no indication of Zion theology, save Psalm 122. (2) Psalms 132–134 have Zion as a central focus. (3) Psalm 132 contains language not found in the rest of the psalms of ascent. (4) Finally the other psalms of ascent are shorter, on the whole. The redactor uses the disparity so that Psalm 122 and 132–134 form an *inclusio* of Zion theology.[18]

The psalms of ascent have characteristics of late Hebrew, that is to say post-exilic Hebrew.[19] Portions of Psalm 132 itself indicate a post-exilic orthography and linguistic evidence. For instance vv. 10 and 13-18 probably have a post-exilic context.[20]

Whereas Hillers argued that conventional wisdom claimed that one would not find a post-exilic reference to the Ark, Patton observes to the contrary that traditions of tent and temple become more intertwined in the post-exilic era than at any time before.[21] The Chronicler's project involves precisely that, the combination of two traditions, namely the tent and the temple. Likewise these two traditions are combined in Psalm 132, as well as in three other psalms (Pss 43:3, 84:2, and possibly 87:2). "Further, the reference to the lost location of the ark in Ps 132:5 would fit the time of the restoration better than that of David or Solomon."[22] All of these observations point to the probability of a late, that is post-exilic date for Psalm 132.

The data used to support the earlier date presents ambiguous information. In terms of linguistic evidence the presence of *yosheb* is ambiguous. While it does occur in early texts it also occurs in late texts. Hence it would be arbitrary to claim that the earliest date should apply. Similarly the reference to the bull of Jacob appears in passages of a later period. (Gen 49:24; Isa 49:26; 60:16) The presence of the term in Second Isaiah would indicate that the Genesis material is from a late redactional strata rather than pre-exilic as construed by Seow.

Now as we close this discussion of the historical context. "The ideological and linguistic connections with the Chronicler, Haggai, Zechariah, and Third Isaiah throughout the psalm confirm what philology and context suggest. Clearly, the psalm contains early motifs and epithets, yet these alone do not necessitate an early date for the composition of the psalm. Methodologically a psalm should be dated according to the latest datable elements it contains, unless those elements are clearly secondary additions."[23] Despite the helpful clarification provided by Patton with regard to the date of the passage is constructive for the debate, but the question as to its meaningfulness is not clear. Hence the historical critical appropriation of the text drives us to another strategy of reading.

II

The exegetical work of Psalm 132 calls us to stand between philosophy of language and linguistic philosophy. Philosophy of language is a subject. It seeks to give philosophically illuminating descriptions of a feature or features of language. However, it is only incidentally concerned with the particulars of any given language. Linguistic philosophy is a method. "Linguistic philosophy is the attempt to solve particular philosophical problems by attending to the ordinary use of particular words or other elements in a particular language."[24] This essay builds on a philosophy of language forged by J. L. Austin and John R. Searle, and advanced by Nicolas Wolterstorff. However, this paper is not a display of philosophy of language. It more closely resembles linguistic philosophy for it attempts to understand the practice of the psalms as a philosophical and theological problem, by attending to the particulars of Psalm 132. One might wonder if what we do in biblical theology might be construed as linguistic philosophy. Thus, this paper will approach the issues of practice and power from the perspective of both a philosophy of language and linguistic philosophy.

A conference on "Practice and Psalms" encourages us to be specific about what we mean by "practice." "By practice I am going to mean any coherent and complex form of socially established cooperative human activity through which goods internal to that form of activity are realized in the course of trying to achieve those standards of excellence which are appropriate to and partially definitive of, that form of activity, with the result that human powers to achieve excellence, and human conceptions of the ends and goods involved, are systematically extended."[25]

A practice has certain characteristics. (1) It involves an attention to rules. (2) It operates under a standard of excellence. (3) It moves out of a history that governs both the standards of excellence and the rules of engagement. (4) It "requires a certain type of relationship between those who participate in it."[26]

Practices live only to the degree that they have a framework. In other words, practices have their context in institutions. Yet they should not be confused with institutions. An example might be helpful here. We can think of prophecy as described by DeVaux as an institution. The institution of prophecy has constituent practices. The literary vestiges of those practices are the prophetic genres.

There are several types of practices. MacIntyre describes games such as chess and other social practices. For the time being two interest us: doxastic practices, those arising from and shaping belief constitution, and social practices. "A doxastic practice is a way of steering one's doxastic constitution."[27] The Hallel psalms challenge listeners to a doxastic practice, where one's life is structured like Psalm 150 where everything we do praises the Lord.

Practices connect with agency. The term agency does not figure in MacIntyre's discussion, nor does the language find a home in Bass *et.al.* *Practicing the Faith*. However, when we pay attention to the original context of MacIntyre's discussion of practice we can easily see the connection to the issue of human agency. MacIntyre's venture was an attempt to develop a viable moral theory. "Practices might flourish in societies with very different codes; what they could not do is flourish in societies in which the virtues were not valued. . ."[28] The idea that one can have virtue posits human agency.

Scripture depends on the radical assumption that God speaks. The speech-action theory opens up new possibilities for the way we construe the biblical text and God as well. This has implications for theological anthropology and epistemology. Speech action theory gives us categories of language to construe biblical texts. Following J. L. Austin we recognize locutionary acts and illocutionary acts. "Locutionary acts are acts of uttering or inscribing words. *Il-*locutionary are acts performed *by way of* locutionary acts, acts such as asking, asserting, commanding, and promising and so forth."[29]

Illocutionary acts are what I will call performative speech.[30] Performative speech organizes power and illuminates the agent and agency. "Acts of promising, and commanding will always reveal something or other about the agent . . . what they reveal about the agent is not that which the agent promised or commanded."[31]

Psalms and practice at work in Psalm 132 open a delicate flower, petals overlapping to create a fascinating design that eludes quantification. The elements of the flower are divine performative speech and human performative speech agency and practice.

Before we can address the issue of divine performative speech we need to take a look at the premise of divine speech. "Divine speech disappeared into divine revelation because speaking of God was taken to be a metaphorical way of attributing revelation to God."[32] The understanding of whether we can have divine discourse effects the method of exegesis that forms the heart of biblical studies.

Issues of authorship may clarify the issue of historical context but are they meaningful? It depends. The Enlightenment created the concept of the author. This view of author came into the domain assumptions of biblical studies. This involved the reconstrual of the affirmation that "God speaks" to the subsequent Enlightenment domain assumption that "God reveals." The meaning of the passage is related to the author and experience of the author, according to the Schleiermacher hermeneutics that dominated the discussion of the nineteenth and early twentieth century. Even today there are those who maintain authorial intention as the location of meaning.[33] As related to issues of Scripture, the argument goes that God spoke to the author and modern readers have only access to the speech of God through the authors of Scripture. In terms of biblical studies this is a deputation model of understanding Scripture. God deputized the biblical writers.[34]

However from the mid-twentieth to the present there have been attacks on the idea of the author. First there was the New Criticism, which claimed that the fascination with the author had outstripped interest in the text.[35] Second there were the French philosophers such as Foucault[36] and Derrida.[37] Finally, reader-response critics, heirs of the New Criticism likewise pay scant attention to the author as an interpretive key. Instead the reader-response style of reading holds to the importance of the interpreting community.[38]

In the area of theology Hans Frei and George Lindbeck takes a similar move. The community of interpretation is the Church. The Christian philosopher Nicholas Wolterstorff sees promise in the hermeneutics of Frei and Lindbeck. Wolterstorff makes two important moves for our purposes. First he re-imagines the authorial located meaning. However, to get at this he makes a case for God as the author of Scripture.[39]

The methodological impact of this can hardly be overestimated. The epistemological model that undergirds historical-critical renderings of biblical texts falls away if Wolterstorff is in fact correct that God is the author of Scripture not merely the dictator. The historical reconstructions can provide edification but not meaning. Second, in order to put this philosophical observation in place Wolterstorff suggests that we use performance interpretation.

Performance interpretation has certain elements that remind us of the interpretive suggestions from Lindbeck. First, interpretations of biblical text "try to get it right." The understanding of musical performance orchestrates his view of performance interpretation. "The score is a set of guidelines for producing a musical performance."[40] Performance interpretation understands the interpretive balance. "The fact that a score's specifications are never sufficient for fully determining its realizations is what makes interpretation not only possible, but necessary. . . . Performers are not thrown entirely onto their own devices for interpretation."[41]

Performance interpretation outlined by Wolterstorff is not so much an exegetical model as it is a set of assumptions about the text, for instance, the notion that church tradition provides a meaningful context for interpreting texts illuminated by church tradition. Here Wolterstorff and the late Hans Frei are on the same page.[42] They share other observations about styles of reading that would be in keeping with performance interpretation, such as the importance of reading the Bible as a single book. Wolterstorff reminds us that this is the traditional practice.

Traditional practice in terms of reading builds on an appropriation model. God spoke in the Bible, thus, the task for the reader is to determine what God is saying. This means we seek the discernment of the authorial discourse, not the presentational discourse *qua* discourse.[43] "So our interest as authorial-discourse interpreters is indeed in what the speaker said—not in what he intended to say, but in what he did say, if anything. But saying is an intentional action."[44] In other words we want to know the agency of God. Once that is in place we are more informed about the strategy for our own agency.

Three core assumptions of performance interpretation resonate with Hans Frei. First an emphasis on reading the Bible as a single book.[45] Second we should read the text with a *sensus literalis*, a plain reading of the text. Third, we should read with a *sensus fidelium*,[46] another way to say that we read in the context of the Church.

Taking Wolterstorff's methodological suggestions, let's take a final look at Psalm 132. The historical-critical material that we have examined before provides a helpful tropological reading, namely outlining the historical particulars which we then construe to make broad observations about human existence and God. In other words, the historical-critic determines the tropos of a given text then extrapolates the meaning of the text. One should complement this with a three-point method that focuses on the *sensus literalis*, reading the text in canonical context, and *sensus fidielium*.

Sensus Literales

The ANE texts that parallel Psalm 132 demonstrate the use of this type of rhetoric for the purpose of legitimating the monarch and royal policy.[47] Seow concludes that Psalm 132 has a background of public display of royal piety.[48] It is too much to venture an annual royal ritual.[49] We can see this all even more clearly when we import the categories of John Austin and John R. Searle.

There are three moves of performative speech. By performative speech I mean language that does more than describe. The first movement is the call to remember. This form of performative speech is not limited to biblical examples but occurs also in ANE.[50] We find two types of parallels in the Hebrew Bible. The first set of parallels remember the deeds of God (Deut 24:9; 25:17) and match Psalm 132 in a call for the recollection of the deeds of David. The second group of parallels are references to individuals. ("Remember the son of Imri . . ." in Neh 3:2 and "Remember Sherebah" in Neh 10:13.)

The second performative speech is introduced by a declarative statement that signals a vow. This declarative statement has an example of synonymous parallelism. We note the verbal parallel "swear" נִשְׁבַּע and "vow" נָדַר . We also recognize the parallelism of the prepositional phrases "to the LORD" לַיהוָה and "the mighty one of Jacob" לַאֲבִיר יַעֲקֹב.

With this descriptive/declarative phase done, we are now prepared to hear the first-person performative speech. This first person speech is quoted performative speech of the past. However, we must recognize that this speech *per se* does not have a clear textual antecedent.

Cohortatives and imperatives often indicate performative speech. This is true in Psalm 132. The quotation of the performative speech paves the way for a series of cohortatives (vv. 7-8). The first cohortative is addressed to the people. The second set of cohortatives is addressed to the LORD. Performative speech acts, as such it invites. The performative speech acts but it also invites action. As such performative speech implies agency and also invites agency of the other.

The second section of the psalm begins in verse 11 which parallels verse 2.[51] This section replaces the performative speech in the mouth of God. The condition clause appears in the second poem as it was in the first. However, now the conditional clause in the midst of performative speech is for the legitimation of the Davidic lineage (v. 12). Now that the status of the royal family is firmly in place, the first person performative speech that follows makes clear the divine affection for Zion. The legitimation of the Davidic household and Zion are connected with satisfying the needy (v. 15).

Canonical Context

A plausible case can be made for reading 2 Sam 6 with Psalm 132. Whether this is a matter of inter-textuality or inner-biblical exegesis is a matter of debate. The inner-biblical exegesis would claim that Psalm 132 is an interpretation of 2 Sam 6. A claim for this as an expression of inter-textuality argues that these are shared tropes. "The procession dramatized the return of the divine warrior to claim kingship in his new abode of rest from which he would demonstrate his beneficence." The ANE parallels indicate the mythological context.[52]

The canonical context and the inner-biblical exegesis discussion has been preoccupied with the matter of historical context. The arguments largely tend to focus on linguistic evidence and theological perspective. Attempts have been made to date this Psalm as early. It does have some language reminiscent of Num 10:35.[53] However, the phrase noted as parallel occurs not only in Numbers, but in late texts such as 2 Chr 6:41; Pss 3:8; 7:7; 9:20; 10:12; 17:13. This indicates that one can make an argument for a late dating of Psalm 132.

Another issue has to do with the sociological context of the passage. Seow rightly notes that this is the only explicit reference to the ark in the Psalter.[54] Mowinckel suggested that this psalm was a ancient royal liturgy. Kraus argues for the connection to an enthronement festival. Dahood and Cross, on the basis of archaisms, want to argue for an early date.[55] However, the archaisms are not thoroughly distributed in the poem.[56]

Sensus Fidelium

The historical-critical treatments of writers such as Seow ultimately fall into a tropological position as one tries to move from historical description to theological reflection. The tropos is the requirement of forging a practice that orchestrates power and politics and ecclesiastical structures. In that sense, we should not be at all surprised that plausible theories can emerge for a late and an early historical setting. Tropes that link political and liturgical power come to the fore in those circumstances when the institutions of a kingship or cult are under fire.

Whether we date the material early or late, the performative language, both human and divine, construe power and institutions. Scholars have been good at being descriptive. However, in terms of practice what would God have us do on the basis of this text?

The performative speech is action. This also means that it conveys a sense of agency. At the same time as it is apparent in Psalm 132, it also incites action, and the concomitant agency related to it. At the level of function of the text in the practice of the Church this psalm mandates that we eschew any sort of obscurantism. The institution of power, politically and ecclesiastically are themselves theological by virtue of the performative speech they embody. Ultimately, we must ask what David and Zion have to do with the construal of power and agency in North America today.

An area for further exploration has to do with the practice of a *sensus fidelium* reading of the Psalms in particular and the Scriptures in general. While this is one of the intriguing ideas put forward by Frei, Lindbeck and Wolterstorff, at the level of practice its implementation becomes troublesome. When one works in the context of the catholic Church universal, how does one read the text *sensus fidelium* in a way that is more than the tropological reading, but ends with authorial intention of a human writer as the arbiter of meaning?

NOTES: CHAPTER 3

[1] J. L. Austin, *How to Do Things With Words*, 2nd ed. J. O. Urson and Marina Sbisa (Harvard: Cambridge, 1962) 1.

[2] N. Wolterstorff, *Divine Discourse. Philosophical Reflections on the Claim that God Speaks* (Cambridge: Cambridge University Press, 1995) 202.

[3] Frank Moore Cross, *Canaanite Myth and Hebrew Epic* (Cambridge: Harvard, 1973) 232.

[4] Ibid., 244.

⁵ Cross, *Canaanite Myth and Hebrew Epic*, 97 n. 24; Dahood, *Psalms 51–100* AB vol. 2 (Garden City: Doubleday, 1970) 242.

⁶ Seow, *Myth, Drama, and the Politics of David's Dance*, HSM 46 (Atlanta: Scholars Press, 1989) 148.

⁷ Ibid.

⁸ Ibid.

⁹ Ibid., 148–49.

¹⁰ Ibid., 157.

¹¹ Ibid., 163.

¹² Ibid., 147.

¹³ D. Hillers, "Ritual Procession of the Ark and Ps 132" *CBQ* 30 (1968) 53.

¹⁴ Ibid., 55.

¹⁵ Ibid., 49–50.

¹⁶ Contra H. Hupfeld, *Die Psalmen II* (Gotha, 1888) 595 and P. Haupt "The Inauguration of the Second Temple" *JBL* 33 (1914) 162f. See Hillers, "Ritual Procession of the Ark," 51.

¹⁷ C. L. Patton, "Psalm 132: A Methodological Inquiry," *CBQ* 57 (1995) 646.

¹⁸ L. D. Crow, *The Psalms of Ascent (Psalms 120–134). Their Place in Israelite History and Religion* SBLDS 148 (Atlanta: Scholars Press, 1996) 143–45.

¹⁹ Patton, "Psalm 132. A Methodological Inquiry," 645–47.

²⁰ Cross, *Canaanite Myth and Hebrew Epic*, 232, n. 56, 238, n. 85.

²¹ Patton, "Psalm 132. A Methodological Inquiry," 648.

²² Ibid., 650.

²³ Ibid., 654.

²⁴ J. R. Searle, *Speech Acts: An Essay in the Philosophy of Language* (London: Cambridge University, 1969) 4.

²⁵ A. MacIntyre, *After Virtue*, Second Edition (South Bend, Ind.: University of Notre Dame Press, 1984) 187.

²⁶ Ibid., 191.

²⁷ Wolterstorff, *Divine Discourse*, 271; The volume *Practicing Our Faith. A Way of Life for a Searching People*, D. Bass, ed. (San Francisco: Jossey-Bass, 1997) explores just such a set of practices.

²⁸ MacIntyre, *After Virtue,* 193.

²⁹ Wolterstorff, *Divine Discourse*, 13.

³⁰ J. L. Austin, *Doing Things With Words*, 5–6.

³¹ Wolterstorff, *Divine Discourse*, 35.

³² Ibid., 10.

³³ E. D. Hirsch, Jr., *Validity of Interpretation* (New Haven: Yale University, 1967) 1–23.

³⁴ Wolterstorff, *Divine Discourse*, 186.

³⁵ Selden and Widdowson, *A Reader's Guide to Contemporary Literary Theory*, 3rd ed. (Lexington: University of Kentucky, 1993) 10–26; T. Eagleton, *Literary Theory. An Introduction* (Minneapolis: University of Minnesota, 1983) 47–53.

³⁶ M. Foucault, "What is an Author?" in the *Foucault Reader*, P. Rabinow, ed. (New York: Pantheon, 1984) 101–20.

³⁷ J. Derrida, *Limited Inc.* (Evanston: Northwestern University Press, 1988).

[38] S. Fish, "Is there a Text in This Class? From *Is There a Text in This Class? The Authority of Interpretive Communities* (Cambridge: Harvard University, 1980) 303–21.

[39] Wolterstorff, *Divine Discourse*, 283.

[40] Ibid., 175.

[41] Ibid., 176.

[42] Ibid., 179.

[43] Ibid., 188f.

[44] Ibid., 199.

[45] Some will notice that this sounds also a lot like the clarion call of Brevard Childs. However, Childs is in no way dependent on these writers and makes little attempt to draw from philosophical sources to buttress his hermeneutical observations and suggestions. So while one might see Wolterstorff as yet another voice of the so-called Yale School, Lindbeck and Frei Childs makes a point of not being lumped into that group.

[46] Wolterstorff, *Divine Discourse*, 218–22.

[47] Seow, *Myth, Drama, and the Politics of David's Dance*, 158–63.

[48] Ibid., 201.

[49] S. Mowinckel, *Psalms in Israel's Worship*; A. Weiser, *Psalms* OTL (Philadelphia: Westminister, 1962).

[50] Hillers, "Ritual procession of the Ark," 53.

[51] E. F. Huwiler, "Patterns and Problems in Psalm 132," in *The Listening Heart* JSOTSup 58 (Sheffield: JSOT Press, 1987) 201; P. Nel, "Psalm 132 and Covenant Theology," in *Text and Context*, W. Claasen, JSOTSup 48 (Sheffield: JSOT Press, 1988) 184.

[52] Seow, *Myth, Drama and the Politics of David's Dance*, 202.

[53] L. Allen *Psalms 101–150* WBC 21 (Waco: Word Press, 1983) 205: Seow, *Myth, Drama, and the Politics of David's Dance*, 145.

[54] Seow, *Myth, Drama, and the Politics of David's Dance*, 145.

[55] Cross, *Canaanite Myth and Hebrew Epic*, 94–97. M. Dahood, *Psalms 101–150* AB vol. 3 (Garden City, New York: Doubleday, 1970) 241.

[56] Seow, *Myth, Drama, and the Politics of David's Dance*, 147.

Discussion: Psalms and Practice

What is a Psalm? What do we mean by "practice"?

Esther Menn's group defined a psalm as devotional singing, but a singing that engages beyond the song. The psalms preach, teach, and pray and are both song and poetry. They contain metaphors that can be material for preaching. The group discovered that sometimes the psalms seem alien, discordant, employing an unknown language regarding enemies, and they wondered what could be done to overcome the alienness of these psalms?

The group continued by reporting that practice involves community, history, rules, the community's standards of excellence, singing, preaching liturgy, memorizing, and the use of psalms in pastoral care. They shared local ideas of the ways psalms were used in their own congregation's liturgical hours.

Michael Jinkins shared that his group talked about the definition of psalms, but was unable to come to any decision regarding a definition. For them, the relationality presented in the psalms was a key issue. A conversation among Gerald Wilson, Harry Nasuti, and Mark Smith about the power of the psalms, and how the language of the psalms somehow moves us was related. The shift in the psalms from being simply about Israel, to identification with "I" and "we," was noted in this group. There is praise in the psalms, but also included are quiet sets of psalms, which sit in silence, waiting for the Spirit to move people through them.

Beth Liebert's group related how the psalms are extensively repeated by psalm-like narratives in both the Old Testament and the New Testament, as well as the nine canonical psalms which can be found in the Qumran. Music may be involved in defining a psalm, but it is not required. This group finally decided to leave the definition of a psalm open, so that there would be room for all things.

Practice is the intention of the psalms, and that practice includes prayer, praise and piety. The liturgical pedagogy of the psalms comes forth only as you use them. They motivate you to learn more about yourself. The psalms also contain ideas of theology.

This group also raised a question of what people remember in music: the melody or the words? They wondered if there is, from the King James edition of the Bible, an English canon in the psalms on which we rely.

The psalms can be used as an entry into biblical theology, but the question must be asked if all of the psalms are still fair game in today's environment. We can interpret the theology of the psalms in two ways: God-talk and systematic. The difference between the two becomes most apparent when we sing the psalms, at that time we are not thinking about theology. Therefore, are they God-talk or not?

What is the connection between theology and practice? The questions raised stayed with us throughout the conference. It's fortunate we did not find the quintessential definition of either psalm or practice!

Alien language and enemies are very real in the psalms. Do we have enemies today? The idea that we have no enemies is strange and the curse psalms imply that they do exist. As Christians, we are counseled to love our enemies, but we can't love our enemies until we first identify them as such. James Howell spoke of pastoral counseling and identified anger in the psalms which can be a very powerful tool in some situations. But a woman who had been raped at knife point heard sermons about loving enemies, and as we talked about her experience, she shared her view that this was the antithesis of any kind of spirituality. Do we find within the psalms a spirituality which allows us to put our arms around the idea of revenge?

In our society we are conditioned to deny we have enemies. We are conditioned to deny our feelings of depression, anger and fear. But if we allow ourselves to be formed by the psalms, we learn that the way to loving our enemies, is to be honest with those feelings and to live through them.

When it comes to loving your enemies, the context of the people you're talking with makes a difference. Vietnam, Egypt, Korea, Philippines, Africa, different cultures provide different answers. The practice of loving your enemy is a local one.

Why is it so hard for those of us in the Church to admit that we have enemies? A very venerable sister once said that she couldn't say the terrible things of a psalm in church, but why can't we say them there? We say them in our halls.

I think that in my teaching, the psalms come to life. Interesting discussions always ensue when I ask my classes, "Have you ever railed against God?" Why do we think it is alien to voice the fact that we have done everything right, and to question where God is in the moment? Can we be mad at God?

The Psalms are unique on this point. Most of the other books of the Bible say that Israel is always at fault, but Psalm 44 says that God is at fault. Haar's dissertation on the psalms is good in that it points out that the psalms call God to account for both God's action and inaction. People outside the Church do not hesitate to fault God, it is those of us in the Church who fail to ask much of God. The biblical witness is filled with tales of the Jewish people telling God exactly what they want. Over and over again, they go out to God and make a deal.

David Blumenthal hypnotizes us with the idea that sometimes God is an abuser. Psalm 44 says "You have rejected and humbled us". The difference between Blumenthal and the Bible is that Blumenthal makes an absolute claim that God is the God of darkness, not only the God of light. Blumenthal further breaks this down to the idea that God is abusive. In order to understand this, we must step outside our own subjective context and say it for other people in their experiential context. The book of Job begins by shifting the own-ness from Job, but ultimately it moves back to him. Blumenthal makes that same move at the outset of the story, but with a different bend. He then assumes a different posture to take it towards God.

What is a covenant with God about, if not a two way deal? As Christians, we cut short the covenant when we don't ask these questions of God. Should we see Blumenthal as a scholar or a practitioner? Why does his idea happen in the context of practice over and against that of theology?

I wanted to have a conference on psalms and practice to bring into conversation about the Psalms excellent scholars, along with people who are pastors, people who are involved with spiritual formation, and people who provide pastoral care. A Valparaiso Project is concerned with the education of religious communities in view of the widespread hunger for knowledge about God. We are not taking advantage of the rich vein of material available. There is widespread hunger for religion in our culture. A hunger for a way of life in tune with God's active presence. A life drawn from sources and places grounded in the ancient wisdom.

The question becomes "How can churches embody this way of life?" Historians working with church and rabbinical literature are trying to help people re-conceive the idea of self-renewal, to help ground us more thoroughly in the way of God.

Does it matter? Do worship and liturgy matter? Yes, but only if we are able to overcome the division between thought and action. When we consider the social practice of physics, we are shown a world we have never seen before. The text belongs to a community that is practicing—a believing and doing community.

Practicing our Faith, edited by Craig Dykstra and Dorothy Bass, has twelve practices that comprise a life for which we are all looking. Practices that help us find ways to sing our lives. In each case, we saw the practices work. They are practices that are common in all religious communities. We are eager to find theologians in the midst of practicing communities who are working at the very important issue of the liturgies of practice.

Part II:
Psalms and Practice
Contemplation and Worship

Introduction

*P*ractice and the psalms are never far from the formation of the soul. This takes place in a number of ways. We explored three of these. First, we looked at prayer. Second the Psalms shape our faith through the process of liturgy. And finally the Psalms shape us as preached Word.

John Endres introduces the spiritual formation discussion in his article "Praying with Psalms: A School of Prayer." The paper began with a course on the psalms during which a student asked ". . . what would you say to someone who belongs to a church that does not believe in prayer?" The question can be rephrased that prayer is performative speech. That is to say that it represents a type of language that shapes not merely describes.

The Psalms genres may seem fixed but, to the degree that they represent prayers, they are as resilient as other prayers. Endres reminds us that the experience of psalms was transformed by Vatican II in two ways, first the Office was now available in the vernacular. Second the Psalms were heard in liturgical fragments. His article begins with this context and suggest ways to connect groups of psalms and the natural moments of Christian spiritual life. This involves praying in and with and through Christ. The spiritual retreat uses a reading strategy of the practice of spiritual disciples called *Lectio Divina*. This style of reading differs from a preoccupation with the original sense of the text. The retreat gives participants an opportunity to avoid an either or reading strategy but rather blending of the two.

Harry P. Nasuti develops a different avenue of spiritual formation and practice in his essay "The Sacramental Function of the Psalms in Contemporary Scholarship and Liturgical Practice." The Psalms are on the one hand a reservoir for pious practice and on the other hand the Psalter is a residue of previous pious practice. Drawing from Athanasius,

Nasuti finds the distinctive voice of the psalms in their ability to "affect" and "mold" a person. Nasuti, like Reid, makes use of speech-act theory of J. L. Austin and John R. Searle. However, he adds to the mix the work of Paul Ricoeur. Hence there is a link between the concerns of these philosophers of language and biblical scholars such as Mowinckel and Breuggemann. The consensus is that psalms have a sacramental power as a means of grace. The power derives from divine agency.

The sacramental power is laid in the manger of the liturgy. The Psalms exist in the liturgy through the lectionary readings. In this collection of readings, the psalms selection is typically responsorial to the Old Testament reading for that Sunday. Nasuti observes that the liturgical context which places the psalm as the response of the people of God to the Word of God dominates. One byproduct of this is the muting of the authorial intention. Nasuti examines Psalm 51 and the Ash Wednesday service to illustrate these observations.

Rolf Jacobson takes a different tact to explore similar themes in his essay "Burning Our Lamps with Borrowed Oil." He notes that the words of the Psalter are not our words, in that sense they are borrowed oil. As we noted elsewhere the residue of pious practice of ages gone. We inherit a language from the Psalms. Hence we receive an interesting rhetorical situation the residue of the ancient practice shapes the rhetoric of contemporary practice. Jacobson notes the use of the first person in many of the Psalms. He introduces a new conversation partner. Whereas Reid and Nasuti worked with speech-act theory and philosophy of language, Jacobson goes to the work on cognitive dissonance to open up the liturgical space as a time when one is shaped not only by words that are not ours in one sense but also by affect that may not be ours either. Jacobson then opens the door to a new appreciation from the categories Brueggemann borrowed from Paul Ricoeur, namely orientation, disorientation, and reorientation. By so doing, Jacobson suggests that cognitive dissonance, disorientation in the rhetorical world of the Psalter can result in a reorientation.

Kathryn L. Roberts reminds us that the Psalter often characterized as the hymnbook of Israel did not function as the *Book of Common Worship* for that believing community. There is no liturgy in the Psalter but rather liturgical pieces. Like Nasuti, she uses Psalm 51 as her test case to outline the dialectical relationship between praise and sacrifice in her essay "My Tongue will sing Aloud of your Deliverance." Roberts invites us to enter the world of sacrifice, despite the preference to privilege passages that annul ritual sacrifice. The result of this anti-sacrifice predilection is the loss of praise as a Christian practice. She makes a case for the commitment to sacrifice as part of a holistic practice of praise.

We encounter the Psalter not only as heard Word through liturgy but also as preached Word in the sermon. Clinton McCann addresses this point. He recounts the burgeoning interest in the book of Psalms generated by renewed interest in the Revised Common Lectionary. At the same time, he notes a decisive hesitance about the preaching from the Psalter. After rehearsing the objections to preaching the psalms, in the field of homiletics and biblical studies both, McCann rebuts them one by one. He points to the matter of practice as aspiration of excellence. He approaches this by pointing out that a major objection to preaching the psalms derives from a difficulty in preaching from poetic texts. Practice has criteria of excellence. Hence the practice of preaching likewise works under these constraints. Then when there is a difficulty in preaching, then it builds a concomitant objection.

McCann makes the point that the present form of the Psalter is the product of a deliberate theological process. Such a process has to be at the heart of something. He then moves to an interesting weaving of exegetical and homiletical work examining Psalms 1 and 2 with contemporary social analysis.

After the example of homiletical reflection in the McCann essay we next turn to James Howell's distinctive contribution to the volume. In his essay, the reader finds a report of the role the psalms made in the shaping of the congregation that heard sermons on selected psalms. Another distinctive element in this essay is the use of boxes to mark excursus. These provide background information that may help put the description of the process in context. Also this essay contains sermon excerpts set off by a distinctive typeface.

Beth LaNeel Tanner gives us a look into the world of suffering and laments. She illuminates the absence of these elements from typical worship. Her essay suggests ways that we might introduce lament into liturgy and dispense with "happy worship." The issue of "happy worship" includes the loss of theodicy. Justice and worship require a place for lament, according to Tanner. Her solution includes "learning laments all over again." This includes a change in the seminary curriculum that finds expression in pastoral care, worship, and Christian education classes.

4

Praying With Psalms
A School of Prayer

John C. Endres, S.J.

*W*hen I began teaching the psalms in 1982, I thoroughly schooled myself in form-critical study of the Psalter, researched the various proposals for early cultic settings of the psalms, and presented this material to students whom I presumed were hungry for this knowledge of Israel's ways of worship and religious practices. Approximately eight weeks into the course, I timidly presented a class one day on "Psalms and Prayer," worried that it might not suit the academic nature of our consortium at the Graduate Theological Union. That day one older student, well known for fairly exotic questions, raised his hand and asked, "Fr. Endres, what would you say to someone who belongs to a church that does not believe in prayer?" The other students laughed, the professor made a humorous remark, and the incident could have been forgotten, except that I began to realize that was how I was presenting the Psalms. Slowly I began to realize that many seminary students were searching for something more—how do the psalms enter into contemporary life, pastoral care, worship, their spiritual lives. They responded as enthusiastically to musical settings of psalms as they did to explanations of Hebrew philology. I began to realize that their responses to the hearing of sung psalms often witnessed a deeper realization of a psalm's depth and power than did the academic study.

Then I began to search for ways to bridge this gap between academy and sanctuary, and it continues to this day. Some time later, I discussed my perceptions about teaching the Psalms with Elizabeth Liebert, a colleague who teaches Christian spirituality at the Presbyterian seminary in our consortium. I talked about my desire to help people both pray with and study Psalms, and she was describing different ways of introducing people to prayer practices for their personal devotion and prayer life. Both of us belong to Roman Catholic religious communities, where the Psalms have played a fairly important role in our community prayer life; moreover, it is normal practice in our groups to set aside six to eight days each year for "retreat," a time of quiet, prayer, and renewal of spirit. Often we make retreats in groups, with a director who gives a couple of talks each day, giving expositions of Scripture for personal prayer, or other types of spiritual experiences. One day we wondered: why not experiment with spending the days of "retreat" praying over psalms in a focused way? So began the development of a retreat focused on prayer with psalms, lasting six to eight days.

Psalm Genres and Types of Prayer

Although scholarly opinions of form criticism are becoming more divided, we found the approach helpful because of the way the psalms are used in the prayer and worship life of the Roman Catholic Church. Priests and religious "said" or sang psalms on a daily basis in the breviary, the offices, the Liturgy of the Hours. However, their experience of psalms changed dramatically after Vatican Council II, when the Office became available in vernacular languages, instead of Latin. Lay Catholics would have known scattered psalm verses from their attendance at Mass, which included selected verses for an *introit* or *gradual* (preferably sung), but seldom would they have heard an entire psalm. Since most Catholic prayer books focused on devotions and litanies, few members of the church would have really experienced the book of Psalms in any holistic fashion. And if they had prayed psalms, it is quite likely that they would have learned them in a Christ-oriented perspective that has a long history in the churches.

The liturgical reforms of Vatican II dramatically altered this landscape for the Psalms. A revised Liturgy of the Word featured a psalm after the first reading on both Sundays and weekdays, a change that introduced many Catholics to more sustained hearing of the moods and language of the psalms than they had previously known. Though people still debate the best way of praying or singing these "responsorial" psalms in the Eucharist, one fact is clear: many more people have an ear for psalms now, and occasionally they will pick up the missallette in the pew and read over the psalm prayerfully before Mass begins.

Some have commented that the psalm touches their lives more than any of the other Bible readings.

A similar transformation of psalmic life occurred among those who pray the Liturgy of the Hours regularly, for new vernacular texts were prepared and disseminated in the early 1970s. Careful focus on the pronunciation or chanting of the Latin Psalter was replaced by understanding of and attention to vernacular texts of psalms. In the English-speaking world, a translation by The Grail became the standard, and its poetic cadences still hold fond memories for many Catholics. During this time some prayer books for Catholics began to feature short collections of psalms as a basis for prayer and meditation, and many came to love certain psalms. The musical settings composed by Joseph Gelineau, S. J., became as popular in English as they had been in French, and these melodies, words, and antiphons still provide for many a rich spiritual entree into the psalms.

On another front, Roman Catholic scholars had timidly entered the world of modern biblical studies on the psalms, beginning in the 1950s. Pius Drijvers, a Dutch Trappist who had studied at the Pontifical Biblical Institute in Rome, wrote an introduction to the Psalms that presented modern biblical approaches to psalms. After the book had gone through several Dutch revisions, a translation in English appeared in 1965: *The Psalms: Their Structure and Meaning.*[1] He contextualized the Psalms in the liturgy of the Church, so he advocated psalm study on the three "organically connected planes" of Old Testament, the Christian Church, and heaven.[2] Much of this book presents the Psalms in Israel's worship life, as he claims to work "in accord with labours of modern exegesis and the leadership of the pope—especially in the encyclical *Divino Afflante Spiritu* of 1943."[3] For him, Gunkel's form-critical approach provides the avenue to modern critical study of the psalms called for by Pius XII.[4] Such study allows one to put each psalm back into its group's particular setting and so to "bring it to life." His description of this approach provided a model for Catholic psalm study:

> . . . the division into groups and into types signifies a great gain for the understanding of the teaching, contents, and theology of the psalms, both from the Old Testament standpoint and when considering them in the light of Christian revelation. Each group is distinguished by its own setting, its own mentality and its own range of thought. Each group has its own central idea and expresses the corresponding attitude of mind. It is for us now to try to discover just what that underlying idea and attitude may be. Our examination of the literary genres will be of great

help in doing this. We can thus "introduce some sort of order into the rather heterogenous mass of 150 psalms", and bring to the fore groups and special themes. When we gradually learn to place that central idea, that theme, that attitude of mind in a Christian perspective, we find a really fruitful way of using the psalms as prayers.[5]

Drijvers was forging a new view of Scripture and of Christian prayer based on a form-critical approach to the Psalms. For him, most psalms originated in Israel's liturgical celebrations, and thus represented the moods and goals of the particular liturgy in which Israel sang them, whether it be praise of God in the Temple, lamentations at a shrine or the Temple, services of thanksgiving, or processions to the Temple. Drijvers' imaginative reconstructions of the different kinds of worship in Israel that stood behind the various genres constituted his way of dealing with issues of *Sitz im Leben.*

Although we possess no written rubrics for Israel's liturgical celebrations, Drijvers found many indications of the particular motions or actions which accompanied a psalm as it was sung or recited: e.g., Pss 100:4; 118:19; 26:6-7; 86:24-25; 66:13-15.[6] His analogy of rubrical language would correspond nicely to contemporary ritual discussion of performative actions and language, thus strengthening a bond between ritual and ritual language, or in Drijver's terms, between liturgy and psalmic language.[7] For example, his discussion of thanksgiving psalms moves from literary genre and structure to imaginative reconstruction of thanksgiving ceremonies in ancient Israel, and then concludes with brief discussion of the Christian Eucharist modeled on Jewish thanksgiving rites.[8] For him, the psalm type represented a class of ritual and worship in Israel which also had it counterparts in Christian worship and prayer. This ritual imagination also emerges in other Roman Catholic commentaries, especially in the two-volume set by Carroll Stuhlmueller.[9] In each case, the perspective on interpretation of the psalms owes a great deal to their usage in Catholic liturgy: as vehicles for prayer of the congregation, and also of the individual.

When we planned a retreat with psalms, this liturgical view of psalms informed much of our vision as we determined the best ways to organize presentation of various psalms to a group gathered for prayer, reflection and meditation. Just as the various types of psalms correspond to liturgies or types of worship, so they may also fit distinct moments in the spiritual life. People attempt to live their lives in ways that connect to the cosmos in which they live, the people with whom they interact, all in relation to the God who creates and redeems them. The stark reality of pain and lament, of concrete thanksgiving for divine intervention and transformation, of praise to the creator and prayer for conversion and forgiveness of sin looms large in the lives of many Christians and engages their imaginations and spiritual lives. Our goal was to connect groups of psalms with these natural moments of Christian spiritual life, to study them through daily exposition of types, and to engage people in prayer exercises with each type, both individual and communal. We determined to include prayer and reflection on lament psalms, especially because they seem to have been largely neglected in much Western Christian worship.[10] Catholic retreats frequently try to balance public presentations and worship with extended times of quiet meditative or contemplative prayer (usually two, three or four hour-long periods each day). We planned days which included two presentations, times of group prayer and worship, but which left plenty of space and time for individual prayer, choosing from the suggested type of psalms for each day.

We have experimented with different ways of ordering the types of psalms through the course of a "week." For example, in 1993, we organized six full days with this pattern:

> PRAISE GOD—PRESENT AND ACTIVE IN OUR WORLD
>   (Hymns of Praise)
> CRY OUT TO GOD—IN OUR NEEDS (Psalms of Lament)
> THANK GOD—PRESENT AND ACTIVE IN OUR LIVES
>   (Thanksgiving Psalms)
> CRY OUT TO GOD—FOR FORGIVENESS OF SINS
>   (Penitential Psalms)
> PSALMS—MIRROR OF OUR LIFE IN CHRIST
>   (Christ and the Psalms)
> WISDOM IN THE PSALMS (Wisdom Psalms and Poems)

We began with hymns of praise, presuming that this style of prayer might provide a bridge from ordinary life, especially given the natural beauty of our location: overlooking a beach on Monterey Bay in Santa Cruz, California. From there we moved to laments, focusing on the myriad of ways in which life experience does not match the beauty of the Creator's vision, for individuals and groups of people. Moving from lament to thanksgiving seemed a natural binding together of types, followed by a second type of crying out to God, for forgiveness of sins. Praying psalms in and with and through Christ connects with so much Christian tradition and spirituality, but we sensed a need to introduce other "types" before this approach. Wisdom psalms, with their focus on affairs of everyday life, seemed an excellent way to begin the transition to ordinary life after leaving this location. We also included some poems of personified Wisdom, Lady Wisdom (Prov 8:22-31; Wis Solomon 7), because the perspective of most wisdom psalms is arguably masculine, and most retreatants have been women; this shift met with strong appreciation. One year it happened that the last full day of retreat was Pentecost Sunday, so this motif of wisdom nicely complemented the celebration of that feast.

The daily program on this retreat follows a regular pattern. Each morning features a biblically-oriented presentation, describing the types of psalms for the day, drawing on contemporary life experiences and also relating them, where possible, to narratives in the Bible. One example is the Hannah narrative in 1 Samuel 1, which sets a situation for lament, shows the prayer at the Shiloh temple (minus the words) and the intervention of the priest Eli (possible oracle of salvation), followed by the return home and pregnancy that she had sought. Her return to the sanctuary, with gifts for a sacrificial offering and celebration, offers hints of an ancient pattern of thanksgiving.

The general structure of the opening talk, which introduces a psalm type, follows the pattern below, as in the case of lament psalms:

> *On Begging God for Help from the Pits* with examples from everyday life in our day.
>
> *How Did Biblical People Complain and Lament?* Some biblical narrative examples of this kind of prayer (e.g., 1 Samuel 1).
>
> *Questions one can ask when reading psalms*
> Who is the Speaker?   person[s] in great distress, oppression
> Who is being addressed?   first, God is directly addressed
> What is the Mood?   anger, hurt, despair, fear, distress, lonely
> What does the Psalmist desire?   that God listen, hear, heal, rescue, save, forgive
> What Images of God do you find?   personal God, who hears my cry, who cares for the lowly," God of covenant (enduring love and loyalty)

A Description of the Structure of Lament Psalms

Addressing God: O LORD, O God
Complaining / Lamenting the Distress I/we experience: "why? how long?"

—against enemies
—against God (as enemy)
—about self (personal experience, feelings)

Petition to God in very strong language, pinpoints what is desired or demanded.

Confessing Innocence of sins that bring on suffering {sometimes}

Confession of Trust in God who has saved us before: "still, nevertheless."

God's word of Salvation [very seldom found]

Vowing to Praise God [occasionally promising thanksgiving sacrifice].

We devised the initial questions to pose when "hearing" a psalm, but the elements of the structure of a psalm are clearly indebted both to Gunkel and to Westermann's helpful delineation of various types of enemies.

One aspect of these talks that cannot be adequately represented in this essay is the musical aspect of psalmody. We always try to hold our sessions in a chapel or room where a piano or keyboard is available, and one member of our group prepares psalm settings coordinated to the type of psalm for the day. We have learned that hearing or singing psalm settings usually evokes the hopes and fears, yearnings and joys of the human heart more pointedly than do the written texts or narratives from the Bible. The music is carefully chosen, tested in advance, and often leads the participants to interiorize both words and situations presented to them. Hearing a psalm setting in a minor key often reflects a mood appropriate to a lament psalm, which also evokes a painful memory. Our goal is to help people bring these feelings and petitions directly to God, in song, in prayer, and in the imagination. We usually listen to a recording of a spiritual, which leads us into a world of pain and hope hidden from the purview of many in the society; images of slavery and its impact on families and personal lives remind the group of important early traces of lament in Israel's story, in Exodus 1–2. We also sing quite a bit at Eucharist and at the morning or evening prayer, so we invited interested retreatants to form a small choir to lead the rest of us in sung prayer; for many of them, this practice added to their prayer experience. After one retreat, a very elderly nun exclaimed joyfully: "We haven't been able to sing this much in many years!"

Each day a second presentation aims at illuminating or introducing various styles of prayer with psalms. These sessions often include some kind of group prayer experience, explained in practical terms and usually situated within the history of Christian spirituality. Morning and Evening Prayer derive from ancient Christian worship traditions, and include singing or chanting of psalms and other hymns, listening to scripture, occasionally a brief homily or reflection, intercessions, and the Lord's Prayer. We usually develop one prayer service for each day of the retreat, tailoring it to the particular type of psalms and worship for that day. On the other hand, in our daily celebration of Eucharist, we normally follow the regular liturgical calendar with its biblical readings; occasionally a brief homily might focus on the way the responsorial psalm invites us to deepen our understanding and experience grasped from the scripture readings.

The ancient Christian practice of *lectio divina* has proven very helpful to many people, especially when it has been properly introduced. This style of prayer invites hearing of individual words, images, lines and pondering them in heart or mind, even ruminating over them until they seem to sink into our consciousness. A style of prayer that was especially fostered in the monastery, it also proves useful today for small groups who wish to hear psalms together, in a quiet and reflective fashion. We introduce the normal steps in *lectio*, both for individuals and for groups: often we spend one or more sessions encountering psalms in this fashion. One might substitute other "texts" for the psalm text at certain times, and we even consider personal life history as a significant "text" for the practice of *lectio*. In such a case, e.g., *Lectio on Life: Grateful Review of Graces in Life*, we invite retreatants to follow the spiritual movement of the psalms presented that day (thanksgiving psalms) rather than the precise words of a biblical psalm. Indeed, some individuals write their own psalms appropriate to the day, while others find a journaling process a very helpful way to articulate to God their own concrete sense of thanksgiving.

A traditional practice in Catholic retreats has been celebration of the sacrament of penance or reconciliation. In our retreat, we introduce that as one appropriate response to a day of prayer on the penitential psalms, an ancient Christian collection of seven psalms particularly appropriate for sorrow for sin. Although they do not constitute a separate genre, we treat them as laments: crying out to God for the gift that is desired: forgiveness of sin and complete restoration to covenantal relationship with God and the community. Our reading of these psalms focuses heavily on what is sought: healing, forgiveness, transformation. Focusing especially on Psalms 32 and 51, we find in these psalms a fairly sophisticated notion of sin in biblical Israel, ranging from rebellious transgression of the decalogue, to perverse activity and even to sins that are actually unintentional. Still, the center of the presentation consists of recognition of particular sins against God and against others, and of the structures of society which almost unwittingly bear and pass on sin. A sense of the abject sinfulness of humans, or a notion of the depravity of the human race, does not seem to feature strongly in these psalms. Nor does it in our presentations and prayer services for that day.

For each day or section of the retreat, we offer a selection entitled "Suggested Psalms." Though not all-inclusive, this page lists a large number of psalms in each category or type. We recommend that retreatants choose one of these psalms, or two at most, to spend time with them in personal prayer at times of their choice throughout the day. Many retreatants will go and spend an hour in prayer with one psalm, and perhaps choose other psalms for other prayer times in that day. They have found a helpful balance between large group prayer and gathering and cherished times of solitude. For many people, these quiet times provide opportunity to relish an image, to speak or chant lines of a psalm aloud, to move with the psalm in physical gestures or dance, to let the psalms "pray themselves" in their hearts.

Such a list of psalms (by type) can also provide nourishment for the person after the retreat has concluded. Or as we have come to reflect on this issue, this prayer pattern (retreat) may not consist of six to eight days set apart and in a different location. For many, this retreat may be concluded in daily life, with special patterns of prayer following this pattern. One might, for example, devote a week or two to each of these types of psalms. For such practice, these lists of psalms have proven helpful and freeing.

From Retreat to Handbook: Praying with Psalms

As we provided materials which could prove useful to people as they returned to everyday life, we began to consider developing a book which would contain the materials we presented in retreats. For several years now, we have been preparing this book, which will be published by Paulist Press. In many ways it mirrors the retreats. The contents of Part I are the following:

Chapter 1: Entering the World of the Psalms
Chapter 2: Approaching the Psalms: Five Styles of Prayer
Chapter 3: Crying Out to God in My Need: Psalms of Lament
Chapter 4: Crying Out to God in Our Need:
    Lament Psalms for the Community
Chapter 5: Thanking God Present and Active in Our Lives:
    Thanksgiving Psalms
Chapter 6: Singing to God in Worship: Psalms of Praise
Chapter 7: Crying Out to God for Forgiveness of Sin: Penitential Psalms

Chapter 8: Wondering at God's Ways: Wisdom Psalms
Chapter 9: Knowing Ourselves through the Psalms:
    Psalms as Mirror of our Lives
Chapter 10: Praying Psalms In, With and Through Jesus Christ:
    Christological Psalms.

For each type of psalm and its day, there is a chapter which introduces that psalm type from a biblical-spiritual perspective. After a presentation of psalms in that genre, following the pattern described earlier
in this paper, there follows a lengthy section describing different ways
people might appropriate these psalms prayerfully. In the actual retreats, we often tailored the prayer suggestions to the composition of
the group (social and religious location) and also to our physical location and season (usually in summer months). The book, we realized,
needed to become much more "catholic" (rather than Catholic), so we
expanded our presentations of the different ways of praying with
psalms and also made a conscious effort to include many more materials from Protestant and Reformed church traditions.

The second chapter describes five prayerstyles that we propose to
people. These include: *Lectio Divina*: An Ancient Way of Praying; Morning and Evening Prayer: A Common Tradition; Handmade Midrash:
Praying Visually; Worshipful Movement: Praying with the Body; and
Psalm-Hymnody: Singing the Psalms. These sections of chapter 2 contain thumbnail histories of the development of each prayer style, and
then offer concrete, practical ideas for ways that individuals and groups
can try these practices. Users can consult sections of this chapter while
they are focusing on the various types of psalms, or they can read them
separately. Chapters 3–10 contain some specific suggestions for these
differing prayer styles, and conclude with a model corporate prayer/
worship service. These prayer services are adapted mostly from Roman
Catholic and Presbyterian books of prayer.

Two Ways of Hearing the Psalms

One of the clearest developments in our presentations over the
years concerned the horizon from which we hear or read the psalms—
our lives or Christ's life—and the writing process has challenged and
helped us to clarify this distinction in a more even-handed way.

We began to discern two basic movements in psalm interpretation in church and academy, which we describe as Human-centered and

Christ-centered, or anthropocentric and christological. The anthropocentric perspective emerges when we pray with psalms appropriate to the various life situations we face, such as joy, sorrow, gratitude, praise, thanks, liturgy. The scholarship of the last century has proven immensely useful for this approach, especially as form critics have attempted to learn what kinds of prayers these were, what types of situations they reflect, and how the psalms address God and describe life and the life-situation of the psalmists and worshipers in Israel. The studies of Gunkel and Drijvers, followed by many contemporary Catholic exegetes (e.g., Stuhlmueller and John Craghan, Luis Alonso Schökel) have clarified relationships between psalm type and prayer and liturgical types.

These presuppositions have been strengthened by important interpreters in the history of the Christian church tradition. John Calvin's introduction to the Psalms, written late in his career (1557), presents a thoroughly anthropo-centered approach:

> I have been accustomed to call this book (Psalms), I think not inappropriately, "An Anatomy of all the Parts of the Soul"; for there is not an emotion of which anyone can be conscious that is not here represented in a mirror. Or rather, the Holy Spirit has here drawn to the life all the griefs, sorrows, fears, doubts, hopes, cares, perplexities, in short, all the distracting emotions with which the minds of people are wont to be agitated.[11]

He then compares his own life and struggles with those of King David (whose authorship of psalms was presumed) and drawing great fruit from the styles, motifs and language of his prayer, as an embattled leader. We occasionally call this an ecclesial approach, since Calvin used it to describe interactions and ways of prayer for a church leader and/ or member.

This approach began to impress itself on us as quite important, and in retreats last summer, we devoted a day to these considerations after praying with psalms of praise, lament, thanksgiving, penitence and wisdom. We described this "new" day as: *Knowing ourselves through the Psalms: Psalms as Mirror of our Lives.* Here we draw on one patristic tradition about the Psalms, contained in the letter of Athanasius of Alexandria to Marcellinus, "On the Interpretation of the Psalms." Most importantly, he describes how the words of psalms that we pray can eventually become our own words, echoing our own hopes, fears, joys and moods. Ambrose of Milan also saw the Psalms as a school for the human soul, using the metaphor of a gymnasium, where one can learn by practice all the virtues. More recently, the revised Liturgy of the Hours in the Roman Catholic Church contains an introduction to praying with psalms that speaks of psalms from two perspectives: prayer through and with Jesus Christ, in the Christian assembly, and also in its original sense:

> each psalm was written in its own individual circumstances . . . each psalm has its own meaning, which we cannot overlook even in our own day. Though the psalms originated very many centuries ago in the East they express accurately the pain and hope, the unhappiness and trust, of people of every age and country, and celebrate especially faith in God, revelation and redemption.[12]

In a typical Catholic strategy, both are presented and valued and no clear choice between strategies is required! Finally, we bring to people the writing on psalms of Kathleen Norris, whose reflections on a life lived with psalms in the monastery are found in her bestseller *The Cloister Walk*.[13] She stresses the ways in which the language and rhetoric of psalms, which weave their way throughout the monastic day, actually provide for people who participate in this prayer pattern a structure for understanding and living their own life experience. In practice, she presents a way of appreciating the forms of psalms as Brueggemann once suggested, as teaching us a "formfulness" for life.[14] We also give examples of ways in which psalms can remind us, on a regular basis, of our own history of spiritual struggles and experiences. We consider as well the special way in which one specialist in pastoral care, Nancy Ramsay, has connected psalm interpretation with an ethic for ministry to victims of child sexual abuse.[15] Her article connects well with this notion of psalms as a mirror of our life because much of the author's reflections on Psalm 23 began with a process of care and recovery from her own experience as a child victim. We have found this particular "turn" to be quite an effective and moving way in which to offer retrospective on the "types" of psalms learned from the form critics.

Another gradual development of ours has occurred in the approach to christocentric interpretation and praying of psalms. Rather than arguing first from the messianic interpretation of psalms in the New Testament, we explore the phenomenon of connecting so many psalms with David in the book of Psalms. Whether or not David wrote any of the Psalms, it is clear that Jewish tradition became increasingly enamored of Davidic authorship (the Septuagint contains more "Davidic" superscriptions than the Hebrew text), so we need to ask why and how this happened.[16] It seems probable that many people felt comfort in praying as David had, and in seeing many aspects of their own lives played out in his life story. Some Jewish commentary on Psalm 90 functions similarly: a psalm of Moses must be good enough for later generations to pray. But we return to Calvin's affinity for David in the psalms, and from these data, we can learn that people often examine their own spirituality by reference to the holy ones in faith who preceded them. We suggest that messianic interpretation of psalms also grew in this fashion, and that it functions thus for many people today. So the first datum is the presupposition, held by many, that Jesus' own Jewish upbringing and prayer life would have included the psalms; so one can claim to pray as Jesus did, especially with the opening line of Psalm 22: "My God, my God, why have you forsaken me?" Moreover the association of particular psalms with each day of the week may have been known and practiced in Jesus' social setting. Those who pray psalms, then, with Jesus' life in mind, can appropriately imagine themselves joined with him in his own prayer life and styles.

Christian exegesis of the psalms also sees them as prophetic. Luke 24:44-45, for example, indicates Luke's appreciation of the messianic interpretation of psalms already discerned in "the law of Moses, the prophets and the psalms." We now know, in addition, that such prophetic understanding of psalms was not unknown in some Jewish groups of that era: the prose colophon to the Psalms Scroll from Cave 11 says of David that "all these [psalms] he uttered through prophecy, which was given him from before the Most High" (11QPs[a] xxvii). Prophetic interpretation of psalms passed from Jewish circles to Christian evangelists, and many studies have demonstrated ways in which the passion narratives seem to have been constructed with a theology of lament psalms in mind. To look at psalms as prophetic of Jesus' passion, death, and resurrection, we present them with a synoptic harmony of the passion narrative in the first three gospels, with all psalm citations in bold. People soon realize why Psalms 22, 31, and 69 are all important in several liturgical traditions for Holy Week.

Messianic, prophetic understanding of the Psalms also has a long and revered lineage in Christian churches: from Augustine to Luther and to Bonhoeffer, we see this way of praying and hearing the psalms. Luther's psalm introductions, conveniently published in a recent psalm book[17], demonstrate his belief that the book of Psalms "promises the death and resurrection of Christ, and describes his kingdom, and the nature and standing of all Christian people."[18] For thirty-five psalms, he notes that they prophesy some aspect of Christ's presence in our world and Christian life. We have provided this list for people to ponder, if they wish, along with other resources for Christ-centered prayer with psalms. These include: selections from Handel's *Messiah* which build on psalms interpreted christologically; in a retreat setting, we would normally listen to these on CD's. We also prepare suggestions of psalms which correlate with episodes in the life of Christ especially during Holy Week; recently, we incorporated a description of the ancient service called *Tenebrae*, filled with laments from the books of Psalms and Lamentations. We translated from the Spanish and incorporated two lists of suggested psalms for persons making retreat after the pattern of the *Spiritual Exercises* of St. Ignatius Loyola; these psalms may introduce or accompany the different suggestions for meditation, contemplation and prayer, especially when focused on the life of Christ.

Obviously we hope to introduce new ways of praying with psalms and occasionally to demonstrate how well they can accompany or structure older ways of prayer and meditation which people still find helpful. We have been encouraged by the prophetic understanding of many psalms in the views of Martin Luther; in fact, we prepared a list of those psalms he considered prophetic of Christ, and now offer them to retreatants, with his brief summary statements. In addition, a new Presbyterian prayer book contains a large collection of psalm texts for daily prayer, and each is followed by a "psalm prayer" of conclusion; for most of the psalms traditionally considered christological, the special prayer beautifully orients worshipers to a Christian understanding of the psalm. By these and other suggestions we hope to help people in the various Christian Churches to rediscover and appreciate some traditional helps to prayer with psalms.

A final project contains a guide to musical resources for those who hope to pray in song, or to listen to psalms sung by others (on tapes, CDs, or from hymnals). We knew that many "hymns" sung in various churches derive from psalms, but comprehensive guides to the psalms set to music (or which inspired hymns) are difficult to obtain. So Elizabeth surveyed a good selection of major church hymnals (one Episcopal, one African American, one Methodist, two Lutheran, one Presbyterian, and three Catholic), and composed a twenty-page appendix, with listings in these hymnals for at least 116 psalms (many of them with more than a dozen settings). Not included are musical books or psalters which present all or most of the psalms along with a musical setting. We are confident that this appendix will facilitate use of the book by a variety of different groups, from various churches, since we offer ways to enrich the experience by using resources from their own church and tradition of spirituality.

By way of conclusion, we have discovered a continuing usefulness of the genres or types of psalms developed by Gunkel. The settings in Israel's worship, which form an important part of form-critical research on the psalms, suggest modes of worship and spirituality which transcend particular centuries or eras of Jewish and Christian worship. We have chosen to focus on traditions of praying with psalms and to try to invigorate different aspects of the Christian life by comparing them to psalm types and by suggesting ways in which the various kinds of psalms can aid people in their prayer life, whether corporate or personal. Our book will present these materials and incorporate examples and parallels from several Christian churches and from different spiritual traditions. In all this work, in retreats and in spiritual conversations with people and in writing this book we have increasingly realized that the book of Psalms has become for us, and for many others, a genuine school of prayer.

NOTES: CHAPTER 4

[1] Pius Drijvers, O.C.S.O., *The Psalms: Their Structure and Meaning* (New York: Herder and Herder, 1965); a trans. from the 5th rev. ed. of "Over de Psalmen," published in 1964.

[2] Drijvers, *Psalms*, 7–8.

[3] Ibid., 12.

[4] Drijvers, *Psalms*, 217, n. 2, notes other European Catholic scholars who have followed Gunkel's approach: E. Vogt, S.J. (who was Drijvers' professor at the Biblical Institute, and was later attacked by conservative factions after the death of Pius XII), J. Steinmann, E. Podechard, A. Descamps, G. Castellino, and A. George.

[5] Ibid., 47.

[6] Ibid., 42.

[7] Herbert J. Levine, *Sing Unto God a New Song: A Contemporary Reading of the Psalms* (Bloomington and Indianapolis: Indiana University Press, 1995). On pp. 24–25 he discusses *performative language*, "a way of making things happen in the social world." Two kinds of ritual activity are described: (1) regulating a pre-existing activity, and (2) "those that actually constitute an activity that is dependent on them, such as blessing, baptizing, circumcising, marrying, or installing a chief or a head of state. In these latter constitutive rituals, the desired outcome does not take place unless the ritual does. And for the ritual to succeed, performative language plays a crucial role" (e.g., words "I do" in a civil marriage ceremony).

[8] Drijvers, *Psalms*, 101.

⁹ Carroll Stuhlmueller, *Psalms 1 (Psalms 1–72)* and *Psalms 2 (Psalms 73–150)* (Wilmington, Del.: Michael Glazier, 1983). Also, Carroll Stuhlmueller, "Psalms" in *Harper's Bible Commentary*, 433–94. J. L. Mays, editor (San Francisco: Harper & Row, 1988).

¹⁰ Cf. C. Westermann, "The Role of the Lament in the Theology of the Old Testament," *Interpretation* 28(1974) 20–38.

¹¹ John Dillenberger, *John Calvin: Selections from His Writings*; Edited with an Introduction (Missoula: Scholars Press, 1975) 23.

¹² Paul VI, "Introduction to the Liturgy of the Hours," #107 in: *The Liturgy of the Hours according to the Roman Rite*, vol. 1 (New York: Catholic Book Publishing Co., 1975) 58.

¹³ Kathleen Norris, *The Cloister Walk* (New York: Riverhead Books, 1996).

¹⁴ Walter Brueggemann, "The Formfulness of Grief," *Interpretation* 31 (1977) 263–75.

¹⁵ Nancy J. Ramsay, "Compassionate Resistance: An Ethic for Pastoral Care and Counseling," *Journal of Pastoral Care* 52:3 (1998) 217–26.

¹⁶ James Luther Mays, "The David of the Psalms," *Interpretation* 40:2 (1986) 143–55.

¹⁷ Bruce A. Cameron, *Psalms with Introductions by Martin Luther* (St. Louis: Concordia Publishing House, 1993). Psalm trans. is the New International Version.

¹⁸ See Martin Luther, "Preface to the Psalms," in: *Martin Luther: Selections from His Writings* (ed., John Dillenberger; Garden City, N. J.: Anchor Books, Doubleday 1961) 38.

5

The Sacramental Function of the Psalms in Contemporary Scholarship and Liturgical Practice

Harry P. Nasuti

*T*he concern of much recent scholarship has been to emphasize the similarity between the book of Psalms and the other books of Scripture. According to such scholarship, what were originally human words to God have now been shaped so as to emphasize their status as a divine Word which is to be studied and contemplated like other biblical texts. Obviously, this recent interpretive trend is a theologically significant move which retrieves a vital aspect of how the psalms function as a book.

Earlier generations of scholars and theologians also noted the connections between the Psalms and the rest of Scripture. Indeed, such figures often claimed that the Psalter contains within itself everything that is to be found in both the Old and the New Testaments. They also claimed, however, that the Psalms have a unique power that is not shared by the rest of Scripture, one rooted in their special ability to have a decisive effect on those who use them.

It is this distinctive power of the Psalms that I would argue is of particular interest to the present conference, since it is precisely this power that comes to the fore in the Psalms' liturgical usage. This is especially (but not exclusively) the case in those liturgies that are based on some form of a lectionary system. With this in mind, this essay first describes some of the ways in which traditional and modern scholarly literature has argued for this distinctive power of the psalms. It then examines the implications of these observations for the way the responsorial psalm may be seen to function in lectionary-based liturgical systems.

The Sacramental Power of the Psalms in the Scholarly Literature

There is no better place to begin a discussion of the Psalms' special nature than St. Athanasius' *Letter to Marcellinus*, a work whose penetrating insights on the Psalms have rarely been surpassed. According to Athanasius, the distinctive nature of the Psalms lies in their ability to "affect" and "mold" a person.[1] Athanasius claims that the Psalms may even be said to "constrain" a person, conforming that person to the text in a special way. According to Athanasius, a person is "enabled by this book to possess the image deriving from the words."[2] That is to say, the Psalms are not simply the means by which one may express an already existing inner state (though they obviously may work in such a way). They also do something to a person that would not happen without their agency. For Athanasius, the Psalms have what one may call sacramental power in that they are the means of bringing about a reality that would not exist without their use.

It is significant that Athanasius grounds the special power of the psalms precisely in the difference between those texts and the rest of Scripture. For Athanasius, those who listen to the other books of Scripture "consider themselves to be other than those about whom the passage speaks, so that they only come to the imitation of the deeds that are told to the extent that they marvel at them and desire to emulate them."[3] On the other hand, the person reciting the psalms utters them "as his own words, and each sings them as if they were written concerning him, and he accepts them and recites them not as if another were speaking, nor as if speaking about someone else. But he handles them as if he is speaking about himself. And the things spoken are such that he lifts them up to God as himself acting and speaking them from himself."[4] For Athanasius, these texts' "astonishing" ability to function in this way is clearly rooted in the workings of grace and the activity of the Spirit.[5]

While modern scholars have not usually focused on the sacramental nature of the Psalms, a recognition of their transformative power has not been completely absent from their work. Perhaps its most forceful advocate—at least on the historical level—has been Sigmund Mowinckel, for whom the Psalms formed an essential part of a cult which he explicitly described as a "sacrament" in its power to bring about a new reality which did not exist before.[6] Mowinckel's specific proposals about the exact historical setting of this cult have generated much scholarly controversy. It is, however, only recently that scholars have begun to unpack the theological implications of his recognition of the sacramental power of cult in general and cultic texts in particular.

Among contemporary scholars who have at least to a certain extent recognized the sacramental nature of the Psalms, one may mention Walter Brueggemann and, especially, James Luther Mays. Brueggeman is explicit in his retrieval of Mowinckel's insights on cultic power.[7] He also breaks important ground in his recognition of their implications for the modern use of the psalms. For him, the psalms can be seen to have transformative power, the ability to "invite and evoke genuine covenanted persons."[8] While Brueggemann's view of the Psalms' sacramental power may ultimately not be quite as far reaching as that of Athanasius or Mowinckel, it is nonetheless clear that he sees the Psalms as active forces and not simply as texts that are at the disposal of the person praying.[9]

One finds a particularly insightful recognition of the sacramental nature of the Psalms in the work of James Luther Mays. For Mays, the Psalms are explicitly a "means of grace," which have the power to "evoke the setting in which prayer occurs."[10] Citing the example of St. Augustine, Mays also talks about the transformative power of the psalms that "inflamed" that Church Father towards God.[11] By entering the "language world" of the psalms, those who have prayed these texts "became the 'I' and the 'we' whose praise and prayers and meditations the Psalms express."[12]

Mays' use of the term "language world" recalls another recent trend in psalms scholarship, namely the growing tendency to see the Psalms in the light of modern literary theory. Especially important in this respect is the use of the speech-act theory of J. L. Austin and John R. Searle. As its name implies, this approach is interested in the ability of texts to perform actions and make things happen in the so-called "real world." Scholars such as Herbert Levine and Anthony C. Thiselton have fruitfully used speech-act theory to examine the various things that the psalms "do" in the lives of those who use them.[13]

Important for speech-act theory is the direction of fit between word and world.[14] When words are used to describe what already exists in the world, they can be seen as moving in a word to world direction. The Psalms often work in this way when they are used as a means of bringing to clearer expression the feelings of those who pray them.

More important for the present discussion, however, is the ability of the psalms to work in a world to word direction. In such a case, the

Psalms do not simply mirror or clarify a state that already exists.[15] Instead, they work to shape the world of the person praying according to the words of the Psalms. As such, they have an effect on the person praying that would not have come into being without their use. Such an understanding of the use of the Psalms is quite congenial to a recognition of their full sacramental power.

One final author who has emphasized this power is Paul Ricoeur. Significantly, Ricoeur sees the Psalms as revelatory "in the sense that the sentiments expressed there are formed by and conformed to their object."[16] As revelation, the word "forms our feelings" in a way which "transcends their everyday, ordinary modalities." Once again, the point is that the Psalms have the power to shape those who use them in a decisive way that would not take place without their agency.

One may conclude this section by returning to Athanasius' assertion that the psalms play a distinctive role within Scripture. If what has been said so far is accurate, the Psalms may be seen as the means by which the rest of Scripture is actualized in the believer. Indeed, they are not so much the human response to what is found in the rest of Scripture as they are the means by which such a response is made possible. They are, in Mays' term, the "means of grace" by which the person praying is formed in a way acceptable to God. They have, in short, sacramental power.

The Sacramental Power of the Psalms in the Liturgy

The rest of this paper will address the question of how taking seriously the sacramental power of the Psalms affects the way one views the role of the psalms in the liturgy. Of particular concern here is the role of the responsorial psalm in those liturgies that are based on a lectionary system. One could, however, also make many of the same points for the use of the Psalms in other liturgical settings.

An integral part of the liturgy of the Word, the responsorial psalm follows the first reading, which is usually taken from the Old Testament.[17] In the Roman Catholic and the standard Episcopal and American Lutheran lectionaries, this first reading is related to the Gospel throughout the year. In the Revised Common Lectionary used by a number of churches (and approved for alternate usage by the Evangelical Lutheran Church in America and the Episcopal Church), this relationship between the first reading and the Gospel is the case for the major festal seasons. Outside of these seasons, the first reading is generally

not related to the specific Gospel passage, since it follows its own sequence according to a *lectio continua* system.

In both of these lectionary systems, the responsorial psalm is tied
thematically to the first reading. In those cases where the first reading
and the Gospel are related, the psalm also serves to anticipate the
Gospel. In such cases, the psalm obviously plays an important role in
setting forth the focus of that particular liturgy.[18]

Even when the psalm is part of a cluster of scriptural texts which center on a common theme, there is, of course, a major difference between
the psalm and these other texts. Whereas the latter present the Word of
God to the people, the psalm is instead the response of the people to that
Word. As such, it plays a crucial role in what has been called "a dialogue
of call and response . . . whose repeated reading is a symbolic rehearsal
of salvation."[19] It is, however, precisely with regard to the psalm's role as
the response of the people to the Word of God that an appreciation of its
sacramental power can make an important contribution.

Crucial here is the fact that the psalm is a *prescribed* response to a
previous divine address and that this response plays a specific role in a
liturgical context. Whether the psalm is one of praise or lament, there is
no guarantee that the psalm accurately reflects what the individual participants in the liturgy feel like praying at that given moment. Rather, the
psalm is what such participants are called upon to pray, because it is the
appropriate response of the Church to a particular divine address.

To appreciate the sacramental nature of the psalm is, however, to see
that it is not only the response that God looks for or even the response
that one should try to have. It is also the response that God makes possible and brings about in those who pray the psalm.[20] Indeed, it is
through the specific agency of the psalm that the person praying is
shaped as a particular type of person, the type of person who, in the language of Athanasius, conforms to the words of the psalm.

Such a view of the psalm fits well with an understanding of the
liturgy as something that God does among God's people so as to enable
them to share more fully in the priestly work of Christ.[21] This is particularly appropriate in the case of the Psalms, since Christian tradition
has long seen Jesus as the one who most appropriately prays the Psalms,
both with reference to his own circumstances (as in the case of Psalm
22) and on behalf of the body of which he is the head (as in those
psalms that ask for forgiveness from sin).[22] Praying the responsorial
psalm unites believers with their Lord, through whom their prayers
have efficacy and in whom these believers become what God wants

them to be. In other words, the praying of the psalm is an event by which God's grace is made manifest in the lives of believers.[23]

When its full sacramental power is understood, the responsorial psalm is properly appreciated as the means by which the Word of God is actualized in individual believers. As such, it is appropriate to recall Athanasius' insistence on the role of the Spirit in the praying of the psalms. Through the Spirit, believers are able to become more fully what they already are, members of the Body of Christ. Like the rest of the liturgy, the psalm is an eschatological reality that helps to bridge the already and the not yet of Christian existence.

The fact that the individual believer prays the responsorial psalm in conjunction with the congregation as a whole underlines its nature as an event that actualizes that believer's proper status as a member of Christ's body. This is especially apparent in those cases where the words of the psalm and the inclinations of the believer are at odds. As an example of this, one may consider the case of the lament psalms.

Despite the fact that recent scholars have seen the lament as a neglected genre in Christian prayer, psalms belonging to this genre are often the prescribed texts in the lectionary system. In such cases, the individual believer is given a text that reflects a clear situation of need. While such a situation accurately describes the reality of some individuals and communities, it does not fit the reality of all those who are asked to pray this type of psalm.

A situation in which non-suffering believers must pray the lament is obviously not meant to be the occasion for a case of emotional pretense. Rather, in such a situation the psalm functions as a means of insisting upon and bringing about a union of such believers both with Christ on the cross and with those other members of the body (in both the local congregation and the wider Church) who pray the lament out of a situation of actual suffering.

As many scholars have pointed out, it is a natural human impulse to resist the lament just as it is to distance oneself from the cross. Because of its sacramental power, the responsorial psalm both insists that believers pray the lament and enables them to do so through the grace of God and the working of the Spirit. It is, of course, important to realize that this union with the rest of the body cannot remain on the liturgical level alone. Unless it is fleshed out by concrete actions in one's ethical and communal life, one runs the risk of mocking the grace of God and the activity of the Spirit.

One may, of course, have a similar difficulty in praying the psalms of praise, especially if one is in a situation where God seems to be distant. Again, the important point is that the psalm is a prescribed response which God's own activity helps to bring about.[24] The psalm is the sacramental means by which believers are enabled to respond as God intends so as to become the people that God wishes.

The Sacramental Power of the Responsorial Psalm: An Example

Before going on to spell out the implications of a sacramental understanding of the psalm for the rest of the service, it might be helpful to look at a concrete example of how the psalm works in its relationship with the other scripture texts in the liturgy of the Word. The example I have chosen is that of Ash Wednesday, obviously one which is full of liturgical significance.

In the Roman Catholic lectionary, the first reading for Ash Wednesday is the well-known call to repentance found in the second chapter of Joel, the "rend your hearts, not your garments" passage.[25] The Revised Common Lectionary gives a choice of first readings for Ash Wednesday, one of which is the Joel passage just mentioned, while the other is the equally well-known "call to proper fasting" passage from Isaiah 58.[26] Both the Joel and the Isaiah passages confront the congregation with God's demand for true repentance, one which goes beyond the externals of a purely religious observance. In the Joel passage, the emphasis is on the need for turning to God with one's whole heart. The Isaiah passage, on the other hand, has a more social reference, with its concern to define a proper fast in terms of "loosing the bonds of injustice."

The responsorial psalm for Ash Wednesday is, not surprisingly, Psalm 51. Identified in its superscription as David's response to Nathan's accusation, Psalm 51 is a thoroughgoing acknowledgment of human sinfulness and a moving plea for divine forgiveness. The psalm has long played an important role in Christian tradition as the most pre-eminent of the traditional seven penitential psalms. It is also the only psalm which Gunkel sees as fully meeting his criteria for the form-critical genre of the same name.

In the liturgy of Ash Wednesday, Psalm 51 is the believer's response to the first reading's call for repentance.[27] The appropriateness of this response is especially obvious when the first reading is from Joel. In that case, the demand to "rend your hearts, not your garments" is met by the request that God create in the believer a clean heart. When the entire psalm is prayed, the demand is further met by the confidence that God will not despise a "broken and contrite heart."[28]

To recognize the sacramental power of this psalm is to understand that praying it is the means by which the believer is formed into a person with such a heart. The psalm enables the believer to repent in the way demanded by the first reading. Through the psalm the Spirit helps the believer to acknowledge his/her sinfulness and beg for God's mercy. In such a way, the psalm functions as a "means of grace" that has a real effect on the believer, not simply as a convenient restatement of sentiments that already existed before the praying of the psalm.

It is not without significance that the divine initiative argued for here is presupposed in the psalm itself. The psalm is filled with explicit requests for God not only to forgive the psalmist's sin but also to change the psalmist's heart. Indeed, the psalm specifically asserts that the only way that the psalmist can praise God is if God first opens the psalmist's mouth. To argue for the sacramental power of this psalm in the liturgy is to recognize the fact that the psalmist could not even make this request unless God were already active.

The psalm is followed by a second reading from 2 Corinthians which contains a classic statement of the Pauline already-not yet.[29] Thus even as Paul addresses the Corinthians as those for whose sake God has already acted in Christ, he begs them to be reconciled to God and not to receive the grace of God in vain. This is indeed the state of the believer in the Ash Wednesday liturgy—already the beneficiary of God's decisive act in Christ by virtue of his/her baptism but in continual need of reconciliation with God and in danger at every moment of not accepting the grace that God is offering. Thus, even as the psalm is a means of God's grace, it is not a once and for all event. There is a need for continued vigilance, a fact emphasized by the psalm verse that is proclaimed before the Gospel: "If today you would hear His voice, harden not your hearts."

The Gospel for Ash Wednesday is taken from the Sermon on the Mount in Matthew 6.[30] In this section, Jesus warns his disciples against performing almsgiving, prayer, and fasting in a public way, counseling them instead to do such actions secretly in anticipation of a reward from God who sees what is hidden. One should note that while this passage works to guard against spiritual exhibitionism, it also assumes that Jesus' disciples will be performing acts of almsgiving, prayer, and fasting—the traditional Lenten disciplines. In the context of the liturgy, the Gospel assumes and builds on the commitment that the congregation has made by praying the responsorial psalm, mandating specific actions and guarding against their misuse.

Implications of the Responsorial Psalm for the Rest of the Service

The argument of this essay is that the responsorial psalm plays an important liturgical role by virtue of its power to shape believers into the type of persons that God wants them to be. As the previous example shows, such a role is significant for how these believers relate to the Scripture readings that precede and follow the psalm. It also, however, is of some importance for the way these believers participate in the rest of the service.

One may begin by examining the relationship between the psalm and the homily. A topic of some concern in contemporary scholarship is whether one should preach on the Psalms. Obviously, as the Word of God, the psalms are texts full of theological import, well worth contemplation and explication in a variety of settings. However, to preach on the responsorial psalm as if it were exactly the same as the other readings would be to fail to recognize the special role that that psalm plays in the liturgy.

As a primary means by which believers are shaped, the responsorial psalm works to establish an identity for such believers. In addressing the congregation, the homilist should take seriously its members' identity as individuals in whom God is already at work in the particular way specified by the response to God's Word found in the psalm—whether that be praise, lament, penitence, or some other concrete mode of standing before God. As such, the homilist can use the psalm to remind these individuals of that to which they have already committed themselves with the help of God's grace. At the same time, the homilist may well need to remind them of the ever-present danger of not living up to this identity in their daily lives. To take the responsorial psalm seriously in the homily is to preach with the eschatological already-not yet of the believer firmly in view.

When the liturgy of the Word is followed by a eucharistic service, the responsorial psalm serves to anticipate the sacramental character of the latter. In the psalm, the members of the body are united with both the head and each other through the activity of the Spirit. It is, of course, precisely such a divinely effected union that forms the basis of both the texts and actions of the eucharistic portion of the liturgy. In such a way, the common praying of the Our Father and the enacted solidarity of the Kiss of Peace continue and intensify the psalm's transformation of the congregation into the community of the Lord. Such a transformation is, of course, effected even more thoroughly by the communion service itself.

Despite their common sacramental thrust, it is significant that the psalm and the eucharistic service obviously differ in their specificity. Thus, the relatively fixed eucharistic service provides a clear representation of the overall relationship between Christ and his body that is the ultimate end of all liturgical and extra-liturgical life. The psalm, on the other hand, is part of the continually varying liturgy of the Word. As such, it provides a specific response to a particular divine Word. The rest of the liturgy provides a context within which to understand the particular response brought about by the psalm, even as that particular response serves to concretize the overall relationship effected by the rest of the liturgy.[31]

Conclusions

This paper has argued that the responsorial psalm plays a sacramental role that accords well with the distinctive power that both Christian tradition and recent scholarship have recognized in the psalms. Precisely because the responsorial psalm is part of a larger liturgical context, its ability to shape believers in a decisive way comes to the fore. In such a context, the psalm functions as the means through which God works to mold those who pray it into individuals more closely conformed to God's will.

Despite the support that the liturgical context gives the sacramental function of the psalms, it would be a mistake to say that it is only in this context that these texts function in such a way. The history of the Psalms' use shows that they have been the means by which God has transformed believers in a variety of public and private settings. There is little doubt that they will continue to function as such in the future.[32]

NOTES: CHAPTER 5

[1] Athanasius, *The Life of Antony and the Letter to Marcellinus*, trans., R. C. Gregg (New York: Paulist, 1980) ch. 10.

[2] Ibid.

[3] Ibid., ch. 11.

[4] Ibid.

[5] Thus, Athanasius notes that the psalms have a "certain grace of their own" and that "each psalm is both spoken and composed by the Spirit, so that in these same words . . .

the stirrings of our souls might be grasped, and all of them be said as concerning us, and the same issue from us as our own words, for a remembrance of the emotions in us, and a chastening of our own life." *Letter*, chs. 10, 12. See also chs. 31 and 33 which talk about the "assistance" and "guidance" that the Spirit gives those who pray the psalms.

[6] See especially his *Psalmenstudien*, vol. 2: *Das Thronbesteigungsfest Jahwäs und der Ursprung der Eschatologie* (Amsterdam: Schippers, 1961 [1922]) 21. Cf. also his *The Psalms in Israel's Worship* (Nashville: Abingdon, 1962) 15–22.

[7] This aspect of Brueggemann's work on the psalms is most evident in *Israel's Praise: Doxology against Idolotry and Ideology* (Philadelphia: Fortress, 1988), though it is also found elsewhere.

[8] Brueggemann, *Praise*, 149, 159.

[9] For an extended analysis of Brueggemann's approach to the psalms, see my *Defining the Sacred Songs: Genre, Tradition, and the Post-Critical Interpretation of the Psalms* (Sheffield: Sheffield Academic Press, 1999).

[10] J. L. Mays, "Means of Grace: The Benefits of Psalmic Prayer," in his *The Lord Reigns: A Theological Handbook to the Psalms* (Louisville: Westminster John Knox, 1994) 40–41.

[11] J. L. Mays, "With These Words: The Language World of the Psalms," in *The Lord Reigns*, 3.

[12] Ibid, 5.

[13] See H. Levine, *Sing unto God a New Song: A Contemporary Reading of the Psalms* (Bloomington: Indiana University, 1995) 79–129, and A. C. Thiselton, *New Horizons in Hermeneutics: The Theory and Practice of Transforming Biblical Reading* (Glasgow: Harper-Collins, 1992) 298–307. For a more general consideration of sacraments as speech-acts, see A. P. Martinich, "Sacraments and Speech Acts," *HeyJ* 16 (1975) 289–303, 405–17, as well as the response by B. R. Brinkman, "'Sacramental Man' and 'Speech Acts' Again," *HeyJ* 16 (1975) 418–20.

[14] For a convenient summary of speech act theory on this point, see Thiselton, *Horizons*, 291–98.

[15] Indeed, they do not even merely commit the person praying to that state, as Thiselton has suggested in *Horizons*, 599.

[16] P. Ricoeur, *Essays on Biblical Interpretation* L. S. Mudge, ed. (Philadelphia: Fortress, 1980) 90.

[17] Throughout most of the liturgical year, this reading is taken from the Old Testament, only being replaced by a reading from the New Testament in the Sundays after Easter.

[18] According to I. Nowell, O.S.B., the psalm "may be a key to all the readings." *Sing a New Song: The Psalms in the Sunday Lectionary* (Collegeville: The Liturgical Press, 1993) 3. This book is a valuable resource for understanding the way specific psalms function in particular lectionary settings.

[19] K. W. Irwin, *Context and Text: Method in Liturgical Theology* (Collegeville: The Liturgical Press, 1994) 88.

[20] Thus, J. D. Crichton, writing about the liturgy of the Word in the Roman Catholic mass, notes that the people "are enabled to respond" to the first reading "by a psalm that continues the theme of the reading, turning it into prayer." *Christian Celebration: The Mass* (London: Geoffrey Chapman, 1971) 74.

[21] On this, cf. Irwin, *Context and Text*, 145, for whom "'active participation' means something more than *doing something* in the liturgy. On a more fundamental level it

means that *God does something among us* at liturgy, namely, to allow us *to take part in* and to become *partakers* and *sharers in* the priesthood of Christ" (Irwin's italics). See also the comments of I. H. Dalmais, for whom the "sacramental character of the Christian liturgy" means that in it "the initiative always belongs to God, who establishes a people for himself, calls it, and gathers it together so that he may enter into communion with it." *The Church at Prayer: An Introduction to the Liturgy*, A. G. Martimort, ed., vol. 1 (Collegeville: The Liturgical Press, 1987) 231. According to P. E. Fink, S.J., liturgy is "first and foremost the *work of God in the people* transforming them, us, and all human life into God's own glory." (Fink's italics) "Liturgy and Spirituality: A Timely Intersection," in *Liturgy and Spirituality in Context: Perspectives on Prayer and Culture*, Eleanor Bernstein, C.S.J., ed. (Collegeville: The Liturgical Press, 1990) 61.

[22] See, for example, the summary statement of A. G. Martimort, in *The Church at Prayer*, 145: "The important place assigned to the psalms bears witness to the Church's conviction, so forcefully expressed by the Fathers and by St. Augustine in particular, that in the psalms the voice of Christ and his Mystical Body is heard; that they are the Lord's prayer to his Father and the prayer of God's people to their Lord."

[23] For the "event" character of the liturgy of the Word as a whole, see Irwin, *Context and Text*, 89. Similar language is also used by Crichton, *Christian Celebration*, 74–75, who further notes that "through the readings and other texts (especially the responsorial psalm) God communicates his grace."

[24] Brueggemann has nicely noted that in situations of need praise can function as an act of hope and social criticism. See his *The Message of the Psalms: A Theological Commentary* (Minneapolis: Augsburg, 1984) 28.

[25] Joel 2:12-18.

[26] Joel 2:1-2, 12-17; Isa 58:1-12.

[27] The Roman Catholic lectionary specifies the use of vv. 3-6, 12-14, and 17. The Revised Common Lectionary specifies vv. 1-17.

[28] When the first reading is from Isaiah 58, the dynamic is a bit more subtle, with the psalm providing what might be seen as a necessary internal counterpoint to the first reading's social message.

[29] In the Roman Catholic lectionary, 2 Cor 5:20–6:2 is read. In the Revised Common Lectionary, the reading extends to 6:10.

[30] In the Roman Catholic lectionary, Matt 6:1-6, 16-18 is read. In the Revised Common Lectionary, the reading extends to 6:21.

[31] One might note that the concrete psalm response of a particular liturgy also exists in the wider context of the liturgical year as a whole. Different responses are called for at other times in that year, all of which form part of the ongoing relationship between a believer and his/her God.

[32] I am most grateful to Thomas Scirghi, S.J., my colleague in the Fordham theology department, for his generosity in reading an earlier draft of this paper and giving me the benefit of his special expertise in liturgical theology. Like the discussions that took place at the Psalms and Practice Conference itself, my conversations with Dr. Scirghi may perhaps be seen as an indication of the usefulness of a collaborative approach to these most "practical" of biblical texts.

6

Burning Our Lamps with Borrowed Oil

The Liturgical Use of the Psalms and the Life of Faith

Rolf Jacobson

A friend of mine grew up as a pastor's kid in the old Lutheran Free Church. For those who may not be acquainted with the Lutheran Free Church, it was a tradition characterized by intense personal piety and tended to avoid rote prayers and liturgies. She tells the story of a time when an old evangelist paid a visit to her home. As they were sitting down to eat dinner, her father began the meal with a prayer. He bowed his head, and began to recite a psalm. I suspect it was Ps 145:15-16: "The eyes of all look to you, O Lord, and you give them their food in due season. You open your hand, satisfying the desire of every living thing." As he was in the midst of praying this psalm, the visiting evangelist interrupted the prayer: "We thank you God," he intoned, "that we do not have to burn our lamps with borrowed oil."

We thank you God that we do not have to burn our lamps with borrowed oil. With this pejorative slam, the evangelist dismissed liturgical and prayer uses of the psalms. With all due respect, I am arguing here that there is something salutary, there is something irreplaceable to be gained when we use the psalms liturgically. Indeed, precisely because some of us arrive at worship burned out, with no oil of our own remaining in our reservoirs, we need to burn our lamps with borrowed oil. And in the psalms such oil is to be found in plenty.

Speaking Another's Words

I wish to take as my departure points for this essay two simple observations. The first observation is that in liturgical traditions that use the Revised Common Lectionary, the Psalter is the only book of Scripture that on an almost weekly basis is placed in the mouths of worshipers. Every week there are four appointed readings: one from an Old Testament book (except during the Easter season when the first reading is taken from Acts), one from a psalm, one from an Epistle, and one from a Gospel. In most congregations that use the Revised Common Lectionary, the Old Testament, Epistle and Gospel readings are read to the congregation, but the psalm is either read *responsively by* the congregation, or sung *responsively by* the congregation. This practice creates an odd dynamic— the congregation burns their lamps with borrowed oil as they speak the words of ancient psalmists, as if they were their own words.

This leads to a second observation. Because many of the psalms are in the first person singular or first person plural, when we place the words of the psalms in worshipers' mouths, we create a situation in which one subject, one self, one "I," speaks the emotionally and spiritually charged words of another subject, another self, another "I." But from this results an interesting thing: The emotions and thoughts of the first self might not be at all consistent with the words of the other self that it is now speaking. Let me offer several examples of the inconsistency I am imagining:

> 1. Imagine that a woman arrives for worship the day after her husband died. She is feeling abandoned, alone, and frightened. The appointed psalm is the twenty-third, so she finds herself saying: "The Lord is my shepherd, I shall not want . . . . Even though I walk through the valley of the shadow of death I shall fear no evil."

> 2. Imagine that a college sophomore is home over break and his parents drag him out of bed to worship. He doesn't believe in God; he is sitting there thinking what a lark this entire affair is. But the appointed psalm is 14, and he finds himself saying, "Fools say in their hearts, 'There is no God.'"

> 3. One more example. Imagine that on Saturday evening a young couple gets engaged. They don't walk into church the next morning, they float in, their toes barely touching the steps as they climb the stairs, sharing their joy with the worshiping community. The entire world is their oyster, but the psalm appointed for the day is Psalm 130. And so the two young folks who are higher than a kite emotionally find themselves saying, "Out of the depths I cry to you, O Lord. Lord, hear my voice . . . my soul waits for the Lord more than those who watch for the morning."

These three examples suffice to illustrate the phenomenon I am getting at. Because many congregations use the psalms as *liturgy*, this odd event occurs where a person speaks words in worship that are at jarring odds with his or her own emotions. It is this disjunction, this disconnect, between the words of the psalms and the emotions, thoughts, and beliefs of the individual worshiper that I will investigate in the remainder of this essay.

Let me state my thesis clearly. Either pastors, liturgists, and theologians must learn to make fruitful use of this disjunction between the emotions of the psalms and the emotions of the worshipers, or we will simply reinforce for people that worship is meaningless. Think again of the example of the sophomore atheist who is being forced to recite that "fools say in their hearts, 'There is no God.'" The imaginary young man might simply find the irony of his recitation ludicrous, and it might just drive him to become more cynical. But I believe that the tension between the words that we place in worshipers mouths and the internal emotional state of the worshipers can be put to creative pastoral and theological use. And I believe that the theory of cognitive dissonance can help us explore this gap and put it to fruitful use.

Cognitive Dissonance and the Psalms as Liturgy

Cognitive dissonance theory holds that the thoughts of individuals need to be consistent and harmonious.[1] When a person holds two or more inconsistent thoughts, that person experiences a cognitive dissonance. For example, a person thinks, "I hate driving" but that person has a daily work commute of one hour. The person will try to resolve the uncomfortable cognitive dissonance, and some of the ways of doing so are:

> **1. Changing Attitude:** The most common way to resolve a cognitive dissonance is for a person to changes attitudes. In my example the person might decide, "I like [or don't mind] driving."

> **2. Adding New Thoughts:** A second way to resolve a cognitive dissonance is for a person to add a thought or cognition: "I hate driving, but I am willing to drive to support my family."

> **3. Changing Behavior:** A person can also resolve a cognitive dissonance by changing behaviors—get a new job, car pool, take public transportation, arrange to work out of the home, get up earlier to shorten commute time, and so on.

I believe that cognitive dissonance theory is helpful in thinking about liturgical use of the Psalms, because cognitive dissonance does not only happen naturally, cognitive dissonance can be intentionally introduced into a subject in order to effect a change in behavior, a change in attitude, or to force the addition of a new thought. It seems to me that the introduction of a cognitive dissonance is exactly how "the power of positive thinking" people affect their changes. Financial self-help guru Suzie Orman tells people to stand in front of a mirror and daily tell themselves, "I deserve to make $80,000." The point is that this new attitude is, of course, at dissonance with the life circumstances of the person, so it is hoped that the person will change her behavior to live up to the new attitude. Analogously, the liturgical use of the Psalms can be employed to introduce new cognitions, new attitudes, and new behaviors into worshipers.

The Liturgical Use of the Psalms and the Life of Faith

One of the tyrannies of our individualistic, western society is the near deification of our emotions. The self-help television shows and the insipid personal therapy culture constantly berate us to "get in touch with your feelings," and "own your emotions." I was once even told by a friend that "feelings are never wrong." And at the time, I believed her! Feelings are never wrong? Of course they are—hatred, envy, lust, despite, jealousy, insecurity, greed, greed, greed!—of course feelings can be wrong. But in our society, emotions have been elevated to such an infallible height that the individual is often left in bondage to his or her own emotions.

But this individual comes to worship, and in worship, this individual can be led to recite the psalms. In this fashion we can use this recitation as an opportunity to introduce a cognitive dissonance into the individual. Thus to the person who is buried under a mountain of sadness, the dissonant cognition can be introduced: "I will give thanks to the Lord with my whole heart" (Ps 111:1). To the person who feels in control of their life, the dissonant cognition can be introduced: "Be gracious to me, O God, for people trample on me" (Ps 56:1). The words clash with the effect. However, the resolution of the dissonance may in fact alter the effect.

In the space I have left, I wish to explore two dimensions of the theological possibilities of what I have been describing. I will interact with Walter Brueggemann's well-known theological typology for appropriating the psalms as he laid it out in his article, "Psalms and the Life of

Faith: A Suggested Typology of Function."[2] As is well known, Brueggemann drew on the work of Paul Ricoeur and proposed that there are psalms of *orientation*, psalms of *disorientation*, and psalms of *reorientation*. I wish stress a point that Brueggemann made in his article: Brueggemann's theological typology of function was never meant to replace or ignore the form-critical categories of praise, lament, or thanksgiving. Brueggemann has been misread by some as offering a rival typology to the form-critical categories. But as Brueggemann wrote:

> Our consideration *of function* must of course be based on the best judgments we have about *form* and *setting in life*. The present discussion assumes and fully values both the method and the gains of form-critical study. It provides neither a criticism nor a displacement of form-critical work.[3]

Precisely because Brueggemann's typology is a hermeneutical appropriation of the psalm texts, I have found it ideal to help think through the possibility of using the psalms liturgically to introduce cognitive dissonances into the worshiping congregants.

Introducing Cognitions of Disorientation to the Oriented

Drawing on the thought of Paul Ricoeur, Brueggemann proposed that "the sequence of *orientation-disorientation-reorientation* is a helpful way to understand the use and function of the Psalms."[4] Orientation is the (artificial?) starting point for this sequence. That is, orientation marks a state of stability and comfort from which the subject begins and to which the subject desires to return. Brueggemann assigns certain creation psalms, wisdom psalms, descriptive praise psalms, and psalms of ascent to this state. These include Psalms 1, 37, 105, 19, 127, 128, 131, 133, and 145. Brueggemann describes orientation as the "mind-set and worldview of those who enjoy a serene location . . . characterized by orderliness, goodness, and reliability of life."[5] In this state, good is rewarded and evil is punished. Creation functions in an orderly manner, chaos is not a threat. Those who fear the Lord are not persecuted by the wicked. The economy is good; husbands don't leave wives; children are not born with birth defects; those who work hard enjoy promotion regardless of their race, gender, or social status. And, most importantly, God is utterly and unquestionably reliable and present.

My experience as a pastor was that on any given Sunday, a significant portion of those worshiping in the pews did so from a state of orientation. They were in a state of orientation not because they were dim-witted, or because they were wicked, but simply because life for them was good at the moment. They had not recently experienced what Ricoeur calls a limit experience, they were not currently in a state of dislocation.

For several reasons, it would be pastorally irresponsible for pastors and worship leaders to abandon their congregants in this state of orientation. First, we know that the state of orientation is not permanent. As one teacher once said, "Because I am a Christian, I know that things are going to get worse." The state of orientation is impermanent; life is finite, and this finitude must come to knock on every door and call on every child of God. Because disorientation is coming, pastors and liturgists should try to equip parishioners against the day it arrives. Second, at any given moment some of our brothers and sisters in the family of God are in a state of disorientation. One of the most goading thorns in the flesh of a sufferer is proximity to those who do not suffer. Think of Job, whose contact with his so-called friends inflamed his wounds and increased his burdens. Think of the suffering lament psalmist, who in suffering, experiences her brothers and sisters as problematic. For the lamenting psalmist, community is not the answer but precisely the problem. The pastor or liturgist owes it to those who are currently in a state of disorientation to disorient the oriented.

One way to do this is to place words of disorientation in the mouth of the congregation by using a lament psalm liturgically. The pastoral goal here would be to introduce a dissonant cognition of disorientation into an oriented person's mind in the hopes that this new thought would eventually be a catalyst that would cause the person to add new cognitions and new attitudes. For example, one of the hallmarks of the state of orientation is the belief set forth in Ps 1:6: "the Lord watches over the way of the righteous, but the way of the wicked will perish." But what if the liturgy invited the worshiper to speak the first words of Psalm 22: "My God, my God, why have you forsaken me? Why are you so far from helping me, from the words of my groaning? O my God, cry by day, but you do not answer me." The worshiper now has two dissonant cognitions: (1) The Lord watches over the way of the righteous; but (2) My God, my God, why have you forsaken me? Not especially that the first person language—"My God, *my* God," "forsaken me," "*I* cry by day, but you do not answer me"—invites the worshiper to make this phrase even more intimately her own cognition.

Brueggemann wrote: "The psalms of lament both individual and corporate, are ways of entering linguistically into a new distressful situation in which the old orientation has collapsed."[6] It is specifically the pregnant power of liturgy as a linguistic event to which I wish to draw attention. Because liturgy places words in the mouth of people, liturgy has an added creative capacity and an extra measure of hermeneutical leverage that sermons and lectures and reading do not.[7] It is easy for the mind to distance itself from the theoretical, abstract words in a sermon in which the pastor may seek to *teach* worshipers about the reality of suffering, but the mind's defenses will be much more vulnerable when it speaks phrases in the first person. "My God, why have you forsaken me." Once such words become my own, once they sink into my heart and mind and soul, it will be impossible for these words to coexist peacefully with the stable cognitions of orientation.

Recall that two of the main ways that the human mind resolves cognitive dissonances are to add new cognitions and to change attitudes. In the present example, the pastoral goal might be something of both. Perhaps the person in a happy state of orientation might add the new cognition, "Sometimes the righteous do suffer." Or a different new cognition might be added, such as: "Perhaps suffering is not a sign of personal failure." Accompanying these new cognitions there may be a new attitude towards those who suffer. Rather than judging sufferers or fearing them, compassion and love might take seed. Such newly added cognitions or newly changed attitudes could serve the subject well also, in the inevitable event of his own suffering. The day of dislocation calls on us all; perhaps we would be better equipped to face it if we already owned the words of disorientation as our own.

Introducing Cognitions of Orientation to the Disorientated

If orientation is the stable starting point for Brueggemann's suggested sequence of orientation-disorientation-reorientation, then disorientation is an inevitable stage of instability through which every life must pass. Just as psalms of disorientation can be placed in the mouths of those who are firm in their orientation, psalms of reorientation can be placed liturgically in the mouths of the disoriented in order to introduce new cognitions.

Earlier I stressed the nature of the psalms of disorientation as linguistic events. I wish to repeat that stress here in my treatment of the psalms of reorientation. As words of reorientation are placed into the mouths and thus entered into the hearts and minds of the disoriented, they do more than simply teach the sufferer a new lesson, they do more than simply give expression to the sufferer's experience. Rather, the words of reorientation create a new life for the sufferer, they evoke new horizons. In the words of the New Testament, they raise the dead.

At this point, perhaps I might be allowed to share a personal experience. As a teenager, I was gravely ill with cancer. Both of my legs were amputated, and I underwent a litany of other treatments. In those years, Ps 27:1 became my favorite Bible verse.

"The Lord is my light and my salvation; whom shall I fear? The Lord is the stronghold of my life; of whom shall I be afraid?" The verse gave me hope when I had little. The verse gave me confidence when all I had was fear. To be frank, I was very afraid in those years. This verse, which speaks of having no fear, did not *match* my experience. Indeed it was contrary to my experience! But these words transformed my experience; they *created* hope.

When the liturgy places the words of psalms of reorientation[8] into the mouths of sufferers, it can introduce a new cognition that one hopes might destabilize the experience of the worshiper. Perhaps a worshiper is thinking, "I feel abandoned and alone." But then the worshiper might find herself speaking the familiar words of Psalm 23: "You are with me; your rod and your staff—they comfort me." Or of Psalm 121: "My help comes from the Lord, who made heaven and earth." The two cognitions are dissonant—I am alone and you are with me—and the human mind will seek to resolve this dissonance: either by changing cognitions, adding new cognitions, or changing attitudes.

Conclusion

I have argued in this essay that a theory of cognitive dissonance lends us a hermeneutical tool to help think about the liturgical use of the psalms and the life of faith. In conclusion, I offer four brief observations and caveats:

> 1. The process I describe does not, of course, apply only to the liturgical use of the psalms, but to the rest of the liturgy as well. It would apply to the confession and absolution, the *kyrie*, the offertory, and so on. But because the language of the Psalter encompasses both the heights and depths of human experience, and because the weekly Psalter is expressly a scriptural lesson, it seems to me that the analysis is especially fruitful for thinking about the liturgical use of the psalms.
>
> 2. The type of cognitive dissonance I am envisioning is not likely to occur after a single recitation of a psalm. In fact, I think the opposite.

Most likely, it is only the week-in-and-week-out reading of the psalms that is likely to be able to introduce a dissonant cognition into a person. But that is why we worship weekly, and that is why we have the annual liturgical calendar.

3. The type of analysis I outline here need not be limited to liturgy. I can imagine pastoral care and catechetical applications of this theory.

4. Given the space and time limitations afforded me, what I have offered here is simply an overture and not a thorough analysis.

NOTES: CHAPTER 6

[1] For the purpose of this essay, I am interacting only with an overview of cognitive dissonance theory. For more information on the theory, see the following: E. Aronson and J. Mills, "The Effect of Severity of Initiation on Liking for a Group," *Journal of Abnormal and Social Psychology* 59 (1959) 177–78 1; L. Festinger, *A Theory of Cognitive Dissonance* (1959); L. Festinger and J. Carlsmith, "Cognitive Consequences of Forced Compliance," *Journal of Abnormal and Social Psychology* 58 (1959) 203–10; L. Festinger, H. W. Riecken, and S. Schachter, *When Prophecy Fails: A Social and Psychological Study of a Modern Group that Predicted the Destruction of the World* (1956).

[2] In *The Psalms and the Life of Faith*, Patrick D. Miller, ed. (Minneapolis: Fortress, 1995) 3–32.

[3] Ibid., 3–4.

[4] Ibid., 9.

[5] Ibid., 10.

[6] Ibid., 11.

[7] In my understanding of the psalms as linguistic events that can create new realities, and specifically in my understanding of the liturgical use of psalms to introduce new cognitions into the minds of worshipers, I may be going slightly beyond Brueggemann. He focuses on the power of psalms to express present reality: "This creative, evocative function of language is precisely what is at work in the Psalms. The Psalms transmit to us ways of speaking that are appropriate to the extremities of human experience as known concretely in Israel. Or, to use Ricoeur's language, we have 'limit-expressions' (laments, sons of celebration) that match 'limit experiences' (disorientation, reorientation)" [Ibid., 27]. While Brueggemann focuses on "matching" the expression to the experience, I am arguing that an expression that is precisely *contrary* to present experience may be introduced in order to initiate a change in experience. It seems to me that this is faithful to Brueggemann's appropriation of the psalms, but it takes Brueggemann in a slightly different direction.

[8] Brueggemann (following Westermann) identifies especially psalms of declarative praise as psalms of reorientation. That is, those psalms that speak of having come through some period of dislocation are psalms of reorientation. This distinction seems correct to me.

7

My Tongue Will Sing Aloud of Your Deliverance
Praise and Sacrifice in the Psalms

Kathryn L. Roberts

For all the insight they provide into the tradition, history, theology, and piety of the religion of Israel, the book of Psalms provides little information concerning the worshiping community's actual religious practices. Like any good hymnal, this collection from the period of the Second Temple is a repository of expressions of worship experiences, but also of accumulated wisdom and theology as these emerged from Israel's social and cultural life. The songs offer glimpses into Israel's theological interpretation of events in the wilderness and pre-monarchical periods, religious life under a king in a palace, and the precariousness of worshiping God without the security of a temple and its establishment. With all of their rich theological insights, these collected expressions of Israel's individual and corporate praise and lament make up the hymn book of Israel, not its *Book of Common Worship*. The Psalter offers up liturgical pieces, but no liturgy.[1] It reveals profound religious faith, but does not directly disclose its praxis. Ritual sacrifice is certainly mentioned in the psalms, but they do not describe and prescribe its cultic practices.

While the psalms do not reveal as much as might be desired regarding the cultic forms of ritual sacrifice, they encapsulate and reveal an internal theological debate on the efficacy of sacrifice in the worship of Yhwh, God of Israel. The corpus exhibits contradictory views as to the meaning and role of sacrifice, thus reflecting the precariousness of its continued significance.[2] Within this collection of various *genre* are found psalms which assume the correctness and efficacy of ritual sacrifice alongside liturgical responses that point away from the outward activity of sacrifice, favoring instead an emphasis on the intention of the human heart.[3] Psalm 51 seems to ascribe to both views, holding these apparently contradictory notions in tension. This essay focuses on Psalm 51, examining this contradictory role of sacrifice in worship, with an eye to questions of its continued meaning for the worship life of the church today.

Psalm 51 is the great penitential psalm of the synagogue and the church.[4] Life in Qumran was immersed in Scripture. Echoes of Psalm 51 are sounded in as diverse settings as the Community Rule and the scroll of Thanksgiving Hymns. The Community Rule regulated life in the wilderness community. The phrase "broken spirit" (51:17 [19])[5] appears there as a description of those fit for participation in the council and governance of the community.[6] In the scroll of thanksgiving hymns found in cave 1, a newly created psalm of personal confession of sin is reminiscent of the penitence of Psalm 51 combined with the imagery of Psalm 139.[7]

The devotional, prayerful nature of the Psalter made it the property of the Christian church in a way that other books in the Old Testament were not.[8] The Psalms became the backbone of the sixth-century Benedictine and the thirteenth-century Franciscan Rules, and Psalm 51 holds a prominent place in both. The "Earlier Rule" of St. Francis requires that "for the failings and negligence of the brothers they should say daily the *Miserere mei, Deus* [Psalm 51], with the Our Father."[9] In addition to commentaries on the psalms by Luther and Calvin, stands the commentary on Psalms 51 and 130, published in 1558 by laywoman Katharina Schütz Zell of Strasbourg.[10] Zell was a vigorous crusader for hospital reform and better conditions for patients without adequate financial means to insure proper medical care.[11] These two psalms and others may have played a role in her pastoral care. Psalm 51 found its way early into the liturgies of the Lenten season and is currently prescribed for the Ash Wednesday readings of Years A, B, and C.

Psalm 51 is part of the Elohistic Psalter, a collection within the larger collection, comprising Psalms 42–83. It takes its name from the substitution of Elohim, God, in place of the divine name, YHWH, customarily translated "The LORD." Although ascribed to "David, when the prophet Nathan came to him, after he had gone in to Bathsheba," the notation is clearly secondary and offers no real help in identifying the author or date of the psalm. Clues internal to the psalm point to the time of the exile at the earliest, with verses 18-19 [20-21] and their reference to building the walls of Jerusalem clearly pointing to the post-exilic period. Ps 51:1-17 [3-19] seems to know Jeremiah, with Ps 51:2, 7 [4, 9] drawing on the language and imagery of washing (כבס) found in Jer 2:22 and 4:14. Ps 51:10 [12] with its petition for a cleansed heart (לב) and a new (חדש) spirit hearken back to Jer 31:31-33, sharing this same vocabulary and essence with the powerful new covenant passage.[12]

While the superscription may not assist in locating the author and dating the psalm, it does the psalm a service by providing it with a plausible context:[13]

> The superscription does not force one to confine the power of those words to that occasion alone, but it does illustrate with power where such words of passionate self-condemnation and extreme plea for transformation and cleansing are appropriate. . . The depth of the sin confessed in Psalm 51 seems to match the depth of the sin committed by David" and his straightforward confession to Nathan in II Samuel 12 in acknowledging, "I have sinned against Yahweh."[14]

Indeed, the depth of the sin expressed and the penitent's confidence in God's forgiveness make Psalm 51 compelling reading for Ash Wednesday or any day when the burden of realized sin becomes too heavy to carry. The psalm is rich and fertile with opportunities for discovering the mercy and faithfulness of God. Since the psalm is too full to be investigated fully in this forum, the emphasis on the agony of confession and confidence in divine mercy must be set aside in favor of questions concerning the human response to such forgiveness.

Psalm 51 is found in the list of psalms that seem to look unfavorably on the necessity of sacrifice as a response in worship, but the psalm also lifts up sacrifice as a requirement of proper piety.[15] After a heartfelt outpouring of penitence, the psalmist cries out:

(14) [16] "Deliver me from bloodshed, O God, O God of my salvation,
    and my tongue will sing aloud of your deliverance.
(15) [17] O Lord, open my lips, and my mouth will declare your praise.
(16) [18] For you have no delight in sacrifice;
    if I were to give a burnt offering, you would not be pleased.
(17) [19] My sacrifice, O God,[16] is a broken spirit;
    a broken and contrite heart, O God you will not despise.

> (18) [20] Do good to Zion in your good pleasure;
>   build the walls of Jerusalem,
> (19) [21] then you will delight in right sacrifices, in burnt offerings and
>   whole offerings;
>   then bulls will be offered on your altar."

Verses 18-19 [20-21] are traditionally considered to be a post-exilic addition to the psalm.[17] The hope is expressed that after the rebuilding of the walls of the ruined city of Jerusalem God will find pleasure in the burnt offerings and animal sacrifices of the people's worship. Verse 18 [19] is consistent with events of the late sixth century B.C.E. when returning Judeans labored to recreate the city and temple precincts in their former glory. The Second Temple was completed by 515 and worship was reestablished. Almost a century later, under the leadership of Nehemiah, the walls were completed in fifty-two days despite opposition from neighboring factions (Neh 1:1–7:5).

Though temple worship and ritual may or may not have already been re-established for several generations, it is worth nothing that it is the walls of the city that the psalmist sees as the final obstacle to proper worship. With the Babylonian exile and the destruction of David's grand temple had gone a never again realized measure of centralized worship and cultic control. Even with the construction of the new temple on the original site, that centralized control in Jerusalem had never regained its former footing. In the years of exile and its aftermath, God's people had begun worshiping locally again, in synagogues. Temple sacrifice, being impossible without a temple, was suspended and other forms of worship, focusing on the reading of Torah, began to come to the fore.[18] Verse 18 [20] may reflect the hope that the walls of the city will provide more than protection from hostile neighbors. It may also be a petition that walls will finally enclose within themselves Zion, the city of God, where proper worship can again delight God and pious humanity.

Ps 51:18-19 [20-21] carefully counters the apparent polemic against animal sacrifice in 51:16 [18]: "For you have no delight (חפץ) in sacrifice (זבח); if I were to give a burnt offering (עולה), you would not be pleased (רצה)," through a repetition of the same language: "Do good to Zion in your good pleasure (רצה) . . . then you will delight (חפץ) in right sacrifices (זבחי־צדק), in burnt offerings (עולה) . . ."[19]

Yet, the shift in attitude toward animal sacrifice is not the most conclusive argument for seeing Ps 51:18-19 [20-21] as a later addition, but the change in the tone and theme. The great penitential prayer of the individual becomes the voice of communal hope in the restoration of the city of Jerusalem in these last two verses and is thereby accessible for worship.[20] The communal aspect of vv. 18-19 [20-21] and not the emphasis on sacrifice may just be the reason for the addition to the psalm. "The most logical explanation is that the original author of this intensely personal psalm of penitence bequeathed it to the cult and that the last two verses were added to adapt it for communal use in the exilic period."[21] It can also be conjectured that for the post-exilic editor the "I" of vv. 1-17 [3-19] acts in a corporate sense, thus providing a consistency with the later addition.[22] Ps 51:18-19 [20-21] then does not function as much to repudiate the earlier stance toward sacrifice as to provide a worship context into which the congregation can be drawn.

For the Christian Church, the addition of vv. 18-19 [20-21] has traditionally been more of a stumbling block. While the psalms have historically been read and preached to the exclusion of much of the rest of the Old Testament, certain aspects of the psalms clearly were not. Psalm 51 is one of ten psalms quoted in the letter of Barnabas, written in the early second century C.E. from Alexandria. The letter is a treatise against Old Testament sacrifice specifically, the cult system, and, in general, other things Jewish. Drawing upon prophetic critiques of sacrifice and citing 51:17a [18a] Barnabas argues that "the sacrifice acceptable to God is a broken spirit," adding that "a smell of sweet savour to the Lord is a heart that glorieth him that made it." Through proof-texting the prophets and by isolating 17a [18a] and bracketing out the remainder of the psalm, Barnabas thus demonstrates that sacrifices are abrogated.[23]

The late twentieth-century Church seems to have adopted the same methodology. The Revised Common Lectionary recommends that the reading for Ash Wednesday, Years A, B, and C be Ps 51:1-17 [3-19]. Ps 51:1-12 [3-15] is commended as an alternate reading for the Fifth Sunday in Lent, Year B, and as the psalm lection on the Eighteenth Sunday in Ordinary Time, Year B. Indications are that the Christian Church seems to be more comfortable with those passages that annul ritual sacrifice than it is with those that affirm its efficacy for the worshiping community. Following Barnabas' methodology serves to confirm for us that sacrifice has truly been abolished.[24] Being assured of our freedom from the Law and its requirements in Christ enables us to distance ourselves from the question of the efficacy of sacrificial language for the Christian church today. It also serves to frame our thinking regarding our grateful responses to God in terms of freedom and individuality, away from questions of duties and imperatives. Worshiping communities uncomfortable with verses 18-19 [20-21] prefer instead the type of freedom articulated in verse 17 [19].

We make the same mistake as Barnabas, however, if we isolate verse 17 [19] from 16 [18], and its larger context, making it a type of proof text, thereby turning Psalm 51 into an anti-sacrifice polemic. This rejection of sacrifice is not as clear cut as it might first appear. In verse 17 [19] the psalmist certainly seems to be saying that sacrifices no longer please God, that God's attentions have turned to the more serious considerations of the condition of the human heart. In line with this idea, Kraus interprets verse 17 [19] as a "rejection of the sacrificial system spoken of by the prophets (Amos 5:22; Isa. 1:11; Jer. 6:20)" that is "taken up here and followed obediently."[25] This thinking, unfortunately, reflects a misunderstanding of the condemnation of the prophets. Amos' attack on the worship life of eighth-century Israel, "I hate, I despise your festivals, and I take no delight in your solemn assemblies. Even though you offer me your burnt offerings and grain offerings, I will not accept them; and the offerings of well-being of your fatted animals I will not look upon; take away from me the noise of your songs; I will not listen to the melody of your harps" does find an echo in Ps 51:16-17 [18-19]. But, the critique is not taken far enough. The very next verse points the reader to Amos' complaint, "But let justice roll down like waters, and righteousness like an ever flowing stream" (5:24). Amos is not preaching against sacrifice and worship, but against *vain* sacrifice and *empty* worship, demonstrated in societal injustice and wrong doing.

Amos confronted religious people whose orders of worship and liturgical disciplines were flawless, but whose lives, lived outside of the context of that worship, were flawed. Isaiah and Jeremiah follow this same course. Isaiah's rousing invective against eighth century worship in Judah contains a call for repentance, cleansing, and the injunction, "Learn to do good; seek justice, rescue the oppressed, defend the orphan, plead for the widow" (1:18). Not to be outdone, Jeremiah's sermon expressing God's displeasure with frankincense, burnt offerings, and sacrifice begins with charges of greed and corruption and the call for a return to the ancient paths" (6:13-19). The psalmist appears to have heard the prophets clearly and to have taken their message to heart. Sacrifices offered from vain hearts are sacrifices offered in vain.[26]

Ps 51:17 [19] says "my sacrifice, O God, is a broken spirit; a broken and contrite heart, O God, you will not despise." As Christians freed from the burden and punishment of sin, we find a resonance with a grateful response that comes from a heart humbled before the throne of grace. Our confession and comfort are that we have a God who sits high and looks low. "For thus says the high and lofty one who inhabits eternity, whose name is Holy: I dwell in the high and holy place, and also with those who are contrite and humble in spirit, to revive the spirit of the humble, and to revive the heart of the contrite" (Isa 57:15).

Lest the psalmist be accused of personally rewriting ceremonial law, this restatement of the parameters of sacrifice must be seen in tandem with verse 16 [18]. "For you have no delight in sacrifice; if I were to give a burnt offering, you would not be pleased" sets the personal statement of verse 17 [19] in focus. Unless the penitent's heart is broken and contrite, sacrifices in and of themselves give God no pleasure. The psalmist's sacrifices can only delight God if the sinner is truly repentant.

Far from being a rejection of ritual, Psalm 51 is rich with liturgical language and cultic acts. Sacrifice is merely the final move in this liturgically motivated response to heartfelt repentance and God's expected forgiveness.[27] The vows of praise of vv. 14-15 [16-17] are cultic acts, expressing more than a relieved, "thank you, thank you, thank you, God!" Westermann makes the helpful distinction between thankfulness and praise in saying:

> A change, however, takes place in our evaluation of things when it becomes clear that in its essence thanking is something secondary, one way of praising. What makes this word so valuable to modern man is just that element in which it differs from praise or goes beyond it. We speak of "thankfulness," and this is the main thing. Spoken thanks is only an "externality," the expression of the feeling of thankfulness. The important thing is the thankful attitude. All this cannot be expressed by the vocabulary for praise. Surely the main difference lies here. The thankful attitude has its origin in a gift or in a helping or saving deed which someone does for me.[28]

In praise the subject shifts its focus from what was done "for me" to the person of God:

> The vocabulary of praise never expresses anything like an attitude or a feeling of gratitude . . . It comes to this, that in the vocabulary of thanks man remains subject, while in the sentences of praise God is subject: "Thou has done . . . thou art . . . God is . . . ."[29]

Praise then is more than an inner experience or feeling. Praise of God is an action, an endeavor that is practiced before others. It is expressed in the form of a vow that is made publicly and carried out liturgically. Its locus is the temple, the place of congregational worship.[30] According to Westermann the vow of praise is a constant component in the Psalms of petition, following immediately after the entreaty. The fact that its placement in the psalm, where form has a tendency to fluctuate, is so constant speaks for "the power and constancy of this motif."[31] Coming where it does after the petition, it speaks of the confidence that God will act and that things are incomplete and open-ended until God does. Publicly committing to a vow of praise puts God on notice. It also serves to put the petitioner on notice: "I *know* then that the matter is not finished when I have pled and God has heard, but that something else must still come. I know that I owe something to God." It is a sign of relationship with God.[32]

In structure the "I" of the psalmist is the subject of the vow and God is the object of the psalmist's devotion. The vow is typically expressed using verbs of vocal expression such as "to praise" (ידה) "to cry out, to sing" (רנן) "to make melody, to sing"(זמר), "to praise" (התהלל), and "to thunder, to shout" (רעם).[33] This same form and structure is found in Psalm 51 where the psalmist ends the plea for cleansing and forgiveness with the vow, "Deliver me from bloodshed, O God, O God of my salvation, and my tongue will sing (רנן) aloud of your deliverance. O Lord, open my lips, and my mouth will declare your praise (הלל)" (51:14-15 [16-17]).

The vow of praise is not a spiritualization of sacrifice nor a replacement of it. Praise and sacrifice are parallel activities, both carried out before other worshipers within the congregation. In the Psalter praise is more than a spontaneous expression of gratitude, it is expressed as a vow and presented as an offering to God.

> I will offer to you a thanksgiving sacrifice and call on the name of the Lord,
> I will pay my vows to the Lord in the presence of all God's people,
> > in the courts of the house of the Lord, in your midst, O Jerusalem.
> Praise the Lord! (Ps 116:17-19)
>
> With a freewill offering I will sacrifice to you;
> I will give thanks to your name, O Lord, for it is good (Ps 54:6 [8]).
>
> Let my prayer be counted as incense before you,
> and the lifting up of my hands as an evening sacrifice (Ps 141:2).

As such, the vow of praise was efficacious in and of itself, on a par with cultic sacrifice. "The formal parallelism encountered between praise and sacrifice argues the case and might lead us to assess words of praise as an offering only slightly less concrete than actual bulls and lambs.[34]

The temptation is, when thinking about sacrifice in Psalm 51, to fall back to "spiritualizing" the psalm or to speaking of the "attitude of the heart." Either of these approaches rolls back the concrete way in which the psalm speaks of sacrifice and its demands. Psalm 51, the great penitential psalm of the synagogue and the church, is not so much a psalm of the individual, as we in the late twentieth century might conceive of the individual, but rather a psalm of the worshiping community. Spoken with the communal "I" it makes liturgical and ritual demands upon the one who takes it seriously. Sacrifice and the vow of praise stand side by side calling the penitent to an accountable response.

Psalm 51 is not spiritualized in the sense that the vows and sacrifices are somehow "symbolic" and not real or tangible. To call cultic actions "symbolic" is "misleading in the implication that the 'real' is somehow elsewhere. On the contrary, the real is summoned up and made present by these cultic acts." This is what we affirm at the baptismal font and at the table. Praise is meaningful in itself, as the act.[35]

Psalm 51 does not release us from costly responses. There is no private piety here. We are still required to make public our praises, to offer our vows of praise in the congregation. We are still required to bring our bulls to the altar. The demand is for more than a change in the attitude of the heart. Psalm 51 challenges us to put our lives, our fortunes, our money where our mouths are: in the praise of the One who delivers through mighty acts. The right attitude of the heart is critical, but only as the active responses flow from it.

The message of Psalm 51 is clearly in line with the prophets:

> With what shall I come before the LORD, and bow myself before God on high? Shall I come before the LORD with burnt offerings, with calves a year old? Will the LORD be pleased with thousands of rams, with ten thousands of rivers of oil? Shall I give my firstborn for my transgression, the fruit of my body for the sin of my soul?" The LORD has told you, O mortal, what is good; and what does the LORD require of you but to do justice, and to love kindness, and to walk humbly with your God? (Mic 6:6-8).

> Why did someone, after having read the Psalm add them, [vv. 20, 21] and why did others accept the addition? Not, surely, just because he and they wanted to push ritual in somehow, but because they felt that, when the experience so poignantly described in the psalm was theirs, they could go on to use the sacrifices of the Temple sacramentally. There were

men who, having cried out for "a clean heart," and "a right spirit," knew that the right use of ritual would help them to find it.[36]

NOTES: CHAPTER 7

[1] Psalms 15 and 24 are considered to be entrance liturgies, 50 and 81 are identified as covenant renewal liturgies, 115 and 134 are liturgies of praise. It should be noted, however, that these texts are lacking liturgical directions. Bernhard W. Anderson, *Out of the Depths. The Psalms Speak for Us Today*, rev. and Expanded (Philadelphia: Westminster, 1983) 239–42. See also Walter Harrelson, *From Fertility Cult to Worship. A Reassessment for the Modern Church of the Worship of Ancient Israel* (Garden City: Doubleday, 1969) 81–99.

[2] "There is no evidence of the thorough and systematic changes that would have been necessary if the Psalter were to become the expression of a single theology." Norman Whybray, in *Reading the Psalms as a Book*, [JSOT Supplement Series 222 (Sheffield: JSOT Press, 1996) 124] points to this apparent ambiguity to address the issue of the collection's theological unity. In his view, the Psalter's contradictions regarding ritual sacrifice are an indication that the collection is not the obvious product of homogenization.

[3] Psalms favorable to the sacrificial system are: 4:5 [6]; 27:6 ; 51:16-17 [18-19]; 54:6 [8]; 66:13-15; 107:21-22; 116:17-19. Ps 26:6; 43:4; and 118:27 mention a response at the altar. Psalms that seem to reject the notion of sacrifice are: 40:6-8 [7-9]; 50:8-15; 51:18-19 [20-21]; 69:30-31 [31-32]; 141:2.

[4] See William L. Holladay's fine tradition history in *The Psalms through Three Thousand Years. Prayerbook of a Cloud of Witnesses* (Minneapolis: Fortress, 1993).

[5] References to numbering in the Hebrew text are in brackets.

[6] Ibid., 105–10.

[7] Ibid., 109–10.

[8] Ibid., 175–78.

[9] Ibid., 178.

[10] Ibid., 198. Also André Séguenny, (ed., *Bibliotheca Dissidentium* (Bibliotheca Bibliographica Aureliana 79; Baden-Baden: Koerner, 1980) 1:118.

[11] Merry E. Wiesner, "Nuns, wives, and Mothers: Women and the Reformation in Germany," in *Women in Reformation and Counter-Reformation Europe. Public and Private Worlds*, Sherrin Marshall, ed. (Bloomington: Indiana University Press, 1989) 21.

[12] Holladay, 58.

[13] In the readings for Year C, in addition to Ash Wednesday, 51:1-12 [3-14] is paired with II Samuel 11:16–12:13a in Ordinary Time.

[14] Patrick D. Miller, Jr., *Interpreting the Psalms* (Philadelphia: Fortress Press, 1986) 53.

[15] Whybray [100–24], and Nigel B. Courtman, in "Sacrifice in the Psalms," [in *Sacrifice in the Bible*, Roger T. Beckwith, and Martin J. Selman, eds. (Carlisle, United Kingdom: Paternoster Press, 1995) 41–58] agree that, despite first impressions, the polarity between what is being expressed in the so-called anti-sacrifice psalms *versus* the pro-sacrifice psalms is not as big a chasm as it might appear. They both allow for a continuum in what the term "sacrifice" may have meant at particular times in the life of worshiping Israelites and later Judeans.

[16] There is a difficulty with the text here. The plural "sacrifices of" (זִבְחֵי) does not fit with the singular "broken spirit." The modern editors of the *Biblia Hebraica* sense the problem and suggest זִבְחִי "my sacrifice" as a solution. This fits better with the first person character of the confession in vv. 1-17 [3-19] and the "objectionable didactic nature of the verse is avoided." See Dalglish, 194. Also Hans-Joachim Kraus, *Psalms 1–59: A Commentary*, trans. Hilton C. Oswald (Minneapolis: Fortress, 1993) 499–500; Marvin E. Tate, *Psalms 51–100*, Word Biblical Commentary, vol. 20 (Dallas: Word, 1990) 7.

[17] Along with Whybray, 105, see also Anderson, 95; Holladay, 58; Tate, 29; Kraus, 506; Artur Weiser, "Psalm 51" in *The Psalms. A Commentary* (Philadelphia: Westminster, 1962) 410; Hermann Gunkel, *Psalms II, 51–100*, Anchor Bible, trans. Mitchell Dahood (Garden City: Doubleday, 1968) 9–10 and *Die Psalmen* (Göttingen: Vandenhoeck & Ruprecht, 1929) 226; E. R. Dalglish, *Psalm Fifty-One in the Light of Ancient Near Eastern Patternism* (Leiden: Brill, 1962) 204–8.

[18] Rainer Albertz, *A History of Israelite Religion in the Old Testament Period* (Louisville: Westminster/John Knox, 1994) 508–23.

[19] Right sacrifices (זִבְחֵי־צֶדֶק) are not a requirement for the ritually correct manner of cultic manipulation of the deity, but rather connote "slain offerings given as a rightful gift." These are offerings rightfully due to God for something that God has done or is about to do for the worshiper and are related to the concept of grant, according to Baruch Levine [*In the Presence of the Lord. A Study of Cult and Some Cultic Terms in Ancient Israel* (Leiden: E. J. Brill, 1974) 135–37]. Levine freely reads: "For you don't desire slain offerings, else I would provide; holocausts you won't accept . . . By your will, repair Zion, build the walls of Jerusalem! Then you will desire slain offerings rightfully due, holocausts entirely consumed; then bulls will ascend your altar!" Cf. Deut 33:19 and Ps 4:6.

[20] Whybray, 106–7.

[21] Dalglish (206) points out that Psalm 130, the only other penitential psalm, has a "similar communal liturgical addition which adapts an individual psalm for public worship."

[22] Ibid., 207.

[23] Holladay, 163. On the subject of the early church and sacrifice see Robert J. Daly, *Christian Sacrifice. The Judaeo-Christian Background Before Origen*, Catholic University of America Studies in Christian Antiquity (Washington, D.C.: Catholic University of America Press, 1978) 422–33. *Barnabas* 2.10.

[24] For summary statements on the question, see Daly on sacrifice in the New Testament, 208–307. Also, Peter M. Head, "The Self-Offering and Death of Christ as a Sacrifice in the Gospels and the Acts of the Apostles" and Roger T. Beckwith, "The Death of Christ as a Sacrifice in the Teaching of Paul and Hebrews" in *Sacrifice in the Bible*, Roger T. Beckwith, and Martin J. Selman, eds. (Carlisle, United Kingdom: Paternoster Press, 1995) 111–29, 130–34.

[25] Kraus, 506.

[26] Weiser interprets the message of the prophets in much the same way, pointing to a new understanding of the more spiritual quality of this view, in which God rejects "the sacrificial cult and its underlying motives," 409.

[27] It is beyond the scope of this paper to investigate the reference to cleansing in "Purge me with hyssop, and I shall be clean; wash me, and I shall be whiter than snow" (51:7 [9]). Kraus says this "alludes to an ancient ceremonial of cleansing" that is no

longer operative in the cult, 504. Weiser agrees, saying that the psalmist borrows from the "ritual language of the cult to illustrate a spiritual process," 406.

[28] Claus Westermann, *Praise and Lament in the Psalms*, trans. Keith R. Crim and Richard N. Soulen (Atlanta: John Knox Press, 1981) 28, Gary A. Anderson, "The Praise of God as a Cultic Event," in *Priesthood and Cult in Ancient Israel*, Gary A. Anderson and Saul M. Olyan, eds. JSOT Supplement Series 125 (Sheffield: JSOT Press, 1991) 15–33, and James L. Kugel, "Topics in the History of the Spirituality of the Psalms," in *Jewish Spirituality from the Bible through the Middle Ages*, Arthur Green, ed. (New York: Crossroad, 1986) 113–44 further develop this notion of the cultic aspect to the praise of God in the psalms and are worthwhile resources.

[29] Westermann, 29.

[30] According to Westermann, the public vow of praise is a motif common not only to Israel, but is found extensively in the psalms of Babylon and Egypt (38–39, 46, 76).

[31] Ibid., 75.

[32] Ibid., 78.

[33] Ibid., 75–76; Anderson, 16.

[34] Kugel, 123–25.

[35] Ibid., 127.

[36] Dalglish, 206. C. Ryder Smith, *The Bible Doctrine of Salvation* (London: Epworth Press, 1941) 85.

8

Thus Says the LORD: "Thou Shalt Preach on the Psalms!"

J. Clinton McCann, Jr.

From the perspective of a scholar like myself who has devoted much of the past ten years to producing resources that facilitate the preaching of the Psalms,[1] there is good news and bad news. Let's start with the good news. First, over the past couple of years, several of my former students have either sent me copies of sermons that they have preached on the Psalms, or they have reported to me that they have preached or are preaching on the Psalms. Then too, several other pastors have informed me that at least occasionally, they preach on the psalm assigned for the day by the Revised Common Lectionary; and at least one pastor whom I know has preached an extensive series of sermons on the psalms.[2] Furthermore, some recent academic and ecclesiastical literature provides encouragement, guidance, and instruction for preaching from the psalms. These resources have been produced by pastors, as well as by professors of both homiletics and Old Testament.[3]

But there is also some bad news. Several of my former students have described to me recently the difficulty of settling on a text or texts for preaching week after week. When I've asked them if they have preached on a psalm, the answer frequently goes something like this: "No; I'm not sure I'd know *how* to preach on a psalm." When I survey pastors and members of congregations about their experience with the psalms in the preaching and hearing of the Word, I often find pastors who have never preached on a psalm and congregations who have never heard a sermon on a psalm. Then too, not all professors of Old Testament and professors of homiletics encourage preaching on the psalms; and some actively discourage it. For instance, Donald E. Gowan, an Old Testament professor, concludes that while the psalms should be used in worship, they should be used "in their appropriate place; we ought to pray them and sing them rather than preach them."[4] David Buttrick, an influential professor of homiletics, recognizes that "the poetry of Israel is preached;" but with scarcely veiled sarcasm, he remarks: "I confess an odd notion that psalms are for singing and not, primarily, for preaching."[5] Hardly an encouragement to preach the Psalms!

Given the persistence of the non-use of the Psalms in preaching and even the active opposition by some influential theological educators to preaching the psalms—that is, given the bad news outlined above—I propose in this presentation to do the following: (1) to examine briefly the possible objections to preaching from the Psalms, objections which probably account for the ongoing non-use; (2) to respond to these objections and to articulate a biblical-theological rationale for preaching the Psalms; and (3) to illustrate timely and faithful directions for preaching the Psalms in a contemporary North American context.

Objections to Preaching the Psalms

The previously mentioned quotes from Gowan and Buttrick imply their rationale for opposing the preaching of the Psalms, and it is primarily form-critical. In short, they suggest, since the Psalms originated as prayers and songs of praise offered by human beings to God, they should continue to be used in exactly the same way. As Gowan succinctly concludes: "We ought to pray them and sing them rather than preach them."

To be sure, this seems like a reasonable conclusion. Indeed, it is reinforced by liturgical traditions that appropriate the psalms not as Scripture (and thus not to be preached), but rather as means of responding to Scripture—in particular, to the first reading or Old Testament lesson in the Service for the Lord's Day. For instance, in a section called "The Service for the Lord's Day: A Description of Its Movement and Elements," the *Book of Common Worship* of the Presbyterian Church (U.S.A.) and the Cumberland Presbyterian Church describes the appropriate use of a psalm:

> The singing of a psalm is appropriate at any place in the order of worship. However, the psalm appointed in the lectionary . . . is intended to be sung following the first reading, where it serves as a congregational meditation and response to the reading. The psalm is not intended as another reading.[6]

By explicitly saying that the psalm is "not . . . another reading," the *Book of Common Worship* suggests that the psalms should not be understood as Scripture, and thus it strongly implies that the psalms are not suitable for preaching. At this point, contemporary form-critical considerations and traditional liturgical practice are congruent. Both suggest that the psalms be prayed and sung, not preached.[7]

There is another possible objection to preaching the Psalms, although perhaps it is less an "objection" than a difficulty—namely, the popularity in recent years of narrative theology and narrative preaching. If narrative is given a privileged place in Scripture, and/or if narrative is seen as the basic structure of human thought and communication, then the Psalms will likely be largely ignored, since they are poetry. To be sure, Robert Alter has argued that many psalms, or at least parts of psalms, can "be thought of as incipient narrative."[8] Thus, the privileging of narrative need not be an insurmountable difficulty for the preaching of the Psalms; however, it has almost certainly contributed to the non-use of the Psalms in preaching.[9]

Responding to the Objections:
A Biblical-Theological Rationale for Preaching the Psalms

As suggested, the objection to preaching the Psalms as articulated by Gowan and Buttrick seems quite reasonable. Indeed, I would be the first to agree with Gowan that we ought to pray and sing the psalms, thus honoring their original intent as well as continuing a long history of traditional use. But, unlike Gowan, I suggest that this need not be done to the exclusion of preaching the Psalms.

What both Gowan and Buttrick fail to realize is that the meaning and usefulness of a text, such as a psalm, are not limited to its original intent or use. To privilege the original intent or use may not be entirely misguided, but it seems to me to be unduly and unnecessarily restrictive. More particularly, what Gowan and Buttrick do not take into account is the fact that individual psalms, which certainly functioned originally in a liturgical setting, were eventually collected in the form of a book. To be sure, the collecting of psalms into a book did not preclude their continuing to be used in liturgical settings; but at the very least, their literary setting within a book provided a new context for interpreting them and also opened up the possibility that psalms could function in new ways. In this regard, it is quite revealing that form-critics have had extreme difficulty in pinning down very precisely the liturgical setting or settings of particular psalms. Almost certainly this is because the process and results of collection have blurred, perhaps intentionally, the evidence of original liturgical setting and use. Furthermore, the process and results of collection have relativized the exclusive significance of what may have been the original intent and use of particular psalms.

To put it another way, the whole collection—the book of Psalms—is greater, or at least different, than the sum of its parts. Admittedly, psalms scholars are still debating the nature and significance of this difference; but some things are clear. For instance, Gerald H. Wilson has demonstrated that the process of collection was not merely random nor haphazard. There was intentional editing; and as for the editorial purpose, Wilson suggests that the final form of the Psalter responds to the critical loss of the Davidic monarchy by directing attention to God's reign. Thus, as a whole, the psalms have taken on a hortatory or instructional function.[10]

In fact, as Wilson and others have suggested, the instructional orientation of the Psalter is clear from its beginning. Citing the introductory function of Psalm 1, James L. Mays also points out that other torah-psalms are scattered throughout the Psalter; and the effect is to give the entire collection a hortatory or instructional orientation. What difference does this make for interpretation of and appropriation of the Psalms? Mays succinctly concludes: "Form-critical and cult-functional questions are subordinated and questions of *content and theology* become more important."[11] One major implication is clear. Given the final form of the Psalter, the psalms are not only to be prayed and sung, but they are also to be taught, learned from, and proclaimed.

To put it yet another way, the traditional characterization of the Psalter as the hymnbook or prayerbook of the Second (or First) Temple may not be entirely inaccurate, but it is certainly inadequate and misleading. In the words of Klaus Seybold, who, like Mays, takes seriously the final form of the Psalter:

> [T]he existing Psalter now takes on the character of a documentation of divine revelation, to be used in a way analogous to the *Torah*, the first part of the canon, and becomes an *instruction manual* for the theological study of the divine order of salvation, and for meditation.[12]

Note that Seybold specifically addresses the issue of how the psalms are to be used. If the psalms are anything like "a documentation of divine revelation," and if they are to be appropriated like the *Torah*, then not only should they be prayed and sung, but they should also be read, meditated upon, studied, and proclaimed.

Brevard Childs, who is also explicitly interested in the use of the psalms in the church, puts the matter even more theologically, and in a sense, even more pointedly for the purposes of considering the preaching of the psalms:

> I would argue that the need for taking seriously the canonical form of the Psalter would greatly aid in making use of the Psalms in the life of the Christian Church. Such a move would not disregard the historical dimensions of the Psalter, but would attempt to profit from the shaping which the final redactors gave the older material in order to transform traditional poetry into Sacred Scripture for the later generations of the faithful.[13]

Without wanting to "disregard the historical dimensions of the Psalter"—that is, without denying that the psalms should be prayed and sung—Childs, like Mays and Seybold, discerns an additional dimension. To borrow Gowan's words, the "appropriate place" of the psalms in worship includes their being preached, because the psalms have been received and transmitted as Scripture. As I see it, the recognition of this reality is a sufficient biblical-theological rationale for preaching the Psalms.

As for the difficulty that the Psalms are not very evidently narrative material—that is, at best they offer only "incipient narrative"—my response is that much of the Bible is not narrative. To be sure, much of the Bible *is* narrative; and I'm even willing to agree with Frederick Buechner that, in a sense, the Bible has "a single plot."[14] But in addition to telling stories or even a single story, the biblical writers also reflected on what the story or stories *mean*. Terence Fretheim calls these reflections "generalizations," and suggests that they "bring a focus to what the story is all about, and make truth-claims which decisively limit the number of possible interpretations." Thus, Fretheim claims, "story and generalization must be kept inextricably interwoven."[15]

I have no objection to the conclusion that the Psalms offer primarily "generalizations" about the character of God and God's relationship to humanity and the world. And, the editors of the Psalter actually encourage the readers of the psalms to interweave them with stories (for instance, the superscriptions that cite incidents in the life of David). My point is that the "generalizations" found in the psalms, as those found elsewhere in the Bible, demand to be proclaimed.

Preaching the Psalms: A Few Key "Generalizations"

This section must necessarily be illustrative, and my intent is to offer several examples of how major "generalizations" from the psalms address what I perceive to be the current crisis in North American culture. As a helpful point of departure, I take Mary Pipher's analysis of the crisis:

> We have a crisis in meaning in our culture. The crisis comes from our isolation from each other, from the values we learn in a culture of consumption and from the fuzzy, self-help message that the only commitment is to the self and the only important question is—Am I happy? We learn that we are number one and that our own immediate needs are the most important ones. The crisis comes from the message that products satisfy and that happiness can be purchased.[16]

The Pursuit of Happiness: Psalms 1 and 2

As Mary Pipher suggests, the current crisis has to do with happiness and how we pursue it. So does the book of Psalms, and this is evident from the very first word in the book: "Happy" (1:1). In a real sense, as James L. Mays suggests, the rest of the entire Psalter offers a commentary on this one word![17] The importance of the word is signaled by its repetition in 2:12, forming an envelope-structure around the first two psalms, which seem to serve as a paired introduction to the Psalter. Plus, the word "happy" occurs twenty-three more times throughout the book.

For the purposes of preaching in the contemporary North American context, it is crucial to note that Psalms 1–2 offer a thoroughly God-centered, rather than thoroughly self-centered, understanding of happiness. For the psalmists, happiness involves unrelenting attention to God and God's *torah*, God's teaching or God's will (1:2)—the precise opposite of the preoccupation with the self that Pipher suggests is causing the current crisis. The truly happy, according to the psalmists, find their "refuge" (2:12)—that is, their strength, protection, and resources for living—in God, not in the self. Again, this is the precise opposite of the autonomy or self-sufficiency that Pipher argues is causing the current crisis. In short, the "generalizations" found in Psalms 1–2 could hardly be more timely!

Psalm 2 moves toward a conclusion by offering a generalized summons, "Serve the LORD" (2:11). Its contemporary edge is captured poetically by writer Anne Lamott:

> It helps to resign as the controller of your fate. All that energy we expend to keep things running right is not what's keeping things running right.

We're bugs struggling in the river, brightly visible to the trout below. With that fact in mind, people like me make up all these rules to give us the illusion that we are in charge. I need to say to myself, they're not needed, hon. Just take in the buggy pleasures. Be kind to the others, grab the fleck of river weed, notice how beautifully your bug legs scull.[18]

Or, in theological terms, "Serve the LORD." To be sure, this sounds hopelessly naive, as naive, in fact, as "the kingdom of God is at hand; repent, and believe in the good news" (Mark 1:15).

When the preacher realizes that both Ps 2:11 and Jesus' "generalization" at the beginning of his ministry announce the presence of the realm of God, then she or he is also reminded that Jesus also taught about happiness. In the Gospel of Matthew, at least, Jesus begins his ministry of proclamation with the Beatitudes, a series of sayings about happiness. The beatitudes can also be accurately characterized as "generalizations," and it is revealing that they initiate a block of material that we usually call a "sermon," the Sermon on the Mount. In short, these "generalizations" demand to be preached, and so do the functionally equivalent "generalizations" in Psalms 1–2.

A Perspective on Suffering: The Psalmic Prayers

The people whom the beatitudes pronounce "happy" are ones who most people would conclude are suffering, and it is precisely these kind of people who always pray the psalmic prayers. This is why they are generally known as "laments" or "complaints." In other words, the happy or "righteous" in the psalms are regularly the "poor," "needy," "meek," "afflicted," "persecuted," and "oppressed."

This recognition leads to an extremely important "generalization"— namely, happiness and suffering are not mutually exclusive. This is why the psalmic prayers regularly juxtapose complaint and praise. The textbook example is Psalm 13, which in tidy, two-verse sections moves from complaint to petition to praise. The move to praise comes with no preparation, no explanation, and no helpful transition. The juxtaposition of complaint and praise constitutes the fundamental interpretive issue in the prayers, and there are several possible explanations. For the purposes of preaching, however, the theological explanation offered by James L. Mays is the most compelling and profitable. Mays contends that the movement is not a sequential one, but rather that the various moods or modes should be understood as simultaneous. His exquisite conclusion is this: "The agony and the ecstasy belong together as the secret of our identity."[19]

To paraphrase this "generalization" in Christian terms, the cross and the resurrection belong together as the secret of our identity. What this "generalization" means is, that for the faithful at least, suffering will be a normal and expected part of their lives. It is at this point that this "generalization" becomes so timely, even urgent, because as Mary Pipher points out, "almost all the craziness in the world comes from running from pain."[20] She also points out the following:

> When we suggest that suffering can be avoided, we foster unreasonable expectations. We are sending the same message that advertisers send. Advertisers imply that suffering is unnatural, shouldn't be tolerated and can be avoided with the right products. Psychologists sometimes imply that stress-free living is possible if only we have the right tools. But in fact, all our stories have sad endings. We all die in the last act.[21]

In a culture that systematically teaches us that suffering is an aberration, the psalmic prayers can remind us of our finitude and fallibility. In short, they can teach us that the agony and the ecstasy belong together.

Failing to learn this lesson, contemporary persons are often ill-equipped to deal with the painful realities of human life. We buy not only the advertisers' products, but we also buy their underlying message. And people who don't *expect* to suffer frequently resort to anesthetizing themselves with substances, with things, with pleasure, or with work. And increasingly and tragically, young people who suffer know no better than to conclude that something must be desperately wrong with themselves or their lives; and they attempt and often complete suicide. For this reason alone, the psalmic "generalization" that the agony and the ecstasy belong together as the secret of our identity demands to be preached!

But of course, even more is at stake. Persons who cannot or will not accept the reality that suffering is a normal part of human life will be ill-equipped to practice the simple things that, according to the Bible, constitute faithfulness to God and authentic human life—things like loving one another (see John 15:12-13) and bearing one another's burdens (see Gal 6:2). It seems to me that the increasing sense of isolation felt by contemporary persons, as well as the ongoing breakdown of basic societal institutions, are linked directly to the increasing inability or unwillingness among us to accept suffering as normal, and indeed, faithful.

If, as is the case in the psalmic prayers, suffering is a sign and/or result of faithfulness rather than unfaithfulness, then we are pushed in a further direction that is also extremely important and timely. Namely, suffering cannot and must not be interpreted as divine punishment. In short, the psalmic prayers obliterate the doctrine of retribution, thus opening the way for the "generalization" that grace is fundamental. This "generalization" is so crucial and timely, because, as I see it, almost no one in our culture believes in grace. Instead, we insist on merit; and the results are disastrous. By the logic of merit, the proud and prosperous can congratulate themselves on their goodness; and furthermore, they can blame the poor and victimized for their victimization. Any accountability toward the dispossessed or complicity in their victimization is out of the question, according to the logic of merit, or to use the more theological designation, the doctrine of retribution.

But the psalmic prayers will not permit this line of logic, nor of course, will the gospel of Jesus Christ. As William Placher has recently put it, "the message of the cross . . . is not just that we should stop scapegoating the innocent, but that we should stop punishing the guilty." He continues as follows:

> There are legitimate concerns about protecting the innocent and rehabilitating those who have gone down wrong paths, but for Christians the condemnation of sinners is no longer possible without condemning Christ. We should not settle for a theology that gives us less than that, for without that we have good news only for those who count themselves among the righteous, and good news only for the righteous is not the gospel.[22]

By obliterating the doctrine of retribution, the psalmic prayers do not settle for a theology less than the radical grace that lies at the heart of the Gospel. Precisely because they articulate this good news, the psalmic prayers, especially Psalms 22, 31, and 69, were primary sources for the Gospel writers as they told the story of Jesus. In short, the Gospel writers interwove the "generalizations" they found in the psalms with the story of Jesus; and this is another reason that the psalms demand to be preached.

From Suffering to Solidarity: The Songs of Praise

In her book *The Amnesty of Grace: Justification by Grace from a Latin American Perspective*, Elsa Tamez points out that if North American Christians actually started believing in grace, then we would begin to accept at least some accountability for what is going on in Latin America and the rest of the world. In her words, the result would be "solidarity."[23]

It is precisely such "solidarity" among all persons that is highlighted in the songs of praise. It is evident in the way the songs of praise invite people to praise God. The invitation is regularly universal. It is extended not simply to Israel or Judah or the righteous, but to all peoples and nations (117:1), all the earth (100:1), all creatures (150:6), and indeed all creation (148:3-4, 8-9). The implications are profound, radical, and timely; for the radical inclusivity of the songs of praise challenges what most of the time we are content to accept as the inevitable *status quo*—permanent divisions between races, nationalities, and social classes. Witness the growing rift in the United States between rich and poor, as well the ongoing tensions between races and persons of different ethnic backgrounds; and witness too the often violent resurgence of nationalism worldwide, as well as the often noted movement toward tribalism rather than "solidarity."

In a word, the songs of praise will not permit the faithful to be content with barriers and divisions. The motivation toward inclusivity is not "political correctness," at least not as we generally use the term today; however, the psalms do offer a "political correctness" of a different kind. The psalmists assert that the world and all its peoples are one, because God claims or owns the world and all its peoples (24:1). In short, "The LORD reigns!" (96:1); and it is this political reality and realm that transcends barriers and invites inclusivity. If this is "political correctness," so be it, although I prefer to call it "biblical correctness." In any case, the Psalms assert that because God rules the world, God will not properly be worshiped until all the world is gathered, or at least until all the world is welcome.

These "generalizations" reinforce those I articulated on the basis of Psalms 1–2 and the psalmic prayers. In short, God's rule calls for submission of the self to God and God's claim, and the result is a community constituted by grace and composed of persons who voluntarily embrace the suffering that inheres in loving other people and bearing others' burdens.

The psalms themselves invite the preaching of the primary "generalization" that lies at the heart of the songs of praise: "Say among the nations: 'The LORD reigns!'" (96:10).

When Jesus came preaching, this is exactly what he said. And so should we! The content and theology of the psalms demand to be preached. Thus says the LORD!

NOTES: CHAPTER 8

[1] See *A Theological Introduction to the Book of Psalms: The Psalms as Torah* (Nashville: Abingdon, 1993); "The Book of Psalms: Introduction, Commentary, and Reflections" in *The New Interpreters' Bible* vol. IV (Nashville: Abingdon, 1996) 641–1280; "Preaching on Psalms for Advent," *Journal for Preachers* 16/1 (Advent 1992) 11–16; and Charles B. Cousar, Beverly R. Gaventa, J. Clinton McCann, Jr., James D. Newsome, *Texts for Preaching: A Lectionary Commentary Based on the NRSV—Year C* (Louisville: Westminster John Knox, 1994).

[2] See James C. Howell, "The Psalms in Worship and Preaching: A Report," chapter nine in this volume.

[3] See, for instance, Elizabeth Achtemeier, "Preaching from the Psalms," *Review and Expositor* 81 (1984) 437–49; W. H. Bellinger, Jr., "Let the Words of My Mouth: Proclaiming the Psalms," *Southwestern Journal of Theology* 27 (Fall 1984) 17–24; William E. Hull, "Preaching on the Psalms," *Review and Expositor* 81 (1984) 451–56; Delmar L. Jacobson, "The Royal Psalms and Jesus Messiah: Preparing to Preach on a Royal Psalm," *Word and World* 5 (1985) 192–98; James Limburg, "The Autumn Leaves: Pages from the Psalter for Late Pentecost," *Word and World* 12 (1992) 272–77; Thomas G. Long, *Preaching and the Literary Forms of the Bible* (Philadelphia: Fortress, 1989) 43–52, which are entitled, "Preaching on the Psalms;" Donald Macleod, "Preaching from the Psalms" in *Biblical Preaching: An Expositor's Treasure*, James W. Cox, ed. (Philadelphia: Westminster, 1983) 102–18; Greg W. Parsons, "Guidelines for Understanding and Proclaiming the Psalms," *Bibliotheca Sacra* 147 (1990) 169–87; Stephen A. Hamilton Wright, "Violent Vengeance in the Psalms: Can It Possibly Preach?" *Journal for Preachers* 14/3 (Easter 1991) 16–21.

[4] *Reclaiming the Old Testament for the Christian Pulpit* (Atlanta: John Knox, 1980) 146.

[5] *Homiletic: Moves and Structures* (Philadelphia: Fortress, 1987) 478.

[6] *The Book of Common Worship* (Louisville: Westminster John Knox, 1993) 37.

[7] Consult the essay by Nasuti who makes the point that the psalms as used in the Revised Common Lectionary are responsorial and thereby replace authorial intention with liturgical one. This is part of the hesitance to compare the psalms readings with the other elements of the lectionary which do still have their own voice and thereby privilege the author's intention.

[8] *The Art of Biblical Poetry* (New York: Basic Books, Inc., 1985) 25.

[9] See Bellinger, "Let the Words of My Mouth," who argues that "part of the task in preaching psalmic poetry is translating it to life story" (21). Bellinger also points out that some psalms "already tell a story" (21).

[10] See Gerald H. Wilson, *The Editing of the Hebrew Psalter*, SBLDS 76 (Chico, Calif.: Scholars Press, 1985) especially 204–7, 214–19; "Shaping the Psalter: A Consideration of Editorial Linkage in the Book of Psalms" in *The Shape and Shaping of the Psalter*, J. C. McCann, ed. JSOTSup 159 (Sheffield: JSOT Press, 1993) 72–82, especially 80–82. For a helpful overview of the work done on the shape and shaping of the Psalter, see David M. Howard, Jr., "Editorial Activity in the Psalter: A State-of-the-Field Survey" in *Shape and Shaping*, 52–70.

[11] "The Place of the Torah-Psalms in the Psalter," *JBL* 106/1 (1987) 12; emphasis added.

[12] *Introducing the Psalms*, trans. R. G. Dunphy (Edinburgh: T & T Clark Ltd., 1990) 27; emphasis added.

[13] "Reflections on the Modern Study of the Psalms," in *Magnalia Dei, The Mighty Acts of God: Essays in Memory of G. Ernest Wright*, F. M. Cross, W. E. Lemke, P. D. Miller, Jr., eds. (Garden City, N.Y.: Doubleday, 1976) 385.

[14] "The Good Book as a Good Book" in *The Clown in the Belfry: Writings on Faith and Fiction* (San Francisco: HarperSanFrancisco, 1992) 44.

[15] *The Suffering of God: An Old Testament Perspective*, Overtures to Biblical Theology (Philadelphia: Fortress, 1984) 24, 23.

[16] *The Shelter of Each Other: Rebuilding Our Families* (New York: G. P. Putnam's Sons, 1996) 26.

[17] *Psalms*. Interpretation: A Bible Commentary for Teaching and Preaching (Louisville: John Knox Press, 1994) 40–41.

[18] *Bird by Bird: Some Instructions on Writing and Life* (New York: Anchor Books/Doubleday, 1994) 180–81.

[19] "Psalm 13," *Interpretation* 34 (1980) 282.

[20] *The Shelter of Each Other*, 143; see 229.

[21] Ibid., 119.

[22] "Christ Takes Our Place: Rethinking Atonement," *Interpretation* 53 (1999) 15.

[23] *The Amnesty of Grace: Justification by Faith from a Latin American Perspective*, trans. Sharon H. Ringe (Nashville: Abingdon Press, 1993) 134; see 134–40.

9

The Psalms in Worship and Preaching
A Report

James C. Howell

T hroughout the history of the Christian Church, the psalms have loomed large in worship, preaching, and devotion. After a period of eclipse, for which observers have devised various explanations, the psalms are now emerging from the shadows to resume their traditional place in services of worship. Some preachers even preach on psalms. The extent of their usage in private prayer, especially among Protestants, is less certain.

During the late spring and the summer of 1998, we focused the worship and spiritual life of Davidson United Methodist Church on the Psalter. I say "we" because it required a high level of planning and cooperation from all the staff and leadership of the congregation. It began when our worship planning team gazed into that long abyss of Sundays called Pentecost, searching for something to give that erratic season some cohesion. Being a pastor with a framed Ph.D. diploma from Duke up in the attic, that parchment having been earned because of research I did once upon a time on Psalm 90, I had always wanted to preach a series of sermons on the Psalms. Before I could get the words out, though, my minister of music proclaimed that he had a special file of anthems on various psalms that he thought the choir might enjoy singing.

So we blocked out Sundays from May through August and selected psalms, striving for diversity of genre, but also in truth gravitating toward our personal favorites. Thomas Merton wisely suggested that having a favorite psalm at some juncture in your life is a special grace from God. We proceeded to select appropriate hymns and prayers for the balance of all the services, and then we got busy, the choir practicing upstairs and the preacher scouring commentaries in quest of the ever-elusive sermon.

But before we began the series itself, we wanted to educate the congregation and get them involved. I led a pair of workshops on the psalms, laying out pretty basic stuff for our people. How did the Israelites worship? and where? What kinds of psalms are there? How were they used? How do we conceive of these words to God becoming the word of God? Why does the New Testament quote psalms so frequently? And how have they been utilized through the history of the Church? We also asked Sunday School classes and other small groups to use a video-based curriculum I had produced a decade before. Most importantly, we asked the entire congregation, in their own private moments, to pray the psalms. We provided a calendar of selections, designed to keep everyone in sync with the psalms that would be read on Sunday morning, to guide their reading and prayer. For instance, on the two days before the worship built around Psalm 73, Psalms 37 and 49 would be read. The day before the sermon on Psalm 24, Psalm 15 would be read, with Psalm 150 the day after.

The good news was that many of our people did, for the first time in their lives, read and pray psalms. They were discussed in classrooms and in living rooms and at a restaurant downtown. So on Sunday, those ancient words to God were very much alive and current, which enriched the series immensely.

The bulletin design was critical. At times we selected settings of the psalm of the day from the United Methodist Hymnal, but on other Sundays, we veered away and explored other modes. Furthermore, each bulletin had an insert. On the front was some simplified summary of what we know about the background, historically speaking, of a given psalm. Again, the intent was to augment the educational process. The back featured insights from the music department on hymnody and the anthems employed.

Psalm 42

After lengthy deliberation, we chose Psalm 42 to kick off the series, guessing that the image of the thirsty deer might capture people's imaginations and invite them to explore other psalms in depth. The insert had to be introductory in nature, and it looked like this:

What is a Psalm?

A psalm is a bit of poetry from the religious life of ancient Israel. Some psalms are prayers, cries to God for help, or else praise or thanks to God. Others are hymns, songs from worship. Still others are reflective meditations. In tonight's Bible study we will consider the kinds of psalms, their place in the life of Israel, and what they can mean for us.

What is special about Psalm 42?

Its was originally joined to Psalm 43 in a single psalm. A refrain, "Why are you downcast, O my soul?" occurs three times (42:5, 42:11, 43:5). The poem was written in "Qinah" meter in Hebrew, a rhythm of three beats, then two—a style frequently used when expressing sorrow. The dominant image in the psalm is of a deer that is desperately thirsty; that is how it is with our souls with respect to God. The Psalmist has much sorrow; "tears have been my bread day and night" (42:3). In the second part of the psalm, we can well imagine a powerful waterfall, such as the one outside the village of Banyas at the foot of snow-capped Mt. Hermon, the source of the Jordan River. The flow of water conveys the quenching of thirst; the sound, the roaring, touches the Psalmist deep inside, somehow enabling him to express the chaos and clamor of his own soul. What the Psalmist wants to do, above all, is return to the Temple in Jerusalem, where he has had profound experiences of God in worship—and hopes to once more.

Thinking toward the sermon, it seems that there is no one right way to preach a psalm. At times the preacher can treat the entire psalm, playing off its structure and inner movement. At other times, a mere phrase or image within the psalm is plenty to handle. Some psalms plead for some obvious New Testament connection. Others may be more justly used precisely by avoiding some very alluring New Testament link. Bruce Vawter, writing of the absence of immortality and resurrection from the thought-world of the psalms, argued that "it seems to be both a fact and a fortunate fact that most of Israel's history was played out in a society which had eschewed this yearning. Which is to say, presumably, that in Israelite society the yearning found fulfillment in other ways. Israel was compelled to examine the meaning of man's earthly existence to a degree and to a depth seemingly without parallel in the thinking of its contemporaries,"[1] issuing in a healthy materialism and an insistence on social justice. I include excerpts from sample sermons for the sake of discussion, with no pretensions to their publishability. Origen steadfastly refused to have his sermons published until he was past age sixty, and I pieced these together as do most pastors—in the all too brief seams of a hectic week.

On Psalm 42, I tried to fix the thirsty deer image in people's minds, but also to explore the image in the light of the fascinating geographical elements within the psalm.

THE SERMON EXCERPT:
Psalm 42: The Beauty and Urgency of My Song

As a deer longs for flowing streams, so my soul longs for you, O God. This Psalmist had seen a deer, probably many of them, thirsty, nosing about, peering into dry riverbeds, searching for water—and he knew that he thirsted for God in the same way. You can create your own image for this quest. In Pat Conroy's novel *The Lords of Discipline*, young Will McLean laments his lack of a romantic life in words that may reflect our anxiety about God:

> I once read in a book that traced the natural history of blue whales that the great creatures often had to travel thousands of miles through the dark waters of the Pacific to find a mate. They conducted their search with the fever and furious attention of beasts aware of the imminence of extinction. As whaling fleets depleted their numbers, scientists conjectured that there were whales who would exhaust themselves in fruitless wandering and never connect with any mate at all. When I read about those solitary leviathans, I feared I had stumbled on an allegory of my own life, that I would spend my life unable to make a connection, unable to find someone attracted by the beauty and urgency of my song.

There's a psychology to this thirst. Our seeking, our song, is indeed urgent—but it has a beauty about it. You don't need me to tell you that we walk around with this gaping hole in our souls, and we will pour anything and everything into it to fill it: stuff, diversions, booze, you name it. We view this thirst as a problem, and one to be solved, and quickly. But maybe that hole isn't a curse so much as a gift. That hollowness is God crying out to you; your song is God's song first! God's Spirit has burrowed out a place, so you would seek after him. Otherwise, you might never sense any need for God. It gets mislabeled—but it is God's call.

Prayer, connecting with God, is never quick and easy. Prayer is like a muscle. It requires use, discipline. All the great masters of prayer teach us this. Henri Nouwen said, "The only way to pray is to pray; the only way to pray well is to pray much." Catherine of Siena wrote, "You, O God, are a deep sea into which, the more I enter, the more I find, and the more I find, the more I seek." Georges Bernanos said we must block out a time for prayer each day: "even if not well used, don't give it to anybody else!"

This leads us to the geography of Psalm 42. The Psalmist knows that God is everywhere; he is praying, after all, near Mt. Hermon. But there is a place, somewhere he needs to go. Henry David Thoreau "went into the woods because I wished to live deliberately, to front only the essential facts of life, and see if I could not learn what it had to teach, and not, when I came to die, discover that I had not lived." The Israelites came out of the woods, and went to the temple, on Mt. Zion, God's holy city. When they thought of that temple, they subscribed to what Amos Wilder once said about Church: "Going to church is like approaching an open volcano, where the world is molten and hearts are sifted. The altar is like a rail that spatters sparks, the sanctuary like the chamber next to an atomic oven. There are invisible rays, and you leave your watch outside."

They knew God certainly was everywhere, but they were aware of it because of what happened in the Temple, in those special meetings in public worship.

Today we celebrate Holy Communion. The Psalmist poignantly remarks that tears have been my bread day and night. Have tears, sorrow, been your bread? At the temple there was another bread, called the "bread of presence," just a loaf of bread that somehow signified to the Jews the very face of God. I wonder if Jesus had that in mind at the Last Supper when he took a loaf of bread, blessed it, broke it, and gave it to them saying, "This is my body, given for you." It was Jesus who said I am the living water, and I am the bread of life. The bread I give for the life of the world is my body. And on the cross, when Jesus flung open a window into the very heart of God, to show us his mercy, his side was pierced, and out flowed water—a sign, a symbol, that this Jesus, whom we worship in this place, around this table, is what we are thirsty for.

Flannery O'Connor was once asked what really mattered in her life. She said that it was this bread: "Holy Communion is the center of existence for me. All the rest is expendable." And so it is. As a deer longs for flowing streams, so my soul longs for you, O God. When shall I come and behold the face of God? God is here. Now. Today. Your beautiful song has been heard.

Psalm 24

For week two we thought it wise to dig into the liturgical context of the Psalter, and found Psalm 24 to be inviting (not to mention the

embarrassment of riches it allows musically). The bulletin insert tried
to help people picture themselves in a crowd of worshipers back in several centuries B.C.E.:

> Psalm 24 illustrates in a remarkable way what the psalms teach us about
> worship in ancient Israel. For the great festivals of the year (such as Pass-
> over), pilgrims would throng to Jerusalem. At the appointed time, wor-
> shipers would gather for a great processional up the long hill called Mt.
> Zion, their destination being the Temple. The shofar, a massive ram's horn,
> would blare, and then trumpets would play, cymbals would clash, dancers
> would dance, and hymns would be sung (such as Psalm 24, v. 1). The epi-
> center of the processional would be the ark of the covenant, carried aloft
> and eventually into the Temple. Children learned the words of the liturgy,
> which we can read in Psalm 24, verses 3-10. The congregation would chant
> verse 3, and the reply to their question would be intoned by the priest at the
> steps of the temple (v. 4). Then, in verses 7-10, we see a back and forth
> litany, a question and answer celebration, the feel of which we have tried to
> capture in this morning's reading of the Psalm. The "gates" and "doors" are
> just that—the way into the Temple, which must be opened for the wor-
> shipers to go in. The "king of glory" is the presence of God, symbolized by
> the ark of the covenant.
>
> What was the Temple like? Israel was a poor land, and most people
> struggled just to eat and maintain a little shelter. But no expense was spared on
> the Temple. It was, for them, the intersection between heaven and earth, a taste
> of paradise, sumptuously appointed and fabulously decorated. Only the high
> priest got all the way to its innermost room (the "Holy of Holies"). And the
> men made it further into the Temple precincts than the women—but the
> women got closer than mere Gentiles.

Handbells opened the service appropriately with Howard F. Starks's
"Psalm for Bells." The congregation sang two hymns: "Come Thou
Almighty King" and "Lift Up Your Heads." The choir mirrored the latter with the great Hal Hopson anthem, "Lift Up Your Heads." Instead of
the responsive setting in our hymnal, we devised a responsive mode of
reading that tried to capture what scholars suggest might have been the
flavor of its liturgical use at those ancient festivals in Jerusalem:

PSALM 24

All sing:	Lift up your heads, ye mighty gates!
Choir:	The earth is the LORD's and the fulness thereof,
	The world and those who dwell therein;

	For he has founded it upon the seas,
	And established it upon the rivers.
All:	Who shall ascend the hill of the LORD?
	And who shall stand in his holy place?
Leader:	He who has clean hands and a pure heart,
	Who does not lift up his soul to what is false,
	And does not swear deceitfully,
	He will receive blessing from the LORD,
	And vindication from the God of his salvation.
Choir:	Such is the generation of those who seek him,
	Who seek the face of the God of Jacob.
All sing:	Lift up your heads, ye mighty gates!
Choir:	And be lifted up, O ancient doors!
	That the King of Glory may come in.
All:	Who is the King of glory?
Choir:	The Lord, strong and mighty, the LORD, mighty in battle!
All sing:	Lift up your heads, ye mighty gates!
Choir:	And be lifted up, O ancient doors!
	That the King of Glory may come in.
Leader:	Who is this King of Glory?
All:	The Lord of hosts,
	He is the King of Glory!
All sing:	Lift up your heads, ye mighty gates!

THE SERMON EXCERPT: Psalm 24: "Holiday"

You have just participated in a glimpse into the worship life of ancient Israel. Psalm 24 was used by the throng of worshipers as they processed up the hill and into the temple precincts in Jerusalem. Pilgrims had made a treacherous journey in great caravans to the great city for one of the great festivals, such as Passover. A holy day, which has come now into English as "holiday."

Holidays, in the sense of holy days, have fallen on hard times. In ancient Israel, and for that matter in ancient Greece, in ancient Rome, and even in the United States until just recently, there were special days set aside for public celebrations, for the honoring of traditions, when all citizens rehearsed the great stories of the past. Those rituals shaped our identity, and gave us clues about what is important, and about how to behave.

At Passover, children could rise from their seats, as they were instructed to do, and ask, "Why is this night special above all nights?" The answer was something rooted in history, and had something to do with God, and justice. Now, if a child rose and asked about any of our holidays, "Why is this day special?" the answer would be something utterly innocuous, like "Because there are bargain prices at the malls."

We have turned holy days into mere vacations. God knows we need some rest. But there is a hefty price exacted from us as people when we embrace the vacation mentality at the expense of holy day. On vacation, you have fun, and more pleasure than usual—but you miss out on stories of heroes, the traditions that shape who we are. Instead we are being reshaped by the ideology of fun and pleasure—and our souls are impoverished, as we look in the mirror to see consumers instead of citizens.

I thought we might put up little tables at the entrances to our church, where instead of getting a nametag, you'd be checked: "Clean hands? Pure heart?" Attendance might dwindle to a mere trickle. And yet somehow church has to be about having clean hands and a pure heart. We come to church, not just to have warm fuzzy feelings and return to our old two-bit life. We come to be changed. Church is about being better. More holy. More compassionate. More committed. More godlike. To be human does not mean to be foolish and flawed. We are made in the image of God, and somehow, we come to church because we are about helping each other to have clean hands and pure hearts.

The way to clean hands and pure hearts isn't by adhering to little rules, to do this or avoid that. Rather, it is an act of the imagination. Will Willimon and Stanley Hauerwas were right: "The primary ethical question is not, What ought I now to do? but rather, How does the world really look? Our ethics derive from what we have seen of God." The God who created the world, and cradles it still in his hands is not done with it, or with us. The future belongs to God. Our culture will treat you like a fool if you avoided some gratification you could have today. But our God is future-oriented, and we bank everything on the God who will one day appear clearly as *The King of Glory*. When we let our imaginations be stretched to see the universe and our lives from God's perspective, then we begin to be better. We plunge into community. We touch lepers. We welcome sons coming home. The Spirit comes. The King of Glory comes in. Who shall ascend the hill of the Lord? He who has clean hands, and a pure heart. May this be our prayer, and our destiny.

Psalm 19

Psalm 19 stood begging for our choir to sing Franz Joseph Haydn's "The Heavens Are Telling," from *The Creation*. The congregation sang "This is my Father's World," and we concluded the service with the Philip Bliss oldie, "Wonderful Words of Life." The printed prayer of confession picked up on the text, reading: "O God of glory, your law is perfect; it revives our souls. Your precepts are right; they rejoice our hearts. Forgive us for straying from your desire for us. Forgive us for the sins that we knowingly commit. And forgive us for the sins that remain hidden from us. Free us from our bondage to our sins, so that we, with the heavens, might tell the glory of God."

C. S. Lewis called Psalm 19 "the greatest poem in the Psalter and one of the greatest lyrics in the world." Its threefold structure sets an example for our own spirituality: (a) Verses 1-6 extol the grandeur of nature. (b) Verses 7-11 praise the greatness of God's law. (c) Verses 12-15 are a deeply personal prayer. The interconnections are profound. God, who ordered the world, also in his mercy gives us directives for how to live in it and take care of it. Just as we are awed by the beauty of nature, we may pause to explore the beauty of God's law. And nature and law are never just out there, somehow removed from us, something we just observe. Rather, they compel us to pray, to get involved, to offer ourselves, to become sharers in what God is about in the world.

The Hebrew word translated as "law" is *Torah*—and *Torah* does not mean "law" in the way we construe "law." *Torah* means "way" or "path," with the connotation that we are on a journey, going somewhere, armed with directions, instructions. God saved the Israelites from Egypt, and led them, not off to a luxuriant island for a vacation, but promptly to Mt. Sinai to learn God's laws. Moses received them, and brought them to the people, as a pattern for how to live as God's saved people—or, as Nahum Sarna put it, "how to stay free." Psalm 19 praises the *Torah* as perfect, sure, right, pure, clean, true, more valuable than gold, tastier than honey, capable of giving life, the source of wisdom. Three translation improvements: verse 7 should say, "The way of the Lord is all-encompassing, restoring human life." Verse 11, which sounds a bit threatening, can be read "By them is your servant instructed; there is great consequence (instead of "reward") in keeping them." And therefore, verse 13 concludes like this: "Then I will be whole (not "blameless"), and *acquitted* (instead of "innocent") of great transgression."

Many Christians mistakenly think that law and grace are somehow antithetical, and that because of Christ there is no law, no requirements, but sheer and total mercy from God, no matter what we may do. It is true that

Jesus died, and that salvation is something we are utterly incapable of earning. But the sense of the New Testament is clearly that because of the great gift of mercy in Christ, we are if anything more motivated and eager to adhere to the ways of God; we are finally enabled, empowered, set free to do God's will. Jesus said, "I came not to abolish the law and prophets but to fulfill them" (Matt 5:17). We live "by every word that comes from the mouth of God" (Matt 4:4). Paul said, "We uphold the law" (Rom 3:31). The letter to the Romans, so full of grace, builds up to chapters 12 and following that tell us much about the demands and shape of the Christian life. The problem is "legalism"—where we begin to use the law as a fence to exclude or judge others, as a weapon of manipulation, or as a prop for our egos (also known as "self-righteousness"). The antidote to an immoral society is precisely the same as the antidote to a smug, holier-than-thou goodness: to look to God's word as a precious, merciful gift, to be treasured and savored.

The sermon gamely strove to establish the inner coherence of creation theology and a sense of Torah as a way or path, hoping parishioners would begin to comprehend what James Luther Mays wrote: "The psalms are the liturgy for those whose concern and delight is the torah of the Lord."[2] To that end, the sermon was punctuated by several local anecdotes and challenges.

Psalm 73

When we selected a date for Psalm 73 in our sequence, we could not have imagined how timely it would prove to be, with several painful losses in the congregation occurring just days before. With a raw edge of grief and minds full of questions, we gathered for worship, with a prayer of confession that was built upon the first portion of the text: "O God, you are our strength, even when our faith fails. We wear our pride like a necklace. We clothe ourselves in judgment without mercy. We covet that which will not lead us closer to you. We turn our backs to your gaze. Forgive us. Work within us, until there is nothing on earth that we desire more than you." The bulletin insert provided some background information.

Psalm 73 is one of the most eloquent, and moving, of all the psalms. It was Martin Buber's favorite; he asked that verses 23 and 24 be inscribed on his tombstone. And last of Charles Wesley's 6,500 hymns was written on his deathbed, and it was inspired by Psalm 73. It begins with a little motto, one of those familiar religious sayings everyone knows and loves: "Surely God is good to the pure in heart."

But this Psalmist has a few questions, and they are intensely personal. Verses 1-12 are an outburst, a cry against the unfairness of life. The Psalmist, in some ways like Job, has been faithful to God—but has enjoyed no great "good" from God. Instead he has faced constant sickness and poverty—all made worse by the fact that he has to look upon wicked people who are all health and prosperity. Aren't there rewards for goodness? and punishments for wickedness? Why does it seem reversed so often? Verses 13-17 form a turning point, as the Psalmist manages not to jettison his faith in God. Somehow, going to the sanctuary of God changes everything. Verses 18-28 then form one of the most beautiful expressions of faith in God, love for God, intimacy with God, in all the Bible.

We sang the Cleland McAfee hymn, "Near to the Heart of God," and the choir did Joseph Swain's beautiful anthem, "O Thou, in Whose Presence." Instead of a responsive reading, we recruited our best lecturers and they recited the entire psalm reflectively. Then came the sermon, aided by liberal borrowing from Clint McCann's New Interpreter's Bible commentary.

THE SERMON EXCERPT: Psalm 73: "Tested by its Own Defeat"

"Surely God is good to the pure in heart." I mean, if we developed a job description for God, that should hover near the top. It is God's job to bless, to protect, to do good, and especially for those who are good. We hear this sort of theology all the time—but its author isn't Moses or David or Jesus or Paul, but rather Benjamin Franklin. It was in *Poor Richard's Almanac* that he penned those sacred words that have so intrigued American culture: "God helps those who help themselves. . . ."

We can explain much suffering, without blaming God. When there is an airplane crash, people always ask, "How could God allow this tragedy?" But God doesn't swat planes out of the air. Rather, when Orville and Wilbur Wright lifted off at Kitty Hawk, and people watched and said, "Now that's a great way to get around," then we signed a contract with death, knowing fully well that some hopefully small percentage of planes would malfunction and crash. Lots of suffering is like that—and I want to say to those who suffer, "Don't take it personally!"

But nothing could be more personal. The "problem of evil" is no intellectual head game, something intellectuals bat about in some ivory tower. Suffering is intensely personal. It strikes, like a fist to your mid-section.

"But then I went to the sanctuary of God." He went to the Temple, the holy place, and somehow, by being in that place, he caught some glimpse of hope. I wonder any more what people think about church buildings. Once upon a time in America, the skylines of great cities featured towering church spires. Now they are dwarfed by towers that celebrate commerce, money. In our anti-institutional milieu, many people feel they can virtually be more spiritual outside the church. Many are cynical about church—and we have labored long and hard to earn that cynicism! But despite whatever may or may not go on inside a church, the very fact that they still stand is awesome. In Lorraine Hansberry's play *Raisin in the Sun*, a suddenly-grown-up girl announces to her mother that she no longer believes in God. Her mother makes a swift path across the room, slaps her daughter on the cheek, and commands, "Repeat after me: In my mother's house, there still is a God." A sanctuary is a protest, a dissenting voice in our culture of skepticism, that there still is a God. Admittedly a sanctuary is mere stone—but Jesus said that even the stones would cry out.

Now, the Psalmist isn't miraculously healed of his diseases. His flesh and heart are still failing. He doesn't win the lottery; Ed McMahon doesn't show up with $10 million. He is still poor; he still suffers. But he affirms now, with great certainty, "Surely God is good to the pure in heart." He believes it now; he understands it now. But he has redefined each term in the equation.

God is no longer the great cashier in the sky, who rings up your good deeds and with a big "thank-you" hands you some payout. No, God is the one whose love never fails, the one who is there, who is not trivialized by human schemes of deserving. For Christians, that God has a face, and the contours of that face are the compassion and wisdom and tenderness of Jesus.

And God is good. But the good that God gives is no "thing." What God gives isn't this or that—but God gives himself. I have things that belonged to my grandfather, Papa Howell: his pocket watch, his mail pouch, his Bible, some tools—and I treasure them above most earthly possessions. But I would eagerly throw them all away to have just one more hour with him, the man himself, talking, laughing, sitting under his oak tree. For me, it is good to be near God. Legend has it that when St. Thomas Aquinas, one of the most prolific and profound theologians the church has ever known, was on his deathbed, a voice was heard from somewhere above: "Thomas, you have written well of me. What reward would you ask for yourself?" And Thomas replied, "Nothing but yourself, O Lord." That was the gist of the last of Charles Wesley's hymns, composed on his own deathbed:

> "In age and feebleness extreme, What shall a sinful worm redeem?
> Jesus, my only hope thou art, Strength of my failing flesh and heart;
> O, could I catch a smile from thee, And drop into eternity."

God is good to *the pure in heart*. And purity of heart is no longer just doing nice things, or avoiding grimy things. What comes out of the heart is—love. The pure of heart love. That's what eternal life is about: it's not that we die, and then God gives us this ultimate prize. Rather, we develop a relationship of love with God now that is so strong that even death itself cannot sever it. Sorrow is always mingled with love— but that is our glory. In Rian Malan's great book about South Africa, *My Traitor's Heart*, the most compelling character is named Creina Alcock. She has suffered much. But late in life, she says this: "Love is worth nothing until it has been tested by its own defeat. Love, even if it ends in defeat, gives you a kind of honor; without love, you have no honor at all. Love enables you to transcend defeat. Love is the only thing that leaves light inside you, instead of the total, obliterating darkness."

We look into the darkness, and it seems no one is listening. But there is a candle, flickering in some dark sanctuary, and it dispels the darkness. Through a window, we see, we are touched, and we know that "it is good to be near God." And then it dawns: "Surely God is good to the pure in heart." And it is enough.

Psalm 47

We returned to the worship theme with Psalm 47, but the sermon focused not on the act of worship itself, but on a notion, just one notion, in the text: The Lord reigns over the nations. The congregation sang Charles Wesley's "Praise the Lord who Reigns Above," and the choir performed the splendid John Rutter setting of Psalm 47, "O Clap Your Hands."

THE SERMON EXCERPT: Psalm 47: *"The Wreckage of Human Earthly Thrones"*

Clap your hands? God has gone up with a shout? Trumpets? Sounds different from our worship. Reminds me of the first time I preached at an African-American Church. The service was raucous, with clapping, shouting, singing, dancing. At first my jaw dropped. Then I re-collected my jaw and began to contemplate the tame words I had typed onto the piece of paper in my pocket—and I became nervous. Finally the preacher urged me into the pulpit, saying, "Brother Howell, come now, unfurl for us the scroll of heaven, so that we might hear the angels sing." This made me very nervous.

Yet the item in Psalm 47 that intrigues me today is verse 8: "The Lord reigns" over the nations. Usually, when it comes to nations and the Lord, nations try to use the Lord, to co-opt and use God for their own purposes. It took Abraham Lincoln, not himself a church-goer, to recognize this in America. In his second inaugural, he said that both sides pray; both sides think God is on their side. But both sides are wrong. His climax: The Almighty has his own purposes.

The Lord is above all that nations do, and much of what they do is evil. We are troubled this week by India and Pakistan, testing nuclear weapons. At one time, smaller powers couldn't compete, and we witnessed the rise of terrorism; now they have weapons of mass destruction. Governments just don't handle technology and power very well. As Einstein put it, "technology can be like an ax in the hands of a maniac." And yet we have to confess that India and Pakistan were tutored for decades by the United States and the Soviet Union, who played a dangerous game of one-upmanship, stockpiling nuclear warheads into six figures.

God is not pleased. God is not mocked. As an undergraduate I wrote a paper on Paul Tillich's view of idolatry—and he suggested that one idolatry is patriotism. No nation can grasp our total allegiance—even our own. Karl Heim once wrote, "The repeated collapse of every earthly imperialism is the most impressive demonstration of the fact that no divinization of any earthly power can stand, that every absolutizing of any earthly absolute always carries within itself the seeds of death. God sets up his throne on the wreckage of human earthly thrones, and the history of the world is strewn with the wreckage of demolished imperialisms and smashed altars, whose debris reveals impressively the sole Lordship of God." Nations come and go. God gets the last word.

There was an earthquake this week—and I don't mean the little 3.2 tremor we had here. I mean the one in Afghanistan, the one where the paper dutifully reported that somewhere between 2,500 and 5,000 people were killed. The next morning I checked the paper for an update, a more exact death toll, stories of assistance. But *The Charlotte Observer* did not contain even once the word "Afghanistan" that day, nor the next, nor the next. All week, I have talked with dozens of people—but I never once heard anyone utter the word "Afghanistan." We did have an earthquake here—and it got my neighbors out into the street, full of hypotheses of what had happened: propane tank explosion? sonic boom? meteor? the rapture? I wish we were the kind of people who would pour out into the street to talk about thousands of our brothers and sisters in Afghanistan.

I can't prove this, but I don't think God even noticed our little 3.2 Richter scale tremor. But you can be sure that God, who reigns over the nations, noticed the horror in Afghanistan. And if you and I are remotely serious about serving the God who reigns over the nations, then we have to care. We have to weep. We have to share.

Jesus, after all, taught a new way of reigning. Pilate asked him, "Are you a king?" And he was—but he wielded power, not by hoisting a bigger sword than the next guy and compelling others into submission. Rather, he invited people to a meal, to eat. And when they got there, he took up the trappings of his reign, a towel and basin, and washed their feet. After he said the blessing, he broke a piece of bread—and I believe that as he looked at it, it dawned on him what probably would happen to him the next day. For he knew that when you reign by washing feet, and taking on the powers that be, they'll break you. I think when he gazed into the cup of wine, he saw blood. He hated bloodshed so much that he even shed his own blood. And reigned—by inviting all people, everywhere, to a table, to eat, to taste a new way of living. And to me, that's something to clap about, to shout about, to sing about. "The Lord reigns over the nations."

Other Psalms

A similar theme emerged when we considered Psalm 46. The congregation obviously enough sang Martin Luther's "A Mighty Fortress," and the choir shared with us John Ness Beck's setting of Psalm 46 from *A Festival of Psalms*. In my sermon I tried to ring the changes on "There is a river," and developed a cadence, trying to build to a crescendo—and in retrospect I would have to say it was unsuccessful, frantic week, with too many meetings, and not enough time to fashion a sermon.

Of course, we had to explore the whole issue of sin and confession (using the familiar Psalm 51), and also the issue of "praise," something that is lost in mainline churches, leaving it to the free or Pentecostal churches. Augustine's classic distinction between *uti* and *frui*[3] was supplied to shape people's thinking in a sermon on Psalm 117:

THE SERMON EXCERPT: Psalm 117

Uti is the love of use. I love money, not in and of itself, not because I want to fondle it in my hands, but because I can use it for something else I really want. *Frui* is the love of enjoyment. I love chocolate, not because I use it for something else; actually, what I "use" it for (raising my cholesterol, fattening my belly) isn't so good—but I still love chocolate, and will do anything to get it, to savor it. This distinction applies to people: you don't want to be used by someone; you want to be loved, just for who you are, quite apart from what you may or may not have done lately. In the same way, God does not exist to be used by us, although we certainly go at God with this motive all the time, hoping to co-opt God to help us get something we really want. God wants to be loved, to be enjoyed, no matter the cost.

Other Sermon Occasions

On two interesting occasions, the sermon zeroed in on just a phrase or image from a psalm. The long and rambling Psalm 108 provoked no sermon at all until I let my imagination play with the admittedly imaginative sentence, "Your faithfulness reaches to the clouds." Playing loosely with the text, and playfully contemplating why "reaches to the clouds" could modify "Your faithfulness," the sermon amounted to my own personal reminiscence on God's faithfulness throughout my own life. Nothing publishable, but this sermon may have been the most effective. Surely if we learn anything about the *Sitz im Leben* of various psalms, we know that worshipers gathered for offerings of thanksgiving, punctuated by a confession, a recital of divine deliverance. The congregation sang "Great is thy Faithfulness," clearly the perfect summation of our service.

The second instance was Psalm 85, which I selected intentionally because I had always been fascinated with the image of the "kiss" between righteousness and peace." The bulletin insert provided a little background.

A National Lament

Psalm 85 is one of the prayers in the Bible that originally functioned as a national prayer for God's mercy and help. In times of national crisis, a great fast would be proclaimed. Citizens would gather in cities, and pray in unison for change. They would repent, plead for forgiveness, ask for a restoration of the ways of God, and search for divine intervention. You might read Psalm 44, Psalm 74, Isaiah 58, and Jeremiah 36 for other public prayers.

> *The Key Verses*
>
> The poetic climax of Psalm 85 comes in verse 10:
> Steadfast love and faithfulness will meet;
> Righteousness and peace will kiss each other.

Jane Marshall's moving "Psalm of Peace" was the choral anthem, and we finished the service singing "Let There be Peace on Earth." The sermon went quite well. I had just finished reading Wendy Farley's eloquent book, *Eros for the Other,* and it provoked my imagination and pushed me toward Shakespeare.

THE SERMON EXCERPT: *Psalm 85: The Kiss*

In verse ten of Psalm 85 they imagine that when the Lord acts, "steadfast love and faithfulness will meet," that "righteousness and peace will kiss each other."

The virtues include righteousness, peace, steadfast love, faithfulness. Unfortunately, we live in a world where virtues have fallen on hard times. They are not nearly as admired as success and pleasure, which seem to be what really drives us. There's a great moment in Mark Helprin's novel *Winter's Tale,* where a father tells his son the most important thing that he needs to tell his son. He says the virtues, honesty, courage, sacrifice, and patience

> are never properly valued until one must lose a great deal for their sake and then they rise like the sun. Little men spend their days in pursuit of wealth, fame, and possessions. I know from experience that at the moment of their death they see their lives shattered before them like glass. Not so the man who knows the virtues and lives by them. The world goes this way and that. Ideals are in fashion or not, but it doesn't matter. The virtues remain uncorrupted, and incorruptible. They are rewards in themselves. The bulwarks with which we can protect our vision of beauty.

The psalm says that these virtues meet, and that they kiss each other. Too often we see them as being separate. In our culture, we hope love and faithfulness coincide, but too often love flares up where there is no faithfulness at all and another marriage is lost. Or, back during the Reagan administration it seemed that the lesson that we were taught, that seemed difficult to argue with, was that at least in our world, peace and righteousness do not easily go together. You had the Ollie Norths of the world who said that if you are righteous you can not have peace. You can only have peace by force and by violence and by deceit. The psalm says that when the Lord comes steadfast love and faithfulness will meet.

Righteousness and peace will kiss each other. I want to talk about kissing this morning. I like kissing. I remember my nearly first kiss with a girl. I was at one of those crazy parties in the seventh grade. As I look back on it, and my memory is foggy on this, we're at somebody's house. . . Were the parents in another part of the house? or had the parents relegated the house to a bunch of seventh graders for the night? I don't know. But we're playing some game and somehow in the course of the game you draw lots. A boy and a girl are sent into this bedroom, into this walk-in closet. They close the door. You are supposed to go in there and kiss. And the game is proceeding, and my heart is just pounding—and I find myself becoming a holy man. I'm praying, intently, that my time doesn't come. Kids are going in and coming out. They're blushing and giggling, and I'm thinking, "Oh God"—and then finally it fell to me and little Marcie Estes. They compelled us to go into this closet. We went in there, and I was so relieved at first when Marcie came up with a brilliant suggestion. She said, "Let's don't kiss, let's just go out and pretend that we did." I thought, "This is great, yes!" We came out, and kind of giggled—and of course later I was a little bit wounded. Why didn't Marcie seize her opportunity?

A kiss. It's an awesome thing. It doesn't suggest possessiveness. It's not even really something you do to get a whole lot of pleasure yourself. You kiss someone because you hold them in a very high regard. You value them, and you're saying through the kiss, "You matter, I care about you, there's a beauty about you." It's a beautiful thing, the kiss.

What it's about was put in front of me in the tenth grade. My English class had to read Romeo and Juliet—and it was lost on me at that stage. But listen: Juliet is up on the balcony and Romeo is beneath. He sees her and he says, "But soft! what light through yonder window breaks. It is the east, and Juliet is the sun." He talks about the brightness of her cheek—that it would shame even the beauty of the stars. He watches her a little longer, and then says, "See how she rests her cheek upon her hand! Would that I were the glove upon that hand that I might touch that cheek."

A kiss—a thing of beauty. In the psalm the kiss is not between people. It is between what seems to us to be mere words: righteousness, peace, steadfast love, faithfulness. But the suggestion is that if they can meet and embrace and kiss, they are not mere ideas. They actually take on flesh and blood. They have a reality, a tangibility about them.

And when righteousness and peace kiss, it is a thing of beauty. Now what is beautiful? You and I know beauty when we see it. I remember I went to the Charlotte Coliseum a while back. I was sitting in my seat for some time. Finally I looked down to my left and there was this woman—and her beauty took my breath away. Now, she was short, and her shoulders were hunched over and her skin looked just like sandpaper. She spoke with a thick accent. She was from Albania, but she spent most of her life in Calcutta. Mother Teresa combined righteousness and love and peace—and it was a thing of beauty.

I was at a bookstore in Charlotte a while back and I bumped into a guy there. I knew him, but he didn't know me. You would recognize him. He has one of those familiar faces that when you see it you say "Ahhh." He's retired now, and it's interesting: in his retirement, instead of doing what sadly I think a lot of retirees do, saying "I'm retired now I can't make any commitments. That's for the young people. I'm enjoying my freedom now. I'm enjoying all those things that I worked for all those years." Instead of doing that he is spending all of his time working on righteousness and peace, building Habitat houses—President Jimmy Carter. The kiss of righteousness and peace. It is a thing of beauty.

But do you know what happens to you and me? We miss out on this kiss, and the reason we miss it is that you and I do what Marcie Estes and I did at that seventh grade party. We go into our closets somewhere, when it comes to our faith, and we negotiate. We work out a little deal with ourselves. And the deal is, "Let's don't really kiss, let's just come out and pretend." We do it really well. We come to church, we smile, and say "I'm a member of Davidson Methodist." Great church, great music. "I'm a Christian." And it's pretending. Our lives remain hollow until we go back into that closet and say, "Lord, I'm through pretending. I'm ready to be serious. I want love, faith, righteousness, peace."

I've asked you to do this before. Pull out your most clever, innovative imagination. Start to think of yourself as a person of righteousness and love and faithfulness and peace. Imagine that you get up in the morning and you do good all day long. Just at every turn you show love, and you make peace, and you exercise faithfulness, and you try to be righteous. You go at it all day long, and you get on a roll with it. The more you do it, the more natural it feels, and it begins to fit like an old glove. You do good all day long. You get ready to go to bed at night and you don't really have any regrets at the end of the day. You think, "Life can not get any better than this." Then you wake up the next morning and it does. That life of righteousness and peace: it just clings to you like a glove. And when you do that, you will discover when you wear that glove that your hand becomes the hand of Christ—and it is at that moment reaching up and touching the very face of God. Steadfast love and faithfulness will meet. Righteousness and peace will kiss each other. It is a beautiful thing.

Conclusion

After four months, we were almost sad to see the Psalm series end. It took concerted planning from the entire staff. But our informal survey of people in the pews led us to believe it had been significant, and extended far beyond worship as lives of prayer were enriched.

NOTES: CHAPTER 9

[1] Vawter, "Intimations of Immortality and the Old Testament," *JBL* 1972, 170.
[2] Mays, James Luther, "The Place of Torah-Psalms in the Psalter," *JBL* 106, 1987, 9.
[3] *de Doctrina Christiana* I.xxii.20.

10

How Long, O Lord! Will Your People Suffer in Silence Forever?

Beth LaNeel Tanner

"Presbyterians Agree to a Truce in the Homosexuality Debate"
"Ninety Methodist Pastors Violate Church Discipline by Presiding at a
    Gay Marriage"
"Leader of the National Baptist Conference Begins Embezzlement Trial
    Today"
"Local Priest Indicted On Multiple Child Molestation Charges"

*T*hese recent headlines are only some of the examples of the pain
that lives inside American churches. Other pain is less public,
but also very present. Death, illness, divorce, theological dis-
agreements, unemployment, all bring almost unspeakable pain on us
personally and on the church as a community. Yet despite the opinions
expressed in much of the recent doomsday literature emerging from
both contemporary culture and the church, these conditions are not
unique to this period in history nor do they originate from a diminish-
ing sense of moral values. On the contrary, pain, suffering, schism, sorrow, and sin have always been a part of the life of the community of
believers, as many texts of the Old and New Testament testify.[1] This dark
reality is especially evident in the cries of lament in Old Testament.

Yet these texts of lamentation have been almost completely erased
from the corporate and private life in the modern church. For example,
the Revised Common Lectionary does not include the darkest of the
laments in the psalter (for example Psalms 69, 88, 109)[2] and often even
when laments are included, the complaint sections are removed from

the reading.[3] Add these omissions to the recent direction of worship that has moved more and more toward contemporary services featuring the popular genre of praise music. Many of these services are, by design, more informal and omit traditional hymns and liturgical components such as the prayer of confession. These factors have contributed, in part, to a sense of "false happiness" as the main purpose and normal state of the Christian Church and of individual Christian lives. In short, to be a Christian in twentieth-century America means to be happy.

This paper will focus first on the state of the Church in general in this period of history. To frame this discussion, I will use the two points stressed in Walter Brueggemann's 1986 article "The Costly Loss of Lament" and illustrate that the Church has suffered directly from this loss over the thirteen years since the article first appeared. Second, this paper will focus on how to begin to reintroduce lament into the liturgy, preaching, and teaching in the Church and how this inclusion can aid the Church not only to speak its pain but also to heal and to begin to move past the damage of the past.

Brueggemann lists the first loss to the Church to be "loss of genuine covenant interaction" since the worshiper "is voiceless or has a voice that is permitted to speak only in praise and doxology. When lament is absent, covenant comes into being only as a celebration of joy and well-being."[4] Certainly we, as pastors and teachers, experience this phenomenon. Parishioners are less and less likely to bring their problems, especially ones associated with shame, to either their pastors or the church family. In the seminary classroom, the introduction of laments into the course curriculum brings a howl of "blasphemy" that must be addressed before a discussion of the importance and power of these texts can begin.[5] Speaking to God in anger, in sorrow, or even in suffering is understood today as against the norm of how we are to worship and even to live. In *Finally Comes the Poet*, Brueggemann warns of the damage that worship does from this perspective.

> Worship in such objectivism may be happy, positive, and upbeat. God seems easily available. Life is good, or is said to be good for those who gather in front of the cameras. Such worship, however, is mistaken, dishonest, and destructive. . . . Such worship is destructive because it requires persons to engage in enormous denial and pretense about how life really is. Such little islands of happiness characteristically fail to take into account the reality of evil and the depth of the crisis of theodicy.[6]

Stephen McCutchan sees the same phenomenon:

> Praise without lament is like relating to a person who always says posi-
> tive things but never utters a critical remark. After a while, the praise
> takes on a false tone. Consider another case. A child gets sick and her
> parents pray for her recovery. . . . When death comes the parents are
> cautioned that they should not blame God for their loss. But if they fol-
> low this advice, what then can be said of their praise of God? How hon-
> est can they be in their worship if they do not acknowledge to God their
> disappointment and anger that their prayers were not answered?[7]

In this type of worship, the observant can hear the echos of the words
of the prophets condemning a pretense of worship without rightness and
trueness of heart (Amos 5:21-24; Isa 1:10-17; and Ps 51:18-19). Under
the cover of dishonest and mindless praise, worship becomes not an avenue for communication, but a conduit for self-interest; an action designed to convince the capricious God not to do you any harm—or, at
least, not any more harm.

Brueggemann's second point about the loss of lament is that it
causes "the *stifling of the question of theodicy*. I do not refer to some es-
oteric question of God's coping with ontological evil. Rather, I mean
the capacity to raise legitimate questions of justice in terms of social
goods, social access, and social power."[8] I would add to Brueggemann's
observation that it is not a question of theodicy but *questions* of theodicy on two fronts, personal and corporate.

McCutchan's example from above aptly illustrates the problem of
personal theodicy; questions that undermine and possibly even destroy
the covenant relationship between God and human. Yet in a search of
the scholarly literature on the use of lament since Brueggamann's 1986
article, I found only six articles pertaining to the use of lament in various aspects of pastoral care.[9] Laments are not the first text that come to
mind when ministers and counselors turn to the Bible for reference.
Based on the scarcity of articles and my own conversations with pastors,
laments rarely come to mind as texts for those suffering and in pain.

Yet I have seen first hand the power and freedom of lament psalms,
even in the artificial setting of the classroom. Each time I present these
bold acts of confronting God in the frank language of the lament, a student has contacted me about how this knowledge of God's love and relationship with the lamenter had helped resolve a deep hurt in their
own life. Lament offers a pathway to voice and work through personal
issues of pain and theodicy, both for seminary students and persons in

the church. It tells us that the pain we feel and the words we want to shout to God have been canonized as Scripture. Personal cries of pain and brash accusations against God are not thoughts to be hidden from the throne of God, but to be deposited with all of their jagged edges and sharp cries before the face of God.

Brueggemann focuses not on these personal aspects of theodicy, but on the corporate process of exploring theodicy that is destroyed when lament is lost. He writes:

> A community of faith that negates laments soon concludes that the hard is-sues of justice are improper to pose at the throne, because the throne seems to be only a place of praise. I believe it thus follows that if justice questions are improper questions at the throne, they soon appear to be improper questions in public places, in schools, in hospitals, with the government and eventually even in the courts. Justice questions disappear into civility and docility. The order of the day comes to seem absolute, beyond question and we are left with only grim obedience and eventually to despair.[10]

I can illustrate his point in my own experience with the Presbyterian Church. I was first introduced to the church's social justice mission in the 1960s. Much of the church's mission was focused heavily on issues of segregation and racism. This period was a time when the mainline churches publically grieved and cried out against itself first, and then after that confession, turned its energy against the parts in the culture that continued to uphold such an evil. To be a Christian meant to stand up against the wrong of society and even to practice civil disobedience in the quest for justice.[11] Then came the Vietnam War and congregations and the denomination were torn asunder, and social justice became not a religious issue, but a political one (i.e., the turmoil over the Angela Davis Defense Fund and seminaries providing safe haven for those avoiding the draft). After the war, the denomination that granted women the right of ordination years before was not so united about the Equal Rights Amendment and abortion wars were fought in the General Assembly and at Coffee Hour. A Christian response to HIV/AIDS and the question of the ordination of homosexual persons further drove us apart. Now in the 1990's, even that initial rallying point of segregation and racism, is an issue we know that we gave up on far too soon, so that much of what was the last point of unity, the justice that we had fought for, is far from being a reality in our world. So that even the action of justice that unified us needs to be lamented again as we again seek to speak a word against racism.

And so today, many discussions of social justice issues in the Church quick changes to issue of politics and the liberal-conservative split. God is either a staunch conservative or an ACLU card-carrying liberal depending on who you ask. God has become the weapon we throw at each other in social justice/political debates and there is little for any of us to be proud of either in social justice discussions in our national meetings or in local Sunday School classes.

Unfortunately thirteen years later, Brueggemann's observations are a living reality in our denominations and congregations. Lament has all but disappeared, replaced by the hollow and mindless praise reflected in much of the contemporary Christian music; while at the same time, theologically grounded social justice conversations have all but disappeared. It is hard to imagine mainline church members practicing civil disobedience for any social justice issue in the last months of the twentieth century. We are as frozen as Brueggemann predicted. Praise stuck in our throats as we approach the throne with anger and sorrow hidden deep in our hearts.

The sorrow and disagreement in our own ranks have taken their toll on our ability as denominations to fight the external evils of culture. Brueggemann argued that this type of paralyzing environment forces us to maintain the status quo and to fear any change; because change causes us to look at the structures and the past realities that, without dragging out the unresolved pain of that past, cannot be questioned or changed. It is this very position that we find ourselves in concerning the current homosexuality debate. Without a resolution of the social problems that have torn us asunder, we cannot begin to have an honest discussion of the current social issues that are at the top of the list. Many theologians and pastors speak the recent troubles in the Presbyterian Church as a strained marriage that is headed for divorce. And looked at from the perspective granted by Brueggemann, we can see it is like a marriage finally brought to counseling; it is not only the issue of homosexuality that we will need to try and resolve, it is all of the hurts and unresolved issues of the last thirty years that must be part of the conversation.

Yet in the midst of this paralysis, there is, I believe, hope; hope for revitalization rather than the certainty of division. I do want to stress that the reasons for our present position are more complex than any single solution can remedy, but I do think that the paralysis will only be broken by restored relationship—real and true relationship with God. One sure and biblical path to relationship is through the avenue of lament. True and genuine lament may not solve the Church's problems, but it will go a long way in restoring right and true relationship with the one God who can then begin new possibilities.

Learning the Laments All Over Again

The first place to begin to learn the lessons of lament is in the seminary classroom. If pastors do not know of relational aspects of the lament genre in the Old Testament, then chances are the congregations these pastors serve will have no access either. Seminary professors designing courses are always faced with hard choices in what to include in core courses and which electives will best prepare pastors for ministry into the few hours allotted for study. As a result of these constraints, the lament literature is often not a top priority in the curriculum.

Yet, Claus Westermann stressed the central place of lament in Old Testament theology. [12] He notes that God cannot be understood only in a series of saving acts; any attempt at a description must also include some verbal communication between God and humans. This conversation is often inaugurated by a human cry; even the central act of salvation in the Old Testament is initiated by the cry of the people in Exod 2:23. [13] Cries of sorrow and need also permeate the whole of the Old Testament witness. [14] Westermann further argues that it is the genre of lament that provides the closest tie between the Old and New Testaments, joining the suffering God with the pain of Jesus on the cross. [15] Lament is central to understanding the true relationship between God and God's humans.

This connection of the suffering of God in the Old Testament with the Jesus of the New also illuminates another problem in modern religious thought. Just as Jesus' prediction of his suffering and death in Matthew 16 stands in direct juxtaposition to the transfiguration in Matt 17:1-9; the understanding of God as lamenter (for example Hos 11:1-11 or Jer 8:18-9:3) is the juxtaposition to the holy unapproachable God of Exodus 24, Isaiah 6, and the book of Ezekiel. Without a full understanding of God, we continue to perpetuate the Western idea of the Old Testament God as distant and removed and Jesus as the available or gracious face of God. Without understanding God as both lamenter and the one who hears the darkest of lament, the portrait of God is skewed. The teaching of lament is not just one of a plethora of options but an essential part of a seminary education, if we are to bridge the gap between the God of the Old Testament and the Christ of the New Testament in the minds of the next generation of preachers and pastors.

The next step is to learn again the power of laments in the congregation. How can a pastor begin to introduce lament into the life of a church? There are variety of ways but the following discussion will stress the use of laments in Christian education, worship and pastoral care.

I start with Christian education because these are texts that deserve to be studied, discussed and contemplated. Just as in the seminary setting, the study of the lament psalms or the confessions of Jeremiah can deepen faith and prayer life in a way that is substantial and biblically based. To teach this depth of relationship is to equip the saints and to be proactive in preparing people for the hard times of life. It also begins to open up the avenues both privately and corporately that Brueggemann has argued have been silenced by our elimination of lament. In addition, study of lament introduces, or maybe even shouts, the fact that the Church and its members are people to whom you can bring your hurts; the church is a place not only to praise but to cry. Reading, discussing, and praying these psalms at all levels of Christian education is one way to reintroduce a discussion of sorrow and of social justice into a congregation.

The second place for the lament psalms is in the liturgy and preaching of the church, even if this means varying the traditional lectionary selections. One obvious time for these selections is in times of community stress or pain. Take for example the funeral of one who died too young or by violence. Even in the gathering for the service, people are not ready to hear a word of praise until they have had a chance to grieve. Sorrow must proceed comfort or understanding. Interestingly, this is the exact direction of the lament psalms: from calling on the Lord, to lifting full bodied and real cries of sorrow, to an affirmation of God's love and comfort. The lament psalms provide the avenue and even the shape for a funeral sermon or meditation. Laments can also be used in the same way in times of community or national distress. In a recent article in *Reformed Worship*, John Witvliet has written an informative article on liturgical lament in times of crisis that will be informative for these types of crisis conditions. [16] Laments can also serve as memory for commemorating events that need to be mourned year after year. J. Frank Henderson has written lament liturgies that include services remembering the Holocaust, the bombing of Hiroshima and Nagasaki, as well as liturgies that cry out against violence of all kinds.[17]

But what about the everyday times when that couple over there are about to divorce; and the couple coming up the aisle have just sent their only child half way across the country to college; and the woman over there is just depressed about her life in general; and the couple in the back just learned they are about to have a baby. Are laments appropriate in the ordinary times of our lives? Again Brueggemann's warning was a warning that we must be proactive in providing avenues for relationship. Laments have a place in the pulpit during the ordinary times where there is grief from the pain of divorce; where there is pain at saying goodbye to a child off to college; where there is disenchantment and a general feeling of dis-ease; where the news of a new child also brings thoughts of how life is about to change. Also laments can, as Brueggemann argued, keep us in touch with the world. Laments in worship and preaching can connect us in a real way to the prayers of the people we are praying for, the people involved in another whole scale ethnic cleansing; or even those across the street who are homeless or hurting. Lament causes people to know that you do not have to wait to calm down to pray; or that a hurt like a child leaving for school is not too insignificant to share with God; or that it is okay to cry out about a general sense of unhappiness. It also provides an new avenue to the pastoral staff. By preaching the laments we tell the world that we are a people willing to hear the laments of the lives of these people of God.

Finally, the laments have a place in pastoral care in any time or sorrow and stress. I have reserved this category for the last discussion, because laments can be the most effective when all of the other above proactive avenues are in place. It is easier for people who have heard these prayers before to pray them in times of pain, than for those to whom this genre is a complete surprise. It provides a place to go, a biblical place to stand in the dark valleys of life.

But even if laments have not been part of a comprehensive program in the congregation, Psalm 109 may be exactly the words a woman who has been raped needs to hear. In fact, psalms can give voice to people who have been silenced by hurt. Therapists have used lament psalms like 109 to give victims of domestic violence a way to voice their hurt, to break their trauma-imposed silence. Others need these powerful words in the hurt of any broken human relationship or in the sorrow of an unexpected of terminal illness. Again, it is the process of the lament psalms that can aid in pastoral care. Even if a person is not ready to voice the assurance that comes at the end of most lament psalms in their own heart, the psalm not only can name their pain, but can give them the place where they hope to stand one day.

This paper has pointed out the missing laments in worship and life of most mainline congregations and the cost of this loss to the church and to God's people. In addition, this paper has suggested ways in which laments can become part of the life of a congregation again. No, it will not solve all of the problems in the world, just as the laments of old did not solve all the problems either. However, they can provide a new way to define true and honest relationship between humans and their God. It is time to balance praise with the legitimate cry of sorrow lifted to God.

NOTES: CHAPTER 10

[1] For example, Abraham's cry to God (Gen 15:3); Hagar's cry (Gen 21:16); the people's cry to God in Exod 2:23; the lament psalms; the book of Lamentations; the cries of Jeremiah; the cry of Jesus from the cross (Psalm 22); or the letters of Paul.

[2] Of the fifty individual laments and the six community laments recognized by C. Westermann (*The Psalms: Structure, Content, and Message*. trans R. Gehrke. Minneapolis: Augsburg Press, 1980), only twenty-five appear in the common lectionary; and of these twenty-five psalms, eleven of them appear either in the season of Lent or during Holy Week. So in times other than Lent/Holy Week, the lament psalm readings (the most common genre in the psalter) appear only eighteen times in three years. Readings from the Book of Lamentations appear only once outside of Holy Week readings and of the five laments of Jeremiah (chs. 11, 15, 17, 18, and 20), only one section, 17:5-10, appears in the three-year cycle.

[3] For example, the lectionary readings include only the first seven verses and the last verse of Psalm 17; the middle verses of comfort in Psalms 36 and 62; and the opening verses of praise in Psalm 63.

[4] Walter Brueggemann, "The Costly Loss of Lament," *JSOT* 36 (1986) 57–71, or in a more recent publication, *The Psalms and the Life of Faith* (Minneapolis: Fortress Press, 1995) 102.

[5] The annotation of Jeremiah's lament (20:7-13) in the *Harper Collins Study Bible* reads that "the complaint is the most blasphemous in the Bible." *The Oxford Annotated Bible* note reads that this complaint is "almost blasphemous." It is no wonder, then, that students see this lament in the same way.

[6] Walter Brueggemann, *Finally Comes the Poet* (Minneapolis: Fortress Press, 1989) 48, emphasis added.

[7] Stephen McCutchan, "Illuminating the Dark: Using the Psalms of Lament," *Christian Ministry* 24 (1993) 14.

[8] Brueggemann, "Costly Loss," 104.

[9] Andre Renser, "Lament: Faith's Response to Loss," *Restoration Quarterly* 32 (1990) 129–42; Barbara Bozak, "Suffering and the Psalms of Lament: Speech for the Speechless, Power for the Powerless [healing for AIDS sufferers]," *Église et Theologie* 23 (1992) 325–28; Karen Johnson, "Can Christians Cry? The Recovery of the Lament Tradition," Unpublished Dissertation, adviser James Limberg, 1993; Cornelius DeBoer, "The Use of Lament in Pastoral Care; Exploring Its Use with Those Working Through the Loss of a Child," unpublished thesis 1993; Robert Morgan, "Cry Unto the Lord: Toward a Theory of Corporate Grief and Its Practice," 1998; and McCutchan's previously discussed article.

[10] Brueggemann, "Costly Loss," 107.

[11] Certainly not all Christians agreed with this stand, but many mainline denominations were very outspoken in their belief of the injustice of segregation and racism.

[12] Claus Westermann, "The Role of Lament in Old Testament Theology," in *Praise and Lament in the Psalms*, trans. K. Crim and R. Soulen (Atlanta: John Knox Press, 1981). Others have also noted the importance of lament. Von Rad, in the section on Israel's response to YHWH's saving acts, discusses "Israel's trials and consolations," in *Old Testament Theology*, trans. D. Stalker (New York: Harper and Row, 1962) 383–441. More recently, Walter Brueggemann in *Theology of the Old Testament* focuses one of the central sections on Israel's counter-testimony (or dispute) again stressing the importance of this aspect of relationship (Minneapolis: Fortress Press, 1997).

[13] Westermann, 259–60.

[14] Westermann, 265–80. For example the individual laments of Hagar in Gen 21; Hannah in 1 Samuel; the lament of David over Saul and Jonathan in 2 Samuel 1; the individual laments of the Psalter; and the laments of Jeremiah. In addition, there are examples of community laments in the book of Lamentations, Psalm 137, and the cries of the people in the wilderness.

[15] Westermann, 278.

[16] John Witvliet, "A Time to Weep: Liturgical Lament in Times of Crisis," *Reformed Worship* 44 (1998) 22–26 and its connected article, Howard Vanderwell and Norma deWaal Malefyt, "How Long Will You Forget Me Forever: A Service of Lament based on Psalm 13," *Reformed Worship* 45, 27–28.

[17] J. Frank Henderson, *Liturgies of Lament* (Chicago: Liturgy Training Publications, 1994).

Discussion: Psalms and Practice
Contemplation and Worship

Questions:

How do we use the Psalms?

How can we nurture the use of the psalms as a resource for prayer and devotional life?

How can we authentically come to terms with christological readings of psalms in Christian prayer?

How can we help people use the psalms as a structure for understanding and living their own life experience?

How can we as scholars and practitioners expand the liturgical and devotional use of the Psalter as songs to stimulate Soul growth?

James: Our group spent considerable time talking about the Psalter in worship and in Christian education, and the connection to its use in contemplative practice. We wrestled about a christological reading of the Psalms and how it is impossible to free ourselves from that way of looking at the Psalms. We discussed a variety of approaches and the importance of gleaning material for other traditions, for example, Jewish resources to help us balance ourselves so as not to have too high a christology of the Psalms, to help us be more trinitarian. The laity and the depth of knowledge of the Psalms they possess these days is something which should be tapped. Pastoral leadership could take advantage of the laity's knowledge of the psalms. We recognized that in different traditions there is a different aesthetic of worship which makes us listen to the Psalms in different ways. There are public psalms and private psalms. We recognized the threatening aspect of the psalms regarding dancing and praising and the unorthodox challenges of the Psalms. The fear of vulnerability people have that would allow them to do that in private worship, but not in public worship. In the Psalms there is a connection between worship and contemplative practice.

Harry Nasuti: We started by looking at various uses of psalms and wondered whether our use of psalms is honest. When congregations use the Psalms, they use them optimistically, like everything is okay. Are they deluding themselves? Individual usage of the psalms may be done in a different way. We questioned whether people choose certain psalms and neglect other psalms. Why do people resist the Psalms? One reason is that the point of resistance can be the point of spiritual growth. Often people can recognize their own spiritual health and allow the Psalms to help them grow. A retreat director could use the Psalms to help us see our own dishonesty. Where are individuals connected socially within congregations? In some classes, there is a mix of groups, and some in the group will latch onto certain psalms which others in the group will resist. The cause for this disagreement is different social situations. Some people identify with the enemy mentioned in a psalm. However, there are communal ways of appropriating the psalms. The American way is very narrow and overly individualistic. We must take note of the canonical shape of the Psalter. We need to increase the honesty of our use of the Psalms. We need to use the power of the metaphor. We also recognize within the Psalms the problem of exclusive language and that christological uses of the Psalms are inevitable.

Terry Muck: We began by talking about how various members in our group experienced psalms in a variety of ways. We grouped the psalms into four categories of usage:

(1) *Lectio divina*, (2) responsively in the liturgy, (3) the office of the hours, and (4) the regular daily use of reading the psalms together in a group.

The power of using the psalms in personal devotions by reading the psalm three times, and asking these questions:

> What does this psalms say regarding Jesus Christ?
> What does this psalms say regarding the community?
> What does this psalm mean for me?
>   Using the psalms in a journaling process.
> Worship leadership?
> Preaching the Psalms?
> Praying the Psalms?
> Teaching the Psalms?

Our questions then became: How can we nurture this in others? How can we pass that on to the Church at large? We then discussed the Psalms as they relate to education, the role of praying the Psalms, putting the Psalms to music and the different ways the Psalms are put to music in different traditions. We ended with a discussion regarding christology.

Cindy: Our group looked at metaphor and the power of metaphor. How do we in our contemplative lives use those metaphors? How do we limit them?

One way we limit metaphors is with our translations. Modern translations limit the power of metaphors. Kathleen Norris' book on metaphors is well worth reading. Hymns are often also mistranslated with regard to metaphor. We shouldn't throw out the kingship of God for the sake of inclusive language. When we do that, we reduce God's kingship to a commonwealth—this means we are all on equal footing with God. We need to realize that God is the king, and we are subservient to God. Who wants a king? Royal language is intense in the gospels. Feminist language is set up against king language. "Lord" is a strange metaphor. "King" is still modeled now, "lord" is not.

The Practice of the Psalms and the Worship of the Church

Do most people in worship have a sense of brokenness to which psalms connect?

Can we talk about a special status of the Psalter as a resource for liturgical practice?

Conveners: Cindy, Rebecca, Steven and Kathryn

Kathryn: We talked about whether people in the pew were happily oriented or aware of their brokenness. We felt that many are in denial about their state and wondered how can the Psalms work to bridge the gap between private pain and all is well? We liked using the Psalter in pastoral care to deal with the inner private pain when the outward persona is all is well. We wondered how we can make the use of the Psalms available to people. The Psalms can be used as a specialized language of the Church. They have an identification role: we become lost in the world and the Psalms bring us back to the church. The efficacy of the "I/we" language draws people back into the psalms. Yet the Psalms make us troubled because God does not make everything okay in the psalms. God does not respond as the Psalms say He will. God is a real disappointment to us. We recognize that preaching in the Psalter is infrequent sometimes because Old Testament preaching is infrequent. Sometimes the Psalter can be used to form a litany that is part of the communal discussion. The Psalter can be used as a communion text and we also realize that the Psalms put God to the test.

Our group recognized that the role of thanks in the psalms takes on a manipulative air. It is sort of like the "Thanks for not smoking" signs—what the sign is really saying is "You aren't going to do that are you?" Is God a great vending machine? Do the Psalms put it that way?

Rebecca: There is a special status of the Psalter which is both Scripture and prayer. There is a continuity of the Psalms. Throughout the psalms the whole Church is revealed in both time and space. There are poor as well as affluent people. The sacramental nature of the Psalms forms and transforms us. It is a counter cultural tool. The Psalms shine the light of judgment on the American sense of judgment. The psalms affirm a godly way of life. What does McCann mean by generalization wisdom? The Psalms are literature that we repeat and are formed by. We stop at some point and step back from them, asking "What have we just said?" What kind of God invites us to pray that way? We feel that psalms should be used in preaching often and liberally. In the Howell article we wondered what his congregation was like. How does the nature of your congregation transfer to pastoral care? What is the nature of sacrifice? What is the meaning of sacrifice? Is praise a sacrifice or something else?

Steven: We wanted to discuss sacramental and put Harry on the hot-seat! How do we understand the term sacramental? The psalms are a means of grace, a way for God to appropriate grace to us. The psalms have an "I" in them, they are individual as well as communal. Acts are the psalms' world view of a sacramental world view. The Psalms encompass the seven sacraments of the Roman Catholic church. We found Rolf's paradigm of dissonance helpful. When reading the Psalms, a fairly common response is anger. "This is not my God. This is not how I feel about my God and my people." Why is it that we can see the feelings of the psalms in the community, but we can not admit the feelings in our faith? Where can we say the feelings that arise? We can say them as we read the psalms. Preaching can use the Psalms. An effective model is to use the Psalms in liturgy and then preach on them. Congregations have taken on a special identity so we can address the congregation as ones who are reformed and committed.

How do we preach the psalms? In what sense is it proper to speak of the psalms as the word of God? Barney shared with our group that he has trouble with the psalms being the word of God, yet the Psalms are included as Scripture in the New Testament. Psalms are the words of the people talking to God. God teaches us how to pray in the Psalms. Why is that any less scriptural than God inspiring other author's formats? God speaks and the people respond. In the Psalms, you have only one side of the argument, the people responding to God. Michael insisted that the Scripture is all word of God and word of community and that that's the mystery and wonder of it.

Mark: We must take into account the ancient consideration about the miraculous material in the Bible. People respond to God as part of this record. How do the psalms conform to this model of revelation or the model of the Torah and the prophets? What comprises a more complex notion is the word of God that he puts in our hearts. It is that notion that leads us back to God. The dialogical model states the whole Bible is the text of God. Yet Barney can not conceive of Psalm 88 being the Word of God.

Is there no bleakness in God? We find bleakness in our lives, in the Bible and in God. God becomes the enemy if you are still talking to Him regarding the human condition, because God does not always respond. There are many cries of misery in the Bible. The wisdom literature is full of misery. The Psalms are connected with the covenant part of the Bible, they presume a theology of covenant. God took us upon Godself in our humanity—that is revelation. God also suffers great pain on our behalf.

Where do we locate the authority of the psalms? All scripture was produced by the human community, but it is the Word of God. The Bible is fully human and fully God.

Larry wanted the group to reflect on why more preachers don't preach the Psalms. Perhaps because narrative theology is in vogue now and some of the painful content of the Psalms does not fit well into that category. The problem is that we are colluding with this idea. In the Psalms, people are in pain, today people want Star Wars instead of pain. There is a pressure on us as preachers not to be direct. We are supposed to preach a lament that moves from prayer to praise, yet many of those in the congregation can not get there. They want preaching about the placidness in the human condition. They don't want to hear about people suffering. But suffering is an illumination of where God is. However, for those in the congregation, it is not only an illumination of where God is, they want to put all of their problems into the context of God as caretaker of all.

Although Bill used the term "generalizations," I'm not very happy with that term. Bill struggled with the notion of how narrative has been very important in our world expression. For him, generalization is what we come to after we have read the story and say "What does that mean?" It is reflection on the narrative.

How do we articulate our belief that the righteous are those who are shaped by the character of God? What is the character of God? What kind of God would do the things depicted in the Bible? How can we understand when the language itself is often abstract?

Part III:
Psalms and Practice
Virtue and Authority

Introduction

$\mathcal{F}$ ormation occurs in contemplation, liturgy and preaching but it also occurs in other action as well. This section explores those elements of practice and the psalms. The first article by Michael Jinkins presents the practice of translation as a way of practicing the psalms. He begins with a look at the work of Levinas, a philosopher of Lithuanian Jewish heritage. Levinas grew up in a multilingual world of Yiddish and Russian. Jinkins through Levinas opens the possibility that the inexact nature of translation belies something more significant in terms of language and practice. Jinkins gives the most extensive treatment of MacIntyre and virtue and practice of any other article in this collection.

Jinkins reminds us that we are largely shaped culturally by a sort of Greekness that now is asked to encounter the Hebrew world of the Psalter. He works with Psalm 37 as a test case for "translation." He compares and contrasts the righteous person in Psalm 37 and the person of virtue in Aristotle's writings. Jinkins excavates Aristotle's intriguing connection between virtue and friendship. Then he, with the help of MacIntyre, critiques Aristotle. The excavation and critique of Aristotle uncovers a social embeddedness in the intimacy of friendship that is as political as it is collegial. This embeddedness finds a context in historical process but not in a *telos*, that is to say linear fashion.

As he turns to Psalm 37, Jinkins ponders the effect and affect of translating the Hebrew from an inherent Greekness that he brings to the text. The issues generated in the psalms text enrich the sense of social embeddedness described in the earlier philosophical discussion.

Cynthia Rigby brings us back to Psalm 51, which was examined in Kathryn Roberts' essay. Rigby does not spend time with the issues of sacrifice but rather the sense of agency. The belief that God has the power to rescue us from adverse circumstances and the conviction that we, as human agents, must choose to act in ways that effect change are not necessarily mutually exclusive. Divine power is at odds with human agency if the omnipotent God "graciously" grants human beings a certain quota of power; divine power buttresses human agency when human agents participate in the power of God. When divine power is understood as a commodity to be distributed, the integrity of human agents is necessarily threatened. When divine power is understood as that which enlivens those who live in covenant relationship with God, human agents contribute to the life of God who has chosen to share life with us.

Rigby sets the stage with a dialogue between the lament and penitential psalms respectively particularly Psalm 22 and Psalm 51. She introduces into this dialogue the provocative work of David Blumenthal that suggests that human beings exercise their agency by blaming the omnipotent God when this God acts or does not act in ways that are "abusive." To this notion of God as abuser Rigby adds the notion of God as Liberator. However, her rendering of Liberator has an interesting twist. For crying out to God involves holding God to account as Liberator, reclaiming our capacity to act as participants in God's liberating activity. God's intervention might not, take the form of "fixing" our circumstances, but of our realization that we have power as agents who exist in the relationship to the power-full God.

Larry Silva stays with the laments. He brings us to the urban neighborhoods and the fields of conflict as he explores the role of the cursing psalms in the process of healing in the conflict ridden world.

Gerald Wilson also brings us back to the exercise of virtue as a practice of reading the Psalms in the urban neighborhoods of North America. Much as James Howell in the previous section gave a report of the preaching of the Psalms, Wilson gives a report of the use of the Psalms in the work of the Contextual Urban Ministry Education Northwest [CUME/NW] program. This work trained women and men for urban ministry using the laboratory of under-served ethnic minority communities and churches in the greater Portland metroplex. The method has been to draw together grassroots coalitions of representatives from ethnic minority communities, Christian service organizations in the urban context, and Christian educational institutions in the order to create a variety of networking opportunities where these constituencies can develop community ownership that build culturally appropriate ways of sharing power and varied educational strategies that address the community.

As this project was going on Wilson was also writing a commentary on the psalms. The juxtaposition of the two events nurture a hermeneutical seed. The essay that follows is part of that seed. His essay moves back and forth from the community of the emerging Psalter to the emerging neighborhoods of the greater Portland metroplex. He is able to distill a few urban survival skills from the psalms. This leads to a provocative rehearsal of how the psalms might shape postmodern praxis.

The final essay by Mark S. Smith brings us back to the basic category questions about the nature of the Psalter that we worked with in the beginning essays by Muck, Bellinger, and Reid. "Taking Inspiration: Authorship, Revelation and the Book of Psalms." This essay addresses the challenge of form-critical thinking to the traditional concepts of biblical inspiration. The Psalter provides an excellent laboratory for such explorations. Recent studies of the superscriptions themselves provide some interesting points linking the traditional view of Davidic authorship of some of the Psalms. The contemporary reader then is confronted with the task of harmonizing text and context. Form-criticism on the other hand makes us aware of the contrast between individual and communal psalms, and therefore raises the issue of individual and communal authorship—and by extension communal inspiration as well. However, the community itself in the course of time conformed its own identity as author to the biblical model of prophetic inspiration. In so doing, the tradition, as early as the late biblical period, harmonized the community authored Psalms with those of the individual. Accordingly, theological reflection on the inspiration of the Psalter requires some reflection on the interaction of the individual and the communal and the ultimately the sublimation of the communal under the rubric of the inspired individual or inspired individuals. These issues of authority, inspiration and practice are as old as the Psalter and as new as tomorrow.

11

The Virtues of the Righteous in Psalm 37
An Exercise in Translation

Michael Jinkins

The true goal of the mind is translating: only when a thing has been translated does it become truly vocal, no longer to be done away with. Only in the Septuagint has revelation come to be at home in the world, and so long as Homer did not speak Latin he was not a fact. The same holds good for translating from [person to person].[1]

nnette Aronowicz, in her introduction to the *Nine Talmudic Readings* of Emmanuel Levinas, writes:

These Talmudic commentaries are . . . an attempt at translating Jewish thought into the language of modern times. That is, they are simultaneously an attempt at letting the Jewish texts shed light on the problems facing us today and an attempt at letting modern problems shed light on the texts. Levinas sometimes refers to this approach as translating the Jewish sources into "Greek," Greek being his metaphor for the language Jews have in common with other inhabitants of the Western world.[2]

In fact, the "translation" task Levinas sets for himself is considerably more subtle and complex than this. Levinas uses the metaphor of "translating from Jewish into Greek" to speak of the dilemma of being both Jewish and European, of ordering (if one is a religious Jew) one's life by a set of texts which most in the contemporary Western world see as irrelevant, quaint, antiquated, or worse, of understanding oneself (whether religious or not) as peculiarly shaped by and interpreted in light of a particular historical legacy, enshrined in a set of stories from which the concept of God is inextricable.[3]

Levinas's own story acts as the parable behind his metaphor. Born in 1906, a Lithuanian Jew, the first language he learned to read was Hebrew. He studied at both a Hebrew school and a Russian *Gymnasium*. His parents could speak Yiddish, but Russian was the language of his home. He learned the classics of Russian and German literature, and attended the universities of Strasbourg and Freiburg where he immersed himself in Husserl and Heidegger. He taught in the universities of Poitiers and Nanterre, his distinguished academic career being crowned by his appointment in 1973 to the faculty of the Sorbonne. Levinas also belonged, throughout his adulthood, to the *Alliance Israélite Universelle,* an organization that sought "to promote the integration of Jews everywhere as full citizens within their states, with equal rights and freedom from persecution."[4] While this integrationist or assimilationist model has been frequently criticized, Levinas believed that it was beneficial and necessary for Jews to become fully integrated into Western culture in order to engage the philosophical, cultural and literary heritage of that culture and to promote a set of ideals he believed were shared by Jewish and Western societies; but Levinas was convinced also that it is beneficial and necessary for Western society to assimilate Jewish wisdom and the Jewish vision of the human person into its culture in order to achieve a genuinely holistic human community, a community enriched by cross-cultural translation, translation from person to person.[5]

Thus Levinas' interest in the Talmud: this quintessentially Jewish set of texts, comprised by layer upon layer of legal, ritual and moral arguments in complex counterpoint, relishing both contradiction and synthesis, becomes the crucial site, for Levinas, of his task of translation. He uses these texts as a window into humanity, warning the reader that for all their "Byzantine" appearance, "these discussions conceal an extreme attention to the Real."[6]

The claim of a translation is that the reader, who does not share the original language of the text, is rendered a version of the foreign text in his or her own tongue. However, as anyone knows who has translated even a simple passage of *Koine* Greek into English, translation involves us unavoidably in a whole series of inexact, sometimes unsavory, though frequently subtle semiotic transactions in both the language of the foreign text and that of the reader. Translations in-evitably lie (or, at least, mislead) in order to tell the truth. Translators are linguistic opportunists. Much is lost, though much is gained. The only way to remain pure in the translation game is not to play. Levinas knows this. He believes, however, that the gains outweigh the losses, for Jews and "Greeks."

The Western world needs the rich wisdom of Jewish culture, its historical-teleological orientation, its vision of humanity, its allegiance to rightness, justice, to Torah and its profound respect for "the other." And conversely Jewish culture, in his view (and here we can discern in Levinas the unmistakable voice of the philosophically sophisticated European scholar who taught phenomenology to Jean Paul Sartre *and* the historically and ethnically sensitive Jew), must remain open "to dialogue and polemic with the West," else it risks the perpetuation of the ghetto and genocide.[7] And so, he writes, "the translation 'into Greek' of the wisdom of the Talmud is the essential task of the University of the Jewish State. . ."[8]

The questions which I wish to raise are these: what would it mean for those of us grounded in the philosophical traditions which Levinas identifies with the metaphor of "Greek" to reflect consciously—and in a manner that deliberately resists putting aside our "Greekness"—on a Hebrew text (in this case, from the psalms)? In other words, how can we go about the translation process Levinas speaks of from the "Greek" side, hearing the Hebrew text in the midst of our Western culture under the influence of our "Greek" thought-forms? What might we learn, for instance, by reading the Psalms, recognizing the parallels, the similarities and the very real disjunctions, incongruities, countervalations and points of incommensurability between certain "Greek" and "Hebrew" conceptions (and in this context to extend the metaphor to reflect the larger history of the Jewish people denoted in the term "Hebrew")?

In order to explore in this very preliminary essay some of the implications of translating the Psalms from Hebrew into "Greek" we shall focus first on one particular Greek understanding (primarily an Aristotelian interpretation) of what it means to be a good person, a person of virtue, one in whom virtue is formed through habitual practice. In this task we shall be guided primarily by Alasdair MacIntyre's analysis of the account of the virtues in Aristotle's ethics. Then, we shall read Psalm 37, with our task of translation from Hebrew to "Greek" in mind, exploring where and how Aristotle's "person of virtue" is like and unlike "the righteous person" described in the Psalms.

I

Moral Goodness, on the other hand, is the result of habit, from which it has actually got its name, being a slight modification of the word ethos. This fact makes it obvious that none of the moral virtues is engendered in us by nature, since nothing that is what it is by nature can be made to behave differently by habituation. . . .

Anything that we have to learn to do we learn by the actual doing of it. . . .9

Aristotle rises like a mountain out of the landscape of Western intellectual history. Ascending him one traces trails like highways in the wilderness leading up to and away from his steep slopes. It is imprudent to speak on many philosophical subjects without at least paying homage to him, and it is quite impossible to discuss what it means to lead a good life without taking him into account. For this reason, in part, I shall restrict our consideration of "Greek" thought to Aristotle; and, I shall restrict our comments to him, in part, also, because Aristotle's understanding of what Sarah Broadie has called "virtue in action"[10] strikingly resonates with the specific Hebrew text I shall translate.

Alasdair MacIntyre says of Aristotle's philosophical theory of the virtues that it is "a theory whose subject-matter is that pre-philosophical theory already implicit in and presupposed by the best contemporary [i.e., Aristotle's contemporary] practice of the virtues."[11] Aristotle's analysis of the virtues assumes the ordinary practice of the Athenian city-state, a social, cultural, and political context in which Aristotle believed "alone the virtues of human life can be genuinely and fully exhibited."[12] The starting point, therefore, for Aristotle's task of the theoretical philosophical examination of virtue is the communal practice of the society from which he emerged, a practice that functions according to a largely tacit pre-philosophical theory and which aims at that vision of the good, that *telos* which is specific and local to the character of the Athenian *polis*, and which is assumed to be universal only inasmuch as it is authentically and really particular.

Aristotle gives a name to "the good," *eudaimonia*, which MacIntyre describes as: "blessedness, happiness, prosperity . . . the state of being well and doing well in being well, of a [person's] being well-favored . . . and in relation to the divine."[13] Those who wish to achieve the goal in life of *eudaimonia* must possess certain qualities, the virtues. However, these virtues are not simply a means to an end, even so good an end as good.

The good life consists in the possession and practical exercise of the virtues themselves. End and means are not only inseparable, the means of virtue embody the end, the good. But, what is perhaps even more significant is Aristotle's understanding of the role of the *polis*, the community, the social context, whose practice provides both the end toward which persons live and the virtues that move persons toward this end.

The vital form of individualism (if we may call it that) running through Aristotle—the emphasis on the virtuous, acting person, the responsible agent—is not simply balanced, as it were, by a general concept of community (as we see in so many current conversations about individualism); to the contrary, Aristotle's individual person is brought into being, is shaped and given humanity, by the community which is prior (in every sense of the word, prior) to the person. MacIntyre's understanding of the cruciality of the community in forming and gifting virtue leads him to ask the Aristotelian question: "What would someone be like who *lacked* to some large degree an adequate training in the virtues of character?"[14] He answers:

> On the one hand one would lack any means of ordering one's emotions and desires, of deciding rationally which to cultivate and encourage, which to inhibit and reduce; on the other hand on particular occasions one would lack those dispositions which enable a desire for something other than what is actually one's good to be held in check. Virtues are dispositions not only to act in particular ways, but also to feel in particular ways. To act virtuously is not, as Kant was later to think to act against inclination: it is to act from inclination formed by the cultivation of virtues. Moral education is an "education *sentimentale*."[15]

Indeed, Aristotle's theory of virtues stresses the role of the community as that which not only forms virtues and confers the vision of the good, but also directs and tutors the passions of the human heart to love and to hate, to yearn and to fear, to hope and to regret in a manner rationally consistent with the virtues of character.[16] The virtuous person, schooled by the community (in the Aristotelian sense), desires the good. S/he does not simply conform to doing the good because to do otherwise is to risk punishment. S/he actively and consciously chooses the particular good because s/he understands and discerns the goodness of the good. MacIntyre writes:

> Such choices demand judgment and the exercise of the virtues requires therefore a capacity to judge and to do the right thing in the right place

at the right time in the right way. The exercise of such judgment is not a routinizable application of rules. Hence perhaps the most obvious and astonishing absence from Aristotle's thought for any modern reader: there is relatively little mention of rules anywhere in the Ethics.[17]

Aristotle seeks a heart formed by concrete obedience, a mind virtuously shaped in the context of a community for the sake of the life of the community. This shaping, he believes, occurs at the most mundane level, as the good person attempts to live appropriately in relationship to others, obeying the acceptable and conventional laws of the *polis*:

> Such law prescribes and prohibits certain types of action absolutely and such actions are among those which a virtuous man would do or refrain from doing. Hence it is a crucial part of Aristotle's view that certain types of action are absolutely prohibited and enjoined irrespective of circumstances or consequences. Aristotle's view is teleological but it is not consequentialist. Moreover the examples Aristotle gives of what is absolutely prohibited resemble the precepts of what is at first sight a completely different kind of moral system, that of the Jewish law. What he says about the law is very brief, although he does insist that there are natural and universal as well as conventional and local rules of justice.[18]

The virtuous person lives neither in abstraction nor in isolation. The virtuous person is a political person, that is, a person living rightly and justly amid a matrix of specific relationships in a particular social environment. It is impossible—it is unintelligible, in Aristotle's view—to speak of the individual except as a *politikon zôon*.[19] Laws can only be understood, therefore, from an Aristotelian perspective, as sets of norms that specify what kinds of behavior contribute to the common life, and the goals and ends of those who live in common and seek to do and to achieve these goals and ends for the sake of the common good. If the virtuous person is, therefore, one who reflects and represents the community, who stands for the community and acts in a manner consistent with the community's valuation of the good, and, consequently, respects and obeys the laws of the community which are based on this valuation, then, conversely, the person lacking virtue manifests his lack of virtue by rejecting the community's valuation of the good specifically by his disobedience of the community's laws.

The virtues of a community "teach its citizens what kinds of actions would gain them merit and honor; the table of legal offences would teach them what kinds of actions would be regarded not simply as bad, but as intolerable."[20] As I have observed elsewhere, the boundaries of a specific community are culturally defined at the points at which members of the community assign blame and praise, punishment and reward.[21] Again, as MacIntyre explains, the community's response to those who transgress the community's laws must take into consideration the transgressor's willful self-exclusion from the community which his transgression implies. And, therefore, "[a] violation of the bonds of community by the offender has to be recognized for what it is by the community, if the community is not itself to fail."[22] The community would, itself, therefore need to have "a broad measure of agreement on the scale of gravity of offences" as well as "a similar broad measure of agreement on the nature and importance of the various virtues."[23]

It is, however, precisely at this point that Aristotle helps us understand that an adequate account of the "good life" consists in more than a narrow account of virtues and vices. One can fail to contribute to the positive good of a community by simply failing to be good enough. One may avoid doing a specific wrong thing because one is a coward or because one is subservient to another vice; and, at the same time, while one avoids doing an evil, one may lack the character necessary to do good. A person, therefore, while failing to contribute to the positive good, might not commit any overt transgressions against the laws of the community.

On the other hand, one who positively transgresses the law of a community does not simply reflect a failure to be good. As MacIntyre writes, "to do positive wrong is not the same as to be defective in doing or being good." It is possible for "a brave and modest" person to commit a murder, "and his offence is no less and no more than the offence of a coward or a braggart." He continues:

> An offence against the laws destroys those relationships which make common pursuit of the good possible; defective character, while it may also render someone more liable to commit offences, makes one unable to contribute to the achievement of that good without which the community's common life has no point.[24]

The virtuous person, therefore, reflects a quality of character which is "the result of fully deliberate activity";[25] and the quality of the virtuous person's character and the quality of his action are mutually congruent, and, taken together, contribute to the integrity of the community. However, the person of virtue is enabled to be and to act in this manner because the community has provided him with all that is necessary to do so.

But this is not all. There is yet another aspect of the "crucial link between the virtues and law," according to Aristotle, because "knowing how to apply the law is itself possible only for someone who possesses the virtue of justice,"[26] which returns us by another road to the practice of virtue in and by the community.

Aristotle observes, in the *Eudemian Ethics*:

> Accordingly Socrates the senior thought that the End is to get to know virtue, and he pursued an inquiry into the nature of justice and courage and each of the divisions of virtue. And this was a reasonable procedure, since he thought that all the virtues are forms of knowledge, so that knowing justice and being just must go together, for as soon as we have learnt geometry and architecture, we are architects and geometricians; owing to which he used to inquire what virtue is, but not how and from what sources it is produced. But although this does happen in the case of the theoretical sciences, inasmuch as astronomy and natural science and geometry have no other End except to get to know and to contemplate the nature of the things that are the subjects of the sciences (although it is true that they may quite possibly be useful to us accidentally for many of our necessary requirements), yet the End of the productive sciences is something different from science and knowledge, for example the End of medicine is health and that of political science ordered government, or something of that sort different from mere knowledge of the science. Although, therefore, it is fine even to attain a knowledge of the various fine things, all the same nevertheless in the case of goodness it is not the knowledge of its essential nature that is more valuable but the ascertainment of the sources that produce it. For our aim is not to know what courage is but to be courageous, not to know what justice is but to be just. . . .[27]

The virtue of justice is what it is by virtue of its exercise, its being in practice. And, MacIntyre observes, "To be just is to give each person what each deserves." The community must come to agreement that there are "rational criteria" by which to measure what the various actions of people deserve; and a community must come to agreement "as to what those criteria are."[28] The community must also recognize that because its laws are general there will be cases in which "it will be unclear how the law is to be applied and unclear what justice demands." In these cases, MacIntyre says, the community itself, as a whole, must learn to "act *kata ton orthon logon* ('according to right reason')."[29] To act according to right reason means to seek an appropriate and reasonable balance, a moderation between extremes. "Aristotle tries to use the notion of a mean between the more or the less to give a general characterization of the virtues: courage lies between rashness and timidity, justice between doing injustice and suffering injustice, liberality between prodigality and meanness. For each virtue therefore there are two corresponding vices."[30] In contrast to the simplistic pseudonymous "Aristotelian" treatise *On Virtues and Vices*, which simply recommends a virtue in contrast to a single vice, its opposite, Aristotle finds virtue specifically in forms of moderation, lying "between vicious extremes of excess and deficiency."[31] Thus, as Hardie says, "the just treatment of one man by another is a mean in the sense that there are two extremes to be avoided, unfair gain and unfair loss."[32]

He continues: "An unjust award which affects two parties, *A* and *B*, may go wrong either by involving undue gain (too much of the useful or too little of the harmful) to *A* and undue loss (too little of the useful or too much of the harmful) to *B*, or the other way round. 'Injustice relates to extremes.'"[33] Justice, therefore, is subject to a kind of contextual variability depending on the vagaries of circumstance; "the very same action which would in one situation be liberality could in another be prodigality and in a third meanness."[34] The virtuous person, consequently, is sensitive to the variability of circumstance, the indeterminate moment. S/he is ruled by that "central virtue" Aristotle designates as *Phronêsis*, a virtue without which "none of the virtues of character can be exercised."[35]

Phronêsis, for Aristotle, is an intellectual virtue, that is, a virtue which "owes both its inception and its growth chiefly to instruction."[36] The intellectual virtues which we receive through instruction are meant to perform a practical purpose: we submit the exercise of our natural dispositions to "right reason" so that our natural dispositions can be transformed into virtues of character. Indeed, our "exercise of intelligence is what makes the crucial difference between a natural disposition of a certain kind and the corresponding virtue. Conversely, the exercise of practical intelligence requires the presence of the virtues of character."[37] Goodness and right reason are necessary concomitants: Aristotle, in the *Nichomachean Ethics*, writes: "Wickedness distorts the vision and causes serious error about the principles of conduct," "[t]hus, it is evident that one cannot be prudent without being good."[38]

And, while the intellectual virtues are derived from instruction, the virtues of character are formed through habitual practice. So writes Aristotle:

> Moral goodness . . . is the result of habit, from which it has actually got its name, being a slight modification of the word, *ethos*. This fact makes

it obvious that none of the moral virtues [the virtues of character] is engendered in us by nature, since nothing that is what it is by nature can be made to behave differently by habituation. . . . The moral virtues, then, are engendered in us neither *by* nor *contrary to* nature; we are constituted by nature to receive them, but their full development in us is due to habit. . . . Again, of all those faculties with which nature endows us we first acquire the potentialities, and only later effect their actualization. . . . But the virtues we do acquire by first exercising them, just as happens in the arts. Anything that we have to learn to do we learn by the actual doing of it: people become builders by building and instrumentalists by playing instruments. Similarly we become just by performing just acts, temperate [or "self-controlled," the word here is *sôphronsunê*] by performing temperate ones, brave by performing brave ones. This view is supported by what happens in city-states [*polis*]. Legislators make their citizens good by habituation; this is the intention of every legislator, and those who do not carry it out fail of their object.[39]

Aristotle stresses, then, that because none of us are "born either good or bad," but become good or bad through the practice of habits, "it is a matter of no little importance what sort of habits we form from the earliest age—it makes a vast difference, or rather all the difference in the world."[40] Again, here we find ourselves in the midst of the community, because it is the practice of the community—frequently the un-self-conscious, taken-for-granted, ordinary practice of the community—that provides us as individuals with that "complex measure" of goodness that is its common expectation, holding us in virtue. The virtuous person—"the community member"—acts in integrity, in wholeness, in moral congruity. Actions and virtues correspond. That radical compartmentalization of public and private morality, that ethical bipolarity, which is condoned in contemporary culture is unimaginable in Aristotle, because it is essentially irrational.

What is more, Aristotle attempts to give a name to the political condition of the virtuous person in his or her relationships with others. When one is known as virtuous in Aristotle's *polis*, one is known as a friend. Friendship, for Aristotle, is the interpersonal expression of one's giving of oneself to the whole, in the totality and integrity, of one's acts which is, itself, a virtue. As MacIntyre writes: "The type of friendship which Aristotle has in mind is that which embodies a shared recognition of and pursuit of a good. It is this sharing which is essential and primary to the constitution of any form of community, whether that of a household or that of a city."[41] However, the friendship Aristotle has in mind cannot confuse community with identity (i.e., with absolute sameness). The friend is not merely a mirror image of myself. Nor does the friend exist wraithlike as the *Doppelgänger*. The essentially narcissistic solipsism of contemporary American culture is foreign to Aristotle; "friend," Aristotle writes, "really denotes, in the language of the proverb, another Hercules—another self," a self as strong, as tenaciously and stubbornly and strangely other, as Hercules.[42] Aristotle continues, "[T]hough by nature a friend is what is most akin, yet one resembles his friend in body and another in spirit, and one in one part of the body or spirit, another in another."[43] Mere resemblance cannot define the bond of friendship, either physical or mental, in appearance, apparel or thought. "[A] friend really means as it were a separate self,"[44] a self who is in community, and is formed by community, but whose identity remains independent from my identity, whose identity cannot be reduced to the identical, whose unanimity must be negotiated, *agreed*-upon. Friends are not twins. But not even identical twins are one. Alterity is preserved in the community of friendship. The adversary is assumed in the community, or community is lost in and to the identical.[45] As a member of the Aristotelian community, the *polis*, one will not necessarily say "my adversary myself," but one must learn to say "my adversary my friend."

Yet, without any loss or reduction of the identity of the one or the other, of the otherness of the other—in fact, with justice that respects the other, and expects reciprocity—friends draw together in the common acts of the *polis*, "for friendship depends on community."[46] "We are to think then," MacIntyre writes, "of friendship as being the sharing of all in the common project of creating and sustaining the life of the city, a sharing incorporated in the immediacy of an individual's particular friendships." He continues:

> This notion of the political community as a common project is alien to the modern liberal individualist world. This is how we sometimes at least think of schools, hospitals or philanthropic organizations; but we have no conception of such a form of community concerned, as Aristotle says the *polis* is concerned, with the whole of life, not with this or that good, but with [humanity's] good as such. It is no wonder that friendship has been relegated to private life and thereby weakened in comparison to what it once was. Friendship of course, on Aristotle's view, involves affection. But that affection arises within a relationship defined in terms of a common allegiance to and a common pursuit of goods. The affection is secondary, which is not in the least to say unimportant.

In a modern perspective affection is often the central issue; our friends are said to be those whom we *like,* perhaps whom we like very much. "Friendship" has become for the most part the name of a type of emotional state rather than of a type of social and political relationship.[47]

MacIntyre observes that "from an Aristotelian point of view a modern liberal political society can appear only as a collection of citizens of nowhere who have banded together for their common protection"; their "moral pluralism" requires that the best they can muster is "that inferior form of friendship which is founded on mutual advantage."[48] Thus we are frequently (and often with tragic consequences) at a loss for how one can oppose us vigorously and remain a friend, that is, remain within the bonds of community. The negotiation of friendship is a political act at the most intimate level, that is, at the most public level. Privacy and intimacy are not mutually inclusive, and intimacy is inevitably political.

MacIntyre is not blind to the objections that "a spokesman for the modern liberal view" might make to Aristotle's moral vision, that he offers "too simple and too unified a view of the complexities of human good," that Athenian society, that Greek culture, offered a rich diversity of values, of conflicting goods, a plurality of virtues so varied, even so contradictory, that it would be a hopelessly reductionist enterprise to attempt to form of them "a simple, coherent, hierarchical unity." The portrait Aristotle paints systematically serves to "exaggerate moral coherence and unity."[49] MacIntyre finds it hard to disagree with this "modern liberal" argument—an argument that becomes only more persuasive in light of questions raised by perceptive postmodern critics[50]—but before dismissing this aspect of Aristotle's thought, MacIntyre wants to examine why Aristotle holds so tenaciously to "the unity of the virtues," "an unnecessarily strong conclusion" even from Aristotle's "own point of view."[51]

MacIntyre explains that Aristotle inherited the concept of the unity of the virtues directly from Plato. With both Aristotle and Plato there is an assumption that the good is essentially monistic, and that the singularity of the good is reflected in a united state, the unity (and therefore the goodness) of which is expressed in its lack of conflict.[52] As MacIntyre writes: "Both Plato and Aristotle treat conflict as an evil and Aristotle treats it as an eliminable evil. . . . For Aristotle, as for Plato, the good life for [humanity] is itself single and unitary, compounded of a hierarchy of goods."[53]

Neither Aristotle nor Plato would have been able to imagine the "good" of a political theory like that of Machiavelli who, in reflection on the first ten books of Titus Livy's history of the Roman republic, understands conflict as contributory to the strength, the political health, and ultimately the stability of a state. Machiavelli held fast to the idea (virtually unknown to the thinkers of antiquity from Plato to Augustine) "that discord can actually strengthen a state and that a republic consists of at least two different *'vivere,'* ways-of-life or communities, not one."[54] Indeed, it was, in this view, in part the loss of public conflict specifically over the nature of the good ("good" for whom?) which led to the corruption and weakness of Rome under imperial rule. Isaiah Berlin, in his classic essay on Machiavelli, and in other essays which explore the moral character of pluralism, and Lewis Coser, in his analysis of "the functions of social conflict," confront us with a vision of reality that does not allow a metaphysical assumption in preference for singularity to obscure our encounter with the obvious: that there are competing goods, frequently incommensurable ultimate ends, and axiological structures based on these ends, in every society, and that the existence of these political and moral countervailing forces is not necessarily evidence of weakness in the society. Their existence, indeed, may be the society's greatest strength, provided there is a fundamental and undergirding respect for others which takes the concrete form of permitting the voices of others to be heard and their values to be taken seriously.[55] Because the competing goods within the society represent entire ways-of-life, and—this must be reiterated—because they are directed toward different ultimate ends (not merely relative goals), individuals belonging to any particular society are faced with agonistic choices, choices which are not simply between good and bad, but between competing visions of the good.[56]

For Aristotle, however, driven by his metaphysical presuppositions regarding the singularity of the good, and "the impersonal unchanging divinity" who supplies humanity with its "specific and ultimate *telos*," conflict within the *polis* is inevitably "the result either of flaws of character in individuals or of unintelligent political arrangements:"

> This has consequences not only for Aristotle's politics, but also for his poetics and even his theory of knowledge. In all three the *agôn* has been displaced from its Homeric centrality. Just as conflict is not central to a city's life, but is reduced to a threat to that life, so tragedy as understood by Aristotle cannot come near the Homeric insight that tragic conflict is the essential human condition—the tragic hero on Aristotle's view fails because of his own flaw, not because the human situation is sometimes

irremediably tragic—and dialectic is no longer the road to truth, but for the most part only a semi-formal procedure ancillary to enquiry.[57]

If we follow MacIntyre's argument further, we find that Aristotle's metaphysical assumptions cause his thought to be strangely at odds with itself: his metaphysics sit askew his politics. The ultimate end of the human life, the life of the person who is *eudaimôn*, according to Aristotle, is metaphysical contemplation. However, in order for a person to be free to pursue such contemplation "material prerequisites and social prerequisites are necessary." The person's social embeddedness, which is a political given, and the individual's involvement in the concern for, the pursuit and accretion of, those acquisitions which constitute the "household," and which make it convenient for one to spend one's time in contemplation, are held to be subordinate to the highest goal of the good life which is metaphysical contemplation itself; yet, as MacIntyre says, "the notion that their possession and practice is in the end subordinate to metaphysical contemplation would seem oddly out of place" in "many passages where Aristotle discusses individual virtues."[58] Herein lies the threatening unreality of Aristotle's ethics that subtly discounts history and the historical actuality of the community, as a movement toward a *telos*, and which consequently undermines its formation of virtues in and among persons.[59]

Aristotle lacks a clear conception of historicity at either the societal or the personal level, which is to say that the static is assumed to be the ideal state of persons and society. MacIntyre explores what he calls "the ahistorical character" of Aristotle's "understanding of human nature," specifically with reference to Aristotle's arguments regarding the identity of the virtuous.

> *Because:*
> - "Freedom is the presupposition of the exercise of the virtues and the achievement of the good," and freedom is a political quality that only has meaning for "members of a community [a *polis*] who both rule and are ruled over" ("The free self is simultaneously political subject and political sovereign."),
> *then:*
> - virtue is impossible for non-Greeks, for barbarians and slaves because these peoples lack a *polis*, in the sense in which Aristotle uses the term.[60]

According to Aristotle, the possibility of becoming a person of virtue belongs, in fact, to an extraordinarily narrow social, political, cultural and racial class of humanity, and remains closed to the greater proportion of the world's population. Even among Greeks, only those of high social status and affluence, possessing wealth, property and the luxury of leisure, "can achieve key virtues, those of munificence and of magnanimity; craftsmen and tradesmen constitute an inferior class, even if they are not slaves."[61] And, because Aristotle did not possess an adequate conception of historical process with reference to human nature and human society ("there is," MacIntyre writes, "no history of the *polis* or of Greece or of mankind moving towards a *telos*"),[62] all classes of humanity are fixed and unchanging; virtue resides in a closed shop. "Thus," MacIntyre continues, "a whole range of questions cannot arise for him including those which concern the ways in which [people] might pass from being slaves or barbarians to being citizens of a *polis*. Some [people] just are slaves 'by nature,' on Aristotle's view."[63] While MacIntyre is correct in saying that these limitations in Aristotle's understanding "do not necessarily injure his general scheme for understanding the place of the virtues in human life," nevertheless they do real damage to our understanding of the process of formation. Formation that is not a historical process, a movement through the rich, complex and profoundly conflicted history of persons and societies toward a *telos* that belongs to the community because the community was created for this *telos*—formation that does not offer the real possibility of growth, even transformation, but that remains, in some sense, a flat series of repetitive acts in various situations serving, by their sheer habitual repetition, to reinforce virtue in the actor—such formation can all-too-easily become an edifying, but sectarian, discipline of a segregated cultural elite. In the end, such formation is easily relativized by those who wish to co-opt a state for their own ends, or for a state that perverts the ends of *polis* to the destruction of its peoples.[64]

MacIntyre closes his analysis of Aristotle's treatment of the virtues by raising several questions, two of which are especially significant in the context of this essay.

In Aristotle's view, the formation of virtues assumes the contextuality of the *polis*, the ancient city-state, a form of social and political life which no longer exists. We must remember that for Aristotle community is not a generalized term (though our discussion has *just* managed to stay on the particular side of Aristotle's usage); community, for Aristotle, is *polis*; community is, in fact, the Athenian *polis*, which did not long survive. MacIntyre asks: can "the kind of self which can exemplify the virtues" "be found and educated," in a manner consistent with Aristotle's account, in other historically-conditioned varieties of society?[65]

Finally, Aristotle's belief in a unity of the soul, and the value he placed on the unity and harmony of the state, led him to believe that social conflict is an evil that must be avoided. This means that Aristotle was blind to what is arguably one of the most crucial aspects of social life—its conflict—and the ways in which the moral character of persons emerges and is shaped and sharpened on the anvil of conflict. The relatively static and ahistorical understanding of formation one finds in Aristotle, despite the undoubted value of his account, does not comprehend that "it is through conflict and sometimes only through conflict that we learn what our ends and purposes are."[66] Is it possible for us, in a manner appropriate to Aristotle's general understanding of virtue, to take account of the fact that the virtuous person frequently emerges as virtuous from the fires that burn but do not consume?

II

> The salvation of the righteous is from the Lord; he is their refuge in the time of trouble. The Lord helps them and rescues them; he rescues them from the wicked, and saves them, because they take refuge in him (Ps 37:39-40).[67]

My purpose in providing this fairly close reading of Aristotle's account of virtue *vis à vis* MacIntyre, again, is to provide a clearly "Greek" conceptual statement regarding goodness alongside which we shall place, a classic text of Hebrew Scriptures, Psalm 37, which speaks in its own terms to the meaning of goodness. As I stated earlier, Emmanuel Levinas suggests in his treatment of the Talmud the method I shall follow in dealing with the psalm.

While Levinas stands ethnically on the Hebrew side of his translation of the Talmudic text, he also stands uncomfortably astride two cultures, a fact that has the effect of lending considerable energy to his endeavor, energy deriving at least in part from the internal conflict of his cross-cultural intellectual experience. He articulates the Talmudic text in a manner that makes it hearable for auditors who may not share his Jewish heritage. As a North American, as a gentile of Northern European extraction, a Christian, and, therefore, as one who is ethnically, culturally and religiously the beneficiary of both the Greek and the Hebrew worlds of faith and thought, I receive the Hebrew text primarily as an integral part of the Christian canon and secondarily as a cultural artifact of and as a religious text for Judaism. In other words, I receive these Hebrew texts already translated into Greek, embedded in a specific form of Greekness. In order for me to gain any access to the Hebrew text *as* Hebrew text, I am looking at it through a complex interpretive matrix that does not belong to the text itself.

When I describe the Aristotelian account of the virtuous person I am pointing out this fact of my relationship to the Hebrew text by pointing to a specific "Greek" representation of the person of virtue which I inherit (and in relationship to which I stand both negatively and positively; neither our relationship to the Hebrew nor the Greek is unambiguous) as a participant in the culture to which I belong. I am, by no means, providing anything like a comprehensive and exhaustive appraisal of the specific "Greekness" through which I read the Hebrew text. I am merely suggesting that by bringing to a level of consciousness the shape of one particular aspect of my intellectual "Greekness," I may be better able to understand the text in translation, better able to recognize its foreignness and alien character, its strangeness, its tenacious theological otherness, and by extension, the transcendence and mystery of its God (the otherness of the one who is altogether, wholly, *other*) who lays claim to the community of faith in which I dwell in our "Greekness" through this Hebrew text.

I hope, therefore, to be better able to touch the power that lies in the differences between the cultural poles that stand on either side of and within the text, and the distance that always remains between us and any text, and within us with regard to every text. I am also suggesting that because this Hebrew text has entered into our "Greekness," through its inclusion in the Christian canon and its use in the practice of Christian Churches over some twenty centuries, it now says certain things as Christian text of Hebrew origin it did not and does not say as Hebrew text; it is a corrupt text, but its corruption is itself a blessing and not a curse.

Our specific concern in translating Psalm 37 from Hebrew, or, more precisely, from the Hebrew text embedded in the "Greekness" of Christian practice, is to understand what it means to speak of "the righteous person," and the formation of this kind of person, in a Western context influenced to some extent by "Greek" notions such as that of the "person of virtue." This explication does not discount the value of "Greek" accretions or of the embeddedness of the Hebrew text in a "Greek" culture for our reading of Hebrew texts. To the contrary, the "Greekness" of the Western context has entered into our reading of the texts because of the various uses to which the Church has put these canonical Hebrew texts in interpreting and making sense of Christian experience, and because of our continuing practice in liturgy and devotion of these texts in Christian communities of faith. We shall note some of these uses in the final section of this paper. It is often through a recognition of these "Greek" accretions in our reading of Hebrew texts and the cultural and theological contextualization of these texts which makes them "Hebrew-Graeco," that we become aware of the historical paths of our practices, our living engagement with these texts over the course of centuries.

We become conscious of the assimilation of these texts into the Church's life and identity (and into the larger Western culture in which the European Church is rooted). Thus we discern also the ways in which these texts have resisted their easy, and sometimes idolatrous, assimilation into "Greek" usage, for the sake of their own otherness and their witness to the Other who remains tenaciously and stubbornly other, between whom and ourselves there is *den unendlichen qualitativen Untershied*.[68] I ask that we hold these concerns in mind as we turn now explicitly to our exegetical task of translation.

Psalm 37 could be described as the psalm of the righteous. Its recurring theme is that of comfort and consolation for those persons who stand for righteousness, for goodness, innocence, and justice, yet who suspect that the righteous do not always triumph and that acts of righteousness are not inevitably rewarded in this world. The entire psalm, which Walter Brueggemann calls "the most obviously sapiential of all the psalms," reads like a collection of proverbs on the tongue of a wise teacher.[69] Psalm 37 might be understood as a homiletical psalm, that is, a homily in the psalmic form.[70] This observation will hold true provided we understand this specific homily as a didactic sermon.

The central teaching of the psalm is this: However difficult their lot, against whatever obstacles are thrown in their way, ultimately the righteous will flourish in the land God has given them because they have chosen the way of the Lord. The way of the Lord, expressed definitively in the Torah, manifesting "the structure of life as Yahweh created it,"[71] takes for the psalmist the concrete shape of a set of social *cum* legal expectations shared by the community that belongs to the Lord. While the teachings of the psalm at first may seem random and unsystematic, indeed repetitive, actually the whole psalm is carefully structured in an acrostic form. Beyond the obvious pedagogical benefits of the acrostic form of the psalm, the form also reflects the subject of the psalm, as if to say: though the world may appear morally chaotic and contingent, a place where the wicked apparently act without fear of consequences, for those persons (the righteous) who can read its secrets aright, there lies at the heart of the world the moral order of its Creator.

Those pupils in righteousness whom the psalm addresses are to understand that the community's standards of religious and social conduct concretely reflect the righteousness of a God who holds each person accountable for his actions. And the person's behavior that conforms to these standards is not an end in itself; "such behavior contributes decisively to the well-being of the entire community."[72] The community that belongs to YHWH mirrors the qualities of life that God wove into the fabric of existence. For the psalmist, therefore, there is a direct positive correlation between the Torah of the Lord and the laws of the community. And, the community whose laws reflect the Torah is a specific community in a specific place; the community "is linked to creation" precisely in the fact that it belongs to the land of Palestine which the Lord has given to the people of Israel; "for land is the specific experience of God's well-ordered creation over which humankind now has dominion."[73] The psalm reflects the Hebrew conviction that social integration into and inclusion in the covenant community which belongs to the land the Lord has given it is somehow equivalent to salvation. A person's integration into the community is expressed in his positive relationship to the laws of the community.

One of the most striking aspects of Psalm 37 is its use of the Hebrew word צַדִּיק (*tsadîq*, the righteous), which one finds in verses 12, 16, 21, 25, 30, 32 and its plural form צַדִּיקִים (*tsadîqîm*) in verses 17, 29, and 39. Psalm 37, in a manner reminiscent of Proverbs, contrasts the way of the righteous from that of the wicked, רָשָׁע (*rāšāts*), and from the first verse admonishes the righteous:

אַל־תִּתְחַר בַּמְּרֵעִים
אַל־תְּקַנֵּא בְּעֹשֵׂי עַוְלָה׃

("Do not burn with anger because of the wicked; do not be envious of the unrighteous")

The contrasts of the ways and the end of the wicked with those of the righteous are typical of wisdom literature: "The wicked borrow, and do not pay back, but the righteous are generous and keep giving" (v. 21). The psalm also contrasts the fate of the righteous with that of the wicked: "For the arms of the wicked shall be broken, but the Lord upholds the righteous" (v. 17); "The Lord knows the days of the blameless, and their heritage will abide forever. . . But the wicked perish. . . ." (vv. 18, 20).

But the psalm is most eloquent when it steps out of this adversarial formula and, beginning at verse 25, speaks of the consequences of righteousness in such a way that the reader sees righteousness as a quality of YHWH's character that YHWH shares with his people. Thus, the consequences of righteousness are not merely rewards, but the natural outflowing of a relationship between the Lord and the people that belong to this particular God and reflects the intention of this God for creation:

> I have been young, and now am old,
>> yet I have not seen **the righteous** forsaken
>> or their children begging bread.
> They are ever giving liberally and lending
>> and their children become a blessing.
> Depart from evil, and do good;
>> so you shall abide forever.
> For the Lord loves justice;
>> he will not forsake his faithful ones.
> **The righteous** shall be kept safe forever,
>> but the children of the wicked shall be cut off.
> **The righteous** shall inherit the land,
>> and live in it forever.
> The mouths of **the righteous** utter wisdom,
>> and their tongues speak justice.
> The law of their God is in their hearts;
>> their steps do not slip (vv. 25-31).

The Lord who can be trusted in all of life has created and intended his people for a life of trustful dependence and goodness (vv. 3-4). This quality of trust, and the goodness and justice that flow from this trust, is the essence of righteousness. The Lord who loves justice forms a righteous people who also love justice (v. 28). The God whose way is wisdom forms a people in whose heart and on whose tongue wisdom dwells (v. 30). The Torah which is the life-giving way of order and rightness permeating God's creation is carved upon the hearts of this people (v. 31). They have been blessed to be a blessing (v. 22); the faithfulness of their God has made them faithful (v. 28); the unstinting liberality of the Lord has made them generous (v. 21); the wholeness of God has shaped in them a peace that runs from generation to generation (v. 37).

The right actions of the righteous are seen, at points, in terms of specific expectations, both positive and negative: "Trust in the Lord, and do good" (v. 3). "Take delight in the Lord" (v. 4). "Commit your way to the Lord: trust in him, and he will act" (v. 5). "Be still before the Lord, and wait patiently for him; do not fret over those who prosper in their way, over those who carry out evil devises" (v. 7). "Refrain from anger, and forsake wrath. Do not fret [this is not merely wringing one's hands, this is fiery fretfulness, jealous anger]—it leads only to evil" (v. 8).

At other times, the righteous of the psalm are shown the path of righteousness *via negativa*, in stark contrast to the path of wickedness: "The wicked plot against the righteous, and gnash their teeth at them" (v.12), therefore, the passage implies, the righteous should not plot against the righteous or grind their teeth in anger against the righteous. (Clearly the implication here is that the one should avoid persecution of the righteous, of brothers and sisters, fellow-members of the community; but, are the righteous also to avoid plotting against the unrighteous? Or would this be taking it too far for the psalmist?) "The wicked draw the sword and bend their bows to bring down the poor and needy, to kill those who walk upright" (v. 14), the plots of the wicked are carried through, in other words; wicked intentions give rise to wicked actions. And the object of their wickedness is "the poor and needy," that is, the humble, the afflicted, the wretched and weak, those in want, whom the text makes synonymous, in its parallel construction, with "those who walk upright" (i.e., the straightforward and just).

Here we see something extraordinarily telling about the identity of the righteous: the righteous are poor and needy, who have nothing to commend them except their utter trust in the Lord, in contrast to the wealthy, the people of leisure, the socially elite, perhaps those who trust too much in their own devices. Full membership in the community is not restricted to the elite. The designation of "righteous" is not just another property available to the privileged. This much is sure. The community consists of all persons in the land, all those with whom YHWH has covenanted. But, there is a zeal in God's inclusiveness that has a bitter edge. The powerful, the elite, the privileged are in great danger of losing their place in Zion. In fact, the socio-economic reversal (God's sovereign exercise of the preferential option for the poor, over against the rich) and the inclusiveness of the psalmist's community (based on the act of YHWH, rather than the instrumentality of the citizens) represent stark and continually surprising points of contradiction between the "Greek" understanding of the virtuous and the Hebrew view of the righteous.

The psalm later returns to the theme of the violence of the wicked against the righteous, observing how "the wicked watch for the righteous, and seek to kill them," but God watches over the righteous and "will not abandon them" to the power of the wicked (v. 32-33). There is an assumption that precedes this promise: while the wealthy and privileged have enormous resources and a variety of means to perse-cute the righteous, the fate of the righteous lies in the hands of one who is more powerful still. Against the wisdom of the psalm, the wisdom of Aristotle represents an altogether more "worldly" vision that gives greater honor to privilege.

A portrait of the righteous emerges in dramatic brush strokes, in fiery, blinding strokes of light against the shadows and half shadows of those who cover their evil deed with the cloak of night (v. 6). The right-eousness of the psalmist is blood-rich and passionate; it emerges from the heart that trusts in God against all odds (vv. 4, 5, 7). The Lord delights in the righteous, his poor, disheveled people who have so little save their trust in God. And the righteous delight in the Lord and find joy in that which the Lord gives them, and in the scornful laughter that peals from heaven at the presumption and the fall of the wicked who oppress them (vv. 4, 11, 13). The righteous may possess very little in earthly terms, but they rejoice more in the fact that they belong to God than that much be-longs to them (v.16). The righteous do not tower above the terrain of his-tory as the privileged, their oppressors and tyrants, do (v. 35).

Frequently humble, often powerless and disenfranchised, giving be-yond their means, hoping against hope, living on faith and often on faith alone, the righteous are formed by the process of trusting God amid the contingencies and vagaries of historical circumstance. Whereas Aristo-tle's understanding of formation was shackled to a static understanding of history, the formation of righteousness in the psalms is dynamic. Conflict is the crucible of formation. The engine that drives Psalm 37 in-exorably from its opening admonition, "Do not fret because of the wicked; do not be envious of wrongdoers" (v. 1), to its closing promise, "The Lord helps them [the righteous] and rescues them; he rescues them from the wicked, and saves them because they take refuge in him" (v. 40), is the psalm's future orientation, its eschatological reference. There is a teleological aspect to the psalms; but the psalmic *telos* has the dynamic feature, when coupled with the Hebrew notion of history, of pulling the entire community toward a sense of wholeness and integrity that becomes God's gift to God's people. And, inextricably bound-up in this teleologically-oriented history is the promise that the entire com-munity will someday enjoy the wholeness of peace and the fullness of justice, and that the suffering of the righteous will not be in vain. The opening admonition of the psalm, after telling the righteous not to burn with anger and envy toward the wicked explains why: the wicked "will soon fade like the grass, and wither like the green herb" (v. 2). In the present the wicked appear invincible, but they "shall be cut off" from the land (v. 9), a circumstance which is synonymous with lifelessness, because no one can live apart from the life-giving land. "Yet a little while, and the wicked will be no more; though you look diligently for their place, they will not be there" (v. 11); and "the wicked perish, and the enemies of the Lord are like the glory of the pastures; they vanish—like smoke they vanish away" (v. 20).

On the other hand, the righteous, the poor and oppressed in the present time, need only "wait patiently" for the Lord (v. 7), "refrain from anger, and forsake wrath" (v. 8), and avoid fretful and, perhaps envious, anger, which leads only to evil (v. 9), because "those who wait on the Lord shall inherit the land" (v. 9), and, again, "the meek shall inherit the land, and delight themselves in abundant prosperity" (v. 11; also vv. 22, 29, 34 where the righteous will "inherit the land"); "their heritage will abide forever; they are not put to shame in evil times, in the days of famine they have abundance" (vv. 18-19).

Righteousness consists in utter dependence on God, the palpable and authentic trust of oneself and one's future in the faithfulness of Yhwh which takes the shape of a quiet confidence when persecuted and which finds in times of oppression reason to hope neither in circumstances nor in vague speculations about what might come to be, but in the justice and providence of Yhwh whose Torah bears witness to the underlying order and rightness of God's creation. Yet, righteousness also entails a positive response to others; "depart from evil, and do good . . . for the Lord loves justice" (v. 27-28). The righteous consciously seek to understand the law of God, to allow that law to become a part of who they are, so that "their mouths" may speak "wisdom," and "their tongues speak justice," and "their steps do not slip" (vv. 30-31). It is on the basis of their conscious adherence to righteousness despite the costs that the people of God are evaluated.

Psalm 37 understands the wisdom of which Abraham Heschel spoke: "A moral deed unwittingly done may be relevant to the world because of the aid it renders unto others." It is possible to do good, and for the good to be truly good for others, and not to realize you have done good. "Yet a deed without devotion, for all its effects on the lives of others, will leave the life of the doer unaffected. The true goal for man [*sic*] is *to be* what he *does*."[74] The virtue of the righteous lies in the choices they make to do the good because it is good to do so, because to do so is in accordance with the Torah, the way of the Lord.

The righteous person does what is right because it is right. Right is its own reward because it is a participation in the character of YHWH, as we have already observed. But righteousness also carries with it certain tangible consequences in the context of the community of faith, among those who seek to live in accordance with the Torah. Those who trust in the Lord receive the inestimable gift of confidence, because they know that their salvation lies in the hands of one who can be trusted. It is in the context of this relationship of trust between the community and YHWH that we discern the formation of the righteous person. "In short, the righteous are persons whose character has been shaped by God's character."[75] And this happens in ways that are so utterly historical that each community's story must be told in order to understand the precise shape of the formation of the righteous among them. Wickedness, conversely, represents an alternative way, a way that violates the bonds of community and the needs of those who are most vulnerable, that glorifies in-dependence from others, and ultimately in-dependence from that other who is the Lord, by refusing to trust in the community and in God, and by declaring a practical secession from the reign of the Lord in "the land." The wicked attempt to sever the connection between actions and consequences, believing that one may sow the seeds of evil and reap a harvest of good results. They seek to glorify themselves at the expense of the community in which alone there is hope of wholeness, thus cutting themselves off from the inheritance of the land that the Lord has given to the righteous (despite what the land titles may read), and excommunicating themselves from the community in which there resides integration, integrity, wholeness, and salvation.[76] The righteous, by contrast, are righteous by virtue of their groundedness in the particular community in a particular place, at a particular historical moment. Their righteousness cannot be abstracted from this historical contextuality.

III

But the Talmud, despite its antiquity and precisely because of the continuity of Talmudic study, belongs, as paradoxically as this might seem, to the modern history of Judaism. A dialogue between the two establishes itself directly. Herein, no doubt, lies the originality of Judaism: the existence of a tradition, uninterrupted through the very transmission and commentary of the Talmudic texts, commentaries overlapping commentaries.[77]

There are several observations I want to make regarding the translation of Psalm 37 from Hebrew into "Greek." As a Christian it is impossible for me to hear the description of the righteous person in contrast to the evil person without thinking of virtue, a conception that bears in its wake a variety of philosophical and religious implications deriving from the "Greekness" of my cultural and educational background. In both the righteousness of Psalm 37 and the "Greek" sense of virtue, the understanding of character, of moral integrity (and integration into the community that defines the morality), while different in definition, bear striking similarities. The community into which the righteous person is integrated, in which the righteous person is formed as righteous, and from which the righteous person emerges, stands in a dynamic analogical relationship to the *polis*. The righteousness itself, reflecting the Torah, the communal structure of life in the image of Yʜwʜ, also stands in a powerfully analogous relationship to the virtuous life, *eudaimonia*, which expresses the law and way of nature and nature's god. It is probably not possible to determine with any precision the extent to which our hearing of the psalmic text is fundamentally shaped by the "Greekness" of our context and faith. Yet, as we have seen, the hearing of the psalm in the "Greek" context is never simply a matter of submitting the "Hebrew" text to "Greek" thinking. Indeed, at many points, the Hebrew text challenges fundamentally the adequacy of our Greek thinking.

Levinas says that "[t]o evoke freedom and non-dogmatism in exegesis today [he is writing in the mid-nineteen-sixties] means one of two things." One must either be a proponent of the historical method, or one must engage in a structuralist analysis of the text. While there is value in the historical critical method, and important things can be learned about an ancient text by use of this methodology, and while we recognize the fact that the text we are translating is indeed a religious text, and there are those who consequently want to relegate it to the general classification of mythological literature, to treat it from the structuralist perspective "as a mythic web of survivals," Levinas insists that we "take the Talmudic text and Judaism which manifests itself in it as teachings."

> Our first task is . . . to read it in a way that respects its givens and its conventions, without mixing in the questions arising for the philologist or historian to the meaning that derives from its juxtapositions. . . . It is only after this initial task of reading the text within its own conventions that we will try to translate the meaning suggested by its particu-

lars into a modern language, that is, into the problems preoccupying a person schooled in spiritual sources other than those of Judaism and whose confluence constitutes our civilizations.[78]

Our concern, then, is to respect the givenness and conventions of the Psalms, תהלים, the *Tehillīm*, the Book of the Praises of Israel, respecting, that is, first their use in the religious, the cultic and liturgical life of the Jewish people. However, because we translate from the "Greek" side, the *textus receptus* is a practiced text, a text in continual use in liturgy and devotion for some two thousand years by the Christian Church. Standing where I stand as a translator, I cannot read it except as such. While I know and respect the fact of the Jewishness of the text; the text comes to those of us in the Church already embedded in Christian faith and practice. The givenness of the text, its conventions—which I wish to respect—must contend with this problem which is a "problem" only in the most formal sense, because it is primarily a gift.

Our access, as "Greeks," to the Hebrew text of the psalms parallels however the access of the "modern" Jew to the Talmud in at least one important respect. In both cases, the common practice of communities invites us into the practice of these texts which has continued virtually uninterrupted for centuries, in the one (the psalms) through a practice of praise, in the other (the Talmud) of scholarly disputation. Neither text is roped off from ordinary usage, in other words; both texts belong to communities which belong to these texts and find in them indispensable matrices of meaning. Thus while we respect the givens and conventions of the text, we must recognize that this respect means that we cannot restrict access to the text from those who bring to it "the problems preoccupying a person schooled in spiritual [and other] sources other than those"[79] which belong to the text and to the religion and culture of the community which produced the text.

The texts of the Psalms are grounded in particular historical experiences of people to whom we have no direct (and only minimal indirect) access. We do not know what specific calamities led one to cry out, "My God, my God, why hast thou forsaken me" or another to pray, "save me, O God, for I take my refuge in thee." But the texts of the psalms have entered both the canons of Judaism and of Christianity as formal statements which in their relative openness invite the one performing or practicing prayer and praise through them to pour into them the concerns and complaints of one's own individual experiences and the experiences of one's community. While we want to hear each text in its own terms, we must remember that hearing a text in its own terms does not exclude (indeed it positively demands) an affective and intellectual connection with the experiences of the practicing community in which we experience the text.

As texts practiced by communities, both the Talmud and the psalms, make claims on those who engage them. Levinas describes these claims as "teachings"; which means that the appropriate posture toward these texts is not that of idle curiosity—scholarly, casual or prurient—but of discipleship; these texts ask us to receive their teachings as willing learners. These texts also, and the communities of practice in which these texts function, wish to teach us in and through their performance and practice. As we read what Levinas called those "square letters" of Hebrew we are drawn into a participation in the communities who teach, learn, are theologically and morally formed through their practice of these texts. In the case of the Psalms, we are invited to praise and worship God, to pray to God, and so to learn to praise and worship and pray. This is inevitably a communal process. By teaching us, the texts make a claim on us which, in some sense, is nothing less than the claim of God. The teachings reflected in these texts make certain radically subjective demands on who we are, what we shall do and what we shall become, which violate the safe distances we attempt to preserve in certain distinctively Western epistemological systems.

One might well ask, however, as one reflects on Levinas' statements about the continuity of Talmudic study and the continuity of the practice of the psalms, where in these texts are the authorial and editorial communities that gave rise to, collected and adapted the texts, and with whom the texts and we (in our communities of faith) are now in "continuity"? This question is vitally relevant to our responsibility to respect the "givenness" of these texts. We are compelled to respond: *These authorial and editorial communities are lost.* The texts now seem to have turned their backs on these communities, so to speak, as the texts turn toward us; the texts so clearly desire us, the contemporary readers, to engage them, they beckon us to enter into them, to know them, as readers and hearers and performers. We have become their focus. Roland Barthes explains that the texts we read *seek us out* and *choose us,* "by a whole disposition of invisible screens, selective baffles: vocabulary, references, readability." The authorial and editorial communities have become lost, then, in the courtship that the texts carry on with us. But, as Barthes observes, they are "lost in the midst of the text," and there, in the midst of the text, *lost,* "there is always the other, the author,"[80] and, by extension, the authorial and editorial communities. To enter into the texts as readers, hearers, performers, translators, and exegetes, is to find, and to risk losing, ourselves among those communities who have found themselves in the texts and have been lost in the process.

Levinas understands the "chief goal of our exegesis" as an extrication of "the universal intentions from the apparent particularism within which facts tied to the national history of Israel, improperly so-called, enclose us."[81] He wishes to move from the particular, the historically conditioned, to the universal, to that which is true in "the unity of the consciousness of mankind," in that fraternal oneness he believes to exist "throughout time and space."[82] This belief Levinas shares with Aristotle, with Plato, with much of Western "Greek" culture.[83] But is this belief anything more than merely the Western assumption of oneness which Levinas believes *because* he stands where he stands with one foot firmly implanted in the "Greek" world? Is it either true or necessary to make such an assumption in order for "Greek" culture to value the Hebrew (or any other) texts which reflect a particularity and historicity other than the "Greek"? Levinas believes that "it is Israel's history which has suggested this idea" of universal fraternity and "the unity of the consciousness of mankind," and that while mankind, "now conscious of its oneness," challenges "Israel's vocation, its concrete universality," it is finally indebted to Judaism for the oneness that allows it to question the particularity of Israel. *And yet*, we might well question Levinas' judgment at this point, because the entire notion of "oneness," of "universality," and "universal fraternity," of the unity of consciousness of mankind have the effect of so flattening out the rich diversity, the plural and concrete actuality and wonder of the particular, the momentary, the unique, the indeterminate moment, the historically real, that one may find it difficult to imagine how anyone who has not assumed *a priori* the value of "universal oneness" could find in it so much to praise and glorify. Such notions of universality and universal oneness are foreign to the psalms (they are truly "Greek" notions in every respect), and one might wonder if they are not just as foreign to the Talmud in which Levinas believes he finds them.

What one clearly does find in the Talmud, as Levinas observes, and also in the Psalms, is a complex meeting place of diverse textuality, of intertextuality, a Grand Central Station of scriptural allusions, of biblical narratives, praise and wisdom texts, covenants, religious codes and laws and the shadows which all of these cast on other texts, of civil and ritual legislation, of preaching, "from a whole stock of Old Testament notions."[84] Levinas writes, speaking specifically of the meanings taught by the Talmudic texts:

> Their meaning is also constituted by a certain number of events or situations, or, more broadly, by certain points of reference contemporary with the Rabbis or sages who speak in the Talmud. Despite the variations of sense that the elements of this signifying inventory might have undergone throughout the ages, despite the contingency of the circumstances in which these signs are inscribed and from which they received their power of suggestion, we do not think that a purely historical approach suffices to clarify this symbolism. Even less does a formalist investigation of the structuralist type seem appropriate to us here.[85]

The meaning of these Talmudic texts does not belong merely to the past, either to be exhumed by the historical critical method or to be formally appropriated as mythological through structuralist interpretation; rather the meaning of these texts is present to us through the mediation of a "living tradition." The Talmud, while ancient, is present to us (is "modern," to use Levinas' term) because it has remained the subject of Talmudic study through the continuity of that study, the communal practices of disputation and commentary that extend from antiquity to the contemporary period. We have access to the ancient texts, therefore, through a living practice, a practice that has never stopped reading into and out of the texts the life of the communities represented there. While Levinas says that biblical thought and the biblical narratives belong "resolutely to history" and they do not "become intelligible without scholarly and critical intervention of the historian," and thus they can become immediately accessible to us by faith alone, do not the psalms represent among the biblical texts an example of the kind of text, not entirely unlike the Talmud, which Levinas understands as present in our contemporary context through a "living tradition," that is, through the continuity of the practice of worshiping, praying, praising communities to whom the psalmic texts lay claim? While remaining ancient texts, while also accessible through faith—and precisely because they are accessible by faith—nevertheless the psalms remain our exact contemporaries through the practice of communities of faith throughout the centuries in a manner parallel to the "uninterrupted . . . transmission and commentary of the Talmudic texts."[86]

Levinas directs our attention to the way the Talmud continues the "'way' of the Bible." He writes: "The Bible furnishes the symbols but the Talmud does not 'fulfil' the Bible in the sense that the New Testament claims to complete and also to continue the Old. That explains the dialectical, argumentative language of the Talmud, conveying the 'biblical myth' *by making matters worse,* if one can express it thus, with an undefinable touch of irony and provocation."[87]

The psalms also convey, elaborate on, make visible and real the Old Testament in the language and form of praise and lamentation; they stand as performative and doxological commentary in a dialectical relationship with the rest of the Old Testament in a manner which, for the Christian Church, is enshrined formally and institutionalized in the role the psalms play liturgically in response to the reading of the Old Testament text.[88] This liturgical use of the psalms reflects an already well-established relationship between the psalms and the other texts of the Old Testament, as historical events and the use of the law in culture and cultus find their lyrical expression in the praise and lament of Israel.[89] Who can doubt that the sorrow of the exilic community during the Babylonian captivity is given expression precisely *"by making matters worse"* in Psalm 137? Or that the expressions of self-righteousness and self-disgust, of vengeance and hope which arise in some psalms make real the historical experience of the community in ways that narratives and legal codes could never accomplish? Levinas explains that the Talmudic "[c]ommentary has always tolerated . . . enrichment of the symbol through the concrete";[90] we might add, in complement, that the concrete has always demanded the realization of the concrete through the symbolic, and has always been something less than actual, somehow less than real, until this symbolic utterance (another type of translation, surely) has happened. The psalms are recognized in the liturgical and devotional practices of the Church as texts which make real and concrete to Christian faith the faith of Israel.

Christian communities, generally following the practice of synagogues, made use of the psalms in their liturgies from the earliest times. Whether the psalms were sung or read in the ancient church is a matter of debate, but the fact of their ordinary use in the Church's worship is well documented, and it is certain that "the singing of the psalms occupied a central place once the daily office developed, both in its 'cathedral' and in its 'monastic' form."[91] The liturgical practice of the psalms was accepted in both the Eastern and Latin Church, and among the churches which emerged as Protestant in the sixteenth-century, especially in the Reformed tradition, where metrical versions of psalms were used as hymns in corporate worship. The Christian Church, from its very earliest beginnings, has found in psalms—in addition to the psalmic reflections on the Torah, the history and prophecy of the nation of Israel, as we have already noted—a lyrically rich reflection on the events of the gospel, especially the passion of Christ. As Dietrich Bonhoeffer observed, "The Psalms have been given to us [Christians] precisely so that we can learn to pray them in the name of Jesus Christ." This is why, he continues, "the Psalter is very often bound together with the New Testament. It is the prayer of the church of Jesus Christ."[92] The Church, for instance, has heard the suffering and death of Jesus through Psalms 22 and 69, and has found in psalms, such as Psalm 34 (note v. 8), 50 (especially v. 14) and 51, Eucharistic and confessional resonance.[93]

Psalm 37, in particular, is used currently at two particular points in the liturgy of those churches that make use of the Revised Common Lectionary; both occurrences are in Year C: (1) as a response on the Seventh Sunday after Epiphany where it is intended to guide the congregation's reflection on Gen 45:3-11, 15, and (2) Proper 22 (27) on the Sunday between October 2 and October 8 inclusive, in reflection on Lam 3:19-26. In the first instance, Ps 37:1-11, 39-40 reflects, perhaps predictably, on an incident from the life of that paradigmatic "righteous man" of the Patriarchal narratives, Joseph, when he revealed his identity to his brothers: "I am your brother, Joseph, whom you sold into Egypt. And now do not be distressed, or angry with yourselves, because you sold me here; for God sent me before you to preserve you" (vv. 4-5). The passage from Lamentations to which Ps 37:1-9 responds actually serves as a sounding board for the psalm, as the admonition of Psalm 37, calls its hearers to trust in the Lord, to wait for the Lord, to commit their ways to the Lord, and is answered by the firm resolution of the righteous person who laments:

> The thought of my affliction and my homelessness is wormwood and gall!
> My soul continually thinks of it and is bowed down within me.
> But this I call to mind, and therefore I have hope:
> The steadfast love of the LORD never ceases, his mercies never come to an end;
> they are new every morning; great is your faithfulness. . . .
> The Lord is good to those who wait for him, to the soul that seeks him.
> It is good that one should wait quietly for the salvation of the LORD (Lam 3:19-26).

The task of translating a text which lives and which is present by virtue both of the faith by which it is apprehended in communities of faith and the continuity of its practice in these communities, makes certain demands on our exegesis which may seem strange to our study of other genres of biblical scripture. Yet, for our study of the psalms, these practiced, living, strangely contemporaneous texts, the demands do not seem outrageous at all.

Conclusion

At the risk of over-simplifying the field of choices one has at one's disposal in translating the Hebrew into "Greek," I propose that there are at least four courses of action available to us:

- We could assume that the Hebrew text and the "Greek" world do not touch at any point. Thus we might say that the world represented in the Hebrew text and the "Greek" world with which we are familiar are so utterly different, so completely separate in cultural and social norms and language, in values and goals, so irreducibly incommensurable that there is no way the Hebrew text can speak in idioms to answer questions raised among "Greeks." While some churches still make claims for this approach, the history of Christian thought has found it wanting, at least since the Marcionite heresy.

- We could decide that the Hebrew text exists for the Church to be subordinated to the "Greek" world of thought. Thus, from the Neo-Platonism of Dionysius the Pseudo-Areopagite and the Aristotelianism of Thomas Aquinas to the Existentialism of Rudolf Bultmann, a variety of "Greek" thought-forms have offered themselves as appropriate interpretive matrices in which to re-structure and re-interpret the faith; but, in each of these cases, the interpretive task was undertaken in such a way that the Hebrew texts being "translated" were subordinated to the "Greekness" of the translators.

- On the other hand, we could decide that the "Greek" world of thought must, in the name of faithfulness, be subsumed by the Hebrew. The Jerusalem Church led by James, and among the Ebionite sect in the first centuries of Christian history, made valiant attempts to reject "Greek" accretions to the Hebrew texts they received while attempting also to claim Jesus as messiah. But the Jerusalem Church did not long survive, and the Ebionites were declared heretical. Tertullian, who demanded to know what Athens has to do with Jerusalem, represents that tendency within the Church to shed that which it cannot shed, its "Greekness," the cultural and intellectual skin inside which it lives; and even Tertullian found it necessary to make his demands in a stylistically elegant Latin.

- In the final analysis, perhaps the only viable alternative for the Church is to try to translate the Hebrew texts in such a way as to recognize the implicit "Greekness" given them by the fact that they find their place for us in a Christian canon and in well-established practices of Christian communities of faith, yet to recognize also and at the same time what Levinas called the "givenness" of the Hebrew texts which keep their distance, their integrity as Hebrew texts even in the canon and practices of the Church.

Levinas, in his preface to "From the Sacred to the Holy: Five New Talmudic Readings," wrote: "What matters to us is to ask questions of these texts—to which Jewish wisdom is tied as if to the soil—in terms of our problems as modern [people]."[94] Wherever we locate that adjective "modern," even if we locate it by dislocating it with the prefix "post," this remains our task, to question the texts we have inherited, respecting them and loving them in their foreignness, expecting to hear from them a "Word of God," but respecting our own moment no less. Because, to pay disrespect to our own moment, and to the claims this moment and this context and their intellectual and cultural forms make on us, leads only to the unconsciously bad exegesis that is bad precisely because it is unconscious, and because unconscious, uncritical. Whatever it is that makes the gospel "foolishness to the Greeks," we "Greeks" had better come to terms with it, so that we may hear the wisdom of God.

In a sense, therefore, this essay has not been so much an essay "about" a kind of translation, as it has been an "exercise" in translation. Thus, the half-title for the essay. What this essay argues for, therefore, is a more conscious articulation of our frequently unconscious "Greekness," in the awareness that the sacred texts we have received in the practice and faith of the Church stand ready to startle us anew. I am reminded again of those words from Karl Barth's essay (some eighty years old now): "The axiomatic is never obvious. The knowledge which the Bible offers and commands us to accept forces us out upon a narrow ridge or rock upon which we must balance between Yes and No, between life and death, between heaven and earth."[95] Perhaps also this is what Levinas meant when he said that the text stands ready to teach us. And when the text teaches, we are taught indeed.

NOTES: CHAPTER 11

[1] Franz Rosenzweig, used by Annette Aronowicz as an epigram in her translator's introduction to Emmanuel Levinas, *Nine Talmudic Readings*, trans. Annette Aronowicz (Bloomington and Indianapolis: Indiana University Press, 1990) ix. The Rosenzweig passage appeared in Nahum Glatzer, ed., *Franz Rosenzweig: His Life and Thought* (New York: Schocken Books, 1961) 62–63.

[2] Translator's introduction to Levinas, *Talmudic Readings*, ix.

[3] Aronowicz notes significantly the fact that "Levinas's first presentation at the yearly Colloquia of French-Speaking Jewish Intellectuals was a paper on Rosenzweig, *'Entre Deux Mondes,'* in *La conscience juive: Données et debats* (Paris: Presses Universitaires de France, 1963) 121–37." Ibid., xxxiv–xxxv. See also, *The Levinas Reader*, Seán Hand, ed. (Oxford: Blackwell, 1989) especially 249–88; and Adriaan Peperzak's preface

to Emmanuel Levinas, *Basic Philosophical Writings*, Adriaan T. Peperzak, ed. Simon Critchley, and Robert Bernasconi (Bloomington and Indianapolis: Indiana University Press, 1996) vii–xv.

[4] Translator's introduction, *Talmudic Readings*, xi.

[5] Ibid., xii–xiii.

[6] Levinas, his own introduction to the *Talmudic Readings*, 5.

[7] Ibid., 9.

[8] Ibid., 10.

[9] Aristotle, *The Ethics of Aristotle: The Nicomachean Ethics*, trans. J. A. K. Thomson, rev. Hugh Tredennick, intro. Jonathan Barnes (London: Penguin Books, 1976) 91.

[10] Sarah Broadie, *Ethics With Aristotle* (New York/ Oxford: Oxford University Press, 1991) 57.

[11] Alasdair MacIntyre, *After Virtue: A Study in Moral Theory* (Notre Dame, Ind.: University of Notre Dame Press, 2nd ed., 1984) 147–8.

[12] Ibid., 148.

[13] Ibid.

[14] Ibid., 149. Italics added.

[15] Ibid.

[16] While a consideration of the comparison between the Aristotelian and a Stoic understanding of habits and virtues is clearly beyond the limitations of this brief essay, it would be fascinating to explore both in relation to the good, and the formation of the good, in the psalms. Compare, for instance, the parallels between Epictetus, *The Discourses*, bk .I. ch. xxvii. Especially at v. 4, which begins: "*Tí oûn pròs éthos éstin eurískein Boéthema; tò enantíon éthos. . . .*" (Cf. bk. II. ch. xviii) and what we see in Aristotle's *Nichomachean Ethics*, bk. I. ch. II. i. However, for Epictetus virtue is removed from passion, Aristotle is much more subtle, his argument carefully nuanced. See *Nichomachean*, bk. II. ch. II. iii–ix. The goodness of the psalms is a goodness of passion, as we shall see, and while Aristotle praises moderation, the psalmist speaks his praise in the extreme.

[17] MacIntyre, *After Virtue*, 150. Though well beyond the scope of the modest paper, one might trace comparatively Aristotle's thought vis a vis MacIntyre with that of Dietrich Bonhoeffer's *Ethics*, Eberhard Bethge, ed. (New York: Macmillan, 1955) especially pt. One, sec. III, "Ethics as Formation," 64–119; note also Bonhoeffer's criticism of Aristotle, 332–35, a criticism which remains trenchant and profound.

[18] MacIntyre, 150.

[19] Ibid., 150. See also: Hannah Arendt, "What Was Authority," Carl J. Friedrich, ed., *Authority* (Cambridge, Mass: Harvard University Press, 1958) 95.

[20] MacIntyre, 151.

[21] Refer to my analysis of John Kenneth Galbraith's social theory in contrast to Bertrand de Jouvenel's perspective on the cultural exercise of power and Robert Putnam's study of democratic institutions in contemporary Italy in Michael Jinkins and Deborah Bradshaw Jinkins, *The Character of Leadership: Political Realism and Public Virtue in Nonprofit Organizations* (San Francisco: Jossey-Bass, Publishers, 1998) ch. 8: "Understanding the Ecology of Leadership and Power," 80–92.

[22] MacIntyre, 151.

[23] Ibid.

[24] Ibid., 152.

[25] Stanley Hauerwas, *Character and the Christian Life: A Study in Theological Ethics* (San Antonio: Trinity University Press, 1975) 38.

[26] MacIntyre, 152.

[27] Aristotle, *Athenian Constitution; Eudemian Ethics; Virtues and Vices*, tr. H. Rackham (Cambridge, Mass.: Harvard University Press, revised edition, 1952), *Eudemian Ethics*, bk. 1. ch. v. 217.

[28] MacIntyre, 152.

[29] Ibid.

[30] Ibid., 154.

[31] Rackham's introduction to *On Virtues and Vices*: in which he observes that the primary interest of this short treatise lies in the way it exemplifies "the way in which Aristotle's reduction to scientific form of the ethical system adumbrated by Plato was later systematized and stereotyped by smaller minds." Aristotle, *Athenian Constitution, Eudemian Ethics, Virtues and Vices*, 484–85.

[32] W. F. R. Hardie, *Aristotle's Ethical Theory* (Oxford: Clarendon Press, 2nd ed., 1980) 201.

[33] Ibid., 201–2.

[34] MacIntyre, 154.

[35] Ibid.

[36] Aristotle, *Ethics: Nichomachean*, bk. I. ch. II, 91.

[37] MacIntyre, 154.

[38] Aristotle, *Ethics: Nichomachean*, bk. VI. ch. XII, 223.

[39] Ibid., bk. II. ch. II, 91–92.

[40] Ibid., bk. II. ch. II, 92.

[41] MacIntyre, 156.

[42] Aristotle, *Eudemian Ethics*, bk. VII. ch. XII., 441. See the trans. note at this point.

[43] Ibid., bk. VII. ch. XII, 443.

[44] Ibid.

[45] Although even a cursory examination of Jacques Derrida's remarkable essay on friendship would take us well beyond our brief analysis of Aristotle *vis à vis* MacIntyre, it deserves careful attention in another place and time: *Politics of Friendship*, trans., George Collins (London/ New York: Verso, 1997).

[46] Aristotle, *The Works of Aristotle*, W. D. Ross, ed. (London: Oxford University Press, 1915) vol. IX: *Ethica Nicomachea*, trans., W. D. Ross, bk. VIII. 8. 1159b.

[47] MacIntyre, 156.

[48] Ibid.

[49] Ibid., 157.

[50] See, for instance: Kathryn Tanner, *Theories of Culture: A New Agenda for Theology* (Minneapolis: Fortress Press, 1997).

[51] MacIntyre, 157.

[52] Note, for example, Plato, Book IV of *The Republic*, trans., B. Jowett, L. R. Loomis, ed. (New York: Walter J. Black, 1942.

[53] MacIntyre, 157.

[54] Bernard Crick, in his introduction to Niccolò Machiavelli, *The Discourses*, trans., Leslie J. Walker (London: Penguin, 1970), 34. See: Machiavelli, *Discourses*, I.3.-I.6.

[55] Isaiah Berlin, "The Originality of Machiavelli," in *Against the Current: Essays in the History of Ideas*, Henry Hardy, ed., intro. Roger Hausheer (London: Pimlico, 1997)

25–79; Berlin, "The Sense of Reality," and "Political Judgment," in *The Sense of Reality: Studies in Ideas and Their History* (New York: Farrar, Straus and Giroux, 1997) 1–53; and Lewis Coser, *The Functions of Social Conflict* (New York: The Free Press, 1956).

[56] Thus John Gray describes Isaiah Berlin's thought as "agonistic liberalism," "a stoical and tragic liberalism of unavoidable conflict and irreparable loss among inherently rivalrous values." Gray, *Isaiah Berlin* (London: HarperCollins, 1995) 1–4, 38–75.

[57] MacIntyre, 157.

[58] Ibid., 158.

[59] Note, in this context, MacIntyre's observation regarding Aristotle's service "of that Macedonian royal power which destroyed the city-state as a free society." Ibid., 159.

[60] Ibid., 158–59.

[61] Ibid., 159.

[62] Ibid.

[63] Ibid., 160.

[64] The distinction between Aristotle's understanding of "formation" and a historically sophisticated conception of formation is made apparent in Hauerwas, *Character and the Christian Life*, 1–45; 179–228.

[65] MacIntyre, 163.

[66] Ibid., 163–64.

[67] All quotations in English are from the NRSV, Bruce M. Metzger and Roland E. Murphy, eds. (New York: Oxford University Press, 1991).

[68] The phrase generally associated with the preface to the second edition of Karl Barth's *Epistle to the Romans*, trans. Edwyn C. Hoskyns (Oxford: Oxford University Press, 1933). Walter Lowe observes in *Theology and Difference* (Bloomington: Indiana University Press, 1993) 3, that the phrase derives from Søren Kierkegaard.

[69] Walter Brueggemann, *The Message of the Psalms* (Minneapolis: Augsburg Publishing House, 1984) 42.

[70] J. Clinton McCann, Jr., "The Psalms," *The New Interpreter's Bible* (Nashville: Abingdon Press, 1996) vol. IV. 828.

[71] W. H. Bellinger, Jr., *Psalms: Reading and Studying the Book of Praises* (Peabody, Mass.: Hendrickson Publishers, 1990) 134.

[72] Brueggemann, 43.

[73] Ibid.

[74] Abraham Heschel, *Between God and Man: An Interpretation of Judaism*, Fritz A. Rothschild, ed. (New York: The Free Press, 1959) 164.

[75] McCann, 829.

[76] The text of this psalm, as received in the context of the Christian canon, seems to lean into the Gospels at many points, but there is one particular echo of the psalm that must be noted. The psalm seems almost to seek resonance with the words attributed to Jesus in the beatitudes where the blessed (the righteous, the poor, bereaved, despised) are contrasted with the wicked (who are now rich, full, laughing):

Blessed are you who are poor, for yours is the kingdom of God.

Blessed are you who are

hungry now, for you will be filled.

Blessed are you who weep now, for you will laugh.

Blessed are you when people hate you, and when they exclude you, revile you, and defame you on account of the Son of Man.

Rejoice on that day and leap for joy, for surely your reward is great in heaven;
for that is what their ancestors did to the prophets.
But woe to you who are rich, for you have received your consolation.
Woe to you who are full now, for you will be hungry.
Woe to you who are laughing now, for you will mourn and weep.
Woe to you when all speak well of you, for that is what their ancestors did to the
false prophets (St. Luke 6:20b-26).

The passage which opens Luke's version of the beatitudes, Μακάριοι οἱ πτωχοί,
uses, in fact, the same word for "poor" which the Septuagint uses (πτωχὸν) to translate
(דל). The Hebrew (psalm) becomes real, as Rosenzweig intimates, only when it is translated into the Greek of the Septuagint; that is to say, the text must step out on its own
among the nations, among the "Greeks"; it has to risk translation into the idioms of
others, strangers, foreigners, and in doing so much risk the vagaries of historical and
linguistic accident where meaning is lost and found in sometimes subtle and infinites-
simal, and sometimes cataclysmic, transactions; it has to make its own way in the world
without the security of "those square letters." But there is a resonance here that goes
further still than the bare fact that a particular word, however crucial that word may be
to the text, is rendered through the Septuagint into the "Greek" world where Jesus'
words and the words of his followers dwell in the practice of Christian communities.
The beatitudes, the parables, the ethics of the kingdom of God which one confronts in
St. Luke, St. Mark, and St. Matthew function in counterpoint to the teachings regarding the "righteous person" which we find in Psalm 37.

[77] Emmanuel Levinas, "Introduction," *Talmudic Readings*, 6–7.

[78] Ibid., 5.

[79] Ibid.

[80] Roland Barthes, *The Pleasure of the Text*, trans. Richard Miller (New York: Hill
and Wang, 1975) 27.

[81] Levinas, 5.

[82] Ibid., 6.

[83] Isaiah Berlin, in his criticism of axiological monism, says that the intellectual
fabric of the Enlightenment, inherited from Plato and classical philosophy, and incorporated into the common thought of Western European culture, holds that "all genuine questions must have one true answer," and that the answer "must be true for
everyone, everywhere, all the time," and that any given answer "must necessarily be
compatible with" other true answers and must "form a single whole." Steven Marcus
quotes and paraphrases Berlin in his review of Michael Ignatieff's biography, *Isaiah
Berlin: A Life* (New York: Metropolitan Books, 1998) *The New York Times Book Review*,
November 29, 1998.

[84] Levinas, 6.

[85] Ibid.

[86] Ibid., 6–7.

[87] Ibid., 7. Italics added.

[88] The psalms are included in the weekly lectionary of readings from the Old Testament, New Testament Epistles and Gospels in the Revised Common Lectionary. They
are intended to be used "to encourage reflection on the first reading" (ordinarily the
Old Testament reading). *The Revised Common Lectionary* (Nashville: Abingdon Press,
1992) 10.

[89] Note Patrick Miller's presidential address to the Society of Biblical Literature, November 1998, published as "Deuteronomy and Psalms: Evoking a Biblical Conversation," *JBL* 118 (1999) 3–18.

[90] Levinas, 7.

[91] Geoffrey Wainwright, *Doxology: The Praise of God in Worship, Doctrine, and Life: A Systematic Theology* (New York: Oxford University Press, 1980) 211.

[92] Dietrich Bonhoeffer, *Life Together/ Prayerbook of the Bible*: Dietrich Bonhoeffer Works, vol. 5, English ed. Geffrey B. Kelly, ed., trans., Daniel W. Bloesch and James H. Burtness (Minneapolis: Fortress Press, 1996) 157–58.

[93] See Michael Jinkins and Stephen Breck Reid, "God's Godforsakenness: The Cry of Derelicction as an Utterance Within the Trinity," *Horizons in Biblical Theology: An International Dialogue*, 19 (June 1997) no. 1. 33–57; Michael Jinkins, *In the House of the Lord: Inhabiting the Psalms of Lament* (Collegeville: The Liturgical Press, 1998) 75–120. also Wainwright, 210–12.

[94] Levinas, *Talmudic Readings*, 92.

[95] Karl Barth, "Biblical Questions, Insights, and Vistas," in *The Word of God and the Word of Man*, trans., Douglas Horton (Gloucester, Mass.: Peter Smith, 1978) 58.

12

All God, and Us
Double Agency and Reconciliation in Psalms 22 and 51

Cynthia L. Rigby

"*A*gency is a power or potentiality for action."[1] Throughout the ages people of faith have struggled to understand the relationship between their agency and the agency of God. If we think we contribute something to the shape of the future, we wonder, have we forgotten the divine providence? If we proclaim our ineptitude and wait for God to act, are we shirking our responsibility? We look to the stories of Scripture and ask: did Sarah overstep her bounds in trying to facilitate God's promise of progeny? Did Judas have any choice but to betray Jesus, if this was the will of God? In matters of salvation, we often ponder how to give God all the credit without removing ourselves from the picture. Why *is* it that we engage in the work of evangelism, if God elects whom God wills apart from our actions? Why work out our salvation "with fear and trembling," if we were indeed chosen "before the foundation of the earth"?

In this essay, I argue that Psalms 22 and 51 suggest an integrated approach to the doctrine of reconciliation that incorporates both divine and human urgency, both Anselmian and Abélardian atonement theories, both substitutionary and representational insights.[2] In these psalms God delivers the psalmists[3] from their incapacitating circumstances *and* the psalmists participate with God in the divine work of reconciliation. Exploring "double agency" as reflected in these psalms, I show how the divine/human relationship the psalmists describe illuminates the character of God's reconciliatory work in Jesus Christ. In short, I argue that these psalms help us understand Jesus Christ as the one who *replaces us* in relation to victimization and guilt (substitution) in order to *create a place* in which we can act as agents in partnership with God (representation).[4]

The approach I take is theological and christological. I begin by explaining why theologians have struggled with the question of human agency when exploring approaches to the doctrine of reconciliation. I then move to consideration of the psalms, analyzing how double agency[5] seems to be in play. Finally, I offer a constructive proposal for how the relationship between divine and human agency in these psalms models a thick approach to atonement that resists setting substitutionary and representational views at odds.

I am motivated by a desire better to understand the character of God's reconciling work in Jesus Christ, and our participation in it. I presume that the character of the divine/human relationship as reflected in the psalms casts light on the character of the divine/human relationship as we participate in it through Jesus Christ. Of course, as a Christian theologian, I have the New Testament revelation—and the history of doctrine—in mind as I read the psalms. But methodologically I am striving not to impose atonement theory on the psalms as much as to learn, from the psalms, how better to conceive the doctrine of reconciliation.

In the course of the essay it is clear that I am in dialog with the great theologians of Christian history who have struggled to understand their place in relation to the divine work of reconciliation. Less explicitly, I am also indebted to David Blumenthal, whose book *Facing the Abusing God* helped open my eyes to how crying out to God—even *blaming* God for shirking on God's promises—can empower human beings to survive and to heal in relation to their sufferings.[6] Here I am presenting a thesis that builds on his provocative insights in developing a constructive possibility that he does not entertain. In psalms such as Psalm 22, I argue, it is certainly the case that psalmists survive and confront God's injustice, moving slowly toward healing. It is surely true that the psalmists praise God for rescuing them once divine intervention occurs. But what is often missed is this: the psalmists do not act only "before" and/or "after" the actions of God. Rather, they participate as partners in the reconciliatory dynamic by naming God's absence, insisting on God's presence, dancing with joy, proclaiming God's truth in public places, feeding and clothing the poor. In short, they *contribute to* their reconciliation both by unrelentingly holding God to account and by engaging in works of love. Human action in both of these cases is *intrinsic* to the reconciliatory dynamic, not prior to it (as in the case of confronting God) nor following from it (as in the case of undertaking works of love). But this last statement is a controversial one, lying at the heart of the problematic I engage.

Background of the Problem

In the history of Christian theology there has been much debate about the dynamics of divine and human action in the event of reconciliation.[7] Related arguments ensued between Augustine and Pelagius in the fifth century, Luther and Erasmus in the sixteenth century, and Barth and Brunner in the twentieth century. Typically the voices that have come to be identified with Protestant orthodoxy are those that argue against the capacity of human agents to exert influence in relation to God. The Reformed tradition, following in the tradition of John Calvin, consistently argues that God is the only subject in the event of revelation.[8] If God determines to reveal Godself, grace is irresistible. If God determines not to reveal, reconciliation does not occur. Either way, Calvin was not concerned with defending human agency. His theological energies were devoted to upholding the divine sovereignty, believing that knowledge of ourselves can come only via knowledge of God.

Since modernity, when (at least for the Western world) the importance of the human agent became the unnegotiable presumption, theologians have been dissatisfied with Calvin's articulation.[9] Schleiermacher—and Bultmann and Tillich following—argued that it is incoherent to think that one can engage the work of theology without attention to human experience, and human agency as integral to this experience. For Schleiermacher, "we know no one so well as Jesus" because Jesus is who we are.[10] We, like Jesus, can achieve God-consciousness by recognizing our absolute dependence on God. For Tillich, theology begins with consideration of culture. His method of correlation holds that the questions human beings ask lead us to encounter the divine answers, and therefore to conscious relationship with God. While both Schleiermacher and Tillich clearly recognize that—ontologically speaking—God's existence precedes our subjective recognition of our relationship to God, they insist that humanity's recognition of its dependence on or acceptance by the infinite is not simply an epistemological matter. Rather, our experience of relationship to God, our asking the questions that lead us to recognize it's character, and our exercising of our agency all *contribute to* our reconciliation.

I argue, though others might disagree, that though Barth insisted that human subjects act (or ask) only in response to the actions (or answers) of the divine Subject, it is nonetheless the case that he—like Schleiermacher and Tillich—insisted that human actions contribute to the divine/human relationship. While clearly the objective reality of God's reconciliatory work in the event of Jesus Christ[11] is accomplished, for Barth, with or without humanity's subjective appropriation of it,[12] our subjective recognition of what God has done with us and for us makes an objective contribution to the reality itself. We are "genuine partners with God," Barth notes, because God has determined, in the person of the fully human, fully divine One, to include humanity as a player in the dynamics of reconciliation.[13] In other words, if we do not recognize the reality of God's forgiveness and love, reconciliation is also *not* accomplished; our recognition of God's completed work (which, I would argue, is an exercise of our agency) then actually contributes something to that which has already been accomplished even without our recognition of it. We are the elect and the righteous; we are becoming the elect and righteous. And the fact that we are the elect and righteous is precisely what makes it possible for us to contribute to our election and sanctification as free, uncoerced, acting subjects.

Perhaps a human analogy, albeit limited, can help with this point. Imagine that one person loves another, but that the beloved does not recognize this love nor respond to it. Imagine that the lover's love is steadfast—it is not dissipated by this lack of recognition. Imagine, though, the dynamic that occurs when the beloved does recognize the love of the lover, and so responds by returning love. Does not the return of love actually contribute something to the love of the lover, to the character of the love that could not have been removed by a lack of recognition, nor even by the rejection of the beloved? Isn't it true *both* that the lover's love is complete and that it is not, apart from the beloved's response to it? And is it not the unconditionality of the lover's love that frees the lover to love freely?

I will now briefly explain the relation of substitution and representation in relation to this discussion, turning to Psalms 22 and 51 to deepen my understanding.

Substitution and Representation

Closely related to the question of the relationship between divine and human agency is that of the substitutionary and representational

offices of Jesus Christ. The substitutionary view of atonement, probably the most prevalent theory of atonement in mainline as well as in
"nondenominational" churches in North America, was articulated by
Anselm in the eleventh century. According to Anselm, the righteous
God cannot act in a way that is inconsistent with God's character, and
so turns away from sinful human beings. But God also desires to be in
relationship to us, and so finds a way to "satisfy" God's honor. Because
the debt to God is accrued by a human being, a human being must pay
the debt. But because human beings are sinful, they are incapable of
paying the debt. God became human in Jesus Christ in order to pay the
debt owed by human beings. Because Jesus Christ was sinless, he himself owed no debt to God. In dying in the place of others as a sinless
human being, Jesus Christ therefore earned a "reward" from the Father.
Not needing the reward for himself, the Son gave the recompense back
to the Father in order to satisfy God's honor in relation to human sinfulness.[14] Our salvation, then, is the recompense paid by the Father to
the sinless Son who took our place on the cross.

Many theologians have taken issue with the Anselmian view. Already in the twelfth century, Anselm was being critiqued for not considering that God could simply forgive, without any requirement for
recompense.[15] Today, feminist theologians are among those concerned
that appropriations of Anselm's theory that emphasize the Father
sending the Son to die tend to portray God as a divine child abuser.[16]
But a third criticism most concerns us here, a criticism that focuses
not on better understanding the character of God, but on honoring
the integrity of human beings. The relevant question is this: if Jesus
Christ takes our place on the cross, what happens to us? Dorothee
Sölle, noteably, has argued that substitutionary atonement results in
the *replacement* of the human agent by Jesus Christ.[17] We are, essentially, eliminated from the reconciliatory dynamic. Freed from penalty,
perhaps, but incapacitated in the process. What kind of reconciliation
is this?

Sölle argues that a more adequate understanding of atonement theory is representational. Following Abélard (a twelfth-century critic of
Anselm), Sölle argues that Jesus Christ does not "replace" us in the reconciliatory dynamic, but rather "holds our place." While a substitute
renders us unnecessary (and, Sölle implies, ultimately worthless), a representative who acts in our stead *until we can act again* affirms our
value as human agents. Sölle's understanding of Jesus Christ's representative work is reminiscent of the Hebrews'[12] image that Jesus Christ

is the one who goes ahead of us, as the "Author and Perfector of our Faith," clearing a space for us so that we, too, can run (vv. 1-2).[18]

Theologians who are concerned with upholding the integrity of the human agent have often, like Sölle, developed representational views. But these views have also not gone uncriticized. On the side of those who advocate for substitutional understandings, there is raised concern that representation both disrespects the divine sovereignty and burdens human beings with responsibilities we cannot always fulfill. Are there not times where, try as we might, we cannot follow the pioneer? When "clearing a space" for us is not enough? When we need to be carried?

It is unfortunate, in my view, when we establish unnecessary either/ors that prevent us from exploring the richness of our relation to God and one another. Why do we have to choose between substitution and representation, between divine sovereignty and human agency? Psalms 22 and 51 contribute to the argument that these are false dichotomies, suggesting ways in which they work in tandem.

Turning to the Psalms[19]

Both "substitution" and "representation" are meant to describe the character of actions taken on our behalf. In the Old Testament the suffering servant, the prophets in general, and specific figures including Moses, Samuel, and Esther acted on behalf of their people, suffering the consequences for their sins,[20] advocating for their just treatment,[21] and/or leading them into life-affirming action.[22] In the New Testament the primary figure who acts for us is Jesus Christ, although it is clear in Acts and in the Pauline epistles that we, being conformed to the image of Christ, are to act on behalf of one another.[23]

Who acts on behalf of the psalmists? The answer, of course, is God. But it is also the psalmists themselves. In Psalm 22 and Psalm 51, God intervenes in a way that delivers the psalmists from their suffering/guilt without removing them from their position as agents in relation to their lives. The work of redemption is all God's doing (the psalmists are helpless; relying on God) and—simultaneously—also the doing of the psalmists (who lament, praise, hold God to account, and engage in works of love). I move, now, to further unpacking this thesis—for it offers insight into how we may understand the dynamics of the divine/human relationship without compromising either on the divine sovereignty or on the integrity of the human agent.

The theology reflected in Psalms 22 and 51 does not portray the relationship of the divine and human agency only as a matter of divine action and human response. Rather, the human agent's cry for divine intervention is intrinsic to his or her deliverance; the songs of praise and re-engagement of life as testifiers to the presence of God are not only humans responding to what God has done, but precisely what God is doing. The psalms bear witness to the fact that we are not *replaced* in the *displacement* of our victimization/sinfulness. Similarly, in the praise to the God who has delivered, or lament to the One who has not, it is not only we who have a place, but God who is at work in and through us.

Double agency is present in Psalms 22 and 51 in the psalmists' plea that God deliver them from suffering/guilt. In both of these Psalms, the psalmists are yearning for a restoration of intimacy between themselves and God. Both experience distance from God, the writer of Psalm 22 because God has not responded to her request for deliverance from the enemy; the writer of Psalm 51 because he has sinned against God. "On you I was cast from my birth," the author of Psalm 22 remembers, begging her God: "do not be far from me" (22:11). The psalmist is desperate that the intimacy between herself and God be restored; her cry for deliverance from the enemy is simultaneously a cry for God to be near her. In Psalm 51, similarly, the psalmist wants the "joy of God's salvation . . . to be restored" (v. 12) via the restitution of intimate relationship with God. "Do not cast me away from your presence," the psalmist begs, "and do not take your holy spirit from me" (v. 11).

The intervention of God, seen clearly in 22:21 and anticipated in 51:13 (where there is indication of a "before" cleansing and the psalmist's role as teacher "after") occurs in direct relationship to the psalmists' pleading. "Save me!" the psalmist cries in 22:20. "Restore me!" the psalmist demands in 51:12. The psalmists yearn for the removal of the divine distance.[24] They know that God is not only transcendent in relation to the creation, but also immanent.[25] And the psalms imply that God acts and will act because the psalmists have requested such action as those who live in covenantal relationship to God. In their incapacity to deliver themselves from victimization/guilt, they are far from passive. There is even a sense in which they *initiate* their deliverance, founding it in an appeal to the history of their relationship with God. The God who initiated covenant relationship with them, the God who has been near to them (22:9-10; 51:12) is being called upon to again draw close.

The psalms invoke no suspicion on the part of the reader that God would have delivered the psalmists apart from their requests. The psalmists, unable to deliver themselves, are delivered only through the action of God, who responds (and, in 51, who will respond) to their cries. They can do nothing but plead and confess, but this testimony to their incapacity to act, and to God's capacity to save/restore, is itself active. There is a sense, then, in which the psalmists' pleas are initiating divine action and simultaneously responding to the divine initiative taken in establishing covenant relationship with God's people. The Tillichian/Barthian debate over whether human questions precede divine answers or divine answers human questions here seems woefully ill-equipped for the task of appreciating the nuanced relationship—the "dialectical dance,"[26] if you will—between the divine agent and the human one. The psalmists are not interested in discerning whether God or human beings acted first, but in advocating for full participation of both God and human beings in the work of life.

If human agency is operative in the divine delivery of the psalmists, God is acting in the psalmists' activities post-deliverance. The psalmist of Psalm 22 moves dramatically from identifying herself as a person who has been victimized (vv. 14ff.) to recognizing herself as a congregational leader (vv. 22, 25); from complaining that she is poor and hungry (vv. 17-18) to proclaiming that the poor will be fed (v. 26). The psalmist of Psalm 51 begs for restoration in one breath and makes the audacious claim that he will "teach transgressors their ways" in the next (vv. 12-13). The descriptions of both psalmists' activities post-deliverance are grounded in the affirmation that God is *not* distant (22:24), that God forgives sins and does not cast us away when we are sinful (51:9, 11). God is immanent; present and active in and through the psalmists' activities. The praise of the Lord by human beings presumes a recognition that God does act; it is those who "fear the Lord" that praise God (22:22-23). It is the Lord who "opens the lips" of the restored one, and simultaneously the restored human being who "declares God's praise" (51:15).

The One Work of Reconciliation

Given the argument that human agency is active in the psalmists' pleas early in the psalms, it is problematic to refer to what happens between 22:21a and 21b, and what presumably will happen in 51:12, solely as God's action. Similarly, given the contention that God is present and at work in and through the psalmists' post-deliverance activities, the psalmist's activities in 11:21bff and in 51:13-19 are not simply human responses to divine action. "Responses to" can mislead us to think that the psalmists are not actively involved in the delivering work of God, and that God is not fully present and working in the restored activities of the psalmists. Similarly, I wonder if the categories "psalm of lament" and "psalm of praise,"[27] while helpful in describing the distinctive strands of the one psalm (e.g., 22, 51) can and have been used to separate sections of the psalm out from one another in ways that compromise on their theological unity and dialectical content. If we imagine God's action as falling into a "space" between the human actions of lament and praise, are we not compromising on the integrity of both divine and human agents? Reconciliation is then understood to be little more than an exchange between contracting parties, rather than a joining together in covenant commitment.

Ultimately, to separate the lament from the praise is to resist participation in the mystery of the divine/human relationship. This relationship, in Psalms 22 and 51, is characterized not by God acting in response to our cries and then us responding to God's acting, but on God and human agents acting *together* in the one work of reconciliation. To separate God's agency from human agency is to deny a message that lies at the heart of these psalms: that God does not sit at a distance from us, but is with us in our suffering and in our praise. Psalms 22 and 51 testify to the mystery of double agency—the basis upon which we address Jesus Christ as both Savior and brother, entering—as creatures—into partnership with the God who has saved us.

Sacrifice, Vows, and Double Agency

The way in which "sacrifice" and "vows" function in each of these psalms helps further to clarify how divine agency and human agency are related. In Psalm 22, the psalmist, celebrating his deliverance, makes vows to God in the "great congregation" (v. 25). These vows—which probably included sacrifices[28]—are part of the active way the psalmist relates to the people around him and to the God who is, indeed, near him. Making sacrifices to God is simultaneously a way both of acknowledging God's agency and participating as a human agent in the divine work. While in atonement theory "sacrifice" is often associated with that which remedies the action of human beings, compensating for their misdeeds and inadequacies,[29] the "vows" of Psalm 22 and the "sacrifices" of Psalm 51 are, rather, human acts that visibly manifest the reality of the divine/human reconciliation.

The understanding of sacrifice portrayed in Psalm 51 displays double agency especially clearly. The psalmist is so aware that what God wants from him is his active engagement that he forswears burnt offerings in verse 16. "For you have no delight in sacrifice;" he declares, "if I were to give a burnt offering, you would not be pleased." Instead, the psalmist indicates that God cares about his spiritual condition as a sinful subject existing in relation to God. God does not want a "sacrifice" to take the place of a "broken and contrite heart." God is not looking for a payment for the psalmist's debt, or a means to satisfy God's honor. God is looking for signs that the psalmist is aware of God's presence with him,[30] in active relation to God, repentant for the ways he has acted against relationship. At the end of the psalm, a verse (18) was later added that insisted again on the importance of "burnt offerings and whole burnt offerings" as good works of God's people.[31] Finally, sacrifice—burnt offerings, *substitutionary* sacrifices—*is* important to the dynamics of reconciliation between the divine and the human. But such sacrifice, when "right" sacrifice, still involves the heart as well as the knife, fire, and economic loss.[32] Substitution, here, is efficacious precisely because it is accomplished within the broader context of representation.

There is one other connection to "sacrifice" that cannot go without mention, for it leads directly back to consideration of what these psalms contribute to discussion of atonement theory. Psalm 22 is commonly associated with Jesus Christ's sacrifice on our behalf, for Jesus cited the first verse right before dying on the cross (Matt 27:46). And yet the psalmist is not Jesus, not a sacrifice that is made for anyone. How do I know this? Because, unlike Jesus, the psalmist is rescued from death, and Jesus is not. Because unlike Jesus, the psalmist offers God vows rather than his own life. If Jesus is asking the Father for a substitute in the Garden of Gethsemane the night before, even as Abraham trusted God to provide a burnt offering and the psalmists trusted God to help, it is Jesus' prayers that are not heard. Jesus died as a victim who God did not rescue from "the mouth of the lion" (22:21).

Setting Psalm 22 in conversation with Jesus' cry of forsakenness leads one to wonder why Jesus was not saved from death and the psalmist was. The presence of God is confirmed for the psalmist, but the presence of the Father is in question at the end of Jesus' life. In setting Psalm 22 and Matt 27:46 in conversation—and asking: where *is* substitution in Psalm 22?—Christians might consider that it is, in fact, God in Jesus Christ who has taken the burden of oppression upon himself so that human beings can find deliverance. From the perspective of eternity, it is the sacrifice of

Jesus Christ on the cross that "saves" the psalmist between 21a and 21b, making it possible for the psalmist to act in vv. 21ff.[33]

The Constructive Argument

While the psalms reveal two acting subjects—the divine and the human—in relation to reconciliation, what does their portrayal of double agency have to contribute to our understanding of atonement theory? In saying that the human is involved in God's work of deliverance and that God is active and at work in the psalmist's response to deliverance, what resources do we have for better understanding the work of Jesus Christ?

First, consideration of Psalms 22 and Psalm 51 clearly does not support the rejection of substitutionary atonement. The unmitigated distress of the psalmists calling upon God to alter their circumstances reflects the incapacity of human beings to save themselves. They need to be delivered by another. While the psalmists certainly exercise agency in soliciting divine action, and while their laments indeed precipitate God's intervening work and are therefore essential to the reconciliatory dynamic, it is by no means the case that the psalmists have the power to remedy their circumstances. There *is* something that "replaces" the victimized psalmist and the guilty psalmist in relation to their victimization and their guilt. The psalmist's victimization is abruptly and definitely removed in verse 22:21. The psalmist anticipates that his guilt will be taken away—to the point where he will "teach transgressors"—by the divine work of restoration (51:13). Replacement is demanded, and it occurs.

But what is it, exactly, that is replaced? Sölle is concerned that, if substitution is the route to reconciliation, reconciliation will not actually occur between God and the person who needs to be reconciled, but only between God and the substitute. Following a strictly Anselmian view, Sölle thinks, we cannot be reconciled by One who dies in our place because at that point we are no longer participating in the divine/human dynamic. We have been replaced. We are unable to act in a way that makes a difference. In a culture which assesses value on the basis of productivity, Sölle adds, replaced persons are worthless.

Psalms 22 and 51 offer resources for developing an approach to substitution that resists the replacement of the individual, and in fact upholds the individual as "irreplaceable."[34] Again, it is clear that the psalmist—as a human being in relationship to God—is anything but replaced by the action of God. The psalmists seem, in fact, to be restored *as* active subjects who are *more* themselves than they were before the divine deliverance, before God acted in relation to their incapacitation. I ask myself, then: what understanding of substitutionary theory is consistent with this?

I propose that attention to the dynamics of Psalm 22 and Psalm 51 supports the understanding that the psalmists *are* replaced, but not in relationship to who they actually are as covenant partners with God. No—it is not the psalmists as such who are replaced, but the *Victim* and the *Sinner* who are replaced precisely so the psalmists can be free to again live in conscious awareness of God's active presence with them.[35] We in our incapacitation are replaced in order to make a place for we who are capable human beings created in relationship to our Creator-God.

It is here, then, that representation comes into play. Substitution alone, traditionally speaking, indicates what it is, exactly, that we are saved *from*. But Psalms 22 and 51 are clear that God acts in relationship to us not only to save us *from* something, but also *for* something. If Psalm 22 ended after verse 21a, and Psalm 51 after verse 12, reconciliation would be incomplete. We would not witness the deliverance of God, which is made manifest in the teaching and praising, the eating and worshiping, the vows and the sacrifices of the human agent. The psalmist claims not only to be "rescued . . . from the horns of the wild oxen" (22:21) but also to go forward and "live for God" (22:29). "I shall live for him." Substitutionary atonement alone—the healing of victimization and sinfulness—does not adequately account for this living of abundant life. The deliverance of the psalmists does not result in quiet thankfulness, happy withdrawal from the world whose burden has been removed. How do we account for the engagement with life—for what we are delivered *for*?

Karl Barth, in his "Doctrine of Reconciliation," explains that Jesus Christ is our substitute precisely so we are free to engage in "other more important and more happy and more fruitful activities" than being caught up in our own self-judgment.[36] (Perhaps he had been reading Psalm 51 before writing this!) The idea is not that God releases us from our burdens so we can act on our own, but that God delivers us *from* that which is incapacitating us *for* active partnership with God. Christologically speaking, Jesus Christ substitutes for us in relation to victimization and sin and represents us in relation to our partnership with God in the ministry of reconciliation. Jesus Christ not only dies on the cross as our Substitute, but lives abundantly as our Representative, exalting us in his resurrection to participation in the very life of God. The life-embracing, God-praising, message-sharing activity of the delivered psalmists is the realization of our true humanity that we experience in covenantal relationship to God through the redemptive work of our Representative, Jesus Christ.

In their beautiful portrayal of double agency as essential to the dynamics of reconciliation, then, Psalms 22 and 51 offer rich resources for reflecting on atonement theory in ways that work to incorporate the human agent as well as the divine agent without compromising on either divine sovereignty or on human responsibility. God, indeed "does it all": delivering us from the oppressor, cleansing us from our sins, acting in and through us in our lives. But we are also actors. In our incapacitation, we cry out for help in the hope that God will deliver. Once delivered, we do not withdraw thankfully into the background, happy that we have been replaced. Rather, filled with the spirit of God, we take our place in relationship to God and continue in the work of reconciliation.

A solely substitutionary view, focused only on replacing us in order to save us *from*, would compromise on the latter verses of these beautiful psalms. A representational view alone, focused only on holding our place and encouraging us to act as agents, would leave us stuck in our incapacity, without deliverance. For we cannot save ourselves in relationship to guilt or victimization. We need God's intervention. We need God to substitute for us precisely so we will have a place in relationship to life.

Conclusion/Implications

Contemporary approaches to the atonement that are attentive to the integration of substitutionary and representational theory, as reflected in Psalms 22 and 51, can make an important contribution to theological discussions in the twenty-first-century North American context for at least three major reasons. First, they will help bridge the rifts between subgroups of Christendom that hold to *either* substitution or representation, either to divine agency or human agency, either to being saved "from" something or saved "for" something. Second, to hold substitution and representation together in our understanding of atonement is faithful to the revelation of God's multifaceted character, as we read about it in the Scriptures. Third, given that human creatures, descriptively, are both incapable of acting to their advantage and creative agents of their lives, a thick approach to atonement is more adequate for addressing their actual life situations. Let me discuss these three points in turn.

As I mentioned in the beginning of this essay, it is not uncommon, in the history of Christendom, for those who espouse an Abélardian view and those who hold to an Anselmian view to be at odds with one another. The weakness of representation is that it errs on the side of works righteousness; the weakness of substitution is that it has been used to justify violence and minimize human responsibility. In my view, both of these critiques must be addressed. As I have discussed, representation promotes human action but has no resources to tackle the dilemma of human incapacity.[37] Substitution, on the other hand, delivers the incapacitated sinner from guilt and penalty, but has no place for the human agent.

Because of the weakness of a solely-representational understanding, proponents of substitution have often rejected liberationist theologies that tend toward a more representational view. With the intention of avoiding works righteousness, advocates of substitutionary theory do not hold that "liberation," understood as behavioral transformation, is "required" for salvation. But the debate over such a requirement is misplaced, from the standpoint of the psalms, because it presumes that changed behavior is something *other than* reconciliation; something that *follows from* God's atoning work. According to the psalmists, the point is not that our works are required in response to God, but that God works to reconcile us in and through our reconciliatory works. Unlike the God of a solely-substitutionary view, the God who delivers does not remain at a distance, taking our place as we watch, gratefully, from the sidelines. Rather, the God who we praise is present when the poor are eating their fill and when "all the families of the nations" are worshiping together (cf. 22:26-27). Attention to representation, as reflected in these psalms, can therefore free substitutionalists from feeling caught between works righteousness and complacency, opening them to consideration of the liberationists' concerns.

Proponents of representation, similarly, can benefit from substitutionary understandings that promote human agency. Feminist theologians are among those who reject substitutionary theory because it is commonly associated with an abdication of responsibility and the minimization of human agency. While the promotion of human agency and responsibility commends itself as long as human beings are relating appropriately, a problem emerges: what happens when we sin? What happens when we *cannot*, of our own energy, get past our jealousy, our hatred, our insecurities? A feminist representational understanding of the atonement that understands Christ as our Representative who substitutes for us when we cannot act—precisely so that we will be free to act again—is consistent with the feminist affirmation of the value of human agency without either leaving the human agent stranded or ignoring the classic Christian doctrine of the divine sovereignty. God may act in and through our actions, but God is not confined by our actions. In our incapacitation, our hope is that God acts where we cannot.

Second, I have tried to show here how an understanding of the atonement that incorporates both substitution and representation is consistent with the dynamics of the divine/human relationship offered in Psalms 22 and 51. I also believe that it is more consistent with the portrayal of Jesus Christ in the Gospels and the epistles. The cross lies at the center of Jesus Christ's redemptive work. And yet we would be mistaken to proceed as though Jesus Christ's redemptive work was accomplished all in one week (the Passion). His teachings, and struggles, and loving of life—his representation of us, culminating in the resurrection—show us what we are to live *for*. The Comforter has come, the Church is in place, the second coming lies ahead. Following the Author and Perfector of our faith, freed by his substitution from our incapacitation, the work of reconciliation continues.

Third, it is my hope that thick description of the dynamics of reconciliation, so helpfully modeled for us in Psalms 22 and 51, will lead to fresh reflection on the relevance of atonement theory to our lives of faith. Recently, a United Methodist minister wrote me a letter responding to an article I authored which suggests an integrated approach to soteriology that takes into account Anselmian, Abélardian, and *christus victor* [38] theories.[39] In indicating his appreciation for the article, the pastor gently alerted me to the fact that I did not seem to realize the direness of the situation: while I argued that we should cease "choosing" one atonement theory at the expense of the others, he explained that too many candidates for ordination cannot articulate *any* approach to atonement!

In my view this is probably not because seminary and divinity school programs have neglected the teaching of atonement, but because what students have learned does not immediately resonate with their experience of life in relationship to God. Being forced to choose between God's agency and our agency, descriptively, does not make a whole lot of sense. The psalmists model an honesty about their participation with God, God's participation with them, and a deep yearning to participate in the mystery of how they—and God—work together in realizing the world that God intends. Perhaps, in joining with them in refusing to simplify the dynamics of reconciliation, we can construct approaches to the atonement that reclaim both God's sovereign involvement and our real contribution, both God's acting for us and our acting with God.

NOTES: CHAPTER 12

[1] Maura A Ryan, "Agency," *Dictionary of Feminist Theologies*, Letty M. Russell and J. Shannon Clarkson, eds. (Louisville: Westminster John Knox Press, 1966).

[2] "Substitution" and "representation" will be described in greater detail below.

[3] Traditionally, Psalm 51 is ascribed to David, written after he had committed adultery with Bathsheba. So I will reference the voice of Psalm 51 with male pronouns. While it is unlikely, from an historical perspective, that any of the psalms were authored by a woman, the belief of the Christian community is that the Scriptures articulate the experience of women as well as men. To remind us of this, I use feminine pronouns in referring to the author of Psalm 22.

[4] As will become apparent, I am profoundly influenced by the work of Karl Barth (e.g., *CD* IV/2) and Dorothee Sölle (e.g., *Christ the Representative*) in the shaping of this question. To some degree I also have in mind Austin Farrar's attempts to articulate "double agency" (cf. *Finite and Infinite*) and John Wesley's insistence that both God and human beings are involved in the work of salvation (cf. sermons including "The Spirit of Bondage and Adoption," in Albert Outler, *John Wesley's Sermons*).

[5] "Double agency," as I use it here, is the idea that God and human beings work synchronically, without compromising on the subjectivity/agency of either.

[6] See David R. Blumenthal, *Facing the Abusing God: A Theology of Protest* (Louisville: Westminster/John Knox Press, 1993).

[7] By *reconciliation* I mean humans existing as creatures in relationship to the Creator God and vice versa. From the vantage point of the human side of the dialectic, I mean living consciously and conscientiously in the recognition of God's presence and God's acts with and for us.

[8] Barth (1886–1968) modified Calvin's position, arguing that indeed God is the only subject in the event of reconciliation. In a brilliant theological move, however, he began his systematic theology with the "Doctrine of the Word of God" rather than the "Doctrine of God," explaining that we know God primarily through God's revelation in Jesus Christ. And Jesus Christ—because he is fully human as well as fully divine—reveals that humanity is included in the divine/human reconciliatory work with no compromise to the divine subjectivity.

[9] For an interesting survey of some approaches taken to this matter since modernity, see Paul Lehmann's *Forgiveness: Decisive Issue in Protestant Thought* (Ann Arbor, Mich.: University Microfilms, Inc., 1963; first published in 1940).

[10] Martin Redeker, *Schleiermacher: Life and Thought* (Philadelphia: Fortress Press, 1973).

[11] Which, Reformed theologians argue, is an *eternal* reality—in effect, then, in relation to the psalmists. (Calvin argues, for example, that when "Abraham's faith is

counted to him as righteousness" Abraham is saved through the work of the one Word that became flesh in Jesus Christ.)

[12] A point that Tillich thought was moot—parallel, analogously, to the argument that a tree makes a loud sound in the forest even when no one is there. *The sound has no import for us unless we are there.*

[13] This last italicized phrase reflects the fundamental difference between Tillich and Barth's understanding of reconciliation. While both hold that the existence of God (which is ontologically prior) is revealed in the context of human experience (which is epistemologically prior), Barth is careful to insist that the ontological priority of God is reflected in the approach that we take to theology, epistemologically. Thus we look not to our experience in and of itself as a theological resource, but to our experience insofar as it has been exalted in the person of the one who is also ontologically prior, Jesus Christ. We look to Jesus Christ to see what true humanity is; because we share in humanity with him we are exalted to partnership with God.

[14] See Anselm, *Cur Deus Homo?* In *A Scholastic Miscellany: Anselm to Ockham,* Eugene R. Fairweather, ed. (Philadelphia: Westminster Press, 1956).

[15] See Peter Abélard, "Exposition of the Epistle to the Romans (An Excerpt from the Second Book), *A Scholastic Miscellany,* Fairweather, ed. 276–87.

[16] See, for example, *Christianity, Patriarchy, and Abuse,* Joanne Carlson Brown and Carol Bohn, eds. (Cleveland: The Pilgrim Press, 1989).

[17] See Dorothee Sölle, *Christ The Representative: An Essay in Theology after the 'Death of God'* (London: SCM Press Ltd., 1967).

[18] Emily Dickinson picks up on this idea beautifully in a poem in which she refers to Jesus as our "Tender Pioneer," where she writes: "Life-is what we make it-Death-We do not know-Christ's acquaintance with Him-Justify Him-though/He-would trust no Stranger-Other-could betray-Just His own endorsement-That sufficeth Me/ All the other Distance He hath traversed first-No New Mile remaineth-Far as Paradise/ His sure foot preceding-Tender Pioneer-Base must be the Coward-Dare not venture-now- [poem #698, in Dorothy Huff Oberhaus, "'Tender Pioneer': Emily Dickinson's Poems on the Life of Christ," in *American Literature* 59:3 (October 1987) 341–58].

[19] Note: biblical references follow the English versification; citations are taken from the NRSV.

[20] As in the case of the Suffering Servant (see, for example, Isaiah 53).

[21] As in the case of Esther, who was called to take risks for the sake of her people.

[22] As in the case of Moses, Aaron, and Miriam in relation to the nation of Israel.

[23] See, for example, Eph 5:21, Phil 2:1-11, Pet 4:10.

[24] This point is made in relation to Psalm 22 in the Peter C. Craigie, *Psalms 1–50.* WBC (Waco, Tex.: Word Books, 1983) 200.

[25] This simple chart shows how the psalmists' concerns regarding the restoration of the divine immanence are related to other central concerns framing this essay:

divine transcendence	divine immanence
humans contribute to God's action	God undergirds human action
substitution (Anselmian emphasis)	representation (Abélardian emphasis)

[26] This is a metaphor used by Barth in *CD* III/4, §54, to describe the relationship between a man and a woman. According to Barth's theological anthropology, man and woman are both question and answer in relation to one another. In encountering a member of the opposite sex, we ask: "who is this one, who is so different from me?" In entering into fellowship with this other, we together reflect the image of God.

[27] For an important study of the distinction and relationship between Psalms of Lament and Psalms of Praise, see Claus Westermann, *Praise and Lament in the Psalms* (Atlanta: John Knox Press, 1981).

[28] Patrick Miller makes reference to the sacrifices that are "brought" in relationship to the offering of vows (v. 25), indicating that they become the meal that satisfies the poor in v. 26. See *Interpreting the Psalms* (Philadelphia: Fortress Press, 1986) 108.

[29] It is in fact the case, according to T. H. Gastor's account in *The Interpreter's Dictionary of the Bible*, that the Old Testament understanding of "the scapegoat" was "representational, not substitutional." Gastor writes: ". . . the scapegoat was not, as modern parlance would suggest, something to which one shifted the blame for one's own transgressions and which was made to pay the price of them. On the contrary, it was a means of removing from the community the taint of sins which had first to be fully and openly confessed. What it removed, therefore, was *miasma*, not responsibility" ["Sacrifices," *Interpreter's Dictionary of the Bible* (Nashville: Abingdon Press) 147–59, 153].

[30] "The 'broken spirit' and 'contrite heart'. . . describe the condition of profound contrition and awe experienced by a sinful person who becomes aware of the divine presence" Marvin E. Tate, *Psalms 51–100* WBC 20 (Dallas: Word Books, 1990) 28.

[31] Ibid., 29.

[32] Miller notes that vv. 16-17 and 18-19 should then not be interpreted as contradicting one another. Rather, their "juxtaposition . . . serve[s] to identify the intimate relation between the spirit of contrition and the actual sacrifices to God" [Patrick Miller, *They Cried To the Lord: The Form and Theology of Biblical Prayer* (Minneapolis: Fortress Press, 1994) 255].

[33] By this argument, we do not read vv. 21 ff. only as prophecy to Jesus Christ's resurrection from death (as many commentators do), but as testimony to the fact that Jesus Christ's substitution on the cross frees us to be exalted with him in his resurrection *in this life* as well as in the life to come. Again, it must be emphasized that the psalmist *does not die* as Jesus does, but is rescued from death for life.

[34] Sölle's term.

[35] Note that, in this understanding, substitutionary atonement makes provision not only for the perpetrator of abuse (the "sinner"), but also for the victim (who God delivers from abuse). This is *contra* the usual understanding of substitutionary atonement, which makes provision for the sinner but not the victim of the sin.

[36] Karl Barth, *The Church Dogmatics*, IV/1, 13 vols. (Edinburgh: T & T Clark, 1936–1969) 234.

[37] It does have the resources to challenge those who *think* they cannot act, but who actually can, to do so.

[38] *Christus victor* is an approach to the atonement that I do not consider in this essay.

[39] See "Are You Saved?," *Insights* 115:2 (Austin, Texas: Austin Presbyterian Theological Seminary, Spring 2000) 3–18.

13

The Cursing Psalms as a Source of Blessing

Larry Silva

*I*n April, 1992, a verdict is announced that acquits white police officers, whose beating of an African-American man was videotaped and broadcast throughout the world. A riot ignites on the streets of East Los Angeles, bringing even more misery to an already depressed and struggling area.

In April, 1998, a bishop in Guatemala is bludgeoned in the garage of his rectory less than two weeks after he delivers a scathing report implicating the military in the deaths of over 160,000 peasants in that country's decades-old civil disturbances. The Pope sends a message of condolence and expresses his outrage at the killing. All who mourn the death of this bishop do so with both anger and fear.

A woman lives in misery for decades because her father repeatedly molested her sexually between the ages of five and ten. The horror of admitting such despicable deeds to her family or even to herself, the hurt that no one—not even God—saved her from these molestations, and the fear that any other man could treat her the same way have all served as bars in a prison of self-hatred and dysfunctional living.

We are painfully aware that the incidents cited above are neither imaginary nor rare. The stories of oppression and violence experienced day in and day out by so many people in all parts of the world form a terrible litany. In the face of such scenes as those recounted above, the human heart bursts with anger and perhaps even hatred of the enemy, whether the enemy is known or unknown. To believe in a God who cares about those who are oppressed or who are the victims of violence may be, for many, the only glimmer of hope. When one can defend oneself, one does so. But when the enemy is too powerful or too nebulous, the natural tendency is to turn to someone with a greater power and a keener eye. The Scriptures, in which God's relations with humanity are recalled as a sacred and living memory, offer a basis for a spirituality of liberation from oppression and injustice. Perhaps the most powerful examples of this spirituality are the prayers of lament. The Scriptures are the Word of God, and it is in them that we find words of wisdom, strength, and guidance as we reflect upon our ethical response to oppression and injustice. But, as Robert McAfee Brown pointed out so well in his book on the Bible in liberation theology, *Unexpected News*, God's ways are sometimes shockingly surprising to us. One shocking surprise is the presence of cursing in the midst of the Scriptures that otherwise portray a God who is slow to anger and rich in mercy.

It can be well demonstrated from the Hebrew and Christian Scriptures that peace is the ideal of God for humanity. God is perennially portrayed in the Bible as forgiving those who turn away from God, never tiring of taking back into good graces those who are unfaithful yet repent. Yet in neither Testament is God portrayed as effete. God's exercise of power may be shockingly surprising either in its wrath or its meekness, but it is a power exercised passionately for the good of humanity and the glory of God's name.

Within our biblical tradition there are resources that can be employed by oppressed peoples to express the real rage they feel in the face of injustice and thus be exorcized of the demonic power of that rage. Perhaps discovering these resources and taking the risk of using them is one contribution we can make to the process of bringing greater justice and healing to the world.

The imprecatory, or cursing, psalms (particularly Psalms 58, 83, 109, and parts of others) are often a source of embarrassment to Christians and other people of good will. The vitriolic language against enemies seems to directly contradict the mandate of Jesus to love the enemy and to turn the other cheek. These psalms are not used in the Roman Catholic liturgy, for example, "because of their unfavorable psychological impact."[1] Yet they have been preserved in the Jewish and Christian canons of Sacred Scripture for centuries. Why? How can such texts be considered the Word of the God, who is Love, who calls us to reconciliation, and who teaches us to love our enemies?

Praying an imprecatory psalm may seem contradictory to the spirit and the ethics presented to us in the Bible, especially, we often presume, in the New Testament. Nevertheless, while they are not the first word or the last word, these psalms are indeed the inspired Word of God. Praying them in the midst of the anger and rage that come from oppression can serve to have a favorable psychological impact on the person or the community, if they are prayed in the context of the whole message of the Bible. The imprecatory psalms are God's wonderful way of recognizing that our human struggles are not always pretty and involve many negative feelings. God-with-us does not want us to ignore these feelings of anger, rage, or vengeance, nor to pretend that those who have faith in God are above such feelings. The covenant relationship of God with humankind demands such an openness and honesty that no such prevarication is tolerated. Indeed these uncomfortable words have more than a cathartic effect and may very well serve as an impetus for change of the oppressive situation.

Referring to both Testaments of the Bible, Jürgen Moltmann states: "Christian theology must be biblical theology. In the Bible we encounter the remembrance of hope, which is both liberating and dangerous."[2]

Dangerous indeed! The words are inflammatory and run the risk of stirring up violent action. But as authors such as Walter Brueggemann and Erich Zenger point out, it is perhaps more risky to exclude imprecation from our prayer vocabulary, for then prayer can lose touch with the realities of injustice and social evil. If the imprecations are used properly, recognizing that they are only a part of the complex message of the Bible and are not the last word, they can release an energy in the community that can give it courage in the midst of struggle and a sense that God understands even their darkest and most dangerous emotions—and can transform them into the true love of enemies in the achievement of justice. It is in risking the use of the passionate language of lament that the prophetic mission of resisting injustice and oppression can be fueled. Once the dark side of the struggle for liberation from enemies is fully recognized and brought to light, there is greater hope for the victory of light over darkness and freedom over oppression.

Walter Brueggemann, in his book *The Prophetic Imagination*, states: "The prophets understood the possibility of change as linked to emotional extremities of life. They understood the strange congruence between public conviction and personal yearning. Most of all, they understood the distinctive power of language, the capacity to speak in ways that evoke newness 'fresh from the word.'"[3]

There is the popular notion, based on a selective reading of New Testament texts, that righteous wrath and imprecations are confined to

the Old Testament and that the Christian gospels have forever precluded the followers of Jesus from engaging in imprecatory fantasies,
much less imprecatory prayers. It is presumed that images of divine or
human wrath against enemies is pre-Christian, un-Christian or less
than Christian. Lest we think that volatile language is confined to the
Old Testament or that the New Testament always calls for a more gentle
approach, let us look at the following words of Jesus himself in
Matthew, the same Gospel in which Jesus says, "Love your enemies,"
and "If anyone strikes you on the right cheek, turn the other also." They
show us that imprecation and righteous wrath are very much a part of
the New Testament's language:

> —"If anyone will not welcome you or listen to your words, shake off the
> dust from your feet as you leave that house or town. Truly I tell you, it
> will be more tolerable for the land of Sodom and Gomorrah on the day
> of judgment than for that town" (10:14-15).
> —"And you, Capernaum, will you be exalted to heaven? No, you will be
> brought down to Hades" (11:23).
> —"You hypocrites!" (15:7)
> —"He turned and said to Peter, 'Get behind me, Satan!'" (16:23)
> —"If any of you put a stumbling block before one of these little ones who
> believe in me, it would be better for you if a great millstone were fastened
> around your neck and you were drowned in the depth of the sea" (18:6).
> —The scene of the Cleansing of the Temple (21:12-13).
> —The scene of the Cursing of the Fig Tree (21:18ff).
> —The series of Jesus' "Woe to you" sayings (23:13ff).
> —"Then he will say to those at his left hand, 'You that are accursed, depart
> from me into the eternal fire prepared for the devil and his angels" (25:41).

Thus we see that imprecation was a part of the vocabulary of the
very one who spoke of peace, forgiveness and love of the enemy. Jesus'
imprecatory sayings were meant to be instructive, to call for radical
change in the ways of those who heard him.

With this positive understanding of the imprecatory psalms as blessings in disguise, let us examine two of them, Psalm 58 and Psalm 109:

Psalm 58 (NRSV)

To the leader: Do Not Destroy.
Of David. A Mik'tam.
  1 Do you indeed decree what is right, you gods?
     Do you judge people fairly?

2 No, in your hearts you devise wrongs;
  your hands deal out violence on earth.
3 The wicked go astray from the womb;
  they err from their birth, speaking lies.
4 They have venom like the venom of a serpent,
  like the deaf adder that stops its ear,
5 so that it does not hear the voice of charmers
  or of the cunning enchanter.
6 O God, break the teeth in their mouths;
  tear out the fangs of the young lions, O LORD!
7 Let them vanish like water that runs away;
  like grass let them be trodden down and wither.
8 Let them be like the snail that dissolves into slime;
  like the untimely birth that never sees the sun.
9 Sooner than your pots can feel the heat of thorns,
  whether green or ablaze, may he sweep them away!
10 The righteous will rejoice when they see vengeance done;
   they will bathe their feet in the blood of the wicked.
11 People will say, "Surely there is a reward for the righteous;
   surely there is a God who judges on earth."

Reflections on Psalm 58

The first item that can easily escape our attention is the superscript, especially the admonition "Do Not Destroy." This may already be a hint that the violence advocated in the psalm is not truly for the purpose of destruction but for instructive purposes, perhaps to rouse the conscience of the community praying the psalm. Gerstenberger says:

> The educative intent of Psalm 58 makes it an INSTRUCTION of the early Jewish community. . . . The ceremony that brought such edifying, comforting, hopeful discourse was that of a volunteer or confessional group intent on fighting for its own rights in the face of powerful counterforces and ready to sustain it with Yahweh's help. Separation from the ungodly in its own ranks proved necessary at this point.[4]
> By cursing the oppressors and their gods, the text actually proceeds to dismantle the oppressive opposition of nonbelievers.[5]

Verse 1 may be addressed to false gods whose worshipers allow them to usurp the rightful place of the LORD, or, if we follow the translation from the New American Bible, "you men of rank," the address could be a sarcastic reference to these "men of rank" who have made themselves gods. Whether they are heavenly gods or earthly "gods," they are negatively affecting life on the earth (v. 2). The image of the first two verses, which are addressed to these "gods," is of shaking one's fist at them in indignation. This is a daring deed, whether they be "men of rank" or heavenly powers.

The venom of verse 4 is a familiar reality to the psalmist, since the venomous nature of verses 6-9 is quite strong. Verse 5 may refer to prophets as "charmers" or to God's own self as the "cunning enchanter," since these wicked people are deaf to the efforts of both to "charm" them back to the right path.

Verses 7-9 are addressed directly to God in the form of curses. They wish grave harm on the enemies. These enemies seem powerful, given the references to teeth, lions and arrows, yet they are presumed to be no match for the power of God. The images of "water flowing off," of slime, of a still-born child, and of wind sweeping them away all conjure up an image of total weakness and helplessness before the power of God. The contrast of these images with the images of strength and power serve as a promise of hope to people who have physical evidence that should otherwise cause them to despair, for God is stronger than their enemies, and they expect vindication from God.

Verse 11 is a subtle reminder to God that God is the primary protector of justice. It is God who takes vengeance, but the just will rejoice in that vengeance, or more precisely perhaps, in their new-found freedom from oppression. Verse 12 seems to be a motivational clause, to remind God of God's love for the just and that, no matter who or what else may pretend to the position, only God is judge of all the earth.

Like most psalms of lament, there is always a reliance on God to avenge the foe and a recognition that the vindication of justice—or even simply the hope that it will be vindicated—leads to praise.

Psalm 109 (NAB)

1 For the leader. A psalm of David.

  I

2 O God, whom I praise, be not silent,
     for they have opened wicked and treacherous mouths against me.
     They have spoken to me with lying tongues,
3 and with words of hatred they have encompassed me
     and attacked me without cause.
4 In return for my love they slandered me,
     but I prayed.
5 They repaid me evil for good
     and hatred for my love.

II

6 Raise up a wicked man against him,
   and let the accuser stand at his right hand.
7 When he is judged, let him go forth condemned,
   and may his plea be in vain.
8 May his days be few;
   may another take his office.
9 May his children be fatherless,
   and his wife a widow.
10 May his children be roaming vagrants and beggars;
   may they be cast out of the ruins of their homes.
11 May the usurer ensnare all his belongings,
   and strangers plunder the fruit of his labors.
12 May there be no one to do him a kindness,
   nor anyone to pity his orphans.
13 May his posterity meet with destruction;
   in the next generation may their name be blotted out.
14 May the guilt of his fathers be remembered by the LORD;
   let not his mother's sin be blotted out;
15 May they be continually before the LORD,
   till he banish the memory of these parents from the earth,
16 Because he remembered not to show kindness,
   but persecuted the wretched and poor
   and the brokenhearted to put them to death.
17 He loved cursing; may it come upon him;
   he took no delight in blessing; may it be far from him.
18 And may he be clothed with cursing as with a robe;
   may it penetrate into his entrails like water
   and like oil into his bones.
19 May it be for him like a garment that covers him,
   like a girdle that is always about him.

III

20 May this be the recompense from the LORD upon my accusers
   and upon those who speak evil against me.
21 But do you, O GOD, my Lord, deal kindly with me
   for your name's sake;
   in your generous kindness rescue me;
22 For I am wretched and poor,
   and my heart is pierced within me.
23 Like a lengthening shadow I pass away;
   I am swept away like the locust.

24 My knees totter from my fasting,
    and my flesh is wasted of its substance.
25 And I am become a mockery to them;
    when they see me they shake their heads.
26 Help me, O LORD, my God;
    save me, in your kindness,
27 And let them know that this is your hand;
    that you, O LORD, have done this.
28 Let them curse, but do you bless;
    may my adversaries be put to shame,
    but let your servant rejoice.
29 Let my accusers be clothed with disgrace
    and let them wear their shame like a mantle.
30 I will speak my thanks earnestly to the LORD,
    and in the midst of the throng I will praise him,
31 For he stood at the right hand of the poor man,
    to save him from those who would condemn him.

Reflections of Psalm 109

The psalmist wastes little time getting to the point. After only the slightest praise after the address in verse 1, there is an immediate and forceful plea to "be not silent." "They" against whom the psalmist is praying are not identified, but we can deduce that they were people with whom the psalmist had a close relationship and that they have now turned against the psalmist by what they are saying to or about him or her. Thus we are brought once again to the realization that even those closest to us can turn against us and that God is sometimes silent in the midst of such injustice. Nevertheless, we can raise our voices to plead passionately for an end to God's silence and for God's movement into action.

Verse 6 seems to plea that the enemy be "given a taste of his own medicine," that is, that someone wicked be raised up against him. Verse 7 may be a disguised recognition that God is habitually merciful to those who plead to him, by requesting that God not be merciful in this case. The following verses are extremely strong in that they seek not only the death of the enemy, but the social dissolution of his family, the blotting out of his name, the destruction of his prosperity, and the condemnation of both his ancestors and his future generations! Verses 14 and 15 appear to be a judgment on his upbringing, for which his parents should be held accountable. Verses 16 and 17 give reasons why this enemy should be judged so harshly. Verse 17 reflects the "eye for eye and tooth for tooth" concept of vengeance. Verses 18 and 19 make it clear that the psalmist's desire is that the enemy's punishment not be superficial or temporary, but that it be profound and perennial. Throughout all these curses, as vitriolic as they are, nowhere does the psalmist suggest being the agent of vengeance. Violence and vengeance are not to be carried out by the person being wronged, but only by God. This is a very important realization, because it establishes one of the boundaries that keep violent fantasies from turning into violent acts.

Section III turns from cursing to lament, that is, from pleading for God's vengeance against an enemy to crying out to God in one's own pain. Especially in verses 22-25 this section is reminiscent of the Suffering Servant Song of Isaiah in the language of misery expressed in the lament. Lament is a recognition that healing is needed in one's own life, no matter what happens to the enemy. It is an acknowledgment that there is an internal enemy that must be dealt with in addition to the external enemy. In the last two verses of the psalm, there is a sense of resolution; that is, that the very act of praying the psalm has caused the psalmist's attitude about the situation to be more positive and trusting. It is the goal of the psalm and of other psalms like it to bring the prayer to a sense of resolution, and ultimately to a sense of peace.

Conclusion

The Badjao tribe from the Sulu area of the Philippines, the so-called "Sea Gypsies," are a peace loving people. They will move away from their own territory rather than make war. Yet there is a genius in their culture that causes them to chant their anger against their enemies. Expressing their rage at their enemies in the safety of their chants affords them the opportunity to deal with their conflicts in a non-violent manner.[6]

Let us return to the scenarios that initiated our reflection and recall that the genius in the Badjao culture is the very same genius of the imprecatory psalms if we but allow ourselves to utilize them.

The riots that broke out in East Los Angeles after the Rodney King verdicts in April, 1992, were precipitated by the verdicts, but were really grounded in the deep-seated sense of frustration and anger in the African-American community in the depressed neighborhoods of the city, an anger that has seethed for generations and that is expressed in ways that are more often than not destructive of the very community that is oppressed. If the imprecatory psalms had been a part of the spirituality of that community—always in the context of the wider and more conciliatory view of Scripture—perhaps that rage could have been focused more clearly on the real problems of oppression, so that constructive action could be taken to break oppression's vicious cycle. As Brueggemann says, "Indeed, poetic imagination is the last way left in which to challenge and conflict the dominant reality."[7] The demons both within and outside the community—the gods of oppression—could thus be directly confronted. The goal of loving one's enemy begins with the recognition that there is an enemy. Naming the enemy with all the power and emotion and passion that the rage of oppression calls forth is the first step in loving, and thereby freeing, the enemy. It is not the last step nor the final goal, but it is a step in the process of liberation that respects the realities of human emotions in the face of injustice.

In the case of the slain bishop in Guatemala, the same principles apply. There is the danger of stirring up violence with strong, passionate and condemning words, but taking the risk of expressing real violent feelings in communal prayer may be the safety valve needed to then move the passion into the non-violent resistance to evil embodied in the overall ethics of the Scriptures. Use of the imprecatory psalms in this context may also serve as a safety valve against the fear of retaliation for speaking out against the crimes perpetrated by an oppressive regime. There is an apocalyptic element to these psalms, then, since they can express in language that is at least veiled by their legitimacy as Sacred Scripture thoughts and feelings that would be too dangerous to express as political rhetoric.

The woman who was sexually abused had her prison doors unlocked by using the imprecatory psalms as the key. In spiritual counseling she learned that the enormous rage she had felt throughout her life could finally be expressed in a real but safe way by praying the imprecatory psalms with passion. The legitimacy of the Psalms as the Word of God allowed her to accept them as good and to use their power to unleash sentiments that she had never before dared to express. She could even shake her fist at God for God's apparent absence and silence, and in doing so found God very close to her and speaking very clearly.

To express outrage and violent thoughts before the God whose most distinguishing feature is loving kindness (*hesed*) seems blasphemous and contradictory to the overriding message of reconciliation and conversion found in the Bible. But God's ways are not our ways, and the imprecatory psalms are indeed a part of the inspired Word of God. Though they are not the last word, they can be an engaging word and a liberating word.

NOTES: CHAPTER 13

[1] *General Instruction of the Liturgy of the Hours,* #131.

[2] Jurgen, Moltmann, *The Experiment Hope* (Philadelphia: Fortress Press, 1975) 6.

[3] Walter, Brueggemann, *The Prophetic Imagination* (Philadelphia: Fortress Press, 1978) 9.

[4] Erhard S. Gerstenberger, *Psalms, Part I with an Introduction to Cultic Poetry* Forms of Old Testament Literature, vol. XIV, Rolf Knierim and Gene M. Tucker, eds. (Grand Rapids, Mich.: William B. Eerdmans, 1988) 235.

[5] Ibid., 234.

[6] *National Geographic Study,* 1966–70.

[7] Brueggemann, *op. cit.* 45.

14

Songs for the City
Interpreting Biblical Psalms
in an Urban Context

Gerald H. Wilson

*A*fter twenty years of teaching biblical studies in a variety of educational contexts from secular research university to Christian
college and seminary, I have for the last four years served as Co-
Director of Contextualized Urban Ministry Education Northwest
[CUME/NW], a non-profit organization developing programs of ministry education for under-served ethnic minority communities and
churches in the Greater Portland metroplex. Our method has been to
draw together a grassroots coalition of representatives from ethnic minority communities, Christian service organizations in the urban context, and Christian educational institutions in order to create a variety
of networking opportunities in which programs can develop with community ownership that are directed in culturally appropriate ways, and
at the varied educational levels necessary to meet the real felt needs of
these communities.

During the same period I have been working under contract on a
two-volume commentary on the book of Psalms. The commentary series intends to be a practical, hands-on commentary, assisting pastors
and lay persons to interpret the psalms and to apply them fruitfully in
their contemporary context. I have found that these two enterprises—
originally distinct and separate—would not stay neatly in their profes-
sional boxes, but continually spilled over into each other, either to
affect the way I tried to do urban ministry education, or to change the
way I interpreted the Psalms.

At last, when I could stand it no longer, I offered to teach a course intended to involve students in investigating how to interpret and apply the Psalms in their own contemporary urban context. This paper is a first step along the road toward that course, which will share the same title and will encourage students and professor alike to explore the intersection of ancient texts and contemporary context even more deeply.

In what follows, I will lay out the insights gained through these interacting pursuits in the following organizational structure. (1) I will consider important issues confronting the urban communities with which I am working. This will provide us with a sort of urban issues backdrop against which to view the Psalms. (2) I will then describe a variety of themes from the Psalter that relate to these earlier urban issues. These will include: (a) ways in which the urban experience is reflected in the Psalter; (b) how the God of the Psalms relates to these urban issues; and (c) a consideration of the experience of the "Faithful Few" in the Psalms. I will then offer, (3) a few Urban Survival Skills from the Psalms. I do not claim this to be an exhaustive study, nor is this the only way one might interpret the psalms in an urban context, but it does reflect my own personal experience of allowing these two areas of my life to rub up against one another—like a couple of treasured stones in a pocket—shaping, smoothing, polishing, highlighting one another.

1. Issues in these urban communities

When I began to explore the varied lives of the ethnic minority persons with whom I was working, a number of common issues related to their urban context began to emerge. Many of these are commonly known from years of social research and activism, but they are real and continuing issues among these particular urban dwellers of minority status.

a. Cultural dislocation, isolation, and assimilation

One primary experience related by almost all my contacts was a sense of cultural alienation induced by their fragile position within the larger society. They were neither familiar with nor an accepted part of the majority cultural patterns. In response to the alien terrain in which they lived, most found themselves "circling the wagons" by forming native cultural associations to preserve their cultural heritage, provide a level of cultural comfort, and to build a hedge against the constant pressure to assimilation with the majority culture patterns and values. Native language, native dress, and celebration of native cultural events marked this attempt to preserve the familiar in a strange and threatening environment.

b. Lack of access to traditional resources

Isolated as they are (both in feeling and in fact) from the surrounding majority culture, these alienated groups felt they had little means to access the traditional resources available in the majority culture. Lack of education, economic stability, or political representation and influence, led to a sense of powerlessness among these groups.

c. Lack of communication skills

Non-existent or poor majority language skills produced a two-way street of mis-communication, and fostered even more isolation and fear. Perfectly capable leaders within their own culture were often rendered ineffective in their attempts to engage a foreign society whose rules and expectations were unfamiliar to them. Many responded by retreating further into their familiar and protective native cultural associations.

d. Prejudice, exploitation, oppression

Many of the ethnic minority persons with whom I work have experienced their contacts with majority culture primarily in terms of *prejudice* because of their lack of majority language skill, formal educational credentials, economic buying power; *exploitation* by employers seeking less expensive labor, merchandizers taking advantage of their lack of understanding; and *oppression* by those who manipulated the relative cultural powerlessness of these invisible people about whom the majority culture knows little and wants to know even less.

e. Erosion of family and family values

These fairly common experiences of minority ethnic persons and communities had negative effects on family values and solidarity. Many second and third generation minority children sought to escape the negative experiences of their parents by flight into assimilation with the majority culture. While this had in some instances salutary effects on the assimilating generation—better acceptance, more access to traditional educational and economic resources, better understanding of majority cultural and political systems—assimilation often drove a wedge between older and younger generations who no longer shared a cultural commonality, and often denigrated the cultural patterns and values of the other.

2. Themes of the Psalter Related to the Urban Context

As these two fields of experience continued to rub up against one another—the psalms and urban ministry—I began to see that there were many themes in the Psalter that were related to the urban context in which I was working.

a. The urban experience reflected in the Psalms

While the cultural experience of pre-exilic Israel was not entirely urban, it did know cities of moderate size, and was especially concerned with the human relationships lived out in Jerusalem—the City of God, the Holy city where Yʜwʜ chose to cause his name to dwell. We must remember, however, that the Psalms were preserved and transmitted to us by the *post*-exilic community of the Jewish diaspora—the majority of whom were dispersed throughout the ancient world and resided in the great cities of their day as an alien minority culture among the dominant majority culture. It should not surprise us then that the Psalms they chose to preserve exhibit many contacts with the concerns of such an alien people. Here are just a few examples.

1. The Psalms reflect the perspective of the few struggling against the many. The enemies who surround the psalmists are *many*. "Ten Thousand are drawn up against me" (3:5). "Those who hate me without reason out number the hairs of my head . . . many are my enemies" (69:4).

2. The Psalms are aware of the abuse of power in all its forms (political, legal, economic, religious). Those persons of power who sit "in the gate" to render judgment in legal matters or to conduct commercial business, "mock the psalmists" who are rendered politically, economically, and even religiously impotent by their ridicule (cf. 69:12).

3. The Psalms describe the denial of God by those in power—either in reality (14, 53), in his effectiveness (3:2), or his concern (94:7). The result of the assumption of God's effective absence is reliance on human power and self-determination. Those in power operate on the assumption that God will not seek out their abusive acts for punishment (10:4; 36:1-4), in effect proclaiming "there is no God!" or at least claiming that God is deaf to the pleas of the afflicted (59:7) or simply unconcerned with their plight (94:7; 10:11).

4. The Psalms describe the suffering of the few in terms of oppression, lack of resources, lack of representation (35:19-21), economic

deprivation, verbal distortion. Terms used to describe the "few" drive their marginalized condition home. They are the "oppressed"; (*'oni*), the "poor, needy" (*'ebyon*), the "weak" (*dal*). As just one example of this common theme, Psalm 73 recounts how reflecting on the injustice of the prosperity that accrued to the wicked almost caused the psalmist to lose faith in God.

5. Diversity is the norm in the Psalms: *many* voices compete to be heard, including the power elite, widows, orphans, aliens, the destitute, the pagan nations, believers, unbelievers.

6. The Psalms are aware of the pain of cultural and religious dislocation and isolation common to transplanted minority culture persons. Psalm 137 reflects the agony associated with loss of place and identity and the lack of concern or understanding displayed by majority culture. Psalm 12 describes the tyranny of articulate speech by which slick, effective speakers oppress and manipulate those unable to counter their arguments.

b. The God of the Psalms and the Urban Experience

The way God is depicted in the Psalms also has implications for urban dwellers. On the one hand, YHWH confronts and challenges the oppressive acts of those in power who would deny the real or effective existence of God in the city. On the other hand, God offers hope to those who are powerless and oppressed. Here are a few ways that the view of God in the Psalms reflects the concerns of the urban setting.

1. God is aware of and concerned with the city. The numerous references to God's presence in and concern with the city makes it clear that he has expectations for justice and faithfulness in the urban context. He is not indifferent to the city. In Psalms 46 and 48 we learn of the City of God—the city where God dwells and his desires are carried out—and learn that such a city is blessed and will not fall. God leads his people to a city where they can dwell (107:4, 7, 36) and builds up Jerusalem (147) and is aware of destructive violence that threatens it (55:9-10).[1]

2. God is not an indifferent observer of city life, but sits as righteous judge and sets standards for those who dwell in the City of God (cf. Psalm 75). He is not a God who takes pleasure in evil . . . the wicked cannot dwell with him (5:4). God condemns the wicked (50:16-21) and judges with equity, righteousness, and truth (Pss 9:4; 11:7; 96:13, 98:9).

3. God defines the proper role of the righteous ruler (cf. Pss 2; 72; 82; 94:20- 21; 146:7-9).

4. God defines the proper role of righteousness in general. Psalm 15 sets out the characteristics of those who may hope to dwell in God's presence on his holy hill. Psalm 24 concurs that only those with clean hands (right actions) and pure heart (right motivations) can ascend the hill of Yhwh. Psalms with protestations of innocence or what amounts to a "negative confession" also point out the awareness of divine standards for dwelling in the presence of God (cf. 7:3-4).

5. Not only does God set the standard for righteous living and leadership, but he shows a special empathy with the oppressed. He is on the side of the few—the poor and needy—those who are powerless against the powerful (146:7-9). When the poor call, Yhwh hears (34:6; 69:33). Those who are concerned for the weak are commended and blessed (41:1). Yhwh becomes a father—legal representative in society—for those who are fatherless (68:5f.).

6. God as king is ultimate authority above all human authority. He is the ultimate court of appeal (laments)—the only lasting, sure foundation of human hope and security. Yhwh is enthroned as king (47). Since Yhwh is king, humans are counseled not to put their trust in human princes, but to trust in Yhwh alone (145).

7. As creator God is in control and provides a secure foundation for life—even when chaos seems to rule. When the foundations are being destroyed what can the righteous do? (11:3). Yhwh, however, is mightier than the destructive forces of chaos (29). Even though the city or temple should be destroyed, God is king from of old, and, therefore offers hope for restoration (74).

c. The Experience of the Faithful Few in the Psalms

In most instances it is the faithful few who are in view in the psalms. Whether it is the individual at odds with his or her community, enemies, or environment, or whether it is the covenant community in conflict with the pagan nations, the psalmist's words often invoke, confront, or encourage the faithful to live out their faith within the challenge of their circumstances. The experience of the faithful few in these psalms is also a fruitful ground of understanding for urban dwellers. Let's look at a few examples.

1. The Psalms speak to the modern urban experience of ethnic and economic diversity, and honors native and alien, the nations and Israelites,

rich and poor alike. This acceptance of ethnic and economic diversity is most clearly expressed in the invocation of all these categories of persons to worship God. While the pagans are often the enemies of God in the psalms and the subject of destructive imprecation; while the rich are often castigated for their participation in the oppression of the faithful poor; rich and poor alike, native born Israelite and pagan born alien all can know and worship Yhwh. "Your ways are known among all nations, all the peoples praise you" (67:1-4).

2. The faithful also learn in the Psalms that their suffering is NOT a portent (sign of divine punishment for sin)—but is instead an indication of a world run amok and the failure of righteous rulership. Ps 71:7 makes this clear when the psalmist counters the common perception of the psalmist's suffering as a "portent" by the confident affirmation "you are [instead] my strong refuge." See also Pss 44:22 and 69:7 where the undeserved suffering of the faithful is given meaning when it is understood as "for your sake"—for the sake of Yhwh—a sign of faithfulness. As in Job enduring faithfulness in the face of undeserved suffering has its own worth—an acknowledgment that God is worthy of our worship and love even when the anticipated blessings of his reign are far from us.

3. The faithful are encouraged to understand that suffering does not negate their faith. Suffering, if otherwise meaningless, is for Yhwh's sake (44:22). It is better to suffer the economic privations of the faithful poor than to enjoy the abundant wealth of the wicked (37:16). Yhwh's love is for the faithful few *better than life itself!* (63:3). See also Psalm 77, where the suffering psalmist makes the conscious decision to trust the evidence of Yhwh's past salvation despite the bewildering contrary evidence of the present (77:10-12). Suffering drives the faithful into the protective care of God rather than away from him. God is the strong refuge in time of trouble (cf. Pss 90, 91, 142, 144, and *many* others).[2]

4. The faithful few are called to eschew the tactics of the enemy. This is clear from the outset of the Psalter when Psalm 1 affirms that the one whose way is known by Yhwh is the one who does not walk in the company and practices of the wicked, sinners, or mockers (1:1). God sends away from his presence all those who do evil (6:8), and the faithful are cautioned "Do not trust in extortion, or take pride in stolen goods, though your riches increase, do not set your heart on them" (62:10). And the faithful deny their involvement by claiming to have avoided "the ways of the violent" (17:3-5), and by guarding themselves from being drawn "to what is evil to take part in wicked deeds with those who are evildoers" (141:3-5).

5. God sets standards for the righteousness of the faithful few as well as the many—the poor and suffering are called to righteous living as much as the wealthy. See the tension between Psalm 15 with its call to a "blameless walk" as prerequisite to entering God's presence and Psalm 101 where the faithful psalmist affirms a blameless stance before crying out to God: "When will you come to me?" (101:2).

6. Psalms seek to undermine reliance on self, human power, and to point to dependence on God alone. "Some trust in chariots and some in horses, but we trust in the name of YHWH our God. They are brought to their knees and fall, but we rise up and stand firm" (20:7). "Do not put your trust in princes, in mortal men, who cannot save. . . . Blessed is he whose help is the God of Jacob, whose hope is in YHWH his God" (146:3, 5; cf. 118:8-9). No one who hopes in YHWH will ever be put to shame (25:3). In the end Israel is called to be like the weaned child at its mother's breast who is stilled, quieted, and at peace in the arms of YHWH (131:2-3).

3. Urban Survival Skills from the Psalms

I have to this point been considering how the themes characteristic of the psalms relate to the concerns expressed and contexts experienced by the urban communities with whom I have been working. Now let me attempt in a brief but (hopefully) coherent fashion to suggest a few ideas regarding urban survival skills that can be derived from the psalms. If the goal is to survive—or even to thrive—as persons of enduring faith in the challenging context of the modern urban setting, what do these ancient poems have to say that can encourage us to keep our feet firmly planted on the "way" that YHWH knows and blesses?

a. The importance of community within community

One of the first and most important lessons the Psalms afford us is the insight that the life of faith—whether expressed as individuals or as a community—is lived out within a believing community. The psalms may speak in singular language and images, but they were most often performed in the midst of community worship. The "I" of the Psalms speaks to the "we" of the gathered congregation. The individual sufferer bears testimony of pain endured and divine deliverance longed for, anticipated, and finally received, not in some isolated hideaway, but in the "great congregation" gathered for worship. Faith in the Psalms is a pilgrim journey through the dark in the company of fellow venturers. The community of faith plays a variety of significant roles in the Psalms.

1. The community of faith can serve to console the suffering and counteract the feeling of isolation that can be experienced by the disadvantaged few among the controlling many. The community can offer praise when individuals cannot (see particularly Psalm 42/43 where the downcast psalmist is renewed by recalling participation in the joyful processions of the faithful to the house of God). The fact that the Psalter is dominated in the first three books by individual lament, but shifts in the final two books to communal praise and thanksgiving is instructive. It brings home the experience that alone and isolated the individual can be overwhelmed by lament. It is within the community of faith that the power to sing the praise of God *in spite of the reality of pain and suffering* is made a reality. When I am unable to praise, the community stands along side to praise for me.

2. It is through the community of faith that the enduring traditions of hope are preserved, reaffirmed, and transmitted to new generations. Here the psalmist declares to Yhwh "Since my youth, O God, you have taught me, and to this day I declare your marvelous deeds. Even when I am old and gray, do not forsake me, O God, till I declare your power to the next generation, your might to all who are to come" (71:17-18). And in 78:1-8 the psalmist recounts not only Yhwh's praiseworthy deeds, but the account of Israel's own faithlessness.

b. The importance of memory

The transmission of the traditions of faith to future generations introduces another survival lesson from the psalms. Memory provides an important foundation for the hope that keeps the psalmists and their followers on the way of faith. The bittersweet memory of Jerusalem motivates the fierce and angry determination not to allow the taunts of the Babylonian conquerors to undermine the hope of the faithful in Psalm 137. We have already seen how memory of participating in the festive processions of temple worship could counter the depressing effects of suffering (42:4). Among the chief focii of memory are (1) the mighty acts of Yhwh (66:1-5 "Say to God 'How awesome are your deeds! . . . Come see what God has done how awesome his works in man's behalf"); (2) moments of personal deliverance by God (66:16 "Come and listen, all you who fear God; let me tell you what he has done for me"); and (3) the traditions of the faithful history of Israel and her God (71; 78; and the other historical psalms). These sorts of memories are the rock on which the faithful of Israel continued to stand secure in spite of their immediate context.

c. Adopting a prophetic voice toward the powers of the city

The psalmists, however, were never content just to rest secure. They consistently raised up their collective voices to confront the powers of their society and to protest the injustice and oppression they and others experienced. Like Jeremiah (4:19; 6:11; 20:9), the psalmists discovered that holding back anguish and critique did not work (Ps 39:1-3), but personal and societal sin must be confronted openly in order for change to occur.

1. The prophetic confrontation can be harsh, as when the psalmists pray for the replacement of faithless leaders and opponents in the strongest terms. See particularly the strong words of condemnation expressed in 109:6-20: "Let him be found guilty . . . may his prayers condemn him . . . may his days be few . . . may another take his place of leadership." Similar sentiments are expressed in 141:5-6: "Yet my prayer is ever against the deeds of evildoers; their rulers will be thrown down from the cliffs."[3]

2. Such harsh critiques are never *just* self-serving tantrums, but seek to educate the community or seek a broader, communal good. Along with the desire for personal deliverance in Psalm 109, the psalmist seeks the removal of a societal threat who "never thought of doing a kindness, but hounded to death the poor and the needy and the brokenhearted." The condemnation of such behavior is admonition to avoid repeating it. The psalmists also identify with the marginalized and oppressed in society, including the poor, the sick and weak, and even aliens and strangers (39:12).

3. In their strong attacks, the psalmists caution against adopting the tactics of the enemy—or of being co-opted by their own attempts to meet power with power.[4]

d. Acknowledging helplessness

The temptation to use and abuse power that is inherent in any attempt to confront and counter entrenched power is often balanced in the Psalms by a relentless call to acknowledge the frailty of human strength and the futility of human control. In the laments this is communicated especially in the theme of innocent suffering—from which there is no apparent escape.[5] If suffering was the result of sin, then there would be a reason for it, and one could DO something about it. One could confess, repent, offer sacrifice, or restitution. But the *innocent* sufferer is forced to acknowledge helplessness and is forced to rely only on the mercy of a God who often seems distant. In some instances such reliance is almost beyond the psalmist for whom God seems to have become the enemy and perpetrator of the suffering the individual experiences (Psalm 88). In these cases the only hope is found in the fact that the psalmist is still in conversation with God.

Along with the helplessness associated with innocent suffering, the psalms stress again and again that human power and claims to control are unreliable sources of security. Even kings and princes fail to save (146:3-5) leaving Yhwh alone as the source of human hope. [6]

e. View of suffering

I have already discussed above the view of suffering characteristic of the psalms.[7] I will limit myself here to a few brief statements regarding how these insights shape the way one responds to suffering in the modern urban context.

1. The Psalms claim that suffering is not always—not even most frequently—a sign of divine punishment or rejection (cf. 71). Innocents do suffer in this mixed up world, and any attempt to justify suffering as the necessary "lot" of a particular group of urban dwellers must be carefully scrutinized for evidence of bias.

2. Contrary to the tendency to label suffering a consequence of "sin" or divine judgment, the Psalms often recognize pain as a sign that all *is not right* in the world. Therefore the psalmists feel constrained constantly to call upon God for redress—to "make things right." [8] The awareness that the world represents a distortion of God's original creation intention in which human relationships to God, other humans, and the world itself most often violate God's purposes, is certainly more apparent to the "have nots" of the city than those who are comfortably in power. The Psalms encourage us to align ourselves with God and seek to transform the urban environment from the "City of Satan" into the "City of God."[9]

3. The Psalms model a relationship with Yhwh built around a continual conversation made up of confession, complaint, protestation of innocence, call to action, confident expectation—as well as the more "worshipful" attitudes of praise and thanksgiving. There are no particularly acceptable attitudes with which to approach God in the Psalms other than the humble recognition that one has no hope other than in Yhwh. This awareness means that all experiences of life in the city need to be brought openly before God.

4. Perhaps one of the most important insights offered by the Psalms for the urban context is that the blessing of righteousness is not to be confused with ease, wealth, and power. These can be experienced without righteousness. Unlike the prosperity preachers of our own day, the psalmists never equate prosperity with blessing. Righteousness is something other than and superior to these physical benefits and pleasures, and those who would be righteous must always hold ease, wealth, and power lightly and cautiously, as the following verses make clear. "Do not trust in extortion or take pride in stolen goods; though your riches increase, do not set your heart on them. One thing God has spoken, two things have I heard: that you, O God, are strong ["power belongs to God"], and that you, O Lord, are loving. Surely you will reward each person according to what he has done" (62:10-12). "Your [God's] love is better than life" (63:3).

5. Despite the many references in the first half of the Psalter to God as refuge, the psalmists make it clear that refuge is in the *midst* of trouble and *not* an escape *from* suffering. God provides protective consolation *during* the experience of pain. The psalmists never look for a pain free utopian existence, but acknowledge that God is worth hanging on to even if death is the only consequence. As a result, suffering can be understood, not as judgment, but as a sign of faithfulness (44:17-22). The ultimate goal of the faithful in the psalms is NOT escape *from* pain, but faithful endurance *in and through* pain.

6. I spoke earlier about how the arrangement of the psalms groups individual lament dominantly in the first three books of the Psalter, while the last two books are characterized primarily by communal praise and thanksgiving.[10] This characteristic shift has one further implication that offers hope for the faithful in the city or outside. The movement from lament to praise drives home the affirmation that lament is not Yhwh's final word. It is most likely that awareness of this fact is the primary reason that the Jewish community chose to call the book of Psalms—with all its diversity—*Tehillim* "Praises." The title seems at first a rather awkward and inappropriate one for a collection as diverse as this one. But the arrangement of the psalms affirms that the anticipated end of God's history with humankind is mirrored in the ecstatic praise of the final hallel (Psalms 146–150) in which the whole creation at last combine voices to give praise to the creator and redeemer of all.

NOTES: CHAPTER 14

[1] See the study by Robert Linthicum, *City of God, City of Satan: A Biblical Theology of the Urban Church* (Grand Rapids, Mich.: Zondervan, 1991).

[2] Jerome F. D. Creach, *Yahweh as Refuge and the Editing of the Hebrew Psalter* JSOTSup 217 (Sheffield: JSOT Press, 1996).

[3] As Christians, we are, of course, often offended by such harsh imprecations against the psalmist's enemies—especially when they involve the innocent children (109:9-12; 137:8-9). If we are honest, however, we may often have flashes of anger in which we wish our opponents' deeds would turn back on them—that they would receive as good (or bad) as they have given. The psalms illustrate that it is okay to acknowledge such anger to God, and leave it there.

[4] See the related discussion above, p. 234, no. 4 and Pss 1:1, 7; 6:8; 17:3-5; 62:10; 141:3-5.

[5] See especially Ps 44:17-22 and Ps 88.

[6] See the related discussion of the limits of human power discussed above (p. 235, no. 6). The similarity of this theme of helplessness to that expressed in twentieth-century Twelve Step groups is remarkable. At one point in the readings presented at every meeting one encounters three "pertinent ideas: (a) that we were [addicts] and could not manage our lives; (b) that probably no human power could relieve our [compulsive behavior]; (c) that God could and would if he were sought."

[7] See p. 234, nos. 2 and 3.

[8] See the discussion and references on p. 234, no. 2 above.

[9] Robert Linthicum, *City of God, City of Satan*, strongly articulates this premise.

[10] See Gerald H. Wilson, "The Shape of the Book of Psalms" *Interpretation* 46 (1992) 129–42.

15

Taking Inspiration
Authorship, Revelation, and the Book of Psalms

Mark S. Smith

I. INTRODUCTION

Over the past century critical scholarship has contributed to the life of the Church (though with some bumps in the road). However, the varied ecclesial bodies, whether they have accepted or rejected historical criticism, have either overlooked, downplayed or set aside historical problems posed to traditional notions of inspiration. When it comes to the book of Psalms, historical scholarship has uncovered a number of difficulties, in particular involving their two different parts, prose labels (also called titles or superscriptions) and poetic texts. The distinction is attested in both ancient and modern texts. One major Greek manuscript, the *Codex Sinaiticus,* distinguished superscriptions from the poems that follow by using red writing for the titles of the psalms.[1] A few of the Dead Sea Scrolls leave a blank line between the titles and the poem proper.[2] Modern Bible translations likewise provide readers with some means of distinguishing the superscriptions from the poems. rsv and njps separate the two by a space. nab and nrsv separate the superscriptions and poems by a space and presents the superscriptions in italics and slightly smaller type. **For the Benedictines of Saint Anselm's Abbey, from whom I first heard the psalms.**

*M*odern translations reflect the scholarly consensus that the superscriptions are prose additions to the prior written poems. The prose labels were intended to provide information about the poems. As Brevard S. Childs observes, "the Psalm titles do not appear to reflect independent historical tradition but are the result of an exegetical activity which derived its material from within the text itself [e.g., the poems]."[3] Childs suggests that superscriptions are to be dated between the book of Chronicles which do not cite the superscription in citing psalms and the Cave 11 Psalms scroll which contains them.[4] In this understanding the psalm titles constitute the first formal comments on the poems, the first attested moment of their interpretation. Many later traditional readers of the psalms instinctively harmonize the poetic texts and the prose context of the superscriptions, just as the authors/redactors who supplied the superscriptions probably intended. As I read psalms with students every semester, one particularly difficulty arises over the superscriptions. Students begin the course first with the assumption that the superscriptions are historically true (and this includes their claims of putative authorship), and that the model of inspiration based on this assumption follows unproblematically.

The superscriptions contain historical and formal claims (if only by way of assumed word use). The critical question involves the degree to which these can be accounted for, in the face of modern knowledge of history and study of genres or forms. This essay introduces and discusses the extent to which the superscriptions can be reasonably harmonized with such information (as well as what guidelines they themselves offer to historical research) in order to consider how traditional notions of inspiration might be made more cogent in the face of historical criticism.

I will address some of these issues in the following order: preliminary considerations of superscriptions; superscriptions and the individual/communal distinction in the poems; genre comments in the superscriptions and form-criticism categories; and finally some limited theological considerations. Before proceeding to the last area an excursus presents a schematic view of what I see as the six basic forms of the psalms and their relations (not so much historically or even genetically, but phenomenologically, as indicated by the texts). To anticipate this discussion, purely formal criteria cannot admit of the categories of "royal psalms," "songs of Zion," or "wisdom psalms"; reconceiving them according to formal categories will simplify the basic categories, and I hope, will also clarify them and their interrelationships.

The final section offers some broader considerations shared by these overall issues bearing on superscriptions and the poems. It is my hope that by retracing some of the steps of how biblical authorship and inspiration came to be conceived, it will be possible to offer some constructive reflections on these theological concepts for the Church today. Fortunately, some recent studies of the labels or superscriptions of the Psalms have suggested such an agenda by studying some of the interesting links between the superscriptions and the content of the poems. Such an agenda tends to focus on the relations between the situation reflected in the biographical data about David in the superscriptions and the content of the situation of the speaker in the poem. Insufficient attention has been paid to the implications which the differences between the superscriptions and the poems may hold for understanding inspiration and revelation. Finally, when it comes to these larger theological issues, I find myself sometimes at a loss for a more precise way to define, delineate and pursue these questions, and I apologize in advance for vagueness in these first groupings of mine regarding these questions.

II. Preliminary Considerations of Superscriptions

Material variation

Superscriptions provide five different kinds of information: (1) ascriptions primarily of authorship or collections; (2) types of psalm; (3) musical information, personnel and titles; (4) biographical information; and (5) liturgical times. No psalm has all five sorts of information, and some have no superscription, either because they never received one (Psalms 1, 2, 91, 93-97, 99, 104, 105, 107, 114-116, 118, 119, 137, for example) or because they form a single poem with the preceding psalm (such as Psalms 9-10 and 42-43). The putative authors vary in the superscriptions:

> 1. "To David," *lĕdāwîd*. The bulk of psalms in the first two books are connected with the name of David (Psalms 3, 4, 5, 6, 7, 8, 9, 11, 12, 13, 14, 15, 16, 17, 18, 19, 20, 21, 22, 23, 24, 25, 26, 27, 28, 29, 30, 31, 32, 34, 35, 36, 37, 38, 39, 40, 41, 51, 52, 53, 54, 55, 56, 57, 58, 59, 60, 61, 62, 63, 64, 65, 68, 69, 70, 86, 101, 103, 108, 109, 110, 122, 124, 131, 133, 138, 139, 140, 141, 142, 143, 144, 145, 151; cf. Psalms 18, 36).
>
> 2. "To Jeduthun," *lîdûtûn/ʿal-yĕdûtûn* (Psalms 39, 62, 77). It may refer to a person known also from 1 Chron 25:1 along with Asaph and Heman, although the form with ʿal would be unparalleled for a person. For this reason Mowinckel denied that a person was involved, and preferred a

cultic interpretation "at/for confession" (from the root *ydh).[5] The root, however, does not show this meaning.

3. "To the sons of Qorah," *libnê-qoraḥ* (Psalms 42, 44, 45, 46, 47, 48, 49, 84, 85, 87, 88).

4. "To Asaph," *lĕ'āsāp* (Psalms 50, 73, 74, 75, 76, 77, 78, 79, 80, 81, 82, 83).

5. "To Solomon," *lišlōmōh* (Psalm 72, 127).

6. "To Heman the Ezrahite," *lĕhêmān hā'ezrāḥî* (Psalm 88). 1 Chron 15:17 and 19 mention Heman with Asaph and Ethan, and 1 Chron 25:1 mentions him in connection with Asaph and Jeduthun.

7. "To Ethan the Ezrahite," *lĕ'êtān hā'ezrāḥî* (Psalm 89). Given the shared clan or family name, Ethan was perhaps related (or, was perceived as related) to Heman.

8. "To Moses, man of God," *lĕmōšĕh 'îš hā'ĕlōhîm* (Psalm 90).

9. "To a lowly one," *lĕ'ānî* (Psalm 102). This psalm is ascribed to a nameless person belonging not to the exalted ranks of Israelite leadership as found in the other ascriptions. Davidic authorship for those psalms bear the superscription *lĕdāwîd* (usually rendered "Of David" [6]). The bulk of these references occur in the first two "books" of the Psalter. For example, the traditional Hebrew text of Jewish tradition (Masoretic text; henceforth MT) attests to Davidic authorship in Book I of the Psalter, Psalms 3, 4, 5, 6, 7, 8, 9, 11, 12, 13, 14, 15, 16, 17, 18, 19, 20, 21, 22, 23, 24, 25, 26, 27, 28, 29, 30, 31, 32, 34, 35, 36, 37, 38, 39, 40, 41; and in Book II, Psalms 51, 52, 53, 54, 55, 56, 57, 58, 59, 60, 61, 62, 63, 64, 65, 68, 69, 70). In addition, relatively fewer MT psalms in other books are connected with David (Psalms 86, 101, 103, 108, 109, 110, 122, 124, 131, 133, 138, 139, 140, 141, 142, 143, 144, 145, 151). A variation in this group is "to the servant of Yahweh, to David" *lĕ'ebed yhwh lĕdāwîd* (Psalms 18, 36). The duplicate psalms, Psalms 14 and 53, contain differences in their superscriptions, also pointing to later editorial processes governing superscriptions. Similarly, the Greek version (Septuagint) and the Hebrew versions often show greater differences in their superscriptions than in the poems.

Material variation within the MT poses few substantial theological difficulties. It is not difficult to posit some means to account for the differences between the superscriptions of Psalms 14 and 53. We might wonder about the differences between the openings of Psalm 18 and 2 Sam 22 ("He said" in Ps 18:2, implying borrowing from a narrative context), but again little theological problem arises from this difference. We may also ask why musical figures mentioned in superscriptions are attested in Chronicles, but not Samuel and Kings while leaders mentioned in superscriptions are known from Samuel and Kings (e.g., David and Solomon). Yet again, theologically, such an issue need not pose a great problem. The same may be said of the question which could be raised as to why all the psalms do not have superscriptions or why those which do not mention all five types of information (mentioned above). Such a disposition of material may remind interpreters that such matters are fully part of historical processes that rarely provide ideal provisions of information. If we were to dwell more theologically on this point, we might be reminded of the fully incarnated character of texts and their contexts; here there is no idealized knowledge accessible even to the chosen.

Textual-theological considerations

The Greek version (Septuagint) of the Bible attributes thirteen more psalms to David.[7] And I would comment further on this difference between the Septuagint and the Masoretic text.[8] Although it is easy to overlook such differences and perhaps dismiss them as theologically insignificant, for Christian traditions (i.e., the Orthodox and Roman Catholics) that so long relied on the Septuagint and then the Vulgate, such differences of authorship are not to be simply dismissed. Instead, traditions accepting multiple textual witnesses require not simply an "historical explanation," but also "theological reflection" on the significance. The question of which textual witness should be accepted becomes acute when dealing with the issue of the different Psalters represented by the different textual versions. From this text-critical situation, it might be argued that the MT is text-critically prior, and therefore it is only reasonable to select MT as the basis for the canonical text.

Given the theological importance which LXX has carried in the history of the Church, I do not feel free to dispense with its historically significant divergent readings. Jewish and Christian traditions have included the book of Psalms in the canon of the Bible, but the form of the book has not been defined in a similar theological way in Christian tradition. Stated differently, Jewish tradition has enshrined the MT and the Protestant churches have followed suit. Yet such an acceptance on the part of the Protestant denominations has not prevented them from using the LXX to correct a text-critical problem in the MT. Roman Catholic scholars likewise regularly use versions in order to produce the most error-free text. Yet both Protestant and Catholic scholars have found some readings in LXX "superior" even when MT is intelligible and not necessarily showing error. In fact, when LXX and MT both show sensible readings, how does a Christian biblical scholar choose since it is the book of the Bible and not the version which has been canonized as such? While different traditions historically have shown distinctive preferences for various versions, there have been no clear guidelines for selection in cases where error is not clearly involved. (Who is to say then variant readings do not deserve a place in translations?) The theological issues are not minor even in matters of textual criticism. Parenthetically, I would suggest that the theological significance of the discrepancy among textual witnesses regarding Davidic authorship partially lies in showing that there is a tradition that discerns authorship over the course of time, rather than a hypothetical original moment that determined the text.

Linguistic matters

David authorship is not an issue only for textual reasons. Linguistic considerations would make Davidic authorship of these psalms highly problematic. The psalms "of David" for the most part could not have been written by David since their grammar points to a later period (unless massive rewriting of psalm texts were to be assumed). David ruled toward the end of what scholars have considered the period of archaic Hebrew[9] and since all the psalms attributed to Davidic (with the possible exceptions of Psalms 18 and 29) are considered to belong to a later stage of Hebrew (the issue is akin to the different stages of English represented by *Beowulf, The Canterbury Tales,* Shakespeare, or T. S. Eliot). Therefore, it would be problematic to accept Davidic authorship, unless one wished to operate on the assumption that these psalms were rewritten in standard biblical Hebrew at a later point; while some grammatical updating is evident (for example, compare Psalm 18 and 2 Sam 22), older texts outside the Psalter tend to be left with their archaic features intact. Accordingly, there is no reason to expect massive rewriting for psalm texts.

Historical information versus Davidic authorship: geography, Temple, city gates, people

Other problems intrude on the superscriptions' ascriptions of Davidic authorship. Geographical references exclusively to the north, for example in Psalm 29, would cast doubt on Davidic authorship. Apparent historical discordances are involved in the question as well. Since it was David's son Solomon who sponsored the construction of the

Jerusalem temple, references to a temple in Psalms perhaps undermine the plausibility of their ascription of Davidic authorship, unless another temple or shrine is indicated by the context (for example, Pss 5:8, 23:6, 26:8, 27:4, 29:9, 36:9, 52:10; 63:3; 68:25, 30, 36; cf. 51:20), an edifice built by David's son, Solomon, only after his father's death; in other words, psalms referring to the Temple could not have been written by David since it did not exist in his time. Taking recourse to suggestions of a temple other than the Jerusalem Temple in David's time is hardly a convenient harmonization, for what Temple did David have? (none according to the historical books). I have entertained the possibility that in some of these cases, it was God's heavenly house being read (or reread?) by the authors of the superscriptions.

Yet one wonders in particular how to make sense of the superscription of Psalm 30: "A psalm of David. A Song for the dedication of the House." In this instance, it is not simply a detail of the poem which undermines information in the superscription; it is information in the superscription itself which belies the apparent claim of Davidic authorship in the superscription. We might discern here a reading of the historical narrative about David's intention to build a house; the poem perhaps was thought to have been written when he thought to build it, only to be precluded by a second oracle from Nathan. Yet this is an *ad hoc* guess, perhaps even a poor one.

Similarly references to gates presume Solomonic building of city walls and gates; yet, Pss 9:15 and 51:20 refers to city gates and these psalms' superscriptions attribute them to David. The gates mentioned in another Davidic psalm, Ps 24:7, 9 would seem to be city-gates as well. Other comments in the Psalms might seem to be problematic if the claim of Davidic authorship in the superscription is taken at face value. For example, what would Ps 14:7 (= 53:7)'s request for "restoring the fortunes" mean in the Davidic era? It might be argued that while David suffered setbacks in his life, Israel's fortunes were not. Finally, in the case of Ps 18:47-51, should readers assume that David, speaking in the first person, refers to himself in the third person? This example points to a particular problem with a number of psalms classified as "royal psalms," an issue we will return to.

III. Individual and Communal Psalms and Claims of Davidic Authorship

Form-criticism has made commentators acutely aware of the formal differences among the 150+ psalms. This section addresses one of the two most basic form-critical distinctions, namely individual versus communal psalms, and how well Davidic ascription comports with this distinction. (The second involves the form-critical assessments of genres or types by scholars and the formal claims made by the superscriptions; this issue is addressed in the following section.) In general, psalms attributed to Davidic fall in the category of what scholars regard as "individual psalms," namely psalms spoken by an individual whether alone or in a communal context. In contrast, the communal psalms in at least the three books of the Psalter are attributed to a communal group (e. g., "the Qorahites"). We can tally the potential correlation:

> Davidic, individual: Psalms 3, 4, 5, 6, 7, 8, 9-10, 11, 13, 16, 17, 18, 19, 22, 23, 25, 26, 27, 28, 30, 31, 32, 32, 34, 35, 36, 37, 38, 39, 40, 41, 51, 52, 54, 55, 56, 57, 58, 60 (to be read as an individual vv 7 and 11 speaking in a communal setting as indicated by "we"; cf. Ps 62:9), 62, 63, 64, 65 (v. 4, despite v 6), 69, 70, 86, 101, 103, 108, 109, 110, 122, 130, 138, 139, 140, 141, 142, 143, 144, 145.
> Davidic, communal: Psalms 20 (cf. v. 7), 21, 124.
> David, unclear: Psalms 12, 14, 15, 24, 29, 68, 133.

In the case of the psalms attributed to David, the vast bulk conform to the expectation that they would be individual psalms. The unclear examples were conformed to this notion that Davidic psalms are individual in character. On this view Psalm 8 is a particularly interesting case. It is generally regarded as a hymn, even though it addresses God rather than some other party (as is the case in most psalms). However, this is an individual hymn, which perhaps accounts for this difference from other hymns. As it stands, it is also the only hymn with a Davidic superscription. It is also the only individual hymn in the Psalter. Given these two correspondences, it might be surmised that the author/redactors responsible for the superscriptions showed some level of consistency in their reading of psalms in the area of singular "I" versus plural "we." (Parenthetically, I would mention as well that some psalms in the heart of Davidic psalms sometimes lack an attribution of Davidic authorship, such as Psalm 33. Interestingly, this psalm is a communal hymn, as indicated by verses 20-22, and therefore one might not expect Davidic attribution given the first person plural verbs. It may be that in later parts of the Psalter a lack of superscription on individual psalms, as in Psalms 71 and 91, should not be considered a lapse, only that other forces may be at work.)

The remaining issue involves those few Davidic psalms which are communal. Psalm 124 would be understood as a psalm in which David speaks for the community. Psalms 20 and 21, however, cannot be conformed to the paradigm in such a manner and so they must be understood differently. Psalm 20 asks God to give help to "you," presumably the figure of the king as he goes out to battle. The community ("we") prays for victory in verse 6 and then pleads: "May the Lord fulfill your every wish." It is clear that the figure of the king is not the speaker, but the second person addressee. Furthermore, an individual speaker emerges in verse 7 ("Now I know . . ."); this speaker refers to "the anointed." *Prima facie*, the king could be speaking of himself in the third person, but the second-person references to the king militate strongly against such a harmonization.

What sense then did the superscription's attribution of Davidic authorship make in this context? In Psalm 21 a similar difficulty obtains. The prayer for the king, mentioned in the third person (verses 2, 8), concludes with the speakers' reference to themselves as "we" (verse 14). In the cases of Psalms 20 and 21, it is the not the number of speaker ("we") that determined ascription of authorship to some plural entity. Instead, the royal content suggested Davidic attribution. Royal content in Psalm 61 would also suggest a comparable reason for its Davidic attribution. The king is mentioned in third person (v. 7) sandwiched by first-person singular references (vv. 6 and 9). The same dynamic is apparent with the Solomonic ascription in 72. Clearly this text concerns Solomon, "the king's son," mentioned in verse 1.[10] Here we may note the contrast of Psalm 89, another psalm that speaks about the dynasty, but it is attributed to a figure other than a king (Ethan). Therefore, it is evident that in Psalms 20, 21, and 72 (as well as 110), content could override formal considerations in attributing putative authorship to David or Solomon (Psalm 127, the second of the two psalms attributed to Solomon, is ambiguous as to the number of the speaker). Yet this number of psalms pales in comparison to the number of individual psalms (and ones ambiguous with respect to the number of speakers) attributed to David; and the exceptions are intelligible in light of the content even if all the ancient considerations do not emerge clearly under modern inspection.

The Qorahite psalms present a different situation:

> Qorahites, individual: Psalms 42–43, 45, 49, 84, 85, 87.
> Qorahite, communal: Psalm 44, 46, 47, 48.

From this distribution, it might be inferred that Qorahite ascription was regarded differently from ascription to Moses, David or Solomon.

It would seem that Qorahites might be regarded not so much as authors as transmitters of psalms both individual and communal for the sake of the temple cult. And this is the picture given them in the books of Chronicles.

Asaph is a different story:

> Asaph, individual: Psalms 73, 77, 78.
> Asaph, communal: Psalms 75, 79, 80.
> Asaph, ambiguous: Psalms 74, 76, 81 (cf. "I" in v 6), 82, 83.

Some psalms of Asaph are individual, but others were capable of individual reading. For example, Psalm 74 could have been understood as a communal lament led by an individual mentioned in passing in verse 12 ("my king"), speaking on behalf of the community. The same applies to Psalms 75 and 83; communal texts on first inspection, an individual voice comes to the fore in 75:10 ("I will declare . . . , // I will sing a hymn . . .") and to a lesser extent in 83:14: ("O my God"). Psalms 79 and 80 have no individual voice, but they could be understood in the same terms. Other Asaphite psalms listed in the third category above are more ambiguous.

Finally, we may note the handful of others attributed psalms:

> Heman, individual: Psalm 88.
> Ethan, individual: Psalm 89.
> Moses, ambiguous: Psalm 90 (communal led by an individual?).
> "A lowly one," individual: Psalm 102.

In three of these four instances, Psalms 88, 89, and 102, the putative author conforms to the number of speaker in the body of the text. In the case of the fourth, Psalm 90, the text is sufficiently ambiguous as to the number of speakers that it admits of a singular speaker.

In conclusion, modern identifications of individual and communal psalms comport with the attributions made in the superscriptions. We might surmise that the ancient writers/editors who prefixed the superscriptions to the poems were fully guided by the information in the poems, just as modern form criticism has been; the ancients were careful readers and knowledgeable, given their frame of reference (as all readers in any era read). In turn, the knowledge evidenced by the superscriptions should urge caution to modern critics as to the ambiguities of the poems, a feature fortunately noted by some modern critics. Indeed, in some cases ambiguity in the bodies of the poems allowed for some latitude in attribution. Poetry is not always so easily harnessed by historical (or historicizing) concerns, ancient or modern. Finally, the significant number of unattributed psalms (Psalms 33, 66, 67, 71, 91–100, 104–7, 111–21, 123, 125, 125–26, 128–30, 132, 134, 135–37, 146–50) would suggest a general lack of knowledge about the processes underlying the attribution of superscriptions and further warns against modern judgments as to the "appropriateness" of the ancient attributions. Stated differently, modern critics cannot afford to assume that they know more than their ancient counterparts who provided superscriptions, given their historical, geographical, and cultural proximity to the authors of the poems.

IV. Poetic forms versus Genre Claims of Prose Superscriptions

The genre designations tend to be passed over quickly in modern considerations of psalms. Instead, analysis tends to move immediately to the formal characteristics of poetic texts. My question in this section concerns the range of fit between genre comments in the superscriptions and the formal designations and delineations produced by scholarly form-criticism. My further issue is whether this discrepancy (if there is one) requires any further theological reflection for reading the book of Psalms. We may begin with a basic listing of genre remarks in the superscriptions:

> 1. *mizmôr*, "song" (Psalms 3, 4, 5, 6, 8, 9, 12, 13, 15, 19, 20, 21, 22, 23, 24, 29, 30, 31, 38, 39, 40, 41, 47, 48, 49, 50, 51, 62, 63, 64, 65, 66, 67, 68, 73, 75, 76, 77, 79, 80, 82, 83, 84, 85, 87, 88, 92, 98, 100, 101, 108, 109, 110, 139, 140, 141, 143). This most common of labels seems not to designate the content of psalms, given the wide variety of types of psalms involved. Rather, the title seems to have become a general designation as in Ben Sira 44. According to 44:5 (manuscript B and Masada), Israel's ancestors include "composers of songs (*ḥwqry mzmwr*)." The word then does not refer to a type of psalm, but to the psalms' musical rendering in the post-exilic temple worship.

> 2. *šîr*, "song" (Psalms 18, 45, 46, 65, 66, 67, 68, 75, 76, 83, 87, 88, 92, 108, 121–34). The title fits most of these texts as hymns. Songs are for celebration, and they call for "dance . . . timbrel and lyre" (Ps 149:2). Hymns call for "blasts of the horn, . . . harp and lyre, . . . timbrel and dance, . . . lute and pipe, . . . and cymbals" (Psalm 150). Accordingly, when lament rather than celebration is the order of the day, people set aside their stringed instruments and desist from "song" (Ps 137:1-4). Some "songs" are provided with specific indications of their usage. Psalm 45 is

"a love-song," and Psalms 120–34 are all labelled as "songs of the ascents" (although the precise referent of the second word is unclear).

3. *těpillâ*, "prayer" (Psalms 17, 86, 90, 102, 142). Psalm 102 is unusual is indicating the sense of prayer as involving a request (typical for laments), in the rest of its superscription ("prayer of the lowly when he is faint and pours forth his plea before the LORD"). Habakkuk 3 also uses *tepillâ* for the prayer there. The designation may refer to its content, but by some point it was used in a very general way for all of Psalms 2–72, as indicated by Ps 72:20: "The prayers of David son of Jesse are finished." Like *tehillâ* (#8 below), *tepillâ* originally was a more restricted term, but became used as a more general designation. The label is also known from psalms in the Dead Sea Scrolls (4Q381 33 8), although the importance of the usage there is unclear.[11]

4. *maśkîl*, "song of adoration" (Psalms 32, 42, 44, 45, 52, 53, 54, 55, 74, 78, 88, 89, 142). The term has been subject of much dispute.[12] It derives from a root (**śkl*) which otherwise is connected to wisdom,[13] but wisdom themes or language do not appear in the psalms which have *maśkîl* in their superscription. Rather, in a number of contexts the word refers to some sort of speech. The clearest of these instances, Ben Sira 32:1d, 2 and 4 (manuscript F), was pointed out by S. Talmon and E. Eshel.[14] Commenting on hospitality to guests, the passage admonishes:

> Worry about them and afterwards go about (your business),
> Tend to their needs and then take your place,
> So that you may rejoice in their honor,
> And lift up (e. g., win) praise (*śkl*) for (your) conduct...
> In place of praise (*śkl*) do not pour out discourse,
> Instead of song (*mzmwr*) do not pour out discourse.

The second example of *śkl* in this passage places it in parallelism with *mzmwr*, "singing" or "song." Given its immediate context, the first instance of *śkl* accordingly means "praise" or the like. Talmon and Eshel therefore read Amos 5:13 accordingly, that "praise will be silent at that time." So too in Ps 47:1 *maśkîl* seems to refer to praise or "song of adoration."[15] The specific connotation of praise suits a number of the psalms reasonably well, specifically with either hymns (Psalm 45), psalms of (or with) thanksgiving (Psalm 54), or psalms of instruction (Psalms 32, 52, 53 [?], 78). While the sense of praise would seem to fit laments poorly (e.g., Psalms 42–43, 44, 55, 74, 88, 89, 142), even in these cases, the laments point to or involve praise (see Pss 42:6, 12; 43:5; 44:5-9; 74:12-17; 89:2-37; cf. 55:17-20).

5. *šiggāyôn*, "lamentation" (?) (Psalm 7). Some scholars have connected biblical *šiggāyôn* with Akkadian *šigû*, originally an exclamation which

secondarily came to designate a penitential prayer.[16] NJPS (1067 n. a) connects this word with the plural form, *šigyōnôt*, in the title to Habakkuk 3 as possibly meaning "psalms of supplication."

6. *miktām* (Psalms 16, 56, 57, 58, 59, 60). The Septuagint translates *miktām* as *stelographia*, writing on stone. For this reason H. L. Ginsberg took *miktam* as an inscription on a stone slab.[17] W. W. Hallo suggests that *miktam* is a letter-prayer as in Isa 38:9. In either case, the word might be a biform of *miktāb*, "letter," or perhaps "inscription." Other views have followed a more strict etymological route. S. Mowinckel takes the term as a "psalm of expiation" (?) based on Akkadian *katāmu*.[18]

7. *tĕhillâ*, "praise" (Psalm 145). This term is very rare in the superscriptions, appearing only in Psalm 145. The only text of this psalm known from the Dead Sea Scrolls calls it *tĕpillâ* (11QPsᵃ 16:7). Originally a word for praise (Pss 22:25, 33:1, 34:1, etc.), *tĕhillâ* becomes the general Hebrew term for the compositions in the Psalter. The earliest known designation for the book is *spr thlym*, "Book of Praises" (see the final section below). The label is also known from psalms in the Dead Sea Scrolls which are not attested in any Bible (4Q380 1 ii 8, 4 24Q381 24 4). It is also a category of compositions created by David according to the Psalms scroll discovered in cave 11 (11QPsᵃ 27:4-5).[19] According to a heavenly liturgy found in a text from cave 4 the angels sing "marvelous praises (*thlym*)" (4Q400 2 4; 4Q403 1 ii 31, 3 2; 4Q405 18 5). Upon the completion of battle, the community is to sing "the hymn of return," according to the War Scroll discovered in cave 1 (*thlt hmšwb*; 1QM 14:2). The biblical book is known as *tĕhillîm* in Jewish tradition. It is tempting to see this designation as a relatively late usage compared with terms such as *mizmôr* or *šîr*. The application of this term to the whole biblical book points to a general understanding of all psalms, whether praise or prayer, as ultimately praise of the God of Israel.

Some psalms have more than a single designation (Psalms 45, 65, 66, 67, 68, 75, 76, 87, 88). Psalms 65–68, 75–76 are called both *mizmôr* and *šîr*; the distinction being drawn between the two terms is unclear. (Both have been translated "song.") In some cases, the first term might refers to the poems' musical rendering in post-exilic Temple worship, while the second designates its content as songs of praise (e.g., hymns); or, when the two terms are juxtaposed, they may represent a double title for "song." As "a love-song" and "psalm of adoration" (*maśkîl*), Psalm 45 uses the first to label its content and the second to designate the psalm's musical usage in post-exilic Temple worship. Psalm 88 is called *šîr mizmôr* and *maśkîl*. Psalm 142 is designated both as a *maskîl* and a *tĕpillâ*, "prayer."

The Dead Sea Scrolls contain types for some psalms which differ in the traditional Hebrew text (MT). For example, Psalm 145 is called *thlh*, "praise," in the MT, but *tplh*, "prayer," in the Psalms Scroll from Cave 11 (11QPs[a]).[20] The last two books of the MT Psalter (Psalms 90–106 and 107–50) often lack superscriptions, but a number of psalms (Psalms 106, 111–13, 117, 135, 146–50, 151) begin with the word *hallĕlûyâ*. In English the form is also known as Alluleia (following the Greek spelling of the word). The designation is grammatically an imperative plus direct object, meaning "Praise Yah." ("Yah" was used as a short form of the divine name, Yʜwʜ, although the linguistic connection between the two is not transparent.) Technically, the word *hallĕlûyâ* is not a superscription as such, but like superscriptions, it stands at the beginning of some psalms and it is used as a term to group a number of psalms together, specifically Psalms 111–13, 146–50. According to L. M. Barré, the different distributions of *hllwyh* in MT, LXX and 11QPs[a] of Psalms 146–50 are not the result of scribal error. Instead, Barré argues that *hllwyh* serves as a conclusion formula in 11QPs[a] but as an introductory formula in LXX, while MT show both usages both, resulting in *hllwyh* functioning as a framing device (known as *inclusio*).[21]

The superscription at the beginning of the Hebrew version of Psalm 151 calls it a "halleluyah" psalm, a label not attested in any other version. This term appears also in 4Q448, col. A, line 1: *hllwyh mzmw[r]*.[22] As the editors of this text note, this word is not used in Qumran community literature. It is also not found in any other extant superscription for this psalm and its presence here is something of a mystery. If the 11QPs[a] scroll were dependent on a Psalter which included 150 psalms as in MT, LXX and Syriac, then this word here might be explained as an extension of the use of this word in the superscriptions in Psalms 146–50.[23]

It seems unlikely, however, that Psalm 151 was composed for or with the collection of Halleluyah psalms of 146–50. (J. Strugnell calls Psalm 151 "very unhalleluyah-like."[24]) Rather, it was attached secondarily to this group at which point it could have received the designation of halleluyah. Another term which is not strictly speaking part of prose labels may function like *hallĕlûyâ*.[25] The word *hôdû* (Psalms 105, 107, 118, 136) is an imperative literally "give thanks." Since this word begins three psalms, it may have been used secondarily to identify minor collections within the second half of the Psalter. It would seem from Psalm 106 which begins with *hallĕluyâ* and then starts the poem with *hôdû* that the two terms were used perhaps in conjunction to structure minor collections in Books IV and V in the Psalter.

Looking at all of the terms for types, some basic distinctions can be observed. E. M. Schuller has thoughtfully raised a number of questions pertaining to the types ascribed to various biblical and Qumranic prayers and has asked whether they "have a technical and consistent usage in this period."[26] Despite inconsistency and a lack of systematic labelling extended to all of the psalms, some basic distinctions seem to hold: "psalm" (*mizmôr*) could apply to any type, while "prayer" (*těpillâ*) refers only to laments or psalms of trust, and "song" (*šîr*) is generally reserved to hymns or psalms of thanksgiving (Psalms 83 and 88 being the only exceptions). Schematized, the genre designations in the superscriptions may be understood in this manner:

GENERAL TERM: *mizmôr*

PRAYER	PRAISE
těpillâ	*šir*
šiggāyôn	*těhillâ*
miktām	*hallělûyâ*
	hôdû
	maśkîl (?)

The genre designations in the superscriptions seem to recognize a fundamental distinction between prayer (request) with its variations and praise (no request, need in background) and its variations. In the area of prayer, *těpillâ* expresses a wish for a change in the speaker's condition. As suggested by the content of the psalms to which they are attached, *miktām* and *šiggāyôn* may be specific sorts of prayer. In the area of praise, *hallěluyâ* and *hôdû* as well as the one example of *těhillâ* psalms, constitute praise (hymns). I am inclined to assign *maśkîl* to praise as well given the discussion of the term above, but there are enough ambiguous or problematic cases for the term to urge caution.

Finally, a few psalms mentions their purpose, perhaps as a clarification or specification of the type:

1. *lěhazkîr*, "to remember" (Psalms 38, 70).
2. *lělammēd*, "to teach" (Psalm 60).[27]
3. *lěʿannôt*, "to answer" (?)/ "to afflict (i. e., for penance)"[28] (?) (Psalm 88).
4. *lětôdâ*, "for thanksgiving" (Psalm 100).

The clearest of these designations, *lětôdâ*, seems to mark Psalm 100 as a psalm to be used to give thanks to God. (If the designation refers to its function, then the line between thanksgiving and hymns is not rigid.) Less clear, the designation *lĕlammēd* might be taken to indicate that Psalm 60, though a lament, was intended to function as a psalm of instruction. The intended purpose of the two *lĕhazkîr* psalms, both laments, is likewise unclear; if this issue were judged on the basis of content, perhaps as laments they are intended to make the God of Israel remember the lamentable condition of the speakers. However, one might wonder why other psalms of lament do not have this label as well. The Jewish Aramaic translation (Targum) of the psalms relates the word to *'azkārâ*, which is part of the cereal offering in Lev 2:2, 9, 16, 5:12, 6:8 and Num 5:16. Perhaps then the word means "to make the offering."[29] Accordingly, it might be suggested that *lĕtôdâ* is not for thanksgiving in general, but either refers to, or is a prayer to be recited for, the thanksgiving offering. The infinitive in Psalm 88 may indicate that this psalm is to function in conjunction with another text. If the following phrase, *maśkîl lĕhêmān hā'ezrāḥî*, were the object of this infinitive, then this label refers not to Psalm 88, but to some other text. It would seem prudent, however, not to make this assumption. These various designations may not date from the same period. From the relatively rarity of these psalms and the restriction of their occurrences, it might be inferred that the designations *miktām* and *šiggāyôn* are older than either the more common designations or the predominantly later ones.

Excursus: The Forms of Prayer and Praise in the Psalter

The discussion above relates to a reading of form-criticism of the Psalms that is more formal than most, if not all, current analyses. Accordingly, it may be worthwhile to explain my basic division of the psalms into prayer (prayer, psalms of trust and laments) and praise (thanksgiving, hymns and psalms of instruction). Despite inconsistency and a lack of labelling in all of the Psalms, some basic distinctions seem to hold: "psalm" could apply to any type, while "prayer' refers only to laments or psalms of trust, and "song" is generally reserved to hymns or psalms of thanksgiving (Psalms 83 and 88 being exceptions). These terms would suggest that such formal observations were concerns of the community which transmitted the psalms in ancient Israel. The ancient distinction made between "prayer" and "song" remains the cornerstone of modern formal study of the psalms.[30]

Form criticism has been very helpful for further analysis of the Psalms.[31] It has been customary among scholars of the Psalms to distinguish the following types: individual and communal laments; psalms of trust and thanksgiving; hymns (with psalms of Yhwh's enthronement and songs of Zion as subtypes); royal psalms; and wisdom psalms. This classification is useful to a point, but if the psalms were to be classified according to form and usage and not content, two basic sorts of psalms might be recognized: prayers, which would include laments and psalms of trust; and praise, which includes hymns, psalms of thanksgiving and psalms of instruction.[32] Furthermore, these types were further defined as individual (spoken by "I" often in a communal context) or communal (spoken by "we") psalms. In the case of laments, for example, a particular psalm may further be categorized as either individual or communal laments. The same is true of songs of trust, psalms of thanksgiving and hymns. Psalms of instruction tend to be individual (though within a group context). In all of these cases, it should be noted that individual psalms as much as communal psalms may be located in the context of liturgy, and because of shifts between "I" and "we," sometimes it is a bit unclear as to whether an individual or communal psalm is involved.[33]

For the most part form criticism has been abundantly helpful for the treatment of psalms, especially laments, songs of thanksgiving, hymns and psalms of instruction. (Songs of trust are not so distinctive from other prayers according to formal criteria, and royal psalms belong to several different formal types, as discussed below.) Prayer seems to be the basic rubric which includes both laments and psalms of trust. As noted above in the discussion on psalm titles, some psalms use the term *tĕpillâ*, "prayer," in their superscriptions, which would suggest that prayer was recognized as a basic rubric for psalms involving request, whether for oneself or for another. The shortest prayer in the Bible is Moses' prayer on behalf of Miriam when he asks God (Num 12:13): "God, please, heal, please, her" (*'ēl nā' rĕpâ' nā' lāh*). Some prayers in the psalms lack the formal elements of either laments or psalms of trust.[34] Prayers which do not belong to these formal types include Psalms 19 (prayer to keep from sin), 20 (prayer for the king), 67 (prayer for a good harvest), and 119 (prayer for instruction).[35] Psalm 67 is a good example of a prayer for the blessing of a bounteous harvest. This prayer for blessing may be contrasted with the lament over drought and famine in Joel 2 and the song of thanksgiving for a good harvest in Psalm 65.

Just as prayer covers the categories of lament and song of trust, so praise (*tĕhillâ*) constitutes the general rubric which would include hymns, thanksgiving and instruction. Thanksgiving psalms and hymns differ in the motive given for praise: thanksgivings is usually given for the deliverance specific to the speaker whereas hymns praise Yahweh for more general reasons not specific to the speaker, such as the greatness of creation or Yahweh's saving deeds on behalf of Israel in the past. Psalms of thanksgiving may include hymnic elements, and it would appear that in the tradition hymns and thanksgiving were closely related as in Ps 22:24-32. Judith 15:14 shows their combination: "Judith led all Israel in this song of thanksgiving, and the people swelled this hymn of praise" (NAB). 1 Macc 4:24 records how upon their return to their army base the force of Judas Maccabee "sang hymns of thanksgiving to Heaven, 'For He is good, for His mercy endures forever.'"[36] The quoted line occurs in the hymns, Psalms 106, 107, 108, 136 and 1 Chron 16:8-36 and 2 Chron 20:21.[37] It would appear that the thanksgiving for military victory was regarded as a hymn.

Psalms of instruction differ from both thanksgiving psalms and hymns in their immediate audience. Psalms of instruction are aimed not at YHWH directly, but at the congregation. The speaker gives witness to the experience of salvation and offers reflections based on this experience. I have included this type of psalm more generally under the rubric of praise, because it offers praise to YHWH indirectly through the experience of teaching. While the immediate audience is the congregation, the congregation is uplifted in hearing the praise of YHWH reflected in the act of teaching.

Prayer and praise represent two related "moments" in the life of prayer and liturgy: prayer or request to YHWH aims for something not yet realized, praise, thanksgiving and instruction addresses something that has already been realized (instruction involves reflection often before a community of believers on what has been realized). Lament, trust, thanksgiving, hymn and instruction are connected in the experience of prayer. Many psalms recount the lament leading to a divine answer which provokes the act of thanksgiving (Psalm 22). Similarly, the lament may incorporate or anticipate a divine answer which turns the words from near-despair to praise (Psalm 40). Many laments, especially communal laments, use old hymnic language to contrast past moments of national glory and the present situation of community distress (Psalm 74). Prayer leads to divine salvation followed by a hymn of praise and acknowledgment of others (Ps 40:2-4).

Some scholars also identify another separate type of psalms known as "royal psalms" (Psalms 2, 18, 20, 21, 45, 72, 89, 101, 110, 132, 144).[38] In form criticism this general category of "royal psalms" has served to group all the psalms dealing with the king either as speaker or topic. This approach to the royal psalms is not consistent with the other form-critical categories for the Psalms which are defined on the basis of form and setting and not content. As a result, royal psalms should be defined along lines of form and setting. Put this way, some royal psalms are actually psalms of prayer (lament or trust) or praise (hymns or thanksgiving); none are psalms of instruction. The royal psalms which presume a royal speaker are individual psalms. For example, Psalm 18 is an individual royal psalm of thanksgiving, and Psalm 89 would appear to be a royal lament (see v. 50). Psalm 144 appears to be a royal prayer. Other royal psalms are addressed to the king. Psalm 2, possibly a coronation psalm, may be viewed as a psalm of instruction. Psalm 45 is clearly a royal wedding song, which may be seen as a hymn to the king and his bride. Psalm 110 might be understood as a hymn exalting the king. Hence, even these psalms which have special royal content nonetheless may be understood as royal variants on individual psalms of different sorts.

The royal psalms in which the monarch is the topic would likewise be classified as communal psalms of various sorts. Hence, Psalms 20, 72, and 132 as well as Habakkuk 3 (see v. 13) are prayers offered on behalf of the dynasty. Psalm 21 is a psalm of communal thanksgiving for the power given to the king by Yhwh. Some scholars have sought to extend the number of royal psalms by understanding the king as the speaker of many anonymous psalms, a view which has waxed and waned in popularity.[39] If the anonymous "I" could be used to identify more royal psalms, the number of such psalms would increase to as much as one-third of the total Psalter, which might be the basis for justifying a separate category of royal psalms. However, as noted by M. Brettler,[40] the arguments are hardly persuasive, and it is wiser to return to the view of a restricted number of psalms with the king as speaker or topic. In retrospect, it is not difficult to venture a guess for the reason why scholars identified "royal psalms" as a separate category. Most, if not all, form-critics were Christians well-versed in the New Testament. Unlike other groups of psalms, the content found in royal psalms played such an influential role in New Testament christology that these psalms already held a distinctive profile for Christian biblical scholars who therefore were predisposed to assign them to a separate category and thereby overlook their formal differences.

The figure of the king is only one of a number of characteristic topics in the Psalter that might be noted in relation to the main Psalm forms or genres. The temple or shrine, Zion (Jerusalem), the king and pilgrimage, likewise serve as the backdrop to a substantial number of psalms. These topics[41] may be correlated to the basic six psalm types (as well as psalmic material in other biblical books) in the following way:

	Temple	Zion	King	Pilgrimage
PRAYER				
prayer	134, 135	Jer 31:23	20, 72 Habakkuk 3	133
lament	3-5, 7	102, 137 (cf. Jer 17:12-13; Lamentations 5)	89 (cf. Jer 22:18, 34:5)	42-43
trust			cf. 21:7f.	23
PRAISE				
hymn		46, 48, 87, 46 122, 134 (cf. Jer 31:23)	45, 110	122[43]
thanksgiving	133	129	18, 21	
instruction	15, 24	50, 81	2	(cf. Isa 1:10-17, 2:3)

Given their topics, it may be supposed that all four themes begin in the period of the monarchy in Israel. Only the pilgrimage tradition would pre-date the monarchy, although none of the surviving pilgrimage psalms are this old.

A similar problem obtains with two other content-oriented categories which biblical scholars sometimes use. Form-critics of the psalms at times discuss "wisdom psalms" and a related group called "torah psalms." These two categories are derived largely on the basis of content and not on a formal basis. Instead, these psalms more precisely belong to a number of different types as illustrated by the schema below:

	Wisdom	Torah
PRAYER		
prayer	36	19, 119
lament		
trust	73	
PRAISE		
hymn	cf. Ben Sira 24	
thanksgiving		
instruction	37, 49, 78, 112, 127, 128, 133	1

Wisdom generally refers to the content of the speaker. So Ps 49:4 declares: "My mouth declares wisdom, the utterance of my heart is full of insight." It is true that some of the so-called "wisdom psalms" contain formulations best known from the wisdom literature of books such as Proverbs; these wisdom formulations include beatitudes ("happy/blessed is the one who"; Ps 112:1), sentence making comparisons ("better is one thing than another") and the address to "my son." However, wisdom in the Psalms just as often constitutes not form, but content such as descriptions of righteous versus the wicked, advice about proper conduct and subsequent reward, warnings about inappropriate conduct and subsequent demise or punishment. Furthermore, these wisdom sentences do not uniformily govern the overall formal construction of the psalms. Instead, they are maleable to a variety of forms. Most of the "wisdom psalms" actually belong to the category of instruction, but a few do not.

Conversely, only one of the "torah psalms" is a psalm of instruction. Both Psalms 19 and 119 contain prayer. While Psalm 19 has been regarded as a hymn plus prayer, the formal characteristic of the hymn, namely the call to others to praise, is absent from this composition; otherwise, this psalm is only clearly marked as a prayer which has used and/or incorporated a long hymnic section, a well-known optional element for prayers. Psalm 119 is more clearly marked as a prayer, containing numerous requests and direct addresses of the deity. Psalm 1 is a special case of an instruction psalm since the implicit addressee to be instructed is the audience of readership of the Psalter itself and perhaps not any audience in a liturgical context. Accordingly, I recognize that the strictly formal approach advocated here is not as clean as I might like, but such a tack is ultimately consistent and it is as equally fair to the texts as a so-called "form criticism" that mixes form and content.

V. Theological Questions

As I hope that the preceding sections suggest, the Psalter provides a particularly interesting test-case for some of the theological problems posed by historical scholarship. In the case of the Psalter, we have information that helps to show how the variety of the Psalter became a single book.

Davidic Authorship

2 Macc 2:13 may contain the earliest attestation to the idea of davidic authorship of the Psalms and perhaps other works as well, possibly a

major section of the Bible; after the prophets this passage mentions "the ones of David" (*ta tou David*).[44] A major halakhic work among the Dead Sea Scrolls, 4QMMT (section C = 4Q397 14-21), line 10, likewise assumes Davidic authorship over some part of Scripture, probably the "Writings" including the psalms: "we have [written] to you so that you may study the book of Moses [and] the book[s] of the Prophets and in Davi[d]. . ."[45] Furthermore, the same text assumes that at least some of the psalms were read in accordance with the superscriptions containing putatively autobiographical information about David: "Think of David who was a man of righteous deeds and who was (therefore) delivered from many troubles and was forgiven."[46] The massive psalms text (11QPs[a]) discovered among the Dead Sea Scrolls claims that David was the author of 360 psalms and 450 songs.[47] Moreover, this scroll attributes to David the extra-canonical psalms 151 (as does the Septuagint), 154 and 155. The Peshitta, a Syriac version of the Old Testament (5ApocSyrPs 1a, 1b, 4, 5) attributes 151–155 to David.[48] In accordance with the post-exilic attribution of various biblical works to famous biblical personages, the idea of Davidic authorship spread to the book of Psalms as a whole (bT. Pes. 117a),[49] although the other authors named in the superscriptions in the psalms were also recognized.

Yet both Jewish and Christian traditions show an awareness that David's is not the only voice of the Psalter. The formulation of the Talmud reflects a compromise formulation: "David wrote the book of Psalms including in it the work of ten elders, namely Adam, Melchizedek, Abraham, Moses, Heman, Yeduthun, Asaph, and the three sons of Korah" (bT. B.Bat. 14b; cf.15a).[50] The number, but not the names, of the ten elders remains consistent in Jewish tradition.[51] John Donne's opinion about authorship in the Psalter, recorded in his "Upon the Translation of the Psalmes by Sir Philip Sydney and the Countess of Pembroke his Sister," was only echoing two millennia of tradition when he wrote: ". . . and as those Psalmes we call/(Though some have other Authors) Davids all . . . ." In sum, the tradition maintains the apparent contradiction of a sense of multiple authors and a general assertion of Davidic authorship not only in the superscriptions, but also in later sources. On one level, the community conformed its identity as author to the biblical model of prophetic inspiration. In so doing, the tradition, as early as the late biblical period, harmonized the communally authored psalms with those of the individual. Accordingly, theological reflection in an era of modern biblical scholarship requires some consideration of the interaction (theologically speaking) between the individual and the communal. Ultimately the tradition sublimated the communal under the rubric of the inspired individual or individuals, yet it hardly erased the communal from its record. Out of respect for the historical tradition passed down, no ideal of scheme of Davidic authorship was imposed consistently. Instead, the model of Davidic piety stands next to the record of twists and turns in the historical development towards a "Book of Praises," as the next section suggests.

The Names of the Book

An analogous issue come to the fore when considering the various *names* for the book. (In contrast, the *order* of the book in the canon provides less direction. In the Christian canon, the book of Psalms appears between Job and Proverbs in the third of four sections, that is before the Prophets, but after the Pentateuch and the historical books. This is consistent with the listing of books by Jerome.[52] However, Luke 24:44 lists the Psalms after the Law and the Prophets. Similarly, Melito of Sardis, Origen and others list Psalms before other Hagiographa.[53] While the Psalms belonged to the Hagiographa in later Jewish and Christian tradition, the date of the beginning of this assignment is unclear.) The oldest attested name is *spr thlym*, "the book of praises," a designation attested in the Dead Sea Scrolls (specifically in 4Q491 17 4, part of a version of the War Scroll, 1QM).[54] This particular text dates to the second half of the first century c.e.; the designation *spr thlym* is presumably older. The early Church Father Origen transliterates the name of the book as *sphar thelleim*.[55] Jewish tradition calls the book *těhillîm*, "praises." The noun derives from the root **hll*, "to praise." It is interesting to note that this word is used only once in the book of Psalms in a prose title to designate a psalm (Psalm 145). Yet David, the author of the psalms by tradition, is reputed to have written 3,600 psalms (*thlym*) according one of the Dead Sea Scrolls, the psalms' scroll from cave 11 (11QPs[a] 27:4-5).

The Septuagint (codex Vaticanus = B) calls the book *psalmoi*, "songs," the basis for the English title, "Psalms" (cf. the Hebrew word, *mizmôr*, "song," used in the first verse of fifty-seven psalms). Luke 24:44 also refers to *psalmoi* for the book. Luke 20:42 and Acts 1:20 refer to the title *biblos psalmōn*, "Book of Psalms." Another English title for the book, the Psalter, comes from the title of the book in the Septuagint, codex Alexandrinus (= A), namely *psalterion*, a word derived from a Greek word for a stringed instrument. Given the musical character of psalms across genre, the Septuagint designation represents a "faithful reading" of the psalms as against their historical background: they were probably sung compositions in ancient Israel and the name given to the book by the Septuagint reflects this feature.

The situation differs for the MT name which illustrates the problem of "the one and the many." First, its name shows the move to call it a book: to be rendered as a book (or a book of five books being a mediating construct) represents a mode of singular reading imposed on a plurality of compositions with their plurality of historical settings and forms. In other words, the move from texts to canonical book called "praises", however much a commonplace or given, represents a massive strategy of reading these texts toward conformity of some sort toward one another, despite the messiness which historical scholarship has demonstrated. The traditions harmonize what critical scholarship shows to have difficulties in harmonizing; it is obvious, however, that such harmonizing activity is hardly impossible. In fact, it is more: it is normative. For Jewish readers the name "the book of praises" provides a theological reading of the psalms as a book which despite its varied genres ultimately serves as *těhillîm*, "praises" or acts of praise. In other words, beyond their original purposes, all the different genres—according to the name of the book—serve a further purpose (and perhaps more ultimate one), namely praise to God.

Taking Inspiration in the Tradition

The collection of the psalms into various forms of "book-ness" encouraged a comparable development in the theological area of inspiration. Such a development may be traced at least in part, thanks to the textual versions of the book. These provide some information about how inspiration was understood (e.g., as prophecy of David). At an early point in the tradition, perhaps by the turn of the millennium, we have two views of the book's place. In one view Psalms stands for a third major section of the Hebrew Bible which it begins.[56] A major legal work among the Dead Sea Scrolls, 4QMMT (section C = 4Q397 14-21), line 10, assumes Davidic authorship over some part of Scripture, beginning with the Psalms: "we have [written] to you so that you may study the book of Moses [and] the book[s] of the Prophets and in Davi[d] . . ."[57] The editors of the *editio princeps* of this text, E. Qimron and J. Strugnell, take "David" as a reference "not only to the Psalms of David, but rather to the Hagiographa."[58] On the other view the Psalms were considered part of the prophets.[59] While Luke 24:44 lists the Psalms after the Law and the Prophets, other New Testament books that cite Psalms refer only to the Law and the Prophets without any indication of a third major section in the Hebrew Scriptures (Matt 5:17; 7:12; 11:13; 16:16; 22:40; Luke 16:29-31; Acts 13:15; 24:14; 28:23; Rom 3:21).[60] (The same two-fold division seems to underlie the Qumran Community Rule, 1QS 8.) A two-part canon might imply the prophetic understanding of Psalms. Even if this is not correct, other evidence suggests such an understanding of the Psalter. At Qumran the Psalms is the only book subjected to one mode of interpretation (known as *pesher*) otherwise known only for prophetic books. In 11QPs[a] 27:11 David is said to have composed Psalms through prophecy, and in Acts 2:30 he is regarded as a prophet (Acts 2:30). It is evident that the Psalms conceived as David's prophecy conforms the book to the paradigm of prophetic inspiration at work throughout much of the biblical corpus not only in the prophetic books proper, but also in the Pentateuch, the product of that prophet of prophets, Moses. And yet it is the very "messiness" of the superscriptions which draws attention to multiple authorship. In some sense such a situation encourages readers to draw a general conclusion about Davidic authorship even as they might recognize other dimensions of authorship. In other words, "harmonizing," a technique of theological "coping" (perhaps associated nowadays more with fundamentalist readings of Scripture) has represented one avenue to preserve the one and the many, at least on the "human side" of biblical authorship.

Yet the book of Psalms poses an additional challenge about inspiration, insofar as it differs from inspiration involved with Pentateuchal or prophetic texts. While most other biblical books represent the divine word issued from God to the Israelite community through various human mediators (such as Moses, priests, prophets or sages), the Psalms is one biblical book where human words *addressed to God* have become God's word. The Psalms not only include, but focus on, human longing and joy as one dimension of God's own message to Israel. Perhaps, because it expresses paradigmatic moments of need (prayer) and equally paradigmatic expression of thanks, praise or instruction (praise), the book continues to inspire people to give voice to the prayer within themselves, just as the psalmist of Ps 40:4 assumed. Or, in another vein, as Martin Buber commented: "For we all are too noisy to hear him; it is our task to make this voiceless voice perceptible giving our tongue to him."[61]

For such a view of a biblical text so central to the life of the Synagogue and the Church, what might inspiration mean? The Psalter captures paradigmatic moments of human need met within the larger context of relationships with the Divine. As only one suggestion about where the Church is at present in seeing historical scholarship meeting up with traditional concepts about authorship and inspiration, we might say that historical criticism has aptly shown the different situations of need (prayer) and recognition of needs met (praise), and it is the later biblical tradition and latter post-biblical theological tradition which could understand not only that these moments of prayer and praise constitute the paradigm of a single life represented by the figure of David, but of a life that would only make sense with God experienced within a community called Israel.

NOTES: CHAPTER 15

[1] See P. W. Flint, *The Dead Sea Scrolls and the Book of Psalms* (STDJ; Leiden: Brill, 1997) 33, n. 22.

[2] See E. Tov, "Special Layout of Poetical Units in the Texts from the Judean Desert," *Give Ear to My Words. Psalms and Other Poetry in and around the Hebrew Bible: Essays in honour of N. A. von Uchelen* (J. Dyk ed.: Amsterdam: Societas Hebraica Amstelodamensis, 1996) 123.

[3] Childs, "Psalm Titles and Midrashic Exegesis," *JSS* 16 (1971) 143.

[4] Childs, "Psalm Titles," 148.

[5] Mowinckel, *The Psalms in Israel's Worship*, 2.213.

[6] The precise meaning of the preposition "to" (*le*) in the psalm titles has been a matter of discussion. The preposition could have referred to either topic ("concerning") or authorship ("by"). Later tradition understood the preposition in the second sense. (This is evident especially in the superscription to Psalm 18 = 2 Sam 22.) It is supported further by other biblical books. For example, Solomon is attributed with the authorship of the Song of Songs in the same manner, with *lĕ-*. See Waltke, "Superscripts, Postscripts, or Both," *JBL* 110 (1991) 584.

[7] The Greek textual witnesses are not uniform on this point, however. A. Pietersma comments: "Uncertainty regarding the precise extent of the Davidic Psalter in Greek remains." (Pietersma, "David in the Greek Psalms," *VT* 30 [1980] 226). For the additions as well as the variations in the Greek forms of this ascription, see A. Pietersma, "David in the Greek Psalms," 213–26.

[8] For the moment I set aside the issue of Psalms 151–55. These five psalms appear in different versions. The Septuagint attests to Psalm 151. The Syriac Church preserved Psalms 151–55. The major psalms scroll from cave 11 at Qumran (11QPs^a) contains the text of Psalms 151, 154, and 155. (For Psalms 152–53 there is no pre-Christian evidence.) The five psalms numbered as Psalms 151–55 have not been included in modern translations or commentaries on the Psalter. The exclusion might be supported on historical grounds, but this argument is not really the point. Let me explain. By tradition the Septuagint is older than the MT. The Septuagint, or at least the Septuagint translation of the Pentateuch, allegedly dates to the third to the second centuries B.C.E., while the MT is thought to go back to rabbinic tradition dating to the early centuries C.E. The reason for the exclusion lies in the traditional religious preference for the Hebrew Masoretic text of the book which contains only 150 psalms. The choice derived from

denominational history: the Masoretic text of Jewish tradition was embraced by the Reformation churches as the basis for the Old Testament text. While both canons of the Old Testament, the shorter Hebrew-Aramaic collection and the wider Greek collection, were used and cited as authoritative in western and eastern Christianity, this issue went unresolved in Catholic tradition until the Council of Trent. In the first decree of the fourth session of April 5, 1546, the Council of Trent listed the sacred books of the Bible, including "the Psalter of David of 150 psalms" (*Psalterium Davidicum centum quinquaginta psalmorum*). Accordingly, the New American Bible (NAB) and Revised New American Bible (RNAB) kept to the shorter canon of the Psalter. At present the Roman Catholic tradition adheres to the shorter canon of the Psalter embraced by Jewish tradition and the Reformers. Yet there is no reason why Catholic Bibles could not add the five psalms, with some qualification made that accounts for the Trent statement. Moreover, there is no reason why the view expressed at Trent could not be revised.

[9] See especially D. Robertson, *Linguistic Evidence in Dating Early Hebrew Poetry* (Missoula, Mont.: Scholars, 1972). See also F. M. Cross and D. N. Freedman, *Ancient Yahwistic Poetry* (SBLDS; Missoula, Mont.: Scholars, 1975; sec. ed.; The Biblical Resources series; Grand Rapids, Mich./Cambridge, U.K.: Eerdmans; Livonia, Mich.: Dove Booksellers, 1997); idem, "Some Observations on Early Hebrew," *Bib* 53 (1972) 413–20; D. N. Freedman, "Archaic Forms in Early History Poetry," *ZAW* 72 (1960) 101–7. E. Y. Kutscher, *A History of the Hebrew Language* (Jerusalem: Magnes; Leiden: Brill, 1982) para. 17, 111–16. Cf. I. Young, "The Style of the Gezer Calendar and some 'Archaic Biblical Hebrew' Passages," *VT* 42 (1992) 362–75.

[10] It is for this reason that the preposition *l-* taken in other superscriptions as indicators of authors would presumably here refer to the topic of the king; if so, *l-* might be viewed in superscriptions as not restricted to putative authorship, but pertaining to the topic of the psalm as in the Ugaritic superscriptions, such as *lb'l*, "regarding Baal" (cf. Ps 45:2). Scholars have long resisted such a conclusion generally for Psalm superscriptions and in general *l-* in superscriptions does not seem to refer to topic. However, a more complex development may lie behind this *l-*: (i) an initial stage where it refers to topics; (ii) a second and overlapping stage where the preposition refers to both the topic and the author; and (iii) a third and overlapping stage where the *l-* of topic drops out of the understanding and the preposition is thought to refer only to authorship. This proposal is, of course, entirely hypothetical.

[11] For greater discussion of these issues, see Schuller, *Non-Canonical Psalms from Qumran*, 25.

[12] See the Briggs', *Psalms* 1.lxi; Kraus, *Psalms 1–59*, 25–26.

[13] So derived by Mowinckel, *The Psalms in Israel's Worship*, 2.209. On the term, see H. Kosmala, "*Maśkîl*," *JANES* 5 (1973).

[14] Talmon and Eshel, "'And the *maśkîl* at that time will be silent' (Amos 5:13)," *Shnaton* 10 (1990) 115–22 (Heb.). The text is published in A. A. di Lella, "The Newly Discovered Sixth Manuscript of Ben Sira from the Cairo Geniza," *Bib* 69 (1988) 233.

[15] So already Ginsberg, *The Israelian Heritage*, 33.

[16] See Mowinckel, *The Psalms in Israel's Worship*, 2.209; *KB³* 949; M. J. Seux, "*Šiggāyôn = šigû?*" *Mélanges bibliques et orientaux en l'honneur de M. Henri Cazelles* (A. Caquot and M. Delcor, eds.; AOAT 212; Neukirchen-Vluyn: Neukirchener Verlag, 1981) 419–38; K. van der Toorn, *Sin and Sanction in Israel and Mesopotamia: A Comparative Study* (Studia Semitica Neerlandica 22; Assen: Van Gorcum, 1985) 117–21.

[17] H. L. Ginsberg, *Louis Ginzberg Jubilee Volume* (English section; New York: 1945) 169f.; followed by Dahood, *Psalms I*, 87.

[18] Mowinckel, *The Psalms in Israel's Worship*, 1.209; *KB*[3] 523. Such a ritual sense is not listed for the Akkadian word in *CAD K*:298–303.

[19] Schuller, *Non-Canonical Psalms from Qumran*, 25, 26.

[20] See E. M. Schuller, "Prayer, Hymnic, and Liturgical Texts from Qumran," *The Community of the Renewed Covenant: The Notre Dame Symposium on the Dead Sea Scrolls* (ed. E. Ulrich and J. VanderKam; Christianity and Judaism in Antiquity 10; Notre Dame, Ind.: University of Notre Dame, 1994) 161–62.

[21] Barré, "*Halĕlû yah*: A Broken Inclusio," *CBQ* 45 (1983) 195–200, especially 198–99.

[22] E. Eshel, H. Eshel, and A. Yardeni, "A Scroll from Qumran part of Psalm 154 and a Prayer for King Jonathan and His Kingdom," *Tarbiz* 60 (1991) 295–327 (Heb.) = *IEJ* 42 (1992) 199–229. See also Halleluyah used to close the considerably later Odes of Solomon 3-42 (see Charlesworth, "Odes of Solomon," *OTPs* 2.736–71), evidently modelled on the biblical examples.

[23] So Strugnell, "Notes," 267; Haran, "The Two Text-Forms," 181. While some scholars accept this theory of dependence (Skehan, Beckwith, and assumed by Strugnell, Haran and Waltke), others dispute it (Sanders, Flint).

[24] Strugnell, "Notes," 267.

[25] See Wilson, *The Editing of the Hebrew Psalter*, 126–29.

[26] Schuller, "Prayer, Hymnic, and Liturgical Texts from Qumran," 161.

[27] Cf. Mowinckel, *The Psalms in Israel's Worship*, 2.217.

[28] So Mowinckel, *The Psalms in Israel's Worship*, 2.212.

[29] See Kraus, *Psalms 1–59*, 29. In support of this theory, Mowinckel (*The Psalms in Israel's Worship*, 1.3) cites Ben Sira 38: 9, 11.

[30] I am aware that such ancient labels are not entirely consistent for a given text. Psalm 145, for example, is called "praise" (*thlh*) in MT but "prayer" (*tplh*) in 11QPs[a]. For a recent discussion of this difficulty, see Schuller, "Prayer, Hymnic, and Liturgical Texts from Qumran," 153–71.

[31] For further details regarding form criticism of the psalms, see Kraus, *Psalms 1–59*, 38–62; Gerstenberger, *Psalms*, 9–22.

[32] Kraus (*Psalms 1–59*, 40) introduced the first two categories on the basis of the Hebrew terminology of the superscriptions and other evidence.

[33] See especially Mowinckel, *The Psalms in Israel's Worship*, 1.12-3, 42-6. On the difficulties as they apply to laments, see P. W. Ferris, Jr., *The Genre of Communal Lament in the Bible and the Ancient Near East* (SBLDS 127; Atlanta: Scholars, 1992) 147–48, 158, 163–64.

[34] Yet such prayers are relatively rare. See Mowinckel, *The Psalms in Israel's Worship*, 1.221–2.

[35] Mowinckel (*The Psalms in Israel's Worship*, 1.221–22) would add Psalm 123, but the complaint of the lament is present in vv. 3b-4. Mowinckel adds Psalms 130 and 131 as well as Psalms 85 and 126. See the discussion of these psalms in the commentary.

[36] J. A. Goldstein, *I Maccabees* (AB 41; New York: Doubleday, 1976) 258, 265–66. See also 4:55, on which see Goldstein, *I Maccabees*, 286–87.

[37] Goldstein, *I Maccabees*, 265.

[38] So Kraus (*Psalms 1–59*, 56–57). Kraus himself settles for Gunkel's basis for such a category, namely they concern kings; yet this is hardly a sufficient formal basis for a

form-critical category. The indigenous phrase which Kraus cites from Ps 45:1, maʿăśay lĕmelek, does not mean "royal composition" (and thereby implying a separate category), but "my composition for a king." It is evident that Psalm 45 involves praise of the king akin to other psalms of praise.

[39] See J. Eaton, *Kingship and the Psalms,* (2nd ed. (Sheffield: JSOT, 1986) 1–11; B. Feininger, "A Decade of German Psalm-Criticism," *JSOT* 20 (1981) 3–4; J. L. S. Croft, *The Identity of the Individual in the Psalms* (JSOTSup 44; Sheffield: JSOT, 1987).

[40] Brettler, *God is King: Understanding an Israelite Metaphor* (JSOTSup 76; Sheffield: JSOT, 1989) 25.

[41] Cf. Kraus (*Psalms 1–59,* 41) who speaks of "theme-oriented form groups."

[42] According to E. M. Schuller, post-exilic examples of hymns of Zion include Tobit 13:9-18, Baruch 4:30-5:9, Ps. Solomon 11, Apostrophe to Zion (11Psᵃ XXII 1-15), 4QPsᶠ VII 14-17, VIII 2-15 and 4Q380 1 i 1-11. Third Isaiah evidently draws on this genre at several points in its praise of Zion. See Schuller, "4Q380 and 4Q381: Non Canonical Psalms from Qumran," in *The Dead Sea Scrolls; Forty Years of Research* (ed. D. Dimant and U. Rappaport, eds.: STDJ X; Leiden: Brill; Jerusalem: Magness/Yad Izhak Ben-Zvi, 1992) 92. See also 4Q179 (J. M. Allegro, *Qumrân Cave 4 - 1 (4Q158-4Q186), with the colloboration of A. A. Anderson* (DJD V; Oxford: Clarendon, 1968) 75–77; Strugnell, Review of Allegro, *Qumrân Cave 4 - 1 (4Q158-4Q186), RQ* [1970] 250–52).

[43] This psalm exemplifies themes of both Zion and pilgrimage, illustrating the spectrum of these topics.

[44] See H. M. Orlinsky, "Some Terms in the Prologue to Ben Sira and the Hebrew Canon," *JBL* 110 (1991) 483–90.

[45] *Qumran Cave 4 V; Miqsat Maʾaśe Ha-Torah* (E. Qimron and J. Strugnell, eds.; Oxford: Clarendon: Oxford, 1994) 58–59, 112 (with my modifications of the translation). The phrase, *bdwy[d],* literally "in Davi[d]," might be an ellipsis for either **bspr dwyd,*" in the book of David" (referring to the Psalms) or **bspry dwyd,* "in the books of David" (referring to the writings). Qimron and Strugnell (*Qumran Cave 4 V,* 59, n. to line 10) take "David" as a reference "not only to the Psalms of David, but rather to the Hagiographa" of which the Psalms were one book in both the MT and the LXX and which heads the MT order of the "Writings." Luke 24:44 similarly refers to "the psalms" as the name for the third major section after "the law of Moses and the prophets" (cf. Acts of the Apostles 28:23; Matt 5:17). L. Schiffman's contention that "David" in 4QMMT refers to "presumably the biblical accounts of the Davidic monarchy" is left unargued and is unpersuasive (see Schiffman, "Origin and Early History of the Qumran Sect," *BA* 58 [1995] 38).

[46] *Qumran Cave 4 V,* 63, to 4Q398 14–17 ii (composite text, section C, lines 25–26).

[47] Sanders, *The Psalms Scroll of Qumran Cave 11 (11 QPsᵃ)* (Oxford: 1965) 91f., Col. XXVII, 4f., 9f.; idem, *The Dead Sea Psalms Scroll* (Ithaca: Cornell University, 1967) 134–37. See Sarna, "Prolegomenon," XIV.

[48] See *OTPs* II: 612–17.

[49] Sarna, "Prolegomenon," XIV.

[50] Sarna, "Prolegomenon," XIV; Leiman, *The Canonization of Hebrew Scripture,* 53.

[51] See Leiman, *The Canonization of Hebrew Scripture,* 165 n. 261.

[52] Leiman, *The Canonization of Hebrew Scripture,* 47.

[53] Leiman, *The Canonization of Hebrew Scripture,* 42; Ellis, *The Old Testament in Early Christianity,* 10–11, 13.

[54] M. Baillet, *Qumran Grotte 4, II (4Q482-4Q520)* (DJD VII; Oxford: Clarendon, 1982) 40.

[55] S. Z. Leiman, *The Canonization of Hebrew Scripture: The Talmudic and Midrashic Evidence* (Transactions of the Connecticut Academy of Arts and Sciences 47; Hamden, Conn.: Archon Books, 1976) 42.

[56] Leiman, *The Canonization of Hebrew Scripture*, 40, 151; Beckwith, *The Old Testament Canon of the New Testament Church*, 111–15, 127, 247, 261; Ellis, *The Old Testament in Early Christianity*, 3, 9 n. 30. For recent substantial discussion, see A. van der Kooij, "The Canonization of ancient Books Kept in the Temple of Jerusalem," 17–40; and B. Lang, "The 'Writings': A Hellenstic Literary Canon in the Hebrew Bible," 41–65, both in *Canonization and Decanonization: Papers presneted to the International Conference of the Leiden Institute for the Study of Religions (LISOR), Held at Leiden 9–10 January 1997* (A. van der Kooij and K. van der Toorn, eds. Studies in the History of Religions LXXXII; Leiden: Brill, 1998). Van der Kooij and Lang, despite their overall differences, both stress knowledge of tripartite canon.

[57] For the text, see *Qumran Cave 4 V; Miqṣat Maʾaśe Ha-Torah* (E. Qimron and J. Strugnell, eds. Oxford: Clarendon: Oxford, 1994) 58–59, 112 (with my modifications of the trans.).

[58] Qimron and Strugnell, *Qumran Cave 4 V*, 59, n. to l. 10. So too E. Ellis, *The Old Testament in Early Christianity*, 10. (Leiman notes a similar usage in Qiddushin 30a; see *The Canonization of Hebrew Scriptures*, 157, n. 210).

[59] On this point, see E. Ulrich, "The Bible in the Making: The Scriptures at Qumran," *The Community of the Renewed Covenant: The Notre Dame Symposium on the Dead Sea Scrolls* (E. Ulrich and J. VanderKam, eds.; Christianity and Judaism in Antiquity 10; Notre Dame, Ind.: University of Notre Dame, 1994) 82.

[60] On this point and the others that follow, see J. J. Collins, *The Scepter and the Star: The Messiahs of the Dead Sea Scrolls and Other Ancient Literature* (ABRL; New York: Doubleday, 1995) 21.

[61] Buber, oral communication to O. Kaiser, "The Law as the Center of the Hebrew Bible," *"Shaʿarei Talmon": Studies in the Bible, Qumran, and the Ancient Near East Presented to Shemaryahu Talmon* (ed. M. Fishbane and E. Tov with the assistance of W. W. Fields; Winona Lake, Ind.: Eisenbrauns, 1992) 103.

Discussion: Psalms and the Practice
Virtue and Authority

Question:

I f you take Psalms seriously as character formative, what kind of person will you become? John could not understand the first two questions so we went to translations. We voiced questions concerning the difficulty we have with metaphors and translations, difficulty regarding christology and ecclesiology. We want to say "Praise the Lord," but how can you bless the Lord who ignores your prayers?

Translation is a problem in the Catholic Church where Aristotle and virtue practice go hand in hand. What about biblical vs. Greek virtues? We had heard that the biblical virtues are generally expressed in more relational terms.

The practice of the Psalter shapes the world for biblical theology. There is friendship on both sides, however the question exists as to whether friendship is a virtue in the Bible. On the Greek side it is, and community is certainly a virtue on the biblical side. We defined friendship as working together toward a common goal. Community is addressing some unfinished things regarding the reign of God. Community is very importantly connected with the lack of power and that which destroys shalom. We don't like to curse any individuals, but there are many individuals who by their actions are working against shalom.

Beth Tanner: We had Michael and Cindy in our group so we were able to look at the revised articles. We talked about the issues of virtue as a quality. When virtue appears to a person in Greek thought, it is grounded in relationship. We believe that virtue and righteousness should be left in tension and that we should not try to resolve them. Let the two stand side by side as in Psalm 37. We talked about how righteousness doesn't take place in a vacuum. It is related to action and is always grounded in the reality of this world in the context of social justice and friendship. In the NSRV, we find the relationship of David and Jonathan expressed by a participle of love. The aspect of friendship does not appear very often in the psalms.

One of the examples of the peril of translation can be found when we use the phrase righteousness vs. wicked. Wicked has almost disappeared from our vocabulary, and we have a great difficulty negotiating this dichotomy. Can we claim ourselves among the righteous? We are not wicked, but we are hesitant to claim ourselves as righteous. Cindy and the group spoke a lot of substitution. In her contemplation, she comes from the Garden of Gethsemane. We spoke of how not only Gethsemane, but of other texts, and how uncomfortable these texts make us. But we must realize that they were difficult texts for the ancients as well as for us.

Beth Liebert: Our group wondered what kind of person you would become if you took the Psalms seriously, then we considered the cursing psalms. Does this imply that some kind of uniform input comes from the psalms? We found four characteristics that could be claimed for a person who is historically located and for communal lives in hope. But what about the cursing psalms? Our first answer was that perhaps they teach us to curse in the right way, with a sort of sympathetic magic. Can we teach this kind of thing today without provoking behavior we don't want? We found no connection between anger and violence in these cursing psalms. This broke our assumed idea that in this culture there is a connection between anger and violence. One of our problems with the cursing psalms is that we think we have to be nice to be Christian. Do Christians have more trouble with the cursing psalms because we think Jesus tells us we must be nice? Cursing is an expression of a strong relationship. The cursing psalms are psalms of covenant. You can throw a desperate situation at God's feet. We found many pastoral examples and ways to work in one to one situations with the cursing psalms. They are a way to bring action to character formation.

Niceness is a truly interesting issue. People want to be good, yet people who question the status quo are often not considered nice. The cursing psalms tell us something about who we are at our darkest moments.

In practice, choice of translation is important. In praise and worship settings, the NRSV is good because it avoids gender specific words. It is helpful to keep the translations in dialogue because of their differences. Comparing translations can be a helpful exercise. We also need to be aware of the cultural differences. Soul is a different word in the

American language, not to be confused with its meaning in Greek history, and heart in the biblical context also involved the mind.

Harry Nasuti spent a lot of time on Esther's paper,[1] which we enjoyed tremendously. We discussed how psalms relate to narrative and meta-narrative. Larry Bethune's paper described poetic texts intersecting with practice and using this intersection as a means of appropriating narrative texts. Out of Esther's paper came an explanation of the way communities provide a setting for texts and for practices based on texts. We discussed the value of one's tradition as a possible means for a free floating use of text, and the need for the community to control this use of text. The most evident topic in Mark's article was inspiration, generating the question "Is inspiration still alive?". Various traditions would find this a good question. Is this a Catholic paper in its concern for inspiration? Is the concern to talk about the forms in the Psalms a historical concern, an inspirational concern, or a theological concern? Bill shared that he read it as a Baptist paper! What is the degree of convergence of the form critical divergence of the Psalms? What do I learn about form criticism from reading the superscription? If the superscriptions are irrelevant, why do we bother? Some of us felt that the only superscription that has any value is 102. The rest of them are not needed, and the issue about inspiration concerned very few of us.

Dorothy Bass: Gerald and Larry were both in our group. Ministry for the city and concern for the poor was our overall concern. What is the authority that we see in the Psalter? One of the ways we found it authoritative, is that it is outside of our ability to change and manipulate. The diversity of the Psalter instructs one, as well as prohibits one. Within the Psalter, the readers who are powerful are those in the community, the powerless are outside the community.

On the theme of narrative psalms, Bill Bellinger's paper calls to mind so many other stories and texts from the Old and New Testaments. This gives one a real sense that these are helpful and authoritative readings. The connections prevent a shallow reading of the Bible.

We had a long discussion about God's preference for the poor. Does that mean God is against those who understand shalom? Does God prefer dependence? After all, the character of the poor is dependent and not self-sufficient. What is the word for the rich in this kind of psalm? We want not to spiritualize the word for the poor, but at the same time we must recognize the other claims made—that we honor the children of the rich who are often poor in some other areas. Gerald's paper addressed how the city is today. Our inspiration was that people from different traditions could find a way to merge. How does the Bible speak to our contemporary countries?

In what sense does inspiration attach itself to the text? Is it the text in a formal form? According to modernists, the text itself has in a way disappeared.

Mark was in our group so we spent most of our time on the psalms superscription. So, how can we take them seriously? They have a complex history. The statement that the superscription can provide an interpretive lens or analogy was one idea discussed. I have experienced the superscriptions like that. Often they can be an interpretative clue to the psalms. Many of the Davidic texts provide a christological reading of the text. David is never called king in any of the superscriptions. Other hermeneutical items in the superscriptions tie the psalms to life experience, but not without some mooring. How can we relate the superscriptions to practice? The Sabbath Psalm and the Pilgrim Psalms brought forth questions of how you actually use them in the liturgy. The superscriptions are not numbered, so how do you use them? In the context of giving an interpretative lens for reading the psalms. We must be aware that the superscriptions are different between the Hebrew and Greek Bibles, and that Psalm 152 is an appendix.

The structure of the Greek Bible is very different. It is not arranged like the Hebrew Bible and our Bible is influenced by the Greek Bible. Our testament ends with prophecy. Notice that the biographical additions in the superscriptions show how David's life was fraught with danger.

There is a clear interest in the narrative superscriptions linking the psalms with David's life. Two scholars have presented a very persuasive theory after accumulating a prayer book. Their work accounts for the emphasis on the terminology of the poor. The psalms are more religious than economic. The lowly connected these Davidic psalms with the times of trouble in David's life. The royal psalms don't show us this.

Rolf shared an idea that emerged for him as to how important a notion of authority is in the practice of feminism. The path of the Bible is a concern for oppressive practices. Gerald's paper, in which the few were being oppressed by the many, makes it impossible to think about practice, without thinking about the authority of the Scripture with relation to agency.

Cindy: Gerald's arrangement is mirrored in the whole inclusive emphasis which is in the psalms. How do inclusivity and exclusivity work together in the Psalms? Is there ever a movement away from the centrality of Zion? There may not be an adequate answer. There is a downplay of human kingship and foregrounding of Yʜᴡʜ in Psalms 144, 145, and 146. In the final *hallel*, the whole community comes to celebrate the kingship of Yʜᴡʜ. The Psalms end with praise. The Zion in the end is a different Zion, and as in Isaiah we must ask, is this the earthly Zion or the heavenly Zion?

Inclusivity is based on those other than us deciding that our particularity is different from their particularity. Then my enemy wakes up and realizes that I was right in the first place. Self tolerance is the only intolerance we have. The psalmists are not very tolerant. Tolerance is a virtue, but it is a democratic virtue, not a Christian virtue.

Is covenant at the center of Creation spirituality? Is it conditional inclusivity? Is it inclusive/exclusive inclusivity? The imperialism of monotheism, is that we are invited to participate in an exclusivity.

NOTES: DISCUSSION

[1] Esther Menn's paper, "'My God, My God, Why have you Foresaken Me?' Shifting Identities of Lamenting Individual and Transformed Community Practices," is appearing in the *Harvard Theological Review*.

Author Index

Abélard 202, 206, 215, 216
Alter, Robert 29, 113
Ambrose 72
Anderson, George W. 4, 32, 33
Anselm 202, 206, 212, 215, 216
Aquinas, St. Thomas 134 195
Aristotle 161, 166, 167, 168, 169,
    170, 171, 172, 173, 174, 175, 176,
    177, 178, 179, 185, 191
Aronowicz, Annette 164
Athanasius 59, 72, 79, 80, 81, 83
Augustine 74, 80, 137, 176, 204
Austin, J. L. 4, 40, 43, 44, 47, 60, 80

Barnabas 103, 104
Barré, L. M. 257
Barth, Karl 196, 204, 205, 209, 213
Barthes, Roland 190
Bass, Dorothy 4, 44, 55
Berlin, Isaiah 176
Bernanos, George 127
Blumenthal, David 54, 162, 203
Bonhoeffer, Dietrich 74, 194
Brettler, M. 262
Broadie, Sarah 167
Brown, Robert McAfee 221
Brueggemann, Walter 29, 30, 60, 73,
    80, 93, 94, 95, 144, 145, 146, 147,
    149, 150, 181, 222, 229
Brunner, Emil 204
Buber, Martin 132, 268

Buechner, Frederick 115
Bultmann, Rudolf 195, 204
Buttrick, David 112, 113

Calvin, John 72, 74, 100, 204
Catherine of Siena 126
Childs, Brevord S. 115, 245
Conroy, Pat 126
Coser, Lewis 176
Craghan, John 72
Cross, Frank Moore 41, 48

Dahood 48
Derrida, Jacques 45
Dionysius 195
Donne, John 265
Drijvers, Pius 64, 65, 72
Dykstra, Craig 4, 55

Eichrodt, Walther 4, 31
Erasmus 204
Eschel, E. 255

Farley, Wendy 139
Foucault, Michel 45
Francis, St. 100
Frei, Hans 45, 46, 49
Frerheim, Terence 115

Gelineau, Joseph 64
Gerstenberger, Erhard 18, 224
Ginsberg, H. L. 256
Gowan, Donald 112, 113, 115

Gunkel, Herman 4, 17, 18, 64, 68, 72, 84

Hallo, W. W. 256
Hansberry, Lorraine 134
Hanson, Paul D. 32
Hardie, W.F.R. 172
Hasel, Gerhard 31
Hauerwas, Stanley 130
Helprin, Mark 139
Henderson, J. Frank 149
Herrmann, S. 31
Heschel, Abraham 186
Hillers, H. J. 41, 42

Knierim, Rolf 4, 29
Koehler, Ludwig 31
Kraus, H. J. 48, 104

Lamott, Ann 116
Levenson, Jon 30
Levinas, Emmanuel 161, 164, 165, 166, 179, 190, 191, 192, 196
Levine, Herbert 80
Lewis, C. S. 131
Lindbeck, George 45, 46, 49
Livy, Titus 176
Loyola, St. Ignatius of 75
Luther, Martin 22, 74, 75, 100, 137, 204

Machiavelli 175, 176
MacIntyre, Alasdair 3, 44, 161, 166, 167, 168, 170, 171, 173, 174, 175, 177, 178, 179
Marcellinus 72
Mays, James L. 80, 81, 114, 115, 116, 117, 132
McCutchan, Stephen 145
Merton, Thomas 123
Moltmann, Jürgen 222
Mowinckel, Sigmund 18, 48, 79, 80, 246, 256

Norris, Kathleen 73, 155

Nouwen, Henri 126

O'Connor, Flannery 127
Origen 125, 266

Patton, Corinne 43
Pelagius 204
Perdue, Leo 28, 29
Pipher, Mary 116, 118
Placher, William 119
Plato 175, 176, 191

Qimron, E. 267

Ramsay, Nancy 73
Rendtorff, Rolf 30
Ricoeur, Paul 60, 80, 94, 95
Robinson, H. Wheeler 32

Sarna, Nahum 131
Schleiermacher, Friedrich 45, 204, 205
Schökel, Luis Alonso 72
Schuller, E. M. 258
Searle, John 4, 43, 47, 60, 80
Seebass, Horst 31
Seow, C. L. 41, 43, 47, 48, 49
Seybold, Klaus 18, 114, 115
Smend, Rudolf 31
Sölle, Dorothee 206, 207, 212
Strugnell, J. 257, 267
Stuhlmueller, Carroll 65

Talmon, S. 255
Tamez, Elsa 119
Terrien, Samuel 31
Tertullian 195
Thiselton, Anthony C. 80
Thoreau, Henry David 127
Tillich, Paul 136, 204, 205, 209

Vawter, Bruce 125
Von Rad, Gerhard 4, 31

Wesley, Charles 132, 135

Westermann, Claus 18, 31, 68, 105, 106, 148
Wildberger, Hans 31
Wilder, Amos 127
Willimon, Will 130
Wilson, Gerald H. 52, 114

Witvliet, John 149
Wolterstorff, Nicholas 4, 40, 43, 45, 46, 47, 49

Zell, Katharina Schütz 100
Zenger, Erich 222
Zimmerli, Walther 31

Scriptural Index

Gen 15:3	151	2 Sam 11:16–12:13a	108
Gen 21	152	2 Sam 12	101
Gen 21:16	151	2 Sam 22	246, 247, 266
Gen 45:3-11, 15	194		
Gen 45:4-5	194	1 Kgs 8:12	41
Gen 49	41		
Gen 49:24	41, 42	1 Chron 15:17	247
		1 Chron 15:19	247
Exod 1–2	68	1 Chron 16:8-36	261
Exod 2:23	148, 151	1 Chron 25:1	246, 247
Exod 15:17	41		
Exod 24	148	2 Chron 6:41	41, 48
		2 Chron 20:21	261
Lev 2:2	259		
Lev 2:9	259	Neh 1:1–7:5	102
Lev 2:16	259	Neh 3:2	47
Lev 5:12	259	Neh 10:13	47
Lev 6:8	259		
		Ps 1	35, 61, 94, 114, 116, 117, 120, 234, 246, 263
Num 5:16	259		
Num 10:35	48		
Num 12:13	260	Ps 1:1	34, 116, 117, 237, 243
Deut 24:9	47	Ps 1:2	116, 117
Deut 25:17	47	Ps 1:6	95
Deut 33:19	109	Ps 1:7	240
		Ps 2	61, 117, 120, 236, 246, 261, 262, 263
1 Sam	152		
1 Sam 1	67	Ps 2:11	116, 117
1 Sam 4:4	41	Ps 2:12	116
		Ps 3	246, 247, 251, 254, 255, 263
2 Sam 1	152		
2 Sam 6	48	Ps 3:2	234

Ps 3:5	234	Ps 17	151, 246, 247, 251, 255
Ps 3:8	48	Ps 17:3-5	237, 243
Ps 4	246, 247, 251, 254, 263	Ps 17:13	48
Ps 4:5	108	Ps 18	246, 247, 249, 251, 252, 261, 262, 263
Ps 4:6	109		
Ps 5	246, 247, 251, 254, 263	Ps 18:2	247
Ps 5:4	235	Ps 18:47-51	250
Ps 5:8	250	Ps 19	35, 94, 131, 246, 247, 251, 252, 254, 260, 263, 264
Ps 6	35, 246, 247, 251, 254		
Ps 6:4	35	Ps 19:1-6	131
Ps 6:8	237, 243	Ps 19:7	131
Ps 7	246, 247, 251, 255, 263	Ps 19:7-11	131
		Ps 19:11	131
Ps 7:3-4	236	Ps 19:12-15	131
Ps 7:7	48	Ps 19:13	131
Ps 8	246, 247, 251, 254	Ps 20	246, 247, 251, 252, 254, 260, 261, 262, 263
Ps 9	246, 247, 251, 254		
Ps 9:4	235		
Ps 9:15	250	Ps 20:6	252
Ps 9:20	48	Ps 20:7	238, 251, 252
Ps 10	246, 251, 252	Ps 21	246, 247, 251, 252, 254, 260, 261, 262
Ps 10:4	234		
Ps 10:11	234		
Ps 10:12	48	Ps 21:2	252
Ps 11	246, 247, 251, 252	Ps 21:7	263
Ps 11:3	236	Ps 21:8	252
Ps 11:7	235	Ps 21:14	252
Ps 12	235, 246, 247, 251, 252, 254	Ps 22	74, 82, 95, 119, 151, 162, 194, 202, 203, 205, 207, 208, 209, 210, 211, 212, 213, 214, 215, 217, 218, 246, 247, 251, 252, 254, 261
Ps 13	35, 117, 122, 152, 246, 247, 251, 252, 254		
Ps 14	91, 234, 246, 247, 251, 252		
Ps 14:7	250	Ps 22:9-10	208
Ps 15	35, 108, 124, 236, 238, 247, 251, 252, 254, 263	Ps 22:11	208
		Ps 22:12	208
		Ps 22:14	209
Ps 16	246, 247, 251, 252, 256	Ps 22:17-18	209
		Ps 22:20	208

Ps 22:21	208, 209, 212, 213, 219	Ps 33	251, 254
		Ps 33:1	256
Ps 22:22	209	Ps 33:20-22	251
Ps 22:22-34	209	Ps 34	194, 246, 247, 251
Ps 22:24	209	Ps 34:1	256
Ps 22:24-32	261	Ps 34:8	194
Ps 22:25	209, 210, 256	Ps 35	246, 247, 251
Ps 22:26	209	Ps 35:19-21	234
Ps 22:26-27	215	Ps 36	151, 246, 247, 251, 263
Ps 23	73, 91, 97, 246, 247, 251, 254, 263	Ps 36:9	250
Ps 23:6	249	Ps 36:1-4	234
Ps 24	35, 108, 124, 127, 128, 129, 236, 246, 247, 251, 254, 263	Ps 37	94, 124, 160, 164, 166, 179, 180, 181, 182, 185, 186, 187, 188, 194, 200, 246, 247, 251, 263
Ps 24:1	120, 128		
Ps 24:3	128		
Ps 24:3-10	128	Ps 37:1	185
Ps 24:4	128	Ps 37:1-9	194
Ps 24:7	250	Ps 37:1-11	194
Ps 24:7-10	128	Ps 37:2	186
Ps 24:9	250	Ps 37:3	183
Ps 25	246, 247, 252	Ps 37:3-4	183
Ps 25:3	238	Ps 37:4	183, 185
Ps 26	246, 247, 251	Ps 37:5	183, 185
Ps 26:6	108	Ps 37:6	185
Ps 26:6-7	65	Ps 37:7	184, 185, 186
Ps 26:8	250	Ps 37:8	184, 186
Ps 27	246, 247, 251	Ps 37:9	186
Ps 27:1	97	Ps 37:11	185, 186
Ps 27:4	250	Ps 37:12	182, 184
Ps 27:6	108	Ps 37:13	185
Ps 28	246, 247, 251	Ps 37:14	184
Ps 29	35, 236, 246, 247, 249, 251, 254, 255	Ps 37:16	182, 185, 237
Ps 29:9	250	Ps 37:17	182, 186
Ps 29:10	35	Ps 37:18	182, 186
Ps 30	34, 246, 247, 250, 251, 254	Ps 37:20	182, 186
		Ps 37:21	182, 183
Ps 31	74, 119, 246, 247, 251, 254	Ps 37:22	183, 186
		Ps 37:25	182
Ps 32	69, 246, 247, 251, 255	Ps 37:25-31	183
		Ps 37:27	186
		Ps 37:28	183, 186

Ps 37:29	182, 186	Ps 46	100, 137, 235, 247, 252, 254, 255, 263
Ps 37:30	182, 183, 186		
Ps 37:31	183, 186	Ps 47	100, 135, 236, 247, 252, 254, 255
Ps 37:32	182		
Ps 37:32-33	184	Ps 47:1	255
Ps 37:34	186	Ps 47:8	135
Ps 37:35	185	Ps 48	100, 235, 247, 252, 254, 263
Ps 37:37	192		
Ps 37:39	182	Ps 49	100, 124, 247, 252, 254, 263
Ps 37:39-40	179, 194		
Ps 37:40	185	Ps 49:4	264
Ps 38	246, 247, 251, 254	Ps 50	35, 100, 108, 194, 247, 254, 263
Ps 39	246, 247, 251, 254		
Ps 39:1-3	240	Ps 50:7	35, 109
Ps 39:12	240	Ps 50:8-15	108
Ps 40	246, 247, 251, 254	Ps 50:14	194
Ps 40:2-4	261	Ps 50:16-21	235
Ps 40:4	268	Ps 51	60, 69, 84, 85, 100, 101, 103, 104, 105, 106, 107, 137, 161, 194, 202, 205, 207, 208, 209, 210, 211, 212, 213, 214, 215, 217
Ps 41	246, 247, 251, 254		
Ps 41:1	236		
Ps 40:6-8	108		
Ps 42	100, 124, 125, 126, 127, 239, 246, 247, 252, 255, 263		
Ps 42:3	125	Ps 51:1-12	103, 108
Ps 42:4	239	Ps 51:1-17	89, 101, 103, 109
Ps 42:5	125	Ps 51:2	101
Ps 42:6	255	Ps 51:3-6, 12-14, 17	89
Ps 42:11	125	Ps 51:7	101
Ps 42:12	255	Ps 51:9	209
Ps 43	100, 125, 239, 246, 252, 255, 263	Ps 51:10	101
Ps 51:11			209
Ps 43:3	42	Ps 51:12	208, 209, 213
Ps 43:4	108	Ps 51:13	208, 209, 212
Ps 43:5	125, 255	Ps 51:13-19	209
Ps 44	35, 54, 100, 139, 247, 252, 255	Ps 51:14	101, 102, 105, 106
Ps 51:15			101, 105, 106, 209
Ps 44:5-9	255	Ps 51:16	101, 104, 105, 108, 211
Ps 44:17-22	239, 240		
Ps 44:22	237	Ps 51:16-17	219
Ps 45	100, 247, 252, 254, 255, 256, 261, 262, 263	Ps 51:17	100, 101, 103, 104, 105, 108
		Ps 51:18	211

Ps 51:18-19	101, 102, 103, 104, 107, 108, 145, 219		251, 254
		Ps 62:9	251
Ps 51:20	250	Ps 62:10	237, 243
Ps 52	100, 246, 247, 251, 255	Ps 63	100, 151, 246, 247, 251, 254
Ps 52:10	250	Ps 63:3	237, 250
Ps 53	100, 234, 246, 247, 255	Ps 64	100, 246, 247, 251, 254
Ps 53:7	250	Ps 65	97, 243, 244, 248, 251, 252, 253, 257
Ps 54	100, 246, 247, 251, 255	Ps 65:4	251
Ps 54:6	106, 108	Ps 65:6	251
Ps 55	100, 246, 247, 251, 255	Ps 66	100, 254, 256
Ps 55:9-10	235	Ps 66:1-5	239
Ps 55:17-20	255	Ps 66:13-15	65, 108
Ps 56	100, 246, 247, 248, 252, 253	Ps 66:16	239
		Ps 67	100, 247, 254, 256, 260
Ps 56:1	93	Ps 67:1-4	237
Ps 57	100, 246, 247, 251, 252, 253	Ps 68	34, 246, 247, 254, 256
Ps 58	100, 218, 220, 223f., 246, 247, 251, 256	Ps 68:5f.	236
		Ps 68:20	34
Ps 58:2	225	Ps 68:25	250
Ps 58:4	225	Ps 68:30	250
Ps 58:5	225	Ps 68:36	250
Ps 58:6-9	225	Ps 69	74, 100, 119, 143, 194, 246, 247, 251
Ps 58:7-9	225	Ps 69:4	234
Ps 58:11	225	Ps 69:7	237
Ps 58:12	225	Ps 69:12	234
Ps 59	100, 246, 247, 251, 256	Ps 69:30-31	108
		Ps 69:33	236
Ps 59:7	234	Ps 70	100, 246, 247, 251, 258
Ps 60	100, 246, 247, 251, 256, 259	Ps 71	100, 239, 241, 251, 254
Ps 60:7	248	Ps 71:7	239
Ps 60:11	248	Ps 71:17-18	239
Ps 61	100, 246, 247, 252	Ps 72	100, 236, 247, 252, 261, 262
Ps 61:6	252	Ps 72:1	252
Ps 61:7	252	Ps 72:20	255
Ps 61:9	252		
Ps 62	100, 151, 246, 247,		

Ps 73	100, 124, 132, 133, 235, 247, 253, 254, 263		253, 254, 255, 256, 258, 259
Ps 73:1-12	133	Ps 89	247, 252, 253, 261, 262, 263
Ps 73:13-17	133	Ps 89:2-37	255
Ps 73:17	134	Ps 89:50	262
Ps 73:18-28	133	Ps 90	74, 123, 237, 247, 253, 255, 257
Ps 73:23-24	132		
Ps 74	100, 139, 236, 247, 253, 255, 261	Ps 91	237, 246, 251, 254, 257
Ps 74:12	253	Ps 92	254, 257
Ps 74:12-17	255	Ps 93	246, 254, 257
Ps 75	100, 235, 247, 253, 254, 256	Ps 94	246, 254, 257
		Ps 94:7	234
Ps 75:10	253	Ps 94:20-21	236
Ps 76	100, 247, 254, 256	Ps 95	246, 254, 257
Ps 77	100, 237, 246, 247, 253, 254	Ps 96	246, 254, 257
		Ps 96:1	120
Ps 77:10-12	237	Ps 96:10	120
Ps 78	100, 239, 247, 253, 255, 263	Ps 96:13	235
		Ps 97	35
Ps 78:1-8	239	Ps 98	254
Ps 79	100, 247, 253, 254	Ps 98:9	235
Ps 80	100, 247, 253, 254	Ps 99	246
Ps 81	100, 108, 247, 253, 263	Ps 100	120, 254, 258
		Ps 100:4	65
Ps 81:6	253	Ps 101	238, 246, 247, 251, 254, 261
Ps 82	100, 236, 247, 253, 254		
		Ps 101:2	238
Ps 83	100, 221, 247, 253, 254, 258, 259	Ps 102	247, 253, 255, 263, 276
Ps 83:14	253	Ps 103	246, 247, 251
Ps 84	247, 252, 254	Ps 104	35, 246, 254
Ps 84:2	42	Ps 104:4	65
Ps 85	138, 247, 252, 254, 271	Ps 104:24	36
		Ps 105	34, 36, 94, 246, 257
Ps 85:10	139	Ps 106	261
Ps 86	247, 251, 255	Ps 107	34, 246, 254, 257, 261
Ps 86:24-25	65		
Ps 87	247, 252, 254, 256, 263	Ps 107:4	235
		Ps 107:6	34
Ps 87:2	43	Ps 107:7	235
Ps 88	143, 157, 243, 247,	Ps 107:21-22	108

Ps 107:36	235
Ps 108	138, 246, 247, 251, 254, 261
Ps 109	143, 150, 221, 223, 225–8, 240, 246, 247, 251, 254
Ps 109:6	227
Ps 109:6-20	240
Ps 109:7	227
Ps 109:9-12	243
Ps 109:14	227
Ps 109:15	227
Ps 109:16	227
Ps 109:17	227, 228
Ps 109:18	228
Ps 109:19	228
Ps 109:22-25	228
Ps 110	246, 247, 251, 252, 254, 261, 262, 263
Ps 111	254
Ps 111:1	93
Ps 112	263
Ps 112:1	264
Ps 114	34, 246
Ps 115	108, 246
Ps 116	246
Ps 116:17-19	106, 108
Ps 117	137, 138, 257
Ps 117:1	120
Ps 118	246, 257
Ps 118:8-9	238
Ps 118:19	65
Ps 118:27	108
Ps 119	35, 246, 260, 263, 264
Ps 120	42
Ps 121	42, 97
Ps 122	42, 246, 247, 251, 263
Ps 123	42, 254, 271
Ps 124	42, 246, 247, 251
Ps 125	42, 254
Ps 126	42, 254, 271
Ps 127	42, 94, 247, 249, 263
Ps 128	42, 94, 254, 263
Ps 129	42, 254, 263
Ps 130	42, 92, 100, 109, 248, 254, 271
Ps 131	42, 94, 246, 247, 271
Ps 131:2-3	238
Ps 132	40, 41, 42, 43, 45, 47, 48, 49, 50, 51, 254, 261, 262
Ps 132:2	48
Ps 132:2-5	41
Ps 132:3-5	41
Ps 132:5	42
Ps 132:7-8	47
Ps 132:8	41, 42
Ps 132:10	41, 42
Ps 132:11	48
Ps 132:12	48
Ps 132:13-18	41, 42
Ps 132:15	48
Ps 133	42, 94, 246, 247, 263
Ps 134	42, 108, 254, 263
Ps 135	34, 254, 257, 263
Ps 136	257, 261
Ps 137	151, 193, 235, 239, 246, 254, 263
Ps 137:1-4	254
Ps 137:8-9	243
Ps 138	246, 247, 251, 254
Ps 139	100, 246, 247, 254
Ps 140	246, 247, 251, 254
Ps 141	246, 247, 251, 254
Ps 141:2	106, 108
Ps 141:3-5	237, 243
Ps 141:5-6	240
Ps 142	237, 246, 247, 251, 255, 256
Ps 143	246, 247, 251, 254
Ps 144	237, 246, 247, 251, 261, 262, 278
Ps 144:15	35

Ps 145	94, 236, 246, 247, 251, 256, 257, 266, 271, 278	Jer 6:13-19	104
		Jer 6:20	104
		Jer 8:18–9:3	148
Ps 145:15-16	90	Jer 11	151
Ps 146	242, 254, 257, 278	Jer 15	151
Ps 146:3	238	Jer 17	151
Ps 146:3-5	241	Jer 17:5-10	151
Ps 146:5	238	Jer 17:12-13	263
Ps 146:7-9	236	Jer 18	151
Ps 147	235, 242, 254	Jer 20	151
Ps 148	242	Jer 20:7-13	151
Ps 148:3-4	120	Jer 20:9	240
Ps 148:8-9	120	Jer 22:18	263
Ps 149	242, 251	Jer 31:23	263
Ps 149:2	254	Jer 31:31-33	101
Ps 150	44, 124, 242, 251, 254, 257	Jer 34:5	263
		Jer 36	139
Ps 150:6	120	Lam	151, 152
Ps 151	246, 247, 257, 265	Lam 3:19-26	194
Ps 152	265, 277	Lam 5	263
Ps 153	265		
Ps 154	265	Hos 11:1-11	148
Ps 155	265	Ezek	148
Prov 8:22-31	67	Joel 2	260
Isa 1:10-17	145, 263	Joel 2:1-2	89
Isa 1:11	104	Joel 2:12-17	89
Isa 1:18	104	Joel 2:12-18	84, 89
Isa 2:3	263	Amos 5:13	255
Isa 6	148	Amos 5:21-24	145
Isa 38:9	256	Amos 5:22	104
Isa 49:26	41, 42	Amos 5:24	104
Isa 53	218		
Isa 57:15	105	Mic 6:6-8	107
Isa 58	84, 89, 139	Hab 3	255, 263
Isa 58:1-12	89	Hab 3:13	262
Isa 60:16	41, 42		
		Jdt 15:14	261
Jer	149	Wis 7	67
Jer 2:22	101		
Jer 4:14	101	1 Macc 4:24	261
Jer 4:19	240		
Jer 6:11	240	2 Macc 2:13	264

Matt 4:4	132	Luke 20:42		266
Matt 5:17	132, 268	Luke 24:44		266, 267
Matt 6	85	Luke 24:44-45		74
Matt 6:1-6, 16-18	89			
Matt 6:1-6, 16-21	89	John 15:12-13		118
Matt 7:12	268			
Matt 10:14-15	223	Acts 1:20		266
Matt 11:13	268	Acts 2:30		268
Matt 11:23	223	Acts 13:15		268
Matt 15:7	223	Acts 24:14		268
Matt 16	148	Acts 28:23		268
Matt 16:16	268			
Matt 16:23	223	Rom 3:21		268
Matt 17:1-9	148	Rom 3:31		132
Matt 18:6	223	Rom 12		132
Matt 21:12-13	223			
Matt 21:18ff.	223	2 Cor		85
Matt 22:40	268	2 Cor 5:20–6:2		89
Matt 23:13ff.	223	2 Cor 5:20–6:10		89
Matt 25:41	223			
Matt 27:46	211	Gal 6:2		118
		Eph 5:21		218
Mark 1:15	117			
		Phil 2:1-11		218
Luke 6:20b-26	200			
Luke 16:29-31	268	1 Pet 4:10		218